KU-493-879

LEEDS BECKETT UNIVERSITY
LIBRARY
20
DISCARDED

Leeds Metropolitan University

17 0127942 2

STREETS

STREETS

Critical Perspectives on Public Space

Edited by Zeynep Çelik, Diane Favro, and Richard Ingersoll

University of California Press   Berkeley   Los Angeles   London

University of California Press
Berkeley and Los Angeles, California

University of California Press, Ltd.
London, England

© 1994 by
The Regents of the University of California

Designed by Alisa Bales Baur

Library of Congress Cataloguing-in-Publication Data

Streets : critical perspectives on public space / edited
    by Zeynep Çelik, Diane Favro, Richard Ingersoll.
        p.   cm.
    Includes bibliographical references.
    ISBN 0-520-08550-7
    1. Streets—History.   2. City planning—History.
I. Çelik, Zeynep.   II. Favro, Diane G.
III. Ingersoll, Richard.
NA9053.S7S82 1994
711'.4—dc20   93-42658
                                               CIP

LEEDS BECKETT UNIVERSITY
LIBRARY
DISCARDED

LEEDS METROPOLITAN
UNIVERSITY LIBRARY
1701279422
B22EV
316040   17.11.95
9. 1. 94
711. 73

On the jacket: Victor Arnautoff, detail of *City Life,* 1934,
fresco, Coit Tower, San Francisco. Collection of the
City and County of San Francisco, courtesy of the San
Francisco Art Commission, photograph by Malcolm
Kimberlin, Reproduction Bureau.

Printed in the United States of America
1 2 3 4 5 6 7 8 9

The paper used in this publication meets the minimum
requirements of American National Standard for Information Sciences—Permanence of Paper for Printed
Library Materials, ANSI Z39.48-1984.

Contents

Streets and the Urban Process

A Tribute to Spiro Kostof

Streets are a primary ingredient of urban existence. They provide the structure on which to weave the complex interactions of the architectural fabric with human organization. At once the product of design and the locus of social practice, streets propose rich questions to historians. Their conception ranges from the most incremental and spontaneous interventions, such as leftover space between buildings, to superbly contrived public works, detailed in plan and section, involving sophisticated engineering and landscaping. The unique characteristics of any street derive from what Spiro Kostof often referred to as "the urban process," that intriguing conflation of social, political, technical, and artistic forces that generates a city's form. The urban process is both proactive and reactive; sometimes the result of a collective mandate, at others a private prerogative; sometimes issuing from a coordinated single campaign, at others completely piecemeal; sometimes having the authority of law, at others created without sanction.[1] One thing is certain: although historical moments in the life of a city can be isolated, the urban process never stops. Unlike works of art—or even certain buildings, which have a more determinate existence— streets are as mutable as life itself and are subject to constant alterations through design or use that foil the historian's desire to give them categorical finitude.

Streets: Critical Perspectives on Public Space takes its impetus from the work of Spiro Kostof and is dedicated to his memory. Initially trained as a connoisseur in the traditional methods of art history, Kostof experienced an intellectual catharsis sparked by the social movements of the 1960s, and he refocused his work almost exclusively on architecture as an urban phenomenon. Already in 1967, before the tide of contextualism had swept over architectural theory, he proposed that historians analyze buildings in their "total context."[2] This desire for a more inclusive method was charted in a lecture course at the University of California, Berkeley, devoted to the urban history of Rome through the ages; it resituated the history of architecture within social and cultural discourse. By shifting the subject of inquiry from architecture or buildings to urban fabric, he made a relatively safe field dangerous: no longer limited to privileged protagonists, fixed chronologies, established technologies, and finite artifacts, the discipline was forced to comprehend the multitude of users, their cultures, and the conflicting interests of any urban situation.

For Kostof, physical form could only be studied through process. Parts of a city can by some extraordinary means be designed as unified artifacts, but more commonly a city's fabric evolves through a complex series of circumstances. The study of architecture as the transcending signifier of urban history allowed for two earth-shattering revelations (at least for the narrow domain of architectural history): first, that all buildings, like all people, are worthy of interest and need to be considered historically; and second, that all cultures are valid and can be meaningfully compared through their urban development. This overture both to the vernacular landscape and to multiculturalism will no doubt prove to be Kostof's most enduring achievement. He was in effect priming the field of architectural history for entry into the territory of "new cultural history," recently defined by Lynn Hunt as "the deciphering of meaning," rather than the "inference of causal laws of explanation."[3] As Kostof put it: "Every building represents a social artifact of specific impulse, energy, and commitment. That is its meaning, and this meaning resides in its physical form." His doubts about positivist conceptions of history were expressed as early as 1967, when he wrote: "Architecture does not reflect the prevalent *Zeitgeist*, it is one of the factors that defines and informs it."[4]

As demonstrated in his essay "His Majesty the Pick," which we have selected to open this compendium of case studies of the urban process, Kostof pursued a panoramic conception of history, with a nearly compulsive desire to narrate the entire scope of the human adventure in a single sitting. His masterful 1985 work,

A History of Architecture: Settings and Rituals, brought the bicycle shed within sight of the cathedral and restored cultural parity between places such as Cairo and Florence in the thirteenth century. In his final works, *The City Shaped*, 1991, and *The City Assembled*, 1992 (the latter with the collaboration of Greg Castillo), Kostof rejected conventional chronological method and investigated the great themes of urban form in a categorical manner based on formal characteristics such as the grid, organic patterns, and grand diagrams. These are open works, meant to stimulate design theory as well as historical analysis, and they offer an inclusive repertoire of topics and examples, ranging from magnificent boulevards to humble back alleys.

Kostof expanded the cultural and geographical boundaries of the field by introducing a multiplicity of centers and by demystifying the "exoticism" of non-Western buildings. In his efforts to revoke the prejudices of the canons of architectural history he pursued an intuitive multiculturalism, a position that has been best outlined by Michael Geyer as "a set of ideas and concepts that explores the diversity and difference of cultural articulation and their uneasy, embattled interactions."[5] Instead of confining the discourse of architectural history to comparative and descriptive tasks, Kostof's desire to investigate the profession, clients, and general mode of production of buildings across cultures affirmed the subjectivity of all building cultures. In an uncharacteristically political statement, he argued for the revision of ethnocentric models in his assessment of American architectural education. American students, he wrote, "are engaged in a reflective process against the authenticated roll call of their own Western traditions, its seeming determinism; and so they expiate the stealthy knowledge that the imperialist urge breeds as readily at drafting tables as . . . in the workings of regimes and the uncharted regions of ill-educated minds. In the end, we are what we know."[6]

Kostof's agenda for an architectural history inspired by differences infuses the essays gathered in this volume, all written by his former students and colleagues. We have attempted to present a great diversity of streets—geographically, chronologically, and socially. Each contribution is a detailed investigation of a single street in a particular city with unique historical conditions, offering focused explorations of the urban process to support Kostof's broader historical sweep and help account for the morphological peculiarities that every city generates through its exceptional situation in time and space.

The organization of this volume is intended as a challenge to hierarchical structures of knowledge. Rather than imposing an arbitrary thematic order, or reverting to chronological or typological categories, we chose to arrange the book according to a neutral geographic itinerary. Starting from the San Francisco Bay area, Kostof's home for over twenty years, the sequence moves west. This new latitudinal strategy eliminates the established order of an architectural history grounded in the evolutionary progress implied by chronological sequences and conditioned by fixed centers, favored periods, and cultural preconceptions. The unusual propinquities of Athens to Tripoli, London to Rabat, or Cairo to Moscow reinforce a broadened, multivalent vision of the world. In violation of this principle, Rome has been granted a unique prominence in this collection, as the only city for which we have allowed more than one essay. We might, perhaps, justify this by noting Rome's particular function in the collective unconscious of the West and the influence of its architectural and urbanistic traditions on the entire global culture. However, the issue is not Rome as the ineluctable center of Western civilization, but how this privileged subject is treated, as Kostof in his multifaceted studies on medieval and Fascist Rome has shown. Furthermore, one case study using a diachronic strategy reveals the strata of meanings one site embodies over time—another theme he pursued.

Several important themes emerge and intertwine in the essays. They concern the anthropological, political, and technical aspects of street making and coalesce into what may be called the discourse of the street. The topics of ritual, ideology, and negotiation merit special attention.

The street as the space for rituals—be they the triumphal processions of ancient Rome, the public drinking ceremonies of the Incas in Cuzco, or the executions at the bridge in papal Rome—is essential to a cultural process that the anthropologist Clifford Geertz suggests is the fulfillment of every society's need to narrate a story to itself about itself.[7] Ritual uses have a peculiar way of adapting to existing spaces and then subsequently determining the character of those spaces. Triumphal arches were first built to mark the traditional path of the victory procession that wound through Rome. In like manner, the plaza space of Hawkaypata in Cuzco had to exist before it could be altered with a layer of sand for storing ritual items. The trident of streets at Piazza di Ponte in Renaissance Rome was apparently designed with military concerns in mind, but soon was adapted to the great spectacle of public punishments because of its advantageous sight lines. The ritual use of a city is evanescent, yet lodged in the collective memory of its streets.

If ritual helps to represent the mythological reasons for a community's existence, ideology conversely gives reason to the myth of order that is promulgated by power in the city. The naming, siting, and form of streets, and the iconography of the buildings and street furniture that help shape them are a means of communicating ideological messages to the public domain. Street making often attempts literally to signify order: the straight axes of Sixtus V's Rome and Stalin's vision of a new well-being under socialism, as expressed in a grand but epidermal package in the design of Gorki Street, are such attempts. The restructuring of colonial capitals by the French in Rabat and the Italians in Tripoli are cases where urbanism was used as an expression of domination. The ideological message of these streets was forged in their form and emphasized in the subtexts of their architectural details. Its aim was to communicate the ability of a regime to provide and control. The presumed semiological control of power over space, however, is at best transitory. Messages of authority can easily be read in an ironic manner or subverted by successive regimes and practices: the automobile, for instance, has usurped the identity of the grand boulevard; the names of the colonial streets in Rabat and Tripoli have been changed and endowed with new symbolism after independence. Any street conceived to convey a message of authority can quickly convert to an "empty signified," as Roland Barthes termed it—a form for which the meaning, despite its precise historical intentions, becomes arbitrary.[8] The ideological aspirations for the new boulevards of nineteenth-century Athens were subjected to similar disjunctions of symbols and meaning; there, Neoclassical monuments were inserted to restore a sense of national identity that drew on the greatness of antiquity but ultimately had little correspondence with the vicissitudes of modern life in a city on the edge of Europe.

Ideology is always present in plans for streets, but authority is often forced to compromise because of the multiplicity of actors in the urban process, and the desired ideological program can easily be muffled. The design of most streets is determined by a series of negotiations involving patrons, technical experts, and governmental agents. The irregular patterns of the streets of Trastevere in medieval Rome, where each building helped reconfigure a previous urban space inherited from antiquity, resulted from a long process of architectural arbitrations and piecemeal changes. During roughly the same period, the even more complex patterns of Palace Street in Cairo, or the market streets in Chinese cities, were incrementally altered in different directions by changing political, religious, and commercial demands over several centuries. A more specific depiction of the negotiation that shapes urban fabric can be found on the levee in nineteenth-century New Orleans, the traditional space of leisure for a city that was trapped in its watery surroundings. The legal contests for development along the levee highlight the contest of competing ideas

of status, conflicting interpretations of public space, and the argument of commercial versus community interests. The design consequences of negotiations are not always irregular or disharmonious: Chicago's Wacker Drive, a two-level street along the Loop, appears to be a unified piece of Beaux-Arts planning but actually involved much compromise by at least five conflicting civic authorities. Commercial interests drive the production of almost every city, since property is one of the most important items of exchange, and negotiation involves many levels, from those in real estate to those of governance, to those of welfare.

Most cities have an existence previous to their major moments of design; that is, they are subject to redesign. Occasionally the design of a street can be followed from its initial formulation to its fulfillment, and the preconceived model encounters the geographical and social contradictions of an existing urban culture. The conventions of Greco-Roman urbanism were inserted into the unique topography and thriving commerce of second-century C.E. Ephesus to create a legible, imperial environment. The eighteenth-century refounding of the Sicilian town of Noto, in the course of which the entire population was moved to a new location after a devastating earthquake, offers a unique opportunity to observe the creation of a Baroque environment designed according to contemporary criteria of seismic safety. The inadequacy of the model and the conflicting interests of local aristocrats, however, led to ineffectual aestheticizing solutions that have proved difficult to maintain. The interventions of even a public-minded patron were often only partly successful, as can be seen in Bute Street, Cardiff. Similarly, an emphasis on aesthetic aspects minimized more urgent issues of infrastructure in the model for the hygienic street at the London World Health Exposition of 1884.

〔In some parts of the world the street no longer seems to be a viable social and cultural space. On one hand, there has been a disengagement from the city because it is a place of uncontrollable diversity, where skid rows such as the Tenderloin in San Francisco threaten middle-class norms. On the other hand, the street has been treated as a nostalgic artifact, to be restored to an ideal state or simulated according to an imaginary historic model. With both the abandonment of the public realm and the recreation of a pseudopublic realm, civic values, such as the street as a space for community, have disappeared. The chief actor in encouraging the demise of the street has been the automobile, which has overemphasized the function of the street for the circulation and storage of vehicles, to the detriment of the social uses of its space. The development of the Silver Spring area of suburban Washington, D.C., for example, demonstrates that the qualities of enclosure and spatial coherence once inherent in street design may lose their immediacy under pressure of the new demands of automobile-bound suburbanites. Expediency of production and marketability of the contiguous private environment become the major factors in the design of streets, and genuine civic functions are no longer associated with the production of the city. The subsequent proliferation of architectural typologies that are not connected to streets, such as the enclosed shopping mall, both in the suburbs and in center cities, have prevailed as internalized, privately managed surrogates for the public street. In Osaka, a multilayered underground shopping concourse is connected to train stations and served by parking lots, but is cut off from the pre-existing network of streets. In this controlled subterranean realm, attempts have been made to reproduce some of the experiences of the traditional street, despite its suspended spatial position. The choice of many cities to conserve or mystify the traditional form of the street according to a preferred historical aesthetic, in order to gratify the expectations of tourists, is another indication that the street as the locus for daily life, including commerce and spectacles, can be subsumed by a purely commercial spectacle. As seen in the renovation of Istanbul's Soğukçeşme Street, daily life becomes a reproduction of itself in such circumstances.

While the death of the street may seem worth struggling against, the historian can neither change the future nor predict further decline; at best, one may change the way the present considers the past. The value of Kostof's work, seen transmuted in these essays, has been to provide a new discourse of the street that comprehends diversity as a biological necessity and otherness as the unique condition imparted by the urban process. If the discussion of the city is free of ethnocentrism and embraces more than aesthetic concerns, then the fear of street life and the superficial desire for a fictional past may have less influence on the production and use of public space.

This publication could not have been undertaken without the generous support of the Graham Foundation, the exceptional trust and care extended by the University of California Press, and the hard work of a most efficient production team. At the University of California Press, we are especially grateful to our editor, Deborah Kirshman, and Tony Crouch, Steve Renick, Lillian Robyn, and Marilyn Schwartz. We are indebted to the members of our independent production crew for their skill, professionalism, and good humor. Our copy editor, Eve Sinaiko, not only cleaned up the text, but also gave us critical input. Cathy Ho prepared and proofread the manuscript with great care, in addition to providing editorial help. Alisa Baur designed the book, demonstrating remarkable patience with the changes it went through. Kathleen Roberts and Cameron Kruger gave support in the coordination of many authors; Richard H. Abramson did this too, and also helped to prepare the illustrations for publication. We thank Maryly Snow for offering her invaluable assistance in securing permission for the jacket illustration at the last moment.

Comments from Christine Boyer, Grahame Shane, and Perry Winston on the manuscript were most beneficial, and the latter's contribution to the organization of the book much appreciated. We were especially fortunate to work with a group of responsive and enthusiastic contributors, brought together by a shared interest in urban process and a shared affection and respect for Spiro Kostof. We hope that *Streets: Critical Perspectives on Public Space* will stand as a modest acknowledgment of our collective debt to an inspiring teacher, thinker, urban historian, and dear friend.

Zeynep Çelik
Diane Favro
Richard Ingersoll

Notes

1 S. Kostof, *The City Assembled* (Boston, 1992), 280.

2 Idem, "Architectural History and the Student Architect: A Symposium," *Journal of the Society of Architectural Historians* 26, no. 3 (October 1967): 189–91. Kostof recommended four methods to approach the total context: to study each building in its entirety because of the "oneness" of architecture; to look at buildings in a broader physical context, later called "setting"; to understand that all buildings of the past are worthy of study because they form a community; and to recognize the nonphysical aspects that are indispensable to understanding a building.

3 L. Hunt, "Introduction: History, Culture and Text," *The New Cultural History*, ed. L. Hunt (Berkeley, 1989), 12.

4 S. Kostof, *A History of Architecture: Settings and Rituals* (New York, 1985), 7; idem, "Architectural History and the Student Architect," 190.

5 M. Geyer, "Multiculturalism and the Politics of General Education," *Critical Inquiry* 19 (Spring 1993): 501.

6 S. Kostof, "The Education of a Muslim Architect," in *Architectural Education in the Islamic World*, The Aga Khan Award for Architecture, Proceedings of a seminar held in Granada, Spain, April 21–25 (Singapore, 1986), 2.

7 C. Geertz, *The Interpretation of Cultures: Selected Essays* (New York, 1973), 448.

8 R. Barthes, "Semiology and Urbanism," 1967, trans. R. Howard, in *The Semiotic Challenge* (New York, 1988), 191–201.

His Majesty the Pick

The Aesthetics of Demolition

SPIRO KOSTOF

Figure 1. Between 1924 and 1932, 5,500 units of mostly low-income housing were demolished to create Via dell'Impero in Rome (now called Via dei Fori Imperiali).

One of the most characteristic self-created images of Benito Mussolini—alongside the fiery orator of the Palazzo Venezia balcony, the general on horseback inspecting the troops or parading at their head, the land tiller winning the grain war, and the paterfamilias surrounded by his wife and children—is the image of the Duce as wrecker, wielding his pick lustily on the roof of some structure in a condemned neighborhood. His own oratory and Fascist literature in general are full of references to *il piccone risanatore* (the healing pick), and once, in a speech of March 18, 1932, he refers to "his majesty the pick." For twenty years, between 1922 and 1942, radio and newsreels made of this humble implement a star, broadcasting its activities in the historic cities of Italy. The proof of this feverish work may be seen today in cities large and small from Genoa to Palermo.

These clearance projects were called *sven-*

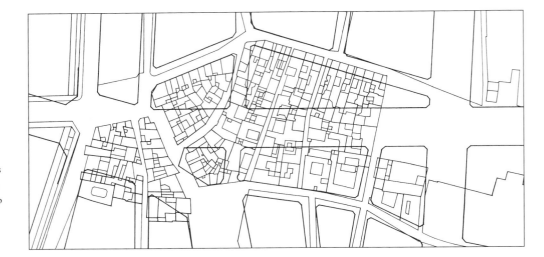

Figure 2. Detail of a plan of Paris, showing Baron Haussmann's demolitions for Boulevard St.-Michel, retraced from an 1855 map in the Bibliothèque Historique de la Ville de Paris.

tramenti, literally, disemboweling, taking the guts out of, making hollow. The word goes back at least as far as Haussmann's use of *éventrement*, and is part of that medical terminology that became common among administrators and planners in the early nineteenth century. It denotes that drastic cure, massive surgery, needed to save a badly infected urban organism. They are there still: those Fascist thoroughfares out of scale with all surrounding urban tissue and vast inarticulate piazzas oozing space in all directions around a historic monument. And then there are those thousands of photographs that have survived—the Duce's sole concession to the few people who complained of patrimony lost. They are the hasty, semiofficial record of what was demolished and they were usually taken when the buildings were already gutted and the shells stood haunting and lifeless, hollow window holes like gouged eyes, a carcass picked clean of life and memory. On occasion, the former inhabitants lined up for one final group photograph in front of the place, the shell that had housed and reared them, where they played and fought and married, a touching portrait on the eve of their uncertain relocation

to an alien, empty, memory-free new ambience (fig. 1). In annual reports, the proud account of all this labor was entered, lists of streets and piazzas that had disappeared forever and statistics of housing units destroyed: twenty thousand in Florence alone between 1927 and 1931, sixty thousand in Genoa, 110 thousand in Milan, and so on, interminably. It was fashionable then to destroy. The Duce was not alone. The rhetoric had been forged in the heat of World War I by the Futurists, the spiritual forefathers of early Fascism, whose hate for old cities was indiscriminate. "Get hold of picks, axes, hammers and demolish, demolish without pity, the venerated cities," Marinetti urged. And Sant'Elia agreed. "We feel we are no longer the people of the Cathedrals . . . but of immense streets . . . of salutary *sventramenti*."

With the birth of the modern movement, the incestuous, urban clutter of those culture-breeding European centuries was now derided and condemned in the name of scientific functionalism. Le Corbusier's Plan Voisin envisaged wiping out most of historic Paris. Oh, there were to be exceptions, of course. "The axis of the undertaking was well-chosen," he writes.

"You can see the Tour Saint-Jacques, which has been spared." The fanaticism may have been polemical, but the point of view it served was no joke. And it made the mid-nineteenth-century vision of Baron Georges Haussmann for this same Paris seem fainthearted by comparison.

Now Haussmann, the "demolition artist," as he was called by his detractors, was of course the great precursor of such pitiless, massive urban surgery (fig. 2). The city as a sleek, efficient machine was his unacknowledged legacy to the modern movement. The scale of later Fascist interventions, their worship of the straight line, monuments that float in seas of space—all this had Haussmann's actualized model to look back upon. Haussmann's treatment of Paris was in fact the first total conceptualization of what we understand by "the modern city." It heralded a technocratically minded, comprehensive approach to town planning in which a rationalized circulatory network would once and for all sweep away the dross of the community's promiscuous life through time. This overarching urban logic was revolutionary. It was the child of the new industrial-capitalist perspective, and so was its guiding concept of obsolescence versus progress, applied now to what was beginning to be called "the urban plant" and its components, in that mechanical analogy of the city that increasingly competed with the pathological.

But the aesthetic or expressive vehicles of Haussmann's *grands travaux* were themselves conservative. The wide and straight tree-lined avenues, the monumental vista, continuous uniform frontages, and spatially profligate piazzas went back directly to Napoleon Bonaparte (figs. 3, 4). And beyond Napoleon the Great were two centuries of Baroque experiment with the sweeping gesture, with a calculated public scenography and willful geometries. But Napoleon's planners had imposed something special on this cumulative body of urban intervention, and that is what

is particularly relevant to the later Haussmann epic. This "something" falls under two headings: first, the still-embryonic notion that planning is a rational amelioration of public life, an effort that considers the grand visual dominion of proposed urban arteries and squares as the frame of coordinated systems of amenities and services—circulation, water supply, sewage, public order, business, entertainment, burial. This is one side of what is new in Napoleonic practice. The other is the willingness to countenance wholesale destruction of the cores of the very old cities of Europe, as demonstrated in the Napoleonic projects for the key stations of his empire, from Brussels and Madrid to Milan, Rome, and Cairo.

At the time of Napoleon, this new, embryonic notion of what planning is all about, and this willingness to destroy the centers of historic cities, were not seen as convergent activities. On the one hand you had civil engineers and administrators who attacked planning in a systematic way, even to the extent of what we would today call regional planning. Their object was to address problems of health and traffic, to see physical design as a remedy for administrative, economic, and social ills, or pressures. The anxiety of historic continuities, the assessment of built heritage, vistas, and memories did not occupy them very much. It was, on the other hand, architects—people concerned with the art of civic design, with formal organization and symbolic presence—who proposed the great forums, the boulevards and *ronds-points* in the thick of historic centers.

Destruction of entire sections of a city was condoned to make room for the public theaters of Napoleon's regime. These theaters were forced upon the old cities in order to reevaluate the monumental achievement of the past in relation to the new master of these old cities, to Napoleon himself. The presentation of ancient monuments in a drama of historical association brings out the comparable—or rather, competitive—grandeur of the present regime in relation to the past. A century later, the Fascist regime had the same idea.

Size, surely, has always appealed to autocratic minds, but earlier autocrats of the Baroque era had sought to gain their grand settings by planting them primarily in unoccupied or underbuilt areas. Versailles was not built at the expense of Paris. The breathtaking Roman avenues of Sixtus V went through vineyards and fields, on the edges of the historic frame of the city, yet within the city's walls. No pope of the seventeenth, eighteenth, or nineteenth century consented to the demolition of the spine in front of St. Peter's. In fact, it wasn't done until the Fascist period. Absolutism trod cautiously when it came to built areas. Single monuments, yes. New facings, cartouches, propagandistic art, but not disembowelings, not *sventramenti*. Napoleon's men were fearless. If the cavernous squares and heroic avenues they proposed had been realized, they would have upset, once and for all, the subtle spatial play between small buildings and large, monumental nodes and the standard tissue that gives these monuments their status, their impressiveness.

The only difference between the Napoleonic and the later work of Haussmann or Mussolini is that they saw traffic and glory as convergent goals. The boulevards that focused theatrically on historic monuments were also now meant to carry fast traffic smoothly through the once-congested, near-impassable tangles of the city (fig. 5). The piazzas where monuments stood in their "necessary solitude," to quote Mussolini, doubled contradictorily as anchors of busy traffic junctions.

Looking further back, beyond Napoleon, and beyond the Baroque, for this enormity of puncturing gargantuan voids in the quick of

aged cities, one earlier example springs to mind. It is the one that would, of course, have come to Napoleon's mind, quite consciously—Imperial Rome. We all know the drastic change that came upon the venerable capital of the Roman Republic when, beginning with Augustus, the emperors put aside its traditions of self-rule for a centralized government on the model of Eastern kingdoms. And no better instance can be cited for our present argument than the complex known as the Imperial Fora. This complex, created additively by a succession of emperors from Augustus to Hadrian, broke through the old walls of the republican city to marry it with the entertainment quarter of the Campus Martius. There one of the great creations of antiquity was carved out to provide a spacious lung for the teeming crowds of the city, which, in the time of Hadrian, probably had about a million inhabitants; it was the largest city that the ancient world had known. But this was achieved at the expense of existing serviceable construction, residential and commercial.

It was in the Hellenistic cities that preceded Imperial Rome that the idea of a city as a work of art, a design to be controlled and orchestrated, first emerged. I don't mean cities laid out all at once for an artificial purpose: colonial implants, military camps, or royal capitals that are born by fiat and forcibly populated. These of course all had regular designs, usually grids of some kind, that were abstract and repeatable. I mean cities that had risen more haphazardly, more organically, and now found themselves, in the Hellenistic period, untidy and congested, with only a focus or two of monumental effort within their tangled and scruffy fabric. In order to give these old Greek cities the highlights of a self-conscious scheme, to run ceremonial axes through them, to monumentalize the approaches and cut into the shape grand formulas, theaters of public life, the Hellenistic planners

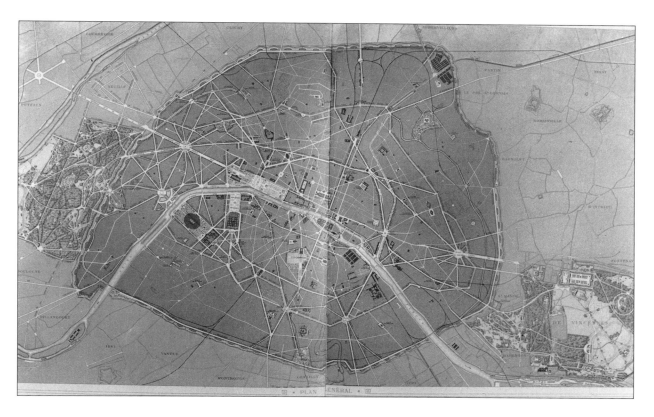

had to demolish some of what was there, displace people and disrupt old habits, as they enhanced and aggrandized. Sometimes the process was in the nature of a face-lift. Creating unified façades through the addition of stone porticoes was one solution. These are the ancestors of Vigevano and Baroque Turin. But Hellenistic and Roman interventions were sometimes much more brutal. The change of the Athenian agora in the second century B.C.E. is one example.

The point is not just the aesthetic change. Town planning is never innocent of political or social ends. The old towns had been self-governing entities. Everyone was theoretically equal, everyone's public life was of more account than his personal fortune. So there was no question of avenues with fancy houses and public display of luxury, distasteful to a culture that equated beauty with morality. Public buildings were symbols of community; they were paid for with public funds and they served high-minded functions: religion, education, the institutional patterns of self-rule.

In the Hellenistic period, urban self-rule is more a form than a reality. The rich live ostentatiously and donate public buildings that bear their names. Extraurban powers, such as the king's, interfere with the structuring of the city fabric. We now have buildings named after individuals, and in such conditions the poor and their buildings are expendable. They are forced to seek their pride in the endowed magnificence of powerful benefactors.

What of the long period between the collapse of the Greek or Roman world and the

Figure 3. Adolphe Alphand, plan of Paris after Haussmann's interventions, from *Les Promenades de Paris*, 1867–73.

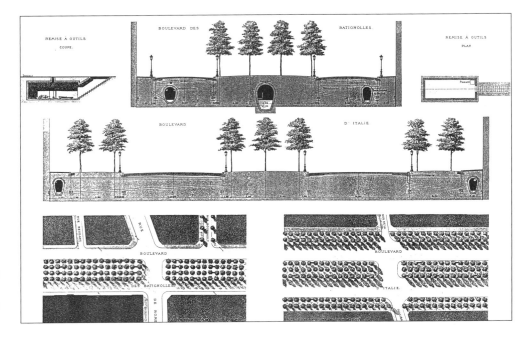

Figure 4. A plate from Alphand's *Les Promenades de Paris,* showing the Boulevard des Batignolles and Boulevard d'Italie in plan and section. The technology of Haussmann's streets includes regular planting, gas lighting, water mains, drains, and sewers.

beginning of the Baroque? What of the Middle Ages and the Renaissance? The classical cities shrank drastically after the fall of the Roman Empire. Those cities that persisted adjusted their proud frames of Hellenistic or Roman times to the new exigencies of a minimal population, of a Christian society in vastly reduced circumstances. In the East something similar was happening. When Islam took over the already rather decrepit cities of the Greco-Roman world, it started to fit them slowly and without any elaborate premeditation into its own way of life. The colonnaded avenues that we admired in the Hellenistic and Roman world became the *suq*s (marketplaces) of later times. Individual bays were covered and made into shops, the whole line becoming rather raggedy and more human, in everyday terms. And the great grids of the formal cities of the Hellenistic and Roman world were carved into little byways, cul-de-sacs, and blind alleys to form superblocks where tribal and ethnic

groups could turn in upon themselves and ignore the abstract formality of the geometric grid. In the Christian West, too, the feudal fracturing of the urban form into defensive rival neighborhoods wrought havoc on the formal geometry of public ways. In Rome the great theaters, the stadiums, the baths, the public colonnades were cut up into little pieces. These vast structures were too expensive to keep, and culturally they were not compatible with the new religion of Christianity. They were fissured little by little into small-scale manageable tissue, eloquent of survival and cultural reevaluation.

The concept of *civitas,* the assembly of citizens, came to supplant the more abstract, artistic notion of the Roman city, or *urbs.* Isidore of Seville writes in the seventh century that what was more important now was "not the stones, but the people." Now, it had been that way once before: the Athens of the sixth and fifth centuries B.C.E. had been a small, moral entity where community was more important than setting. With the Hellenistic era had come the notion that urbanism was not the faith of public life, but the art of public living. And now, in the early Middle Ages, we are back again to a basic grouping and crowding that corresponds to the realities of daily existence, not to the lavishly subsidized and highlighted theater of urban pomp and circumstance of the Hellenistic era and the Roman Empire.

The difference between the classical polis of the Athens model and the medieval city was, of course, self-rule. The classical Greek city governed itself, or believed it did so. The medieval city was the creature of a lord, a bishop, an abbot, or some other feudal authority. The struggle for self-government began again in earnest only in the twelfth century, rather late in the story. But when it did, when the communes began to rise against the feudal masters and demand charters of self-government, demolition came back as an instrument of the people. The classic example is late-medieval Florence.

Florence had been a perfect Roman city once, with a grid. It had been eaten into in the ways we have described. Thoroughfares, often whole neighborhoods, were obstructed and sealed off by feudal lords whose towers rose on the skyline of the city. Lesser infringements cluttered the city form everywhere, so the charge of the young republic, beginning in the twelfth century, was two-pronged: to unstop urban passageways, weave together all quarters of the city, and thus eradicate pockets of resistance against its authority; and to conceive of the city form once again as an intentional design that confirmed the supremacy of the commune, the people, and their institutions. Now the first of these objectives was of course achieved by legal constraint, by financial settlement, by the use of force. The government adopted a building code; statutes affecting the

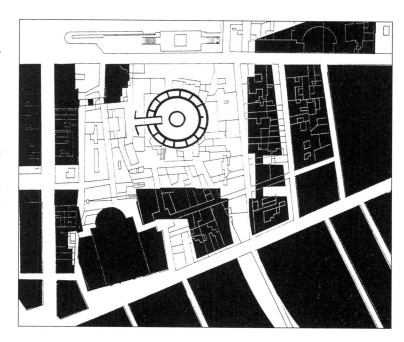

appearance and care of open spaces and public works were enforced so that everything was regulated, from balconies, porticoes, and outer stairs, to street traffic and pavement. This was no mere aesthetic compunction. It was designed to allow no overwhelming private privileges, such as feudal towers, that would create extravagant accents in the standard fabric. The height of feudal towers was systematically reduced. The property of offending nobles was razed. New public building was undertaken to make the prestige of the commune evident to itself and to the outside world.

The city as a work of art goes beyond mere practical amelioration, political control, and the presumption of monumentality. It strives for what we might call perceivable order, which in turn relies on the ability to see the city as a ceremonial symbol. We have two direct indications that this trend existed in thirteenth-century Tuscany. first, we know of the drawing-up of town plans as a way of conceiving of the

Figure 5. Plan showing the imposition of Mussolini's design over the existing fabric of a Roman neighborhood to create Piazzale Augusto Imperatore in Rome, 1934–40.

city in its totality; second, we know of the appointment of town architects. In thirteenth- and fourteenth-century Florence, an effort was made to combine the two great ideals of the Greco-Roman world—self-rule and the noble formalism of the Hellenistic planned city. So, for example, wide, straight streets again became a goal. The benefits of rectifying irregularities were said to be health, convenience, and beauty—words that we shall hear again and again from demolishers of all stripes in succeeding centuries. The details of Arnolfo di Cambio's Florentine master plan include a new cathedral and the palace of the people in the Piazza della Signoria. These were connected by a widened axis, the present Via Calzaioli, with Or San Michele, the city's granary and a monument to her guilds, halfway in between. Perhaps the most important point: all of this was done in a participatory atmosphere. Artists as well as the people generally were active in this. Taxes and labor from the people went to the building of the new walls. Citizens' commissions oversaw street clearance and urban-renewal projects. The guilds supervised construction of public buildings. There were competitions and juries, and the citizenry at large was, in fact, invited at times to testify on the projects. And the city form was coaxed into shape, with a little widening here and a little straightening out there.

That method continued in the Renaissance. Ideal schemes for perfect overall forms stayed in treatises. Reality forced a respect for built things, as long as they were serviceable, as long as they could be kept standing. Urban stock was not casually expendable. So the new style had to rely on exemplary accent to make its point. Renaissance churches and palaces, prominently situated, would ennoble an old town. That is the story of Pienza, Mantua, Urbino.

But there were some important attitudinal changes. The destruction of contiguous tissue, of temporary accretions, in the name of morality and decorum, which had started with pre-Renaissance Florence, now becomes a common solution. And this works against the medieval notion that large public structures must harbor humble attachments, that families of uses are more important than the purity of architectural forms. Then, with Via Giulia in Rome, we have a very early example of a straight street that is cut willfully through a built area, running counter to the existing street net.

Such behavior, however, was exceptional. In the Renaissance, cities changed primarily through individual negotiations between owners and builders on the one hand and the citizens' commissions responsible for streets on the other. The law begins to favor large, dignified buildings in the new manner, and it provides that neighbors be obliged to sell adjacent property to those who propose to upgrade their building or to build a new one from the ground up. An owner could also barter privately for public land in order to adjust the shape of a block, to alter the alignment of neighboring façades, or even to change the width and direction of a street. That is the way—not through any great Renaissance master plan—that we get the great rectangular block of the Palazzo Farnese, with its front piazza. And that is the way in which, through a matter of three centuries, the medieval fabric of the city of Rome, which was basically composed of two- and three-story single-family dwellings, slowly begins to congeal, consolidate, and enlarge itself into large apartment blocks. It was, in fact, this piecemeal way of changing the fabric of the city that was most crucial to the Renaissance and the Baroque, rather than those great gestures that we like to talk about.

With the Baroque, and beginning with Michelangelo, of course, all those things that we associate with the Baroque come in: dynamism, impetuous reach, sensate passage through space, and a new notion of the grand vista. Renaissance streets, even when they are straight, like Via Giulia, are essentially connecting channels of communication. They facilitate traffic and encourage the exploration of a quarter. But they are not conceived of as grand vistas with worthy termini. In Sixtus's famous scheme for Rome, he sends these impetuous avenues in all directions. You have bifocal framing of stretches of straight lines. You see out to something worthwhile at the end: an obelisk, an arch, or a monument of some kind. This idea is, of course, at the basis of so much of Napoleon's, Haussmann's, and Mussolini's later planning.

In the hands of the unscrupulous, this kind of mentality could have meant disaster to old city fabrics. It didn't. Common practice was gentler and a lot more could be done with mock effects than with downright destruction. The example of Baroque Rome is a wonderful case in point. To carve out a space in front of Santa Maria della Pace you don't demolish an entire area. You open a little piazza that will look enormous because of the narrow way you are going to be brought into it, and you drop curtains that shield from the eye the irregularities that lie behind. Rome is marvelous in the way it takes areas that are a jumble in terms of open space and, by a single justified gesture—a fountain, an obelisk—galvanizes and pulls together that space without doing anything to its edges. You can see what the gigantic, oversized *Triton* fountain has done for Piazza Barberini. Nothing is done around it; that fountain and its great jet are enough to pull the square together. This is in fact a new piazza, without actually having much new construction around it. A more famous case is the Piazza del Popolo. There, the idea of two small matching churches, set like a triumphal arch of Christian intent at the end

of the piazza, leading to the city, is enough to transform this jumble of an ancient Roman gate, an obelisk, and various kinds of buildings around it. The French model of the royal *place*, with uniform façades and a single crown line on all sides, or, for that matter, the residential squares of London, unfold relatively harmlessly at the edges of town, and are therefore of only marginal interest here.

By 1750, the major changes that concern European urban structure may be enumerated. first is the cultural revolution, challenging the mid-eighteenth-century primacy of that classical language that had been ruling Europe since the early Renaissance. Archaeological revivalism begins with an interest in all the past and its varied manifestations, introducing an emotional note into matters of urbanism. Slowly, very slowly, the notion is established that the fabric of a city, with all the styles represented in it, records the continuity of the race and that therefore planning cannot simply be content with motives of health, comfort, and beauty. Memory as guiding principle of planning comes into play.

Second, in association with revivalism, is the notion of picturesqueness, in which various things stand together, so that uniformity of design and other tenets of classicism will be brushed aside. An example is Nash's Regent Street and Regents Park complex in London, where a whole series of episodes exist together. Incident is worked into the scheme. This picturesqueness makes use of a technique of Karl Friedrich Schinkel, who carefully sites single buildings in a way that recalls neighbors without forced parody. Thus he seeks to unify an environment pictorially. Now, both the picturesque aesthetic of the Nash variety and Schinkelesque environmentalism make what exists acceptable and thus reduce the urge to demolish the old for the sake modern perfections.

Third, these compromises with the ideal notion of classical design represent the decline of autocratic rule. The age of grandeur is over. With the political and military revolutions of the end of the eighteenth century, we begin to come to grips with the triumph of capitalism and the bourgeoisie. This is one side of the change in the social order that preoccupies the nineteenth century. The other side is, of course, industrialism and its corollaries: swelling urban population, critical changes in transportation, and the rise of a new class of professional administrators, destined to cope with nightmarish problems of sanitation and general welfare. Both sides affect the old cores radically. The bourgeoisie wants now to reshape cities in its own image, to make its own businesses, residences, and places of entertainment the monumental core of the city, replacing the princely palaces and royal churches of the Baroque period.

This is the triumph of Haussmann, who is, to be sure, working for the emperor, but a bourgeois emperor, and the monied class that props him up. Upper-middle-class merchants, financiers, and manufacturers, liberal in their business practices but politically right-wing, demand law and order, favorable conditions for the conduct of their affairs, nice places to live, and cultural and recreational centers for their leisure hours. They want plumbing to work, they want the sewer mains to be in order, and these requirements Haussmann's *grands travaux* meet admirably. He reduces urban tensions and unrest by demolishing old neighborhoods that were chronic trouble spots (fig. 6). He rationalizes and streamlines the street network for rapid communication and weaves into it adequate business facilities. The mansard-roofed apartment houses that line his great boulevards provide gracious living for families no longer content with having apartments in the side streets of the old parts of the city, but not rich enough

to own townhouses of their own. At the same time, in the execution of this remarkable feat, Haussmann proved himself the most able of the new breed of professional planners. Now, this group functions completely differently from the designers of late-medieval Florence, and I think Haussmann himself feels that. At one point in his memoirs, he makes a lengthy distinction between a commune and a prefecture. He says, "The commune is almost as old as the family; it is not simply a territorial division, it is a collection of people tied together by concerns at once moral and material. With us, [it has] become an integral and subordinate part of the State. . . . By contrast, the Department [of the Seine] . . . is above all an administrative division." Exactly so. It is a lot easier to see the city as plant, a design on paper you can update and modernize as needed, without having to worry about it as a collection of people for whom it must struggle to maintain a moral and material fit.

Isn't this really the same argument we have today—the struggle between representative government and municipal bureaucrats on the one hand, and neighborhoods on the other? Aren't the aesthetics of demolition a polite cover for something far more basic? If what we look like, in urban terms, is what we are, he who decides what we are going to look like is also deciding what we are, what we were, what we are going to be. Who is going to do this? Will it be the ruler? Will it be the people? The civic government? One side of the argument is the choice between the total power and action of central authority (Haussmann, with the aid of Napoleon III), and the piecemeal, compromising urbanism of representative government. But there is another side to the argument. You may see the city as a collection of people, of generations, fixed to a place with conviction, proud of its past, aware of its traditions, solici-

Figure 6. Demolitions for the Rue de Rennes according to Baron Haussmann's renewals.

tous of its future; or as an amenity where people live and work as suits their convenience, where their commitment is conditional and short-term. But in both these contexts, demolition is not a simple matter of health, economics, traffic, beauty; it is a statement of purpose, made by a society to itself and to those who will view it in the future.

The nineteenth century was really very confused about that. The cities were changing fast, alarmingly fast. The development of the periphery dissipated the traditional energies of the city, confused its identity. The Baroque city, however explosive within, was a closed city. The new Vienna, the new Paris were not. In the past, the city had been the rock of existence for those who lived there. It was the familiar, slowly changing backdrop of the evolving generations, the material covenant of spelled-out relationships. You were born in

it to stay; you knew it well; it had palpable shapes and it commanded deep allegiance. Now the city behaved erratically. It showed a protean impatience beyond the common will. Waves of immigrants jostled it rudely; it pushed out messily, shapelessly; it was too big to comprehend, except on paper. Charles Baudelaire spoke best and most simply of the changes Haussmann had wrought for Paris: "The old Paris," he said, "is no more. The city's form, alas, changes faster than the human heart."

One reaction to this was to cling to what was there: urban conservation. It was a minority view, slow to mature, gaining real strength only toward the end of the century. And even then, the initial fight was for monuments, buildings of artistic or historic interest. Haussmann challenges his detractors in his memoirs to show "even a single old monument worthy of interest, one building precious for its art, curious by its memories," that his administration destroyed. He doesn't see the irony in his words because he has a very special definition of *worthy*. He doesn't see the irony in the list of 19,722 houses destroyed by him in greater Paris, of which 4,300 or so were in the old core. It is okay because they were worthless, unhealthy. He says he has built forty-three thousand new houses or repaired old ones, so what is the fuss? People can move and live somewhere else.

Painfully, slowly, the awareness of contexts dawns, and that primarily in Germany, where the concept of *Stadtbild,* or the general physiognomy of a place as a monument, finds expression. The city and its landscape, its identity, its character, after the war of 1870, became a concern in Germany. The patriotic movement called the *Heimatschutz* began to equate conservation with nationalism. Around 1900 some really remarkable prescriptions come out of Bavarian and Hessian law and local building regulations of such towns as Hildesheim.

In the streets and open places . . . those parts of any building which can be seen from any street or public place must be carried out in architectural forms that agree with those previously in use in Germany up to the middle of the seventeenth century. Further, the new work must as far as possible be in harmony with its nearest surroundings and especially with any conspicuous building that gives character to a whole neighborhood. As a rule, new buildings must be built so that the general appearance of the surroundings is not interfered with. This applies especially to materials, including those used in the roofing and the ornamentation, and to coloring.

The nationalistic argument supported the aesthetic theories persuasively put forth by Sitte, Stübben, Brinckmann, and others: that straight, wide avenues can be boring and vacuous; that the small incident, the twisted street, the rounded corner, the little planted oasis unexpectedly come upon were superior to mansarded boulevards, *ronds-points* and imposing *places*. This helped to stem for a while the Haussmannization of European cities. It became aesthetically chic to tolerate the clutter of old cities, to change them gently, lovingly. Thus, Rome could produce Corso Vittorio Emanuele, gingerly threading its way among important buildings.

But what the *Heimatschutz* crowd was getting at was something beyond mere theory of form, beyond the selective memory of monuments. The burgomaster of Hildesheim, in a speech to a conference on the care of monuments, held in Düsseldorf in 1902, gave the classic defense of this point of view:

Does a civic administration exist merely for the sake of enabling people to fulfill the needs of daily life as well, as cheaply, and as completely as possible? Is the city there for this alone? . . . Does the well-being of men consist only in bodily things, or is there not something far higher, the spiritual well-being of men, and does it not contribute greatly to this when they feel in close relation to the past, and take delight in realizing how the city has gradually built itself up, and how not only the streets, but every single public building, each individual house, even each piece of carved ornament, has grown in the course of time to be what it is? To make this feeling real is the task of the civic authorities.

To accomplish this task civic authorities need, first, to curb the profit machine, the new, all-consuming speculative greed. Many cities can't or don't. Florence, once a model of civic mettle, lost its historic downtown to speculation. It substituted a grid that was supposed to bring back the Roman grid and didn't; and it

acquired a most authentic looking Renaissance downtown, almost all of it ersatz 1880s stuff, totally without authenticity, standing on an area of seventy thousand square meters that was wiped clean of 26 old streets, 20 piazzas, 341 houses, and 451 shops.

Second, to achieve the burgomaster's task, civic authorities are needed who are elected and accountable to the people, not appointed and ultimately responsible to the state. The commune that Haussmann was glad to be rid of, the representative apparatus of civic administration that Mussolini and his proclaimed archetype, Augustus, abolished as soon as possible are essential. With this elective body out of the way, the stage is set for the regime to remember selected great deeds suitable for the glorification of its own aims. Then, in the name of saving monuments, of decorum, health, *grandezza,* the regime will attack the most defenseless, unresisting bits of city, the live tissue around the solid anchors of historic piles, the tissue that happens unfailingly to be the densest and most restive neighborhoods of working-class families, the urban poor, small craftspeople or *artigiani* (fig. 7). In the process, the regime manages to eradicate from the heart of the city an unwanted, volatile social element, that most likely to become antagonistic to or disillusioned with the government.

Figure 7. Mussolini's demolitions for Via dell'Impero, Rome.

The hate of totalitarian rule for incidental form is understandable. The urban clutter that Fascists disparagingly called local color is the sum total of small idiosyncrasies, hundreds of semiwitting acts of taking possession of a city. It is eloquent of the continuous rhythms of a common humanity that survives regimes, digests extravagant triumphs and defeats, and goes on weaving a pattern of personal joy and pain and decency. It is incompatible with what the Fascists called *gerarchia,* where individualism did not exist outside of the place to which each person was assigned in society, according to his or her function in a chain of authority that culminated with the Duce. Fascist *sventramenti* are bothersome because they remind us of a people's long acquiescence. Similar totalitarian schemes should bother us today, what-ever their source: dictators, spineless city councils that cannot stand up to private interests, form givers like Le Corbusier.

Contextualism is not a war won. It is never won with finality. The city form always demands vigilance. Not to be bothered by the loss of past buildings, big and small, is to have no sense of community beyond our immediate needs and pleasures. To feel that loss, to resist it, is to remember the times when all too spinelessly we surrendered our destiny to high designs, and to refuse to allow it to happen again. To kill is not to heal. To destroy is never a wise way to foster love. ∎

Note

This essay was initially presented as a lecture at Cornell University in autumn 1976. It was first published, in a slightly different form, in a 1982 issue of *Design Quarterly.*

1

SAN FRANCISCO

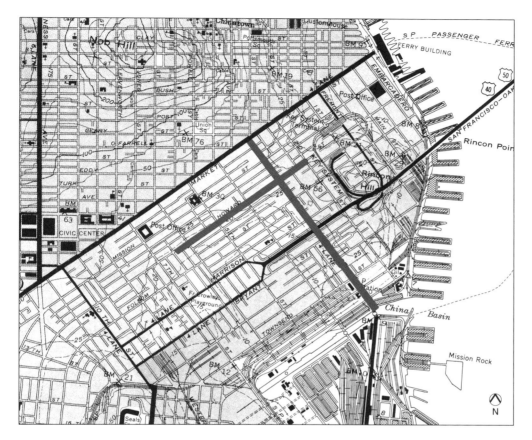

Third and Howard

Skid Row and
the Limits
of Architecture

PAUL GROTH

Figure 1. Detail from a
1947 United States
Geological Survey map of
San Francisco. The single-
laborer's sections of
Third and Howard Streets
are marked in gray.
Note proximity to docks
and railroad yards.

Third and Howard Streets in San Francisco began life as wide, simple demarcations of large blocks south of Market Street. They were part of the first large addition to the city's street plan. Architecturally and technologically, Third and Howard were like most other downtown streets in American grid-plan cities. Within the fairly classic scheme of the South of Market addition, Third and Howard were little different in prominence than their sibling streets (fig. 1). However, by the 1890s, the people who owned and leased property along Third and Howard Streets, together with the people who were their customers, had made these streets into nationally known examples of an important American street type: skid row. Third and Howard—especially the block of Howard between Third and Fourth Streets—had become a vortex of northern California's huge migrant labor force. These special streets mixed cheap work, cheap rooms, cheap clothes, cheap liquor, and cheap thrills for people with very low incomes. Until the 1950s, Third and Howard teemed with sidewalk life day and night; their land and buildings brought sure and steady profits to owners and predictable services to their customers. For those urban critics who consider street life a sign of urban health, Third and Howard merit attention.

By 1915, Third and Howard both had fairly imposing commercial architecture that compared in mass and ornament with the nearby

Figure 2. The last two blocks of Third Street in 1929, looking toward the financial district. Worker's hotels vie with downtown offices in permanence and prominence.

downtown business district (fig. 2). Nevertheless, the people and the street life of Third and Howard remained outside the social limits of what imposing architecture can achieve; even the best of architectural definition could not gain respect for skid rows and their citizens. Nor could it save them from eradication.

By the 1950s, most Americans had learned to use the term *skid row* pejoratively, for any place seemingly frequented only by single elderly and unemployed men. However, before 1950, places such as Third and Howard were socially and culturally very different. The term *single-laborer's zone* is more fair and more appropriate. Even if people from the middle and upper class had rarely been to a single-laborer's zone, the

names of such places evoked vivid images, and were typically the names of streets: in New York, the Bowery; in Minneapolis, Upper Hennepin Avenue; in Baltimore, Pratt Street; in Chicago, the Main Stem on West Madison Street; in Los Angeles, South Main Street.[1] These districts needed a special kind of downtown street because they had a very particular kind of economy and culture.

Low wages and a misunderstood subculture kept the life of San Francisco's casual laborers focused on streets such as Third and Howard. Other urban people with low income were merely *down* on the socioeconomic ladder; the men and women on Third and Howard, however, were often both down and *out*. They lived outside of a private household of any sort and were ostracized from the rest of the city. Although unwelcome, they were nonetheless essential as laborers until the 1950s. Nels Anderson, an ex-hobo who later became a University of Chicago sociologist, defined the true hobo as the "in-between worker, willing to go anywhere to take a job and equally willing to move on later."[2] In remote locations, hobos dug ditches, carted bricks, and tended animals in the construction of railways, highways, mines, and oil fields. In farm regions, hobos followed the harvests of grain, corn, fruit, potatoes, beets, cotton, or hops. During the winter, smaller numbers of men did lumbering or cut ice. In city locations, gangs of casual workers toiled over the menial tasks involved with building industrial plants and street railroads, paving streets, laying pipe and wire for gas and electric systems, erecting new buildings, and lugging materials during industrial and shipping peaks at docks, warehouses, and factories.[3]

In the economy of the nineteenth and early twentieth century, demand for hobo labor fluctuated wildly. When work was plentiful, hobos came to the city to sign up at special employment agencies catering to casual laborers; the agencies then sent them out in the appropriate numbers. When there was no work, the laborers flocked back to the urban districts that catered to them. Some California farm workers migrated to and from San Francisco for over fifty years.

To outside observers, gangs of hired laborers seemed to be members of a single category: tramp. However, casual workers themselves pointed out vital differences within their caste, often using a three-line rule of thumb: a hobo works and wanders; a tramp dreams and wanders; a bum drinks and wanders. Hobos, tramps, and bums all appeared unattached to a family; they had few possessions, enjoyed recreational drinking, worked intermittently, and traveled often. The categories of tramps and bums did the most to give casual laborers a bad reputation, yet they made up only a small share of the whole group.[4]

Photographs and reports from the turn of the century show that worker's districts were not full of elderly, hard-drinking men, as the 1950s stereotypes of skid row suggest. At the turn of the century, at least one casual laborer out of eight might be under twenty years of age, and most were in their middle years.[5] In some regions of the United States, new immigrants and racial minorities made up significant parts of the casual-labor markets. Through the 1920s, in San Francisco, Japanese and Chinese workers were hired from separate, "Oriental" employment agencies. In other cities, blacks were the more significant racial minority in the single laborer population. Although skid rows were very predominantly a male realm, a few women did live there as well. During the Depression, women were as many as one out of ten migrant workers; observers estimated that from fourteen thousand to fifty thousand women were on the road nationally. Yet before World War II, in large cities most casual laborers were white, American-born men whose rent payments and retail business commercially supported a special part of the city.[6]

Large cities had more than one single-laborer's zone, and San Francisco had three: Third and Howard Streets in the South of Market, the waterfront/Barbary Coast area, and Chinatown. Third and Howard was by far the most populous of the city's single-laborer's zones and the most infamous and worst-feared part of the much larger district known as the South of Market.[7] Several neighborhoods comprised the whole of San Francisco's South of Market. Most of them were packed with immigrant families living in tiny cottages and flats. The South of Market flour and sawmills,

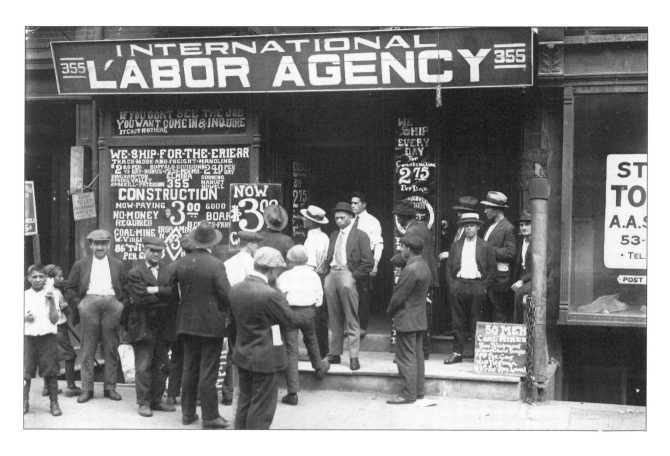

Figure 3. A labor agency on New York's Lower West Side, 1910, photographed by Lewis W. Hine.

refineries, printing plants, and machine shops generated large numbers of jobs for skilled workers as well as unskilled casual laborers. A 1914 survey estimated that, in addition to the large numbers of family-tied workers in the district, the Third and Howard area housed forty thousand single men at the peak of the winter. About a third of these men were permanent city residents; the rest knew Third and Howard Streets only as a part-time home base. Migrants typically arrived in the Southern Pacific Railroad's freight yards; from there they walked north along Third Street. By the time they reached the corner of Third and Howard they would have found all that they needed to be at home for the day, week, or month.

During the day, the busiest parts of Third and Howard's street life were the several employment agencies that occupied rented storefronts (fig. 3). On the one block of Howard Street between Third and Fourth were seven major employment agencies that competed with each other. Other agencies were close by. Early in the day and in times of high employment, the agency clerks filled their shop windows and the interior walls with chalked placards listing jobs. At the beckoning of "800 HANDS TO COLUSA—SOUTHERN PACIFIC RR," or "40 SHOVELERS—4TH STREET," the men would be off to work for the day or the month. Outside the labor agencies, still more men would stand and wait to register for work, or for other listings to appear. In slack times, the sidewalks outside the labor agencies were still the prime loitering and meeting spot of the worker's zone. In 1907, in Omaha's great hobo employment center, Douglas Street, officials estimated that they could see a thousand men passing time on the streets and sidewalks.[8] This was not Parisian boulevard life, but was nevertheless a distinctly street-centered life.

At the sidewalk edges of Third and Howard Streets began various retail outlets for those with low incomes. This retail street life expanded into most ground-floor spaces along each block. Prominent first-floor elements were workingmen's saloons, boldly advertising their nickel beer. Along Third Street, men found the greatest concentrations of worker's saloons, many with back-room bookie joints, legal in California until 1938. By 1910, San Francisco's saloons no longer served a free lunch, but they offered hearty 10¢ to 15¢ meals with the purchase of a glass of beer. Nearby was a distinctly grubby class of poolrooms and penny arcades. Added to the mix along the ground floors were occasional amusement halls; concert saloons, with their cheerful and gladdening bathing beauties; and, later, cheap all-night movie theaters. The saloons and entertainment establishments were frequented not only by the neighborhood residents but also by working men from throughout the city, and by adolescents who stole away to see something of life other than what the purveyors of the dominant urban culture thought appropriate for them. The South of Market also had fifty-one secondhand clothing stores, twenty-one of them on the core block of Howard Street alone. Retailers offering new clothing called themselves "outfitters": they sold the serviceable boots, Levis, heavy shirts, and gloves needed for distant work camps. Trunk shops and commercial storage-locker businesses catered to men leaving town for a season. Radical bookstores supplied reading material aimed at a workers' revolution. A

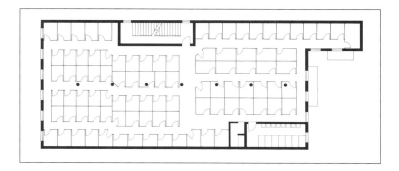

third of San Francisco's pawnshops were also in the district. Nearby were charity missions and the Salvation Army "institute," or wood yard, a vacant lot where men cut and stacked up cords of wood in exchange for meals and a place to sleep. There were barber colleges offering free haircuts; medical and dental schools offering low-cost clinics. Greek migration was strong in San Francisco after 1910, and the local colony of Greeks began to run South of Market tea- and coffeehouses and inexpensive restaurants. In the evenings, some of the shops offered exotic dance shows. Houses of prostitution or assignation were never far away, but a typical single-worker's zone had fewer women and children visible on its streets than any other residential or commercial district of the city.

Inexpensive eating joints filled the interstices of the South of Market. For breakfast, San Francisco's Bolz Coffee Parlor promised "three of the largest doughnuts ever fried and the biggest cup of coffee in the world" for 10¢. Coffee Dan's advertised "one thousand beans with bread, butter, and coffee" for 15¢. On a crash economy program, a man or woman could eat three meager meals a day for as little as 30¢ in the mid-1920s. At such rates, neither food nor service enticed the diner's palate. Overworked waiters got plastered with food; stale bread and sour milk were common. The cheapest meals were the free mission provisions.[9]

Figure 4. A typical lodging-house floor plan: a loft space with cubicle partitions. Based on the Kenton Hotel on the Bowery in New York City, built c. 1900.

Figure 5. Bush Street in San Francisco, a socially respectable street of middle-income residential hotels, photographed in 1946. In the 1990s, this street remains virtually intact.

The busy street scenes of Third and Howard make better sense with an understanding of the upstairs life in the buildings that lined the streets. On the upper floors of at least half of the buildings along Third and Howard were residential hotels of the very cheapest sort: lodging houses that catered specifically to people with a very low income. Cheap lodging houses were home to people largely living outside of the family and without access to the rest of the city; they were the ultimate "no-family house."[10] The prices (those given here are for the 1920s) separated lodging-house amenities into three levels: full private rooms for 25¢ to 40¢ a night; semiprivate cubicles or open wards for 15¢ to 25¢ a night; and flophouses that charged from 5¢ to 10¢ a night for a dry space on an open floor. The lower the price, the more one lived in a group. The higher the price, the greater the privacy, although in none of these hotels were conditions particularly conducive to staying indoors.

The private room for 40¢ a night was about ten feet square and might have two chairs and a dresser in addition to the bed, but it was usually in a building that offered no lobby or dining room—simply a warren of rooms. The 25¢ cubicle or ward-style lodging house was even more spartan and usually less well-maintained. The patrons called the cubicles "cages" or "cribs": the floors were filled with stalls made of partitions about seven feet high, and just large enough for one chair, a bed, and some hooks on the wall (fig. 4). A layer of wire mesh over the tops of the partitions (for security) gave them their nickname. The cubicle room's great significance was that it still offered its renter a private, locked space. At the next lower price level were open dormitory wards—areas crowded with rough, homemade bunk beds or cots. In such a dormitory area, each guest had at the most a locker for clothes. Even lower were flops—usually loft spaces with no permanent

installations whatsoever, rarely even beds. Some had mattresses or piles of rags with a blanket available; others had long rows of canvas hammocks. In a few dormitory wards, most flops, and all free missions, tenants could gain access to the room only after dark; at 6:00 A.M. all the sleepers would be roused and moved out. For single hobos, housing options other than these cheap lodging houses or missions were slim. Their chances of securing a polite apartment or a room with a family were no more likely than attaining a berth on a luxury ocean liner.[11]

For San Francisco's lodging-house residents (as for the residents in more expensive rooming houses in other neighborhoods) the reality of hotel life was that their home was scattered up and down the street. Permanent residents in hotels slept in one building and ate in another. The surrounding sidewalks and stores functioned as parts of each resident's home. The dining room was in a basement near the corner of the block and the laundry was three doors over. The parlor and sitting room were at a bar, luncheonette, billiard hall, or a favorite corner. If compared to a private single-family house of the time, places like Third and Howard were thus hallways and dwelling spaces as well as streets. Men loitered on the sidewalks throughout the year, night and day, no matter what the weather, literally because they often had no place to sit indoors other than seats for which they were required to pay "rent"—seats in a saloon, card room, cheap theater, or other commercial establishment.[12] Even if one had a cubicle or room, there were still other reasons to be on the street: the often horrible interior conditions of cheap lodging houses—poor heat, ample vermin, bad ventilation, almost complete absence of maintenance and cleaning, and the noxious odors from fouled bedding and people who bathed and washed infrequently. Along Third and Howard, life

Figure 6. Cheap lodgings on a waterfront street in San Francisco, 1913. These structures had survived the 1906 earthquake and fire and could thus remind San Franciscans of Victorian single-worker's streets.

Figure 7. The Central Hotel, a cheap Third Street hostelry built in 1909 with 440 small rooms, as it appeared in 1991. Originally, the structure had storefronts across the first floor, including a large saloon and dining room run by the management of the hotel. This is the only remaining worker's-hotel structure on either Third or Howard.

on the sidewalk might be the best life one could arrange.

Obviously, for the men and women who lived mostly on the sidewalks of Third and Howard, the overarching advantage was low price and the fact that they were accepted there. But the streets of skid row offered other advantages. The indigent elderly clung tenaciously to the advantage of ambulatory independence; as long as they could walk, they could meet their own needs. For the men and women of Third and Howard, the streets of cheap hotels and cheap services were also more than simply a place to be. They were a significant part of hobo identity, just as suburban houses became important for the family identity of the middle and upper class. Single laborers lived largely within a nonmaterialistic and highly verbal subculture, which relied heavily on storytelling and social drinking. Recent research suggests that among no-family people

setting in large part can *become* life-style. The hotels, street corners, and retail businesses of cheap lodging-house districts—even though fluidly used and seen as essentially interchangeable—provided an essential and meaningful backdrop for the single laborer's social world.[13]

Even with their omnipresent fire escapes, the upper façades of the tall brick buildings of Third and Howard's cheap lodging houses gave little hint of the minimal conditions inside the buildings and looked much like residential hotels in more polite districts (fig. 5). In San Francisco, this had been different before 1906, when the old, deteriorated exteriors of lodging houses typically matched bad interior conditions. In the nineteenth century, run-down and cheaply constructed wooden lodging-house exteriors stood out like sore thumbs (fig. 6). The buildings, like their residents, were social embarrassments, cultural concerns, and eyesores. However, between 1900 and 1920, San Francisco's skid-row landowners rebuilt with more polite façades—exterior images that better matched the new commercial world of downtown. In other cities, with no single inducement like San Francisco's 1906 earthquake and fire, skid-row landowners did similar reconstruction. Much of the rebuilding was a response to the production peaks of the early 1910s and World War I.

These newer canyon walls along Third and Howard were remarkably schizophrenic structures. The façades and interiors were disassociated; the exterior design and building materials said little or nothing about the uses of the upper floors or the people who lived inside them (fig. 7).

The interiors of lodging houses told their residents immediately and constantly about their income, their place in society, and their cultural alienation (fig. 8). The interiors of cheap lodging houses were embarrassing necessities for agricultural and industrial production, and for commercial and transportation service. In contrast to the interior conditions along Third and Howard, the architectural exteriors could easily be mistaken for decent lofts or small office buildings of the period. Admittedly, institutional forces encouraged owners to build this way. But beyond fire and zoning codes, neither city nor state bureaucracies stipulated that owners of purpose-built lodging houses commission the construction of nice façades. Indeed, *nice* is the word for the lodging-house façades built after 1900: they were dressed up, made more presentable than their forebears.

The presentable yet schizophrenic façades built along streets like Third and Howard after 1900 were clearly one strategy that landlords used to erase embarrassing images of the social and economic marginality of their properties and to erect reassuring images of greater cultural uniformity. Of course, landowners also built polite exteriors for personal reasons: for

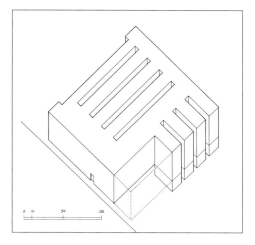

Figure 8. Axonometric drawing of the Central Hotel, showing the minimal light wells, up to four stories deep, that serve its 440 tiny rooms.

future flexibility and better resale values, for individual pride, or for the desire to be more respectable business people. Yet the new lodging-house façades also made the walls along Third and Howard into a different kind of place: architecturally, at least, with new buildings on either side, the Third and Howard Streets of 1915 could be seen more as socially satisfactory, minimally threatening, and permanent. The public could imagine that the people inside the new buildings were perhaps not so drastically alien a subculture as the sidewalk scenes suggested. The resident hobos could appear to share with downtown business people the bridge of commercial culture. For the hobos themselves, the better downtown architectural images may also have helped them to feel more a part of the great commercial core of the metropolis—that is, as long as they were outside, on the street.

In the long run, the exterior respectability of the rebuilt Third and Howard Streets proved to be insufficient to repel a long and partially planned attack on the social and commercial life of the district. One thrust of the attack came from workplace changes that began gradually in the 1920s and were complete by

Figure 9. A view along Howard Street in 1953, showing the older population left after World War II. The imposing structures that can be seen in the background have now been replaced by the Moscone Convention Center.

the 1950s. During the 1920s, production owners began to mechanize manual-labor chores in manufacturing, farming, mining, road building, lumbering, and warehousing—the tasks that were the mainstay of casual-labor demand. As the remaining migrants began to drive rickety automobiles to their work, new countryside skid-row conditions appeared in West Coast auto camps. These became rural slums well before their chronicling in John Steinbeck's *The Grapes of Wrath*.[14] The exigencies of the 1930s filled the hotels along Third and Howard, but with men and women more desperate than those of a decade earlier. Having gradually lost

the business of younger, robust migrant workers, districts like the South of Market began to be more identified with an elderly home guard.[15] After a brief return to a full-house and full-sidewalk status during the high-production period of World War II, Third and Howard came to be seen by the mid-1950s mostly as a settling place for formerly migrant people too old or too infirm to work or unwilling to go back on the road (fig. 9). In spite of these outsider's impressions, a vital community remained, smaller in numbers but still essential to the urban work force.

A parallel attack on skid-row vitality came

from urban reformers and large-scale real-estate interests. From 1900 to 1980 San Francisco's city officials, housing activists, and urban planners worked to eliminate the neighborhood centered on Third and Howard. Like the majority of middle- and upper-income city residents, the reformers considered Third and Howard's people and street life economically expendable as well as culturally dangerous to the future of the city. These critics of skid row wanted both the environment and the people of Third and Howard to vanish. Using the different tools of social reform, enforced building codes, zoning, active public disinvestment, and eventually outright demolition, they fought the small-scale real-estate management processes by which the area was becoming more permanent.[16]

If architecture could have helped any skid row to survive these pressures, surely it would have served well for San Francisco's Third and Howard Streets. In the 1950s, San Francisco's casual-labor market remained stronger than that of many other urban areas. Furthermore, the city's warm winters and cool summers drew hobo retirees with good savings from all over California and the United States. The hotel and retail buildings of Third and Howard were typically forty years old in the 1950s, but were still in the hands of the families that had built them and still repairable. In spite of all this, the enemies of Third and Howard eventually prevailed—not in down-sizing the district but in eradicating it altogether in a spectacularly scaled urban clearance program. The bulldozing, however, encountered a nationally important series of political demonstrations and resistance activities in the 1960s and 1970s.[17] The proper commercial buildings of Third and Howard, no matter how imposing, did not compensate for the investment competition for their central urban location. Neither could they counter middle- and upper-class aversion to the people on the street and to the sidewalk life, which remained largely misunderstood by outsiders. The same was true of skid-row streets in other cities. The lives of the casual laborers and commercial services of Third and Howard were beyond the social limits of what architectural façades could achieve.

In the 1990s, the outlines of Third and Howard Streets survive on city maps, but with a much-reduced and very changed sidewalk life. On the central block of Howard—the block between Third and Fourth, where most of the large employment agencies were located—stands the entrance to the Moscone Convention Center, the centerpiece of the Yerba Buena urban-renewal area. People much like those who once lived on Third and Howard now dwell in the few remaining cheap downtown hotels—if they are lucky—or are homeless on the city's streets. The 1990s street life of downtown is much poorer than the World War I mixture of life-styles and housing types, of which the old Third and Howard were an important part. ■

Notes

1 The term *skid row* was derived from the old Skid Road section of Seattle, where loggers lived next to the street where logs were skidded down to the waterfront. See S. Wallace, *Skid Row as a Way of Life* (Totowa, 1965), vii, 13–45. See also K. Jackson, "The Bowery: From Residential Street to Skid Row," in R. Beard, ed., *On Being Homeless: Historical Perspectives* (New York, 1987), 68–79; J. Schneider, "Skid Row as an Urban Neighborhood, 1880–1960," in J. Erickson and C. Wilhelm, eds., *Housing the Homeless* (New Brunswick, 1986), 167–89; and L. Blumberg, et al., *Liquor and Poverty: Skid Row as a Human Condition* (New Brunswick, 1978), which uses San Francisco as one of three case studies.

2 N. Anderson, *The Hobo: The Sociology of the Homeless Man* (Chicago, 1923), xviii–xiv.

3 On this labor force in California, see J. Nylander, "The Casual Laborer of California," Master's thesis, University of California, Berkeley, 1922.

4 Anderson, *Hobo*, 87–89, 172–73; C. Hoch and R. Slayton, *New Homeless and Old: Community and the Skid Row Hotel* (Philadelphia, 1989), 41; Wallace, *Skid Row*, 18–19.

5 Hoch and Slayton, *New Homeless and Old*, 37–40.

6 On Chinese, see N. Shumsky, "Tar flat and Nob Hill: A Social History of San Francisco in the 1870s," Ph.D. diss., University of California, Berkeley, 1972, 49–51. On blacks, see J. Schneider, "Tramping Workers, 1890–1920: A Subcultural View," in E. Monkkonen, ed., *Walking to Work: Tramps in America, 1794–1935* (Lincoln, 1984), 212–34. On women in lodging houses, see "Ten Cent Lodgings," *San Francisco Chronicle* (October 5, 1890), 9; and L. Weiner, "Sisters of the Road: Women Transients and Tramps," in Monkkonen, ed., *Walking to Work*, 171–88.

7 The key sources here are A. Averbach, "San Francisco's South of Market District, 1850–1950: The Emergence of Skid Row," *California Historical Society Quarterly* 52 (September 1973): 197–218; and California, State Relief Administration, *Transients in California*, Sacramento, 1936, typescript report.

8 N. Anderson, *The American Hobo: An Autobiography* (Leiden, 1975), 85.

9 F. Riesenberg, Jr., *Golden Gate: The Story of San Francisco Harbor* (New York, 1940), 250; Heller Committee for Research in Social Economics, University of California, *The Dependent Aged in San Francisco*, University of California Publications in Economics 5:1 (Berkeley, 1928), 73; Anderson, *Hobo*, 33–35.

10 I have borrowed the term "no-family house" from Lars Lerup, who uses it for a conceptual house design.

11 On cheap lodging houses, see P. Groth, *Living Downtown: The History of Residential Hotels in the United States* (Berkeley, 1994), chapter 5; on range of privacy, Hoch and Slayton, *New Homeless and Old*, 44–45, 60–61.

12 See C. Bauer and D. McEntire, "Relocation Study, Single Male Population, Sacramento's West End: Report Number 5" (Sacramento, 1953), 4–5.

13 Setting becoming life-style is a common thread in J. Spradley, *You Owe Yourself a Drunk: An Ethnography of Urban Nomads* (Boston, 1970), 252–62; H. Siegal, *Outposts of the Forgotten: Socially Terminal People in Slum Hotels and SRO Tenements* (New Brunswick, 1978), 42–44, 51, 68; Anderson, *Hobo*, 40–57, 87–106; and Wallace, *Skid Row*, 125–34, 166, 179–202.

14 See N. Hayner, "The Auto Camp as a New Type of Hotel," *Sociology and Social Research* (March–April, 1930): 365–72.

15 Averbach, "San Francisco's South of Market District," 210; Heller Committee, *Dependent Aged*, 63–64. See also Schneider, "Skid Row," 173–80; Anderson, *Hobo*, xix, 41–45, 74, 107–19.

16 On the designer's role in the elimination of skid-row hotel life, see P. Groth, "Non-People: A Case Study of Public Architects and Impaired Social Vision," in R. Ellis and D. Cuff, eds., *Architects' People* (New York, 1989), 213–37.

17 C. Hartman, *Yerba Buena: Land Grab and Community Resistance in San Francisco* (Berkeley, 1974). The Moscone Center is the keystone of the Yerba Buena redevelopment program.

OSAKA

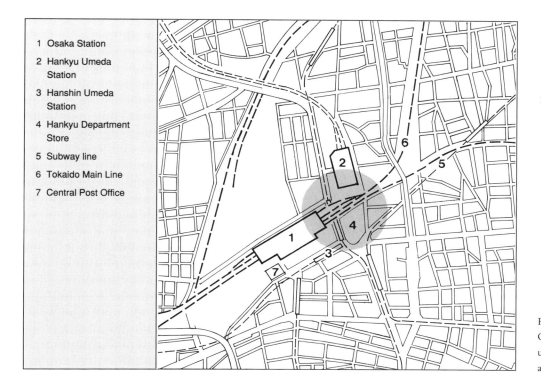

1 Osaka Station

2 Hankyu Umeda
  Station

3 Hanshin Umeda
  Station

4 Hankyu Department
  Store

5 Subway line

6 Tokaido Main Line

7 Central Post Office

**Underground
in Umeda**

MARC TREIB

Figure 1. The Umeda/
Osaka Station district. The
underground commercial
area is shaded.

The bombings and fires that accompanied the Allied invasion of Japan at the close of the Pacific war tore the infrastructure of the major cities and ruptured the traditional patterns of their streets. In central Nagoya and Tokyo, for example, the intricate networks of roads and alleys that had for centuries teemed with commerce and social exchange disappeared; in the postwar period, straight, fast arteries replaced these narrow, meandering roads. Certain districts managed to maintain their historical character for a time, in spite of extensive reconstruction, changes in consumer patterns, and the impact of advertising and electronic media. But on the whole, the Japanese metropolis underwent a substantial metamorphosis.

This resulted in a new transportation nexus, focused on the stations for the national railroad. Here intersect the worlds of taxi and bus, car and subway, private and trunk line, pedestrian and shopper. And here, below the ground, the historical street type—varied in architectural scale and texture, and free of vehicles—continues to exist in a transmogrified form. Despite the modern structural matrix that configures them, the shops, restaurants, and passages of the underground embody a centuries-old attitude toward the street and a customer attraction that depends on a traditional concept of space. The underground development around the Umeda Station in Osaka, which developed rapidly in the late 1960s and early 1970s, provides the most extensive and extreme instance of what has now become a national pattern (fig. 1). As such, this project indicates a contemporary attitude toward commerce, circulation, and social space that reflects a continually evolving model of the street in Japan.

The construction of Japan's rail system played a key role in the rapid industrialization that followed the country's forced opening to the West in the second half of the nineteenth century. Until 1877, railroad construction was a government monopoly, but thereafter private interests were allowed to enter the interurban transportation theater. In 1906, once their military value was recognized, the major rail lines were again nationalized. At that time, only 30 percent of the existing lines had been built by the state, based primarily on British models.[1] Major trunk lines were superimposed upon the Edo-period land routes that linked the shogunate with points throughout the country. On the Tokaido, long Japan's principal road, the first segment of rail construction was completed in 1872, linking Shimbashi in Tokyo with Yokohama and its port. In 1874, Osaka and Kobe were connected, and three years later, Osaka and Kyoto. By 1889, the project to join the principal cities of Honshu by rail had been realized. As the shrine had been to the village, as the castle had been to the city, the new imperial capital of Tokyo (literally, the "eastern capital") became—and has remained—the conceptual center of the nation as a whole. Even today, rail routes are termed "upbound" (toward Tokyo) and "downbound" (away from Tokyo).

Historically, Osaka (formerly Naniwa) served as Kyoto's port.[2] Because Osaka occupies a peninsula extending to the sea, the principal passenger rail station was established on the main Tokaido line at Umeda, barely an hour from inland Kyoto. Just a short detour from the trunk line, the Umeda/Osaka Station became the local pivot between Osaka and Kyoto, Nara, Kobe, and the Wakayama peninsula, with direct traffic extending northward to Tokyo and to points south on Kyushu. The prominence of the Umeda site is reflected in the agglomeration of governmental services and major architectural devel-

opments around the station; the area remains one of the busiest in all Osaka.[3]

The Umeda/Osaka Station development today is arguably the largest and most complex of all the underground developments in Japan, and as such it illustrates practices and trends found throughout the nation's principal cities.[4] Characteristic of these transit-node projects is a symbiotic economic relationship among rail line, passengers, consumer products, rental space, and services. As a result, the development in and around these stations accrues in layers, like deposits of sand and debris that, under pressure, come to compose sedimentary rock. In the earliest phase, the construction of the Osaka railroad station established the armature for all future development. The subsequent construction of municipal subway or private rail lines overlaid the national railroad station, and fixed this momentary pause in the trunk lines as the heart of a spatial network. Just as an obstruction in a stream causes more and more detritus to collect, reinforcing its importance as a disturbance, the station amalgamates its constituent parts and has become, over time, a small village.[5]

The physical development around, over, and under stations objectifies patterns of economic development as well as those of commuter rail traffic. Throughout Japan, but weighted toward the eastern coast, corporate railroad companies serve regional markets. Tokyu and Odakyu in Tokyo, Meitetsu and Kintetsu in Nagoya, and Hanshin and Hankyu in Osaka are large conglomerates whose economic interests center on rail lines and land development, but expand into many other industries and institutions.

Hankyu Railway, which controls a substantial portion of the Umeda Station area, was founded by Ichizo Kobayashi in 1906 as the Minoo Arima Railway, and became one of the most successful transit firms in Japan. In 1982 the company's profit ratio was the highest among Japan's private

Figure 2. Hankyu Umeda Station, Osaka, 1971. The station area is a nexus of transportation modes: buses, taxis, cars, and foot traffic. In the background is the Hanshin Department Store, Hankyu's competitor.

railroads. Kobayashi understood the inherent relationship among railroads, land development, and consumer goods, and under his directorship, Hankyu established business practices that have been emulated all over Japan. In 1929, the Hankyu Department Store was opened in Umeda, adjacent to the station, drawing commuters traveling on the Japan National Railroad and the Hankyu and Hanshin lines. The Hankyu Umeda is said to have had the largest gross sales in the country, with 1982 sales of almost $1 billion (fig. 2).

To maximize economic return is a long-term economic goal. Japanese entrepreneurs realize this in part through more immediate short-term projects, such as real-estate developments. In and around the station, the corporation builds department stores and other commercial facilities, office space, and parking (in the case of Umeda, on the roof of the station complex), and may even acquire control over surface transportation systems, such as bus lines and taxis.

Throughout the process, the value of land around the lines and stations continually increases. The nature of the transactions at these complexes is highly symbiotic: rail passengers become shoppers at the railway's department store, conveniently linked to the station, and may even work in one of its office buildings. Conversely, department-store patrons rely on the railway for their transportation. Transformed by the extensive commercial development that characterizes the underground shopping center, the station serves as a consumer destination as well as a point of passage or transfer. The station's subterranean commercial development assumes the role of the historical street.

Entire districts in cities such as Osaka and Tokyo have become indelibly linked with the rail lines and department stores that serve them. In Tokyo, Tokyu is synonymous with the district of Shibuya, Odakyu with that of Shinjuku, and Seibu with Ikebukuro; in Osaka, Kintetsu dominates the Namba quarter, and Hankyu

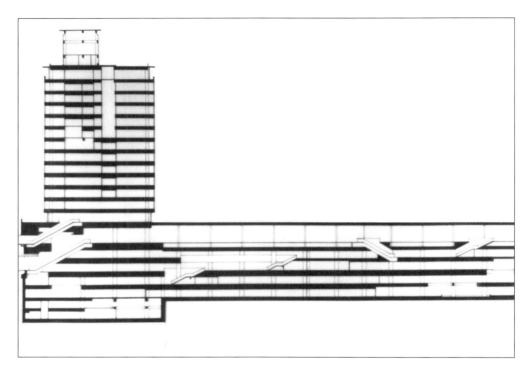

Figure 3. Hankyu Umeda Station, Osaka, 1971. Section through the terminal building.

the Umeda area, although Hanshin also evinces a strong presence. Of these, the Umeda district has been—until the last decade—the most extensive, with an interrelated network of over 650,000 square feet, extending over two thousand feet from north to south, and five hundred feet from east to west. More than one million people pass through the station area each day, and a good portion of them stop at some point to eat or to shop.[6]

Although the Umeda/Osaka Station of the Japan National Railroad has existed in some form since 1874, the opening of the first subway lines connecting Umeda to Shinsaibashi in 1933, and Umeda to Tennoji in 1936, provided the stimulus for new commercial markets. Subterranean passenger movement between the subway and rail lines became both a logistical and an economic consideration. During the war years, the railroads were turned to military service; in the aftermath of the extensive bombings of Osaka efforts were directed toward restoring antebellum services, rather than augmenting them. But with the "economic miracle" of postwar recovery, the domestic transportation market began to boom. Extensive development in the Umeda Station area began in the early 1960s, when population density, passenger traffic, and land values made underground development cost-effective. Prior to this time, hotel and commercial structures such as department stores tended to exploit the air rights above and around stations, rather than the ground below them. The adaptation of building form to accommodate lower-level traffic was limited, although the basement floors of department stores, for example, might be given over to food sales—a high-traffic commodity—and opened to passengers in transit on the subterranean level. The inauguration of the shopping

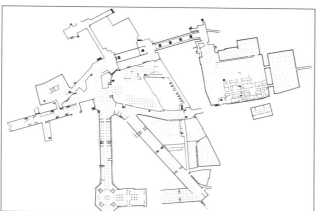

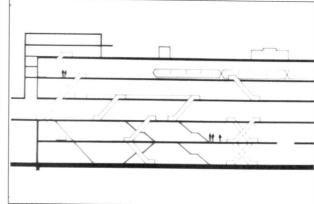

malls Hankyu San Ban Gai, around 1970, and Hankyu five, in 1973, created vast new underground worlds of three to five levels, zones in which—however ironically—aspects of the traditional world of the Japanese street reappeared. The small-scale pedestrian orientation and variegated texture that characterized Japanese urbanism until the modern era underlie the new shopping district. As the combined shop and dwelling of the traditional town had opened to the street, so the new commercial spaces open to the promenade: shops with walls of sliding glass; restaurants with terraces. History has been reformed in several levels below the street.

The presence of an extensive network of underground shops and services is hardly perceptible from the streets that surround the station, indicated only by signs announcing the location of rail companies, tracks, ticket windows, and department stores. The entrances to the transit precincts are scaled for large numbers of people, commuters more often than consumers. Even within the extensive station buildings, there is no hint of the pleasures of the subterranean realm. Within, one exists in "short space": the density of crowds—especially at rush hours—and the complexity of circulation patterns hardly allow the eye to see more than

fifty feet ahead. Like the seventeenth-century Japanese stroll garden, this is a world of hide-and-reveal in which space is not perceived as a totality, but rather as a conglomerate of fragmented experiences and views.[7]

The design of the Umeda complex grappled first with basic functional issues (fig. 3). The typical problems of moving people horizontally and vertically were solved with elaborately treated stairs, elevators, and, more prominently, escalators. These provide a dynamic spatial vision that animates the upper levels, exciting the clientele with views of crowds being displaced simultaneously horizontally and vertically (figs. 4, 5). The internal environment is fully air-conditioned throughout the year, maintaining an ideal temperature and moderate humidity. All construction is designed for seismic safety, scaled to accept large numbers of people, and brightly illuminated to eliminate all gloom. It is a sparkling world, clean and ordered—everything that the metropolis as a whole is not. If there is a reference to traditional architectural typologies, it is not that of the railroad station but that of the hotel lobby or the department store itself, or the American shopping mall. The complexity of the surface street has been sanitized and regulated by corporate interests; the

(left) Figure 4. Hankyu Umeda Station and San Ban Gai shopping development, Osaka, 1971. Detailed section, showing train-level and underground shopping floors.

(right) Figure 5. Hankyu Umeda Station and San Ban Gai, Osaka, 1971. Plan of the first underground level, showing the connection to the Hankyu Department Store.

eclectic architectural decor that ranges in references from classical Greece to vernacular Japan. Circulation is rarely direct and paths are almost never obvious, despite the straight regulating lines dictated by the structural grids. While the complex is less than labyrinthine, movement to a desired point is often a challenge to one's navigational skills.

A Japanese citizen reads the city in a far different way than an American, weaned on the simplicity of the grid. The majority of Japanese streets are not named, so that one relies instead on the indigenous *banshi* system, which orders space concentrically, focusing on a loosely defined district center. In the absence of precise route identification, people use visual clues, architectural or graphic. This need for landmarks allows the entrepreneur to entice the wandering shopper with extravagant or intensely illuminated displays; conversely, the shopper does not consider strolling without a precisely defined route a great inconvenience.[8]

The Umeda shopping complex employs a palette of architectural devices to mitigate the user's apprehension at being underground, within a hermetically sealed environment (fig. 6). Light is dramatic and floors tend to be of a pale color, for maximum reflective value. Shops and restaurants have glass fronts, adding the visual appeal of objects and services to the path, as well as additional sources of light and color. Animated water enlivens the circulation flow of the lowest level, dividing the main walkway into two paths and giving an impression of a width greater than its physical measure. The sound of moving water screens mechanical and human noises and provides comfort through associations with the distant natural world (fig. 7).[9] Uniting the various underground levels is a design challenge. Water, directed by gravity, is used to establish connections and conjure images of the world

Figure 6. Hankyu Five shopping center, Hankyu Umeda Station, Osaka. The Neo-Neogothic arches lend a somewhat medieval structuralist air to the pedestrian concourse.

underground version has been "conditioned" for both climate and shopping.

Functional issues are one thing, psychological comforts yet another. For many, the idea of being several floors below ground in seismically active terrain is not appealing; nor is the complete absence of windows and natural ventilation. This is the world of mechanical environmental conditioning and of an

Figure 7. San Ban Gai, Hankyu Umeda Station, Osaka, 1971. The "river" and its bubbling jets of water mask the sounds of the industrial systems necessary to service the underground complex. The ceiling lighting is ambient; incandescent and spot lights from shops and restaurants modulate the illumination along the promenade.

Figure 8. San Ban Gai, Hankyu Umeda Station, Osaka, 1974. "Classical" statuary lends a spurious touch of class to this café along the promenade.

Figure 9. Andō Hiroshige, *Night Scene at Saruwakacho*, color woodblock print, from One Hundred Views of Famous Places in Edo, 1856. The street façades of the shops and residences lining the street comprise a membrane that changes the degree and location of permeability throughout the day and night.

San Ban Gai, Hankyu five appears almost medieval. As usual, the architectural imagery is far from cohesive, however, and the Umeda underground complex is a collage of disparate and contrasting elements, rather than a unified architectural vision. Shops may be modern, or have a neofolk motif; Western themes confront the native Japanese styles; plastic models of food in inexpensive restaurants confront high-end Western clothing; the classical statue confronts the wooden clog (fig. 8).

Imagery, like the brick in Hankyu five, is only a veneer; meaning is borrowed from diverse sources and applied almost indiscriminately. In planned Western cities, the street pattern prevails and establishes a hierarchy of spatial importance: Haussmann's nineteenth-century renovation of Paris, for example, emphasized the intersection, the *place*, and the park. At Hankyu Umeda, however, the fragment rather than the overall configuration engages the visitor. While the subterranean street layout is basically orthogonal, there are few signs by which to read the geometry as a whole. As in the historical city, one is rarely aware of the greater plan beyond the immediate vicinity. Architectural imagery subsumes the greater "urban" order.

In contrast to castle towns and imperial cities, the traditional villages of the Japanese countryside acquired their irregular configurations over time, their layouts reflecting the pragmatic adjustment to factors such as land form, drainage, prevailing breezes, and the cosmological concerns of geomancy.[11] To the unpracticed eye, these patterns evince no sense of order; their streets appear as footpaths that have been incrementally widened over time to accommodate wheeled traffic and growing numbers of people. Despite the presence of these linear paths, space has been perceived primarily as a loosely concentric field: "room," house, garden, neighborhood, district, and ultimately city are conceived as a series of

above ground. Important transition points, such as escalators, feature devices such as a cascade that extrudes pencil lines of water, falling unchecked through three levels.

A multitude of design features adds architectural character to an engineered street. In Hankyu five, a thin brick veneer on the walls creates a dark space, with illuminated stained-glass windows that suggest both the churches of Gothic France and the Cannery shopping complex in San Francisco, built in 1968.[10] In contrast to the high light levels and modernity of

LEEDS METROPOLITAN UNIVERSITY LIBRARY

nested zones, modified by topography. Even within the few (usually monumental) cities planned on the grid, such as the early capitals of Nara and Kyoto, the spatial identity of place has traditionally been linked less to the linear street than to areas surrounding the intersection of streets. Similarly, one experiences the Umeda underground world as a district with only vaguely defined borders and, perhaps, the escalators or "river" as its central locus. The street functioned as the essential public space of Japanese towns and cities, nevertheless. Here was the stage for trade, social intercourse, circulation, religious processions, play, and even the public humiliation of criminals.[12] With land limited and commerce rooted in propinquity, the urban form was tightly integrated. In the middle and lower strata, business and residence commonly shared the same quarters. With its origins in village agriculture and trade, the urban street became an external corridor lined by semipermeable barriers that modulated social zoning from public to more secluded areas—an identity echoed in the modern underground "streets" of the Umeda complex (fig. 9).

The romantic idiom of the underground shops in the Umeda complex stands in direct contrast to the pragmatic structuring of its spaces, determined by engineering requirements. Its pedestrian passages tend to be linear, like their historical predecessors (although there are some convolutions and dead ends). There are no automobiles; they have been parked four and five levels above. Instead, the pedestrian reigns supreme in a nearly perfected world. Within the Umeda shopping complex, urban life and transactions have returned to the personal level, urban life with an emphasis on the pedestrian and a fabric of small shops that is becoming increasingly rare in urban Japan. And while it is far from Hankyu's intended project, these underground ways re-create, if not in its precise form, the essence of the historical street, tens of meters beneath the earth. ∎

Notes

1 W. G. Beasley, *The Modern History of Japan*, 3d rev. ed. (Tokyo, 1986), 137.

2 Having been founded according to the dicta of geomancy, which required mountains to the east and north and a river flowing from east to west, Kyoto was landbound except for river traffic. Because so much of the country is mountainous, and wheel traffic was consequently quite slow, major shipping had traditionally been by sea. Osaka became the merchant city; Kyoto the cultural center.

3 Facing the station, for example, is Tetsuro Yoshida'a 1935 Central Post Office building, recognized as a landmark Modernist structure of reinforced concrete. More recently, Hiroshi Hara has been designing a major complex of highrise hotels and office buildings that vastly increases the density around the station.

4 A more recent complex, from the mid-1980s, attached to the Kintetsu Namba Station, boasts a larger square footage than the Umeda complex. Recent hotel and office construction, however, may tip the balance again toward Umeda.

5 A comparison might be drawn to villages such as Ouchi, in Aizu Prefecture. The linear configurations of such villages resulted from their function as post towns or way stations, and are a direct reflection of movement translated into architectural form. Like the railway station, they suggested a pause in motion, rather than its complete arrest. Although vast numbers of people pass through Japan's stations each day, they rarely stop for more than a brief pause.

6 "Redevelopment of Umeda Hankyu," *Process Architecture* (March 1984): 106. Land ownership in the Umeda district extends beyond the holdings of one corporation and includes the rival Hanshin Railway, but Hankyu maintains the prevailing interest.

7 Under the influence of Zen Buddhism, the garden was treated as an object of contemplation; it was looked upon, but it was not entered. By the Edo period (1603–1867), people again moved through the garden, but the long vista characteristic of the formal French garden, for example, vanished. Instead, space was layered, partially screened, and

revealed only by movement through it. Landscape composition used bushes, trees, and other features to hide a distant view, thereafter revealing it, for heightened dramatic effect.

8 For a discussion of cognitive structure, graphic place representation, and building imagery, see M. Treib, "Reading the City: Maps, Signs and Space in the Japanese City," *Idea* (Japan, November 1979). For comments on the *banshi* system, see B. Rudofsky, *The Kimono Mind* (Tokyo, 1965), 264–66. Kevin Lynch distinguishes between using landmarks and paths as a means of urban navigation. In the United States, where the street and highway have such prominence, it is no surprise that we rely primarily on paths, planning our travel in terms of blocks, turns, and street names. See K. Lynch, *The Image of the City* (Cambridge, Mass., 1960). In Japan, subway and rail systems begin to define location; the process is completed using local landmarks such as banks, markets, office buildings, and shops. Building imagery thus acquires increased importance.

9 These watercourses may refer to gardens as far back as the Nara period (710–94), when the meandering stream, the *yarimizu*, was a central element.

10 The architectural imagery of both the Hankyu five and the Cannery, by Joseph Esherick and Associates, is sufficiently similar to suggest a comparison. In the renovation of the Cannery, the brick arch was used as a design motif; remarkably similar forms also appeared beneath the streets of Osaka, a few years after the completion of the San Francisco project.

11 *Kaso*, or geomancy, concerns the design of cities, buildings, and rooms in accordance with cosmological forces. Based to a large degree on the Chinese *feng shui*, the Japanese *kaso* conflates direction, color, animal and life force. Günther Nitschke, drawing on Japanese sources, describes Japanese spatial planning as having passed through three phases. The first, apparent disorder, is an intuitive process by which incremental decisions congeal to order hamlets and villages, with no suggestion of conscious forethought. The subsequent stage, geometric order, evidences a formal approach to organization, free to some degree of the exigencies of the particular site. The final stage, sophisticated order, eschews the obvious geometry of the previous stage to understand and reapply the more natural organization of the first stage—but in a highly conscious and aesthetically conceived design. See G. Nitschke, "Ma: The Japanese Sense of Place," *Architectural Design* (May 1966).

12 Soon after its first appearance, the railroad station came to deflect the public focus from the street, and in some ways became the equivalent of the Western plaza. Lafcadio Hearn wrote in 1894 of an incident at the Kumamoto railroad station in which the widow of a murder victim confronted the murderer. This story reveals that by the end of the last century, only some two decades after the arrival of the railroad, the station had become the point of intersection between the town and lands beyond. See S. Hirakawa, "A Case of Sympathetic Understanding of the Inner Life of Japan: Lafcadio Hearn's 'At a Railway Station,'" *Japan Foundation Newsletter* (1979).

With complete industrialization, the railroad station as the transportation node acquired increased prominence. Even today, the *eki-mae*, or area in front of the station, is usually the most active part of any town. When land around the station was restricted, development moved above or below ground. See M. Treib, "Dichotomies of Dwelling: Edo/Tokyo," in *Tokyo: Form and Spirit*, ed. M. Friedman (New York, 1986), 116–17.

3

KAIFENG AND YANGZHOU

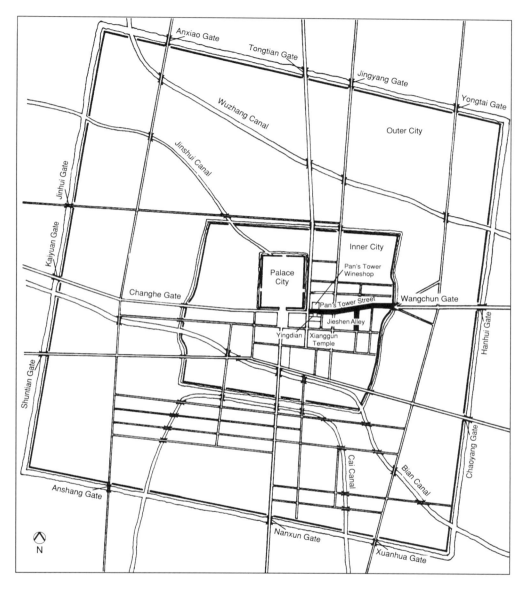

The Birth of the Commercial Street

HENG CHYE KIANG

Figure 1. Schematic plan of early-twelfth-century Song Kaifeng, with an irregular network of streets, some of which are oblique. Pan's Tower Street is marked in black.

Chang'an in the Sui (581–618) and Tang (618–906) periods and Kaifeng in the Northern Song (960–1127) represent two stages in the development of the Chinese medieval city. These capital cities reflected the respective periods that produced them: one rooted in a strong aristocratic power with a highly hierarchical social structure, the other shaped by a pluralistic, mercantile society managed by pragmatic professional bureaucrats. While the medieval capital of Chang'an was a controlled, highly disciplined city with restricted commercial activity that recalls the capital cities of the Six Dynasties period, Song Kaifeng established a new urban

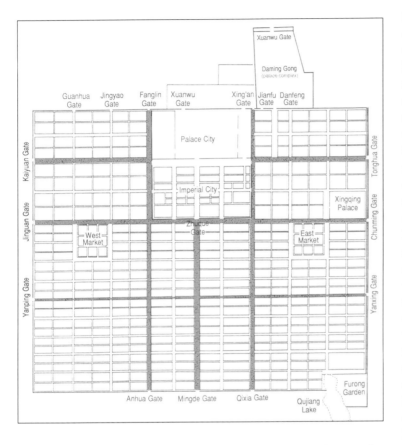

Xuanwu Gate

Daming Gong
(palace complex)

Guanhua Gate | Jingyao Gate | Fanglin Gate | Xuanwu Gate | Xing'an Gate | Jianfu Gate | Danfeng Gate

Kaiyuan Gate

Jinguan Gate

Yanping Gate

Palace City

Imperial City

West Market

Zhuque Gate

East Market

Xingqing Palace

Tonghua Gate

Chunming Gate

Yanxing Gate

Furong Garden

Anhua Gate | Mingde Gate | Qixia Gate | Qujiang Lake

Figure 2. Tang-period Chang'an and its "Six Streets," marked in gray.

structure with pluralistic streets (fig. 1). The emergence of this new urban paradigm is one of the most dramatic and important changes in Chinese urban history. Integral to this transformation, the open commercial street appeared as one of the constituents in a constellation of important urban changes that happened during this crucial period. This new paradigm remained dominant until contact with the West and the advent of modern technologies, industries, and government during the last one hundred and fifty years once again altered the urban landscape.

The structure of Chang'an in the Sui and Tang was extremely controlled. Although it was the biggest—and, with about a million inhab-

itants, the most populous city in the world—its urban landscape was very different from that which we would imagine of a prosperous and boisterous city.[1] Eleven north–south and fourteen east–west major streets divided the walled city into 108 *fang*, or wards (residential quarters) and two designated markets (fig. 2).[2] Along the central axis a great street, the Street of the Vermilion Sparrow, measuring 120 *bu*, or about 155 meters wide, cut the city into two halves. Like all other roadways in the city, this *tianjie* ("heavenly street") was made of compacted earth and flanked on both sides by open ditches and three-meter-high mud walls.[3] In fact, in Chang'an, there were six principal avenues, commonly referred to in contemporary writings as the "Six Streets." These were the three north–south and three east–west arteries that led to the gates of the city. Each measuring between 120 and 134 meters wide, these avenues were also wider than the others (fig. 3).[4] On both sides of the streets were ditches, about three meters wide, that helped not only in draining water off the slightly elevated roadways, but also in irrigation. Locust trees, willows, elms, and, at times, fruit trees lined the major avenues.[5] Behind the trees, earthen walls defined the sides of rectangular wards containing houses, religious establishments, and occasionally some official buildings. In the middle of each side, a public gate allowed residents to enter and leave the ward. Except for religious institutions or mansions of senior court officials, houses of private citizens were forbidden to have individual gates in the walls, and hence were denied direct access to the main streets during curfew hours.

At night, these extraordinarily wide streets became vast expanses of a closely patrolled no man's land. The residents of Chang'an who lived in the wards were subject to stringent supervision and forbidden to leave the wards during curfew hours. The keys of the gates were kept by the ward headman and unless a permit was issued, as in the

Ward Walls | Ditch | Roadway | Residential quarters

 Figure 3. A schematic cross-section of a typical street, 120 meters wide.

case of an emergency, illness, or marriage, no one was allowed out in the main streets at night.[6] Guards stationed in police posts, located at junctions of the avenues at the corners of the *fang*, enforced compliance. An entry in the treatise on officials in the *Xing Tangshu* [new history of Tang] records this close supervision:

At sunset, the drums were beaten 800 times and the gates were closed. From the second night watch [9–11 P.M.], mounted soldiers employed by the officers in charge of policing the streets made the rounds and shouted out the watches, while the military patrols made their rounds in silence. At the fifth watch [3–5 A.M.], the drums in all the streets were beaten so as to let the noise be heard everywhere; all the gates of the wards and markets were then opened.[7]

The main streets were also devoid of commercial activities, which were restricted to the fortresslike East and West Markets in the city. There trading was permitted only during certain hours of the day. At noon, the opening was signaled by two hundred beats of the drum; one and three-quarters hours before sundown, three hundred gong beats were sounded to indicate the closing of the market.[8] The image of a quiet night life and good order in Tang Chang'an was clearly described in a poem written by Bai Juyi (772–846) in 827:

Hundreds of houses, thousands of houses—
    like pieces on a great chess-board
The twelve streets like the orderly paths between
    vegetable plots.

In the distance I see faint and small the torches
    of riders to Court,
Like a single constellation of stars lying to the west
    of the five Gates.[9]

In fact, Chang'an behaved very much like a collection of semiautonomous walled cities or urban "villages" separated by wide avenues, within a fortified precinct (fig. 4). This was especially so when each residential ward had small-scale businesses that catered to everyday needs. Toward the end of the Tang dynasty, commercial activities began to be found, at first discreetly and later on a larger scale, within the residential wards. This was part of a long process, starting during the second half of the eighth century, in which a number of significant changes took place, including the appearance of commercial activities outside the markets, the disregard of curfew, and the tearing down of ward walls. These changes helped to erode the Tang urban structure and to create an alternative in which the open commercial street played an important role.[10]

Such urban changes were already present during the second half of the Tang period in many cities. This was especially obvious in the increasingly prosperous Yangtze region. Distant from the weakened central authority, Kaifeng, Suzhou, and particularly Yangzhou— the most prosperous port city at the time— began to defy the stringent regulations of enclosed wards and temporal constraints by the first quarter of the ninth century, if not earlier. Many poems written during this period sing of the new developments in city life. In Yangzhou, night markets, once forbidden, now flourished, as affirmed in a couplet by Wang Jian (c. 768–830):

Night markets—lamps in thousands lit the
    azure clouds,
Lofty towers—red-sleeved ladies and guests
    throng.[11]

Two lines from another poem, "Touring Huai-nan," by Zhang Hu (792–852), also clearly describe bustling night life beyond the confines of designated markets in Yangzhou:

The ten-*li* long street links markets to markets,
On Bright Moon Bridge, I look at "spirits and
    sylphs."[12]

As these poems suggest, commercial activities appeared and even thrived outside the previously restricted market wards in Yangzhou. Typically, these spontaneous markets flourished around bridgeheads and along water routes. Later, they expanded to fill entire streets, and business hours extended into the night.

Yangzhou was not unique; there were similar developments in other cities as well. During the Tang dynasty, Kaifeng, located along the Grand Canal, which brought supplies from the south to the capitals of Chang'an and Luoyang, quickly grew to be one of the most important commercial nodes of the empire. Spurred by the dramatic increase in trade, the old, strict urban structure was breaking down. Wang Jian wrote that this busy city had markets around water gates and bridges patronized by drinkers throughout the night.[13] Farther south, Suzhou too was a busy city with bustling night markets that attracted the attention of Bai Juyi, who described it as "more populous than Yangzhou," with "wards more active than half of Chang'an,"

and of Du Xunhe, who left us descriptive lines such as "Night market sells lotus roots, spring boat ships damask robes."[14]

Chang'an also experienced this phenomenon, although it took longer for the central authority to accede finally to the forces of change. The city and its structure had belonged to the preceding Sui dynasty, heir to the sinicized non-Han Northern Dynasties, whose institutions were concerned with the functional, hierarchical organization of society.[15] The Sui and the early Tang administrations adopted and further refined these institutions. The rigid urban structure, with its strict functional segregation and close supervision, recalled the highly hierarchical societies of the Northern and Sui dynasties. Early in the sixth century, when Luoyang was the capital of the Northern Wei, for instance, the strict social hierarchy of society had been reflected and reinforced by the rigid segregation of populations in their respective wards. The northern portion of the walled inner city was mainly dedicated to the palace and its parks. Government offices, monasteries, and residential quarters of officials and gentry made up the southern section. Outside the walls commoners lived in wards, the composition of which depended on the social status of their inhabitants. Hence, nobles and officials were allocated wards different from those of craftsmen and merchants, subject southern Chinese, aliens, and the like, creating a situation in which the inhabitants were very conscious of the location of their domiciles. On many occasions subject nobles from conquered territories, ashamed of living in the wards of aliens or subjugated people, petitioned the central authority for permission to move to other districts.[16] Even commoners, sensitive to the social stigma attached to certain wards, composed a song for one such residential precinct:

Northeast of Luoyang is Shangshang Ward,
For ages the home of spiteful Yin descendants,
Now forsaken by all except the lowly potters,
It brings only disgrace to its residents.[17]

The autocratic control of the city was equally evident in the manner in which Emperor Wen of the Sui dynasty dealt with the urban conditions of Kaifeng when he stopped there in 595, on his way back from the *feng* sacrifice at Tai-shan. He found a city in which commercial activities flourished and ward walls had been torn down to provide direct access to the streets for houses and shops alike. Offended by the sight of opulence and the proliferation of "unscrupulous" characters, Emperor Wen curbed commercial and artisanal activities, blocked gates that had been illegally opened to provide direct access to the streets, relocated boat dwellers who had settled outside the city walls, ordered refugees from the north to return to their land, and prohibited, among other things, people from living from nonagricultural occupations.[18] Emperor Wen's reaction was typical of the prevailing official attitude toward merchant activities and illustrates the strict control that the government was able to exercise on the population.

Gradually, the aristocratic and centralizing nature of the Sui and early Tang administration gave way to a government managed by career Confucianist bureaucrats and a progressively mercantile economy.[19] Thanks to the long period of stability during the first half of the Tang period, the economy expanded. After the An Lushan rebellion and subsequent unrest of 755–63, the government's control over the market system and trade began to break down. Shops and workshops started to appear outside the designated market wards. Initially, such commercial activities took place on a very discreet scale within the residential wards, but this soon increased. Wards located close to markets and

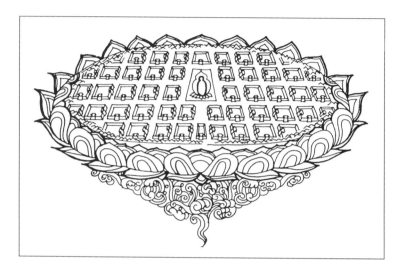

palaces were especially successful in attracting businesses. Night life thrived in these wards.

As early as the second half of the eighth century, inhabitants within the enclosed wards pierced private gates in the ward walls and even tore down wall sections. This practice was widespread enough to warrant the attention of the imperial court. In repeated attempts to curb these acts, the Tang government issued several imperial edicts prohibiting *qinjie*, or "encroaching on the street," between the mid-eighth and mid-ninth centuries.[20] *Qinjie* consisted of punching doors in the ward walls, tearing down wall sections, or building structures beyond the street limits.

A memorial from the Left and Right Patrol Officers to the emperor in 831 described the critical extent of the situation. It complained that commoners opened gates in the walls, disregarded curfew hours, and made it difficult for the guards to apprehend criminals. It also pleaded that the emperor issue an order similar to those decreed during and around the Zhide (756–58) and Changqing (821–24) reigns, whereby no one except officials above the third grade and *sanjue* houses was allowed to have doors

Figure 4. A reconstructed representation of the Buddhist Huayan world as depicted in a Tang mural in Dunhuang cave number 85. The world is represented as a lotus flower on which are laid out the neat, walled wards of a Tang city with a rectilinear grid as unyielding as that of Chang'an. In place of the walled administrative precinct at center is the image of the Buddha atop a lotus. Most wards had four gates, one on each side, but some had only two, as in this image.

opening directly onto the avenues.[21] The Left Patrol Officer further complained that in addition to the official guard posts, structures belonging to commoners and officials were erected in the middle of the avenues, once again complicating the maintenance of order. An edict calling for their removal was issued. Another imperial decree in 840 abolished the night markets that had developed in violation of the regulations during this period of urban ferment within the capital.[22]

Enforcement of official mandates, however, was problematic. Judging by the frequency of these edicts, the success of such restrictive measures was at best short-lived. After 860 the empire was besieged by popular uprisings and in 881 the capital was temporarily abandoned to rebels led by Huang Chao; such concerns were probably set aside in the face of these disturbances. The prolonged death throes of the dynasty during the last twenty years before its collapse in 906 left the cities even less ordered. The capitals were destroyed; Chang'an was reduced to "earth-heaps and waste-land."[23]

The interregnum of a half-century that separated the fall of the Tang dynasty and the foundation of the Northern Song dynasty was a crucial transition period for the development of the Chinese city. China, once again torn into short-lived feuding kingdoms, lacked a strong central authority with the will and the means to impose strict urban controls. Further erosion of the urban structure was evident in a 931 memorial to the Later Tang emperor, which complained of numerous intrusions on public roadways in the capital city of Luoyang.[24] An imperial edict issued twenty-five years later, during the reign of Chai Rong (also known as Emperor Shizong of the Later Zhou dynasty), acknowledged the inevitable breakdown of the walled-ward system in Kaifeng when he allowed citizens to use 20 percent of the public roadway for their own

purposes. For public streets fifty *bu* (paces) wide, inhabitants on both sides of the thoroughfares were permitted to use up to five paces to plant trees, dig wells, or even to erect mat awnings or shelters. In the case of narrower roads twenty-five to thirty paces wide, up to three paces could be used. Just a year earlier, finding the city too congested, the emperor had ordered the building of another expanded circuit wall. Instead of master-planning every detail of the city, as the Sui rulers had done in Chang'an, Emperor Shizong specified only the layout of military camps, roads and alleys, granaries, and administrative bureaus.[25] The rest—residential and commercial facilities—was apparently left to the initiative of the common people.

Relative stability during the short reign of the Later Zhou dynasty (951–60) brought a renewed economic vitality to the capital Kaifeng. Artisans and merchants flocked to the city and shops spilled beyond market confines into the congested streets. Together, economic forces and the pragmatic ideology of the new ruler laid the foundation for the blossoming of a new urban form.

The battle to dismantle the existing rigid urban structure was, however, not easily won. During the early Northern Song period, the central authority tried hard to revive the system of walled wards in Kaifeng.[26] After the founding emperors had consolidated the empire, the Song rulers Zhenzong (998–1022) and Renzong (1023–63) turned their attention to the increasingly cluttered capital. During the long period of relative peace, the population in Kaifeng as well throughout China grew rapidly—a result, in part, of agricultural advancements. The adoption of new strains of early-ripening Champa rice allowed for multiple harvests per year; improvements in agricultural technologies brought about dramatic increases in

production. At the same time, surplus labor began to specialize, resulting in ample consumer goods for the growing urban population. The Song saw a period of unprecedented growth. The capital region, which had 180,000 households during the years 976 to 984, had to shelter 230,000 households between 1078 and 1085. Yet in physical size, the intramural city was not much bigger than it had been during the Later Zhou dynasty.[27] Kaifeng quickly became crowded. Houses and sheds invaded public roadways. Simultaneously, commercial activities bloomed. Shops expanded beyond the last semblance of the wards; they first lined and later encroached upon the streets and avenues. These developments became the target of the central authorities, who still preferred the orderly and easily controllable city of the Tang era.

In 1002, for instance, Emperor Zhenzong issued an edict. In spite of widespread protest from the rich and the powerful, the streets were cleared of encroaching shops and the curfew of the previous era was reimposed.[28] In the ensuing years, the central authority repeatedly tried to

maintain the fragile urban order. Again, the frequency of such edicts, however, points to their ineffectiveness.

Although decrees were issued to dismantle structures encroaching the roadway, there was no further mention of ward walls. Instead, repeated references were made to wooden road markers, beyond which all building was forbidden.[29] This was probably because the low earthen walls of the wards were no longer intact and buildings, especially shops, had been erected beyond the original perimeters. Many of these must have actually infringed on the roadways, making the streets narrower than their intended sizes as indicated by the road markers.

The Song emperors' decrees acknowledge the breakdown of the old urban structure and the emergence of a new kind of street—an acknowledgment the Later Zhou conceded when Chai Rong laid down the guidelines for the use of road shoulders. Toward the end of the eleventh century, the Song authorities actually went a step further, giving in to the phenomenon of unmanageable street encroachment.

Figure 5. Street scene by an unknown artist from *Lady Wenji's Return to China*, color on silk, Northern Song, eleventh century. Note the plurality of activities in the narrow street—restaurant, wineshop, peddlers, tradesmen, ox cart—in front of a large residence.

Figure 6. Street scene by
Zhang Zeduan, from
*Going up the River during
Qingming Festival*, ink
on silk, Northern Song,
early twelfth century.

Instead of suffering demolition, offending builders were charged a rent for the infringement of roadways during Emperor Zhezong's reign (1086–1100).[30] The pragmatism of the Song reign turned an urban problem into a money-making opportunity and accepted the birth of a new urban system. The rigid physical and temporal urban constraints on the city were finally abandoned. The developments that occurred in Song Kaifeng also took place in most other major Chinese cities, such as Suzhou, Yangzhou, and Hangzhou. By the beginning of the twelfth century there was no turning back. A new urban ambience and lifestyle were celebrated in paintings such as *Qingming shanghe tu* (Going up the river during Qingming Festival) and in contemporary writings (figs. 5, 6, 7). The memoir *Dongjing menghua lu* (A record of the dream of splendor in the eastern capital), written by Meng Yuanlao, recalls life and festivities in Kaifeng shortly before its fall in 1127 (see fig. 1).[31] In one of the accounts, he describes a busy entertainment and commercial district immediately southeast of the Palace

City, where the major east–west thoroughfare took its name, Panlou jie, or Pan's Tower Street, from a prominent wineshop located along it. Before the tavern, the street is busy with shops and stores displaying gems, silks, and fragrant herbs. South of the street, the Yingdian (Accipiter Inn) lodges only traveling merchants who trade in hawks and falcons. An alley, called Jieshen, with stately, imposing houses and broad, awe-inspiring gates, branches off to the south. Here gold, silver, and colored silk are bought and sold: "Every transaction involves thousands and tens of thousands of cash; it truly startles one to see or hear it." East of the Accipiter Inn and on the north side of the street is the Pan's Tower Wineshop. Below the wineshop, commerce goes on day and night, with the things traded varying throughout the day. Between three and five in the morning, a market gathers. Stores and stands buy and sell clothes, calligraphy and paintings, precious baubles, rhinoceros horns, and jade. At dawn, food items such as sheep's head, tripe and lung, red and

white kidneys, udders, tripe, quails, rabbits, doves, wild game, crabs, and clams arrive at the market. Next come the various tradesmen to peddle miscellaneous small items and materials. After meals, delicious sweets and snacks of all sorts are sold. Toward evening, merchants sell garments, household implements, precious trifles, toys, and the like. The Xu family's Calabash Mutton Stew Shop, another popular eating place in the capital, is located farther to the east. South of the street is a large entertainment district formed by several *wazi*, or "pleasure precincts;" among them are more than fifty theaters, large and small. The bigger of these can accommodate several thousand spectators. Commerce flourishes in these precincts too. Fortune-tellers and hawkers of herbs, food and drink, old clothes, and paper cutouts display their wares here.[32] Pan's Tower Street was only one in an extensive network of commercial streets that served and animated the Northern Song capital. Urban land, much of it in the hands of the officials, the gentry, and the monied merchant class, was used to produce a

city for their own consumption—a city crisscrossed by streets lined with shops, taverns, restaurants, pleasure precincts, and brothels, offering a plurality of services matched only by the purchasing power of the new social classes. The perceptive account of Meng Yuanlao records a flourishing cityscape of commercial streets.

Unlike Sui-Tang Chang'an or Luoyang, Song Kaifeng and most other Song cities had much narrower streets; the widest in Kaifeng measured only about 60 meters (40 *bu*) wide.[33] Most other streets measured around 30 to 37 meters (20 to 25 *bu*) in width. Oblique streets, unimaginable in the earlier checkerboard grid, now appeared (fig. 8). The divisive open ditches of the previous period were concealed. Crisscrossing the city were streets lined with large and small shops with open fronts, such as those along Pan's Tower Street and those depicted in *Going up the River during Qingming Festival*. Merchants displayed their wares at the front of these, while artisans worked in the back. The many taverns, teahouses, and restaurants in the

Figure 7. Street scene by Zhang Zeduan, from *Going up the River during Qingming Festival*, ink on silk, Northern Song, early twelfth century.

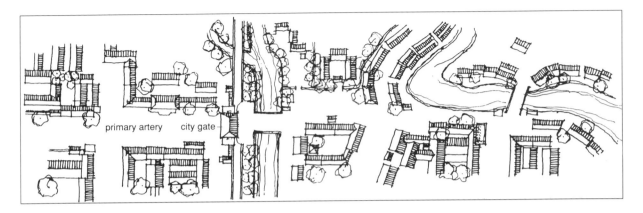

primary artery   city gate

Figure 8. Schematic plan of a section of Kaifeng, as depicted in Zhang Zeduan's painting *Going up the River*. Notice the absence of a clear grid, the oblique streets, the encroached, narrow primary artery leading to a city gate, and the multifunctional character of the streets.

capital added gaiety and color to the streets, with their large, richly decorated entrance scaffoldings, or *cailou*. Many of these food and wine establishments had an upper level; some were even three stories high. Huge pleasure precincts with numerous theaters, shops, and restaurants provided entertainment venues for the populace. Nearby, food hawkers set up tables and stands selling all sorts of snacks to tease the appetites of passersby. Corner eateries boasted tables and benches set outside, under light mat awnings or huge parasols. At the busier junctions and bridgeheads, peddlers, one after another, displayed their goods on low tables or on the ground. Local inhabitants on foot and on horseback, itinerant merchants, animal trains, mule and bullock carts, and palanquins crowded the narrow streets. Business went on all day, and in busier localities continued through the night.

As Spiro Kostof has pointed out, "Power designs cities, and the rawest form of power is control of urban land."[34] The strong, autocratic grip that the Sui emperors had over their capitals, coupled with a rigid social order, produced an equally strict urban order of walled, monofunctional wards separated by wide, policed streets, confining citizens to easily controlled quarters. The government's disdain for commercial activities and merchants alike relegated them to closely supervised, enclosed markets; trade, if needed, was primarily for the consumption of the court. Although this system was adopted during the early Tang period, the second half of the Tang saw a gradual erosion of the urban structure, thanks to a weakened central government, an expanding economy, and the emergence of a prosperous urban class. The half-century-long interregnum, which decimated much of the aristocracy and the gentry, brought an end to the "apogee of the power of the great aristocratic clans" and paved the way for a new social order.[35] Under the more pluralistic Song society, commerce, once considered a necessary evil and kept to a minimum, flowered. The imperial coffers, which had depended mainly on agricultural taxes, now derived a large income from commercial taxes. Even officials and gentry, attracted by profit, participated in commercial ventures once regarded with contempt. In fact, many of the rental properties that encroached on the public roadways were built and owned by high officials themselves, making it ever more difficult for the central authority to rid the streets of these structures. Once confined to the walled enclosure of the Tang markets, the commercial street was finally liberated. ∎

Notes

1 For Chang'an, see E. Schafer, "The Last Years of Chang'an," *T'oung Pao* 10 (1963): 133–79; A. Wright, "The Cosmology of the Chinese City," in W. Skinner, ed., *The City in Late Imperial China* (Stanford, 1977), 33–73; N. Steinhardt, *Chinese Imperial City Planning* (Honolulu, 1990), 93–121.

2 When the palace complex, Daming Gong, was added northeast of the city in 634, a new imperial avenue cut two big wards into four smaller ones, increasing the original 108 wards to 110.

3 In most such cities, the *tianjie* is usually the main north–south street leading to the palace. Sometimes the term was also used to designated all the major streets in a city.

4 Only the southernmost east–west principal street measured significantly less, but was still a very impressive 55 meters wide. See "Tangdai Chang'an cheng kaogu jilue" [A brief archaeological record of Tang-period Chang'an], *Kaogu*, no. 11 (1963): 595–611.

5 The planting of fruit trees was ordered in 740. See *Tang huiyao* [Collection of important Tang documents], henceforth abbreviated as THY (Shanghai, 1991), vol. 86, 1864.

6 The etymology of the word *fang*, or ward, may have something to tell us of the nature of the Tang city—or for that matter, imperial cities prior to the Tang period—and the reason for such tight control. *Fang* was written with the *tu*, or earth radical. However, this word had its roots in the homonym, *fang* with the *fu*, or mound radical, which means "to defend or to guard against." One common interpretation suggests that the walls of these wards were as much for the protection of the inhabitants of the wards as for the control of them within the wards, guarding against popular unrest. These walls also made it easier for the police to ensure the security of the city and facilitated the arrest of criminals. See E. Balazs, *Chinese Civilization and Bureaucracy* (New Haven, 1964), 69.

7 See *Xing Tangshu* [New history of Tang], ch. 49, part 1, 8a–b; passage translated by Balazs in *Chinese Civilization*, 69.

8 THY, vol. 86, 1874.

9 Bai Juyi, "Deng Guanyintai wang cheng" [Watching the City after Ascending Guanyin Dais], *Quan Tanshi* [Complete Tang poems] (Beijing, 1960), c. 448, 5041; translation modified from A. Waley, *Chinese Poems* (London, 1961), 161.

10 For the gradual erosion of the Tang ward system, see Kato Shigeshi, "Sodai ni okeru toshi no hattatsu ni tsuite" [The development of cities during the Sung period], in *Shina keizai shi kosho* [Studies in Chinese economic history], Toyo bunko ronsho, no. 34 (Tokyo, 1952–53), 93–140; He Yeju, *Zhongguo gudai chengshi guihua shi luncong* [Discussion of the history of ancient Chinese city planning] (Beijing, 1986).

11 Two lines from the quatrain "Watching the Market of Yangzhou at Night," by Wang Jian. See *Quan tangshi* [Complete Tang poems] (Beijing, 1960), vol. 301, 3430.

12 *Quan tangshi*, vol. 511, 5846.

13 Ibid., vol. 300, 3406. See Wang Jian's poem "Sending Off Bianzhou's Master Linhu."

14 *Quan tangshi*, vol. 447, 5033–34; vol. 691, 7925.

15 Gernet, *A History of Chinese Civilization* (Cambridge, 1982), 204. See also Tanigawa Michio, *Medieval Chinese Society and the Local "Community,"* trans. J. Fogel (Berkeley, 1981).

16 Ho Ping-ti, "Lo-yang, A.D. 495–534: A Study of Physical and Socio-Economic Planning of a Metropolitan Area," *Harvard Journal of Asiatic Studies* 26 (1966): 52–101.

17 Quoted and translated in Ho Ping-ti, "Lo-yang, A.D. 495–534," 87–88. From a sixth-century account of the city by Yang Xuanzhi, *Luoyang jialanji* [Record of the monasteries of Luoyang], 38b. See also W. J. F. Jenner, *Memories of Luoyang, 495–534* (Oxford, 1981).

18 *Sui Shu* [Official history of Sui] (Beijing, 1973), vol. 56, 1386.

19 *The Cambridge History of China*, vol. 3: Sui and T'ang China, 589–906, part 1 (Cambridge, 1979), 14–15.

20 Dali second year, or 767; Zhenyuan fourth year, or 788; Taihe fifth year, or 831, and Dazhong third year, or 849. See *THY*, vol. 86, 1867–68.

21 *Sanjue* houses were those located along the periphery of the ward, with three sides blocked by other properties. See *THY*, vol. 86, 1867.

22 *THY*, vol. 86, 1875.

23 Schafer, "Last Years of Chang'an," 168.

24 *Wudai huiyao* [Important documents of the five Dynasties] (Shanghai, 1936), vol. 26, 315.

25 Ibid., 320.

26 For Kaifeng, see E. A. Kracke, Jr., "Sung K'ai-feng: Pragmatic Metropolis and Formalistic Capital," in J. W. Haeger, ed., in *Crisis and Prosperity in Sung China* (Tucson, 1975), 49–78.

27 The outer city was enlarged slightly during the first ten years of Shenzong's reign (r. 1068–85). The perimeter of the outer wall was extended from an initial 48 *li* 233 paces to 50 *li* 165 paces. The Song *li* is about the length of the Tang *li*, which is equivalent to 360 paces, and measures about 531 meters. There was also a shorter Tang *li* that consisted of 300 paces, or 442.5 meters. See *Zhongguo gudai duliangheng lunwenji* [Papers on ancient weights and measures of China] (Zhengzhou, 1990), 235, 242. Part of the population lived in suburbs located outside the walls. See Kracke, "Sung K'ai-feng," 66.

28 See *Xu zizhi tongjian changpian* [Continuation of the comprehensive mirror for aiding government], henceforth abbreviated as *CP* (Shanghai, facsimile ed., 1986), vol. 51, 6b–7a.

29 These were issued in 1012 (*CP*, vol. 79, 14b), in 1024 (*CP*, vol. 102, 9a), in 1034 (*CP*, vol. 115, 16b; vol. 116, 7b), in 1036 (*Song huiyao jigao* [Collection of important documents of Song, Beijing, 1936], vol. 19815, 2b), and in 1059 (*CP*, vol. 190, 21b–22a).

30 This practice was implemented by 1079 and was still in use before the fall of Kaifeng. See *CP*, vol. 297, 16a–b.

31 Meng Yuanlao belonged to an influential clan whose members held official positions during the last years of the Northern Song administration. The memoir was written in Hangzhou; a preface was added in 1147. On Meng Yuanlao, see S. West, "The Interpretation of a Dream," *T'oung Pao* 71 (1985): 63–108.

32 This description is based on a passage in Deng Zicheng, *Dongjing menghua lu zhu*, henceforth abbreviated *MHL* (Beijing, 1959), 67. See also a translation of the same passage in W. Idema and S. West, *Chinese Theater 1100–1450* (Wiesbaden, 1982), 14–15.

33 Since Song Kaifeng was inherited from the Later Zhou, the streets were probably no wider than those prescribed by Chai Rong. Although *MHL* recorded that the avenue south of the Palace City was 200 paces wide, I believe that this is true only for a section that functioned, in reality, as a public square, rather than a street.

34 S. Kostof, *The City Shaped: Urban Patterns and Meanings through History* (London, 1991), 5.

35 D. Twitchett, "The Composition of the T'ang Ruling Class: New Evidence from Tunhuang," in A. Wright and D. Twitchett, eds., *Perspectives on the Tang* (New Haven, 1973), 47–85, 52.

4

MOSCOW

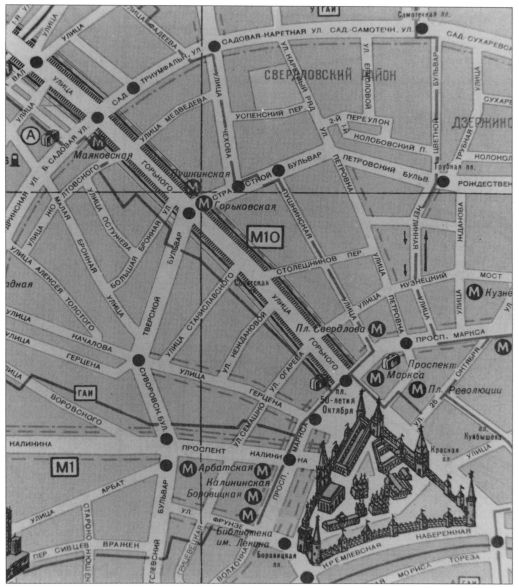

Gorki Street and the Design of the Stalin Revolution

GREG CASTILLO

Figure 1. Plan of central Moscow. Gorki Street is marked with heavy, striped borders.

During the climax of the Great Purges in the late 1930s, as a generation of Bolsheviks disappeared silently in nighttime arrests, Moscow's dailies heralded the arrival of a Renaissance in socialist construction. Tverskaya Street, the Kremlin's northern approach, was being remodeled as a broad new boulevard, renamed in honor of Maxim Gorki, the dean of Soviet writers (fig. 1). The namesake project marked the first full application of the state-approved Socialist Realist aesthetic, developed in part by Gorki, to the art of urban design.

The street's reconstruction was acclaimed as an opening episode in Moscow's Stalin-era Ten Year Plan of Great Work. The "magnificent distances" of scores of such boulevards would soon traverse the capital; as their prototype, Gorki Street was immediately declared a success. Its architect-in-charge, Arkady G. Mordvinov, was well rewarded for his efforts. He was fêted by V. M. Molotov at the 1938 Party Congress and awarded the presidency of the Academy of Architecture, a seat on the Mossovet (Moscow's city council), and a position on the Supreme Soviet. It was an unprecedented ascent to power, one that had few rivals within the history of the Soviet architectural establishment.

Gorki Street was promoted as an example of a new kind of boulevard: the "socialist *magestrale.*" In fact it followed the conventions of nineteenth-century street design in its broad pavements, elegant lamps, and ensemble architecture (fig. 2).[1] But what really distinguished this socialist brand of aesthetic reform from predecessors was its long-term viability. Soviet planners were endowed with unlimited powers of expropriation and condemnation by a 1918 decree abolishing private land ownership in cities. Socialist Realism was thus spared the fate of the American City Beautiful and Haussmann's Paris, urban-reform traditions that were eventually broken by the price tag attached to their vision of urban harmony. In the USSR, by contrast, new six- to eight-story street façades stretching up to half a kilometer in length could be created in the heart of the city at a single stroke. Unified compositions of such superblocks were to define a new Moscow, "bringing home to everyone the overall image of the city."[2]

The paradigm established by Gorki Street reached the administrative capitals and new industrial towns throughout the Soviet Bloc, and here too Mordvinov played a part. He advised in the reconstruction of Sofia, Bulgaria, the Eastern Bloc capital that most precisely conforms to the Moscow precedent. He also guided the socialist building program of Bucharest, playing tour guide when its Romanian architects failed to produce a satisfactory design and were sent to Moscow on an edifying field trip.[3]

Mordvinov's professional achievements were seen as such only within the confines of this empire. In the West, Soviet urbanism's claim as the legitimate expression of built socialism was challenged on two fronts. Writing from exile, Leon Trotsky condemned Stalinist traditionalism as a reversion to petit-bourgeois norms and values. "Every regime has its monumental reflection in buildings and architecture," he argued in *The Revolution Betrayed.* "Characteristic of the present Soviet epoch are the numerous palaces and houses of the Soviets, genuine temples of the bureaucracy."[4] On the other hand, proponents of Soviet avant-garde architecture and urbanism, now elbowed out of their position of State patronage by Neoclassicists, reproached Stalinist culture largely on aesthetic grounds.

Over the past fifty years these two critiques— one ideological, the other aesthetic—have fused and hardened into a single verdict. Anatole Kopp, one of the first Western chroniclers of Stalinist architecture, regards Socialist Realism as an apostasy so repugnant that it hardly merits reflection. The leftist architectural historians Manfredo Tafuri and Francesco Dal Co dismiss Socialist Realism as "an eclecticism that was unashamedly kitsch." Even that champion of postmodern Neoclassicism, Charles Jencks, scorns its products for their "coercive and boring symbolism," melding "the repressive forms of czarism . . . and the signs of bourgeois power."[5] The implications for scholarship are clear: if Stalinist architecture is beneath contempt, it is surely outside the bounds of serious inquiry.

Figure 2. Blocks A and B (1937–38) were the first elements of Mordvinov's reconstruction of Gorki Street to be completed. Block B's triumphal archway, visible at far left, leads to older buildings walled off from the street by the precinct's reconfiguration in a superblock pattern. This view faces south, with the spires of the Kremlin's corner Arsenal and Nikol'skaya towers visible on the right.

The price of this aesthetic and ideological prejudice is high. Denying Socialist Realism and its representative urban environments their scholarly due forfeits a fuller understanding of Soviet cultural history—and not just its Stalinist installment. In settling for a caricature of Socialist Realism as the absolute repudiation of Soviet Modernism's promise of social and technological reform, conventional connoisseurship rehashes the politically expedient revisionism of the Khrushchev era and its quarantine of all aspects of Stalinist culture within the boundaries of an unequivocal periodization of history. Architectural historians rarely question this historiographic convention. But breaks *and* continuities between Modernism and Socialist Realism are chronicled in the reconstruction of Gorki Street, an artifact of a self-proclaimed urban Renaissance that coincided with a reign of urban terror.

As a starting point for the 1935 Stalin Plan for Moscow—"the international capital of workers and toilers of all lands"—the choice of Tverskaya Street takes some explaining. Initial Soviet urban-renewal projects had focused on working-class quarters long deprived of infrastructural investment, while Tverskaya Street's prerevolutionary associations were exclusively czarist and mercantile. Running from the former city ramparts downhill toward the Kremlin, it was the terminal stretch of the royal route linking Moscow to the heart of autocracy in St. Petersburg.

Despite this ceremonial function, the thoroughfare retained a ragged informality, acquired in the late seventeenth century through continual private encroachment onto the street space. The nineteenth-century literary critic V. G. Belinski describes it as an ungainly agglomeration in which one house "has run several steps into the street to have a look at what's going on there, while another has run back a few steps as if out of arrogance or

Figure 3. Tverskaya Street, as it appeared in October 1918 on the eve of the first anniversary of the revolution. The Moscow City Soviet (Mossovet) is on the left, looking north. A banner hanging across the street reads *Sovetskaya Ploschad*, or "Soviet Square," the new name of the plaza to the right of the view.

modesty."[6] A boom in banking and large-scale institutional construction in the Kitaigorod, the old commercial center alongside the Kremlin, provided an influx of displaced shops and new businesses, beginning in the 1860s. By century's end, Tverskaya Street was lined with grandiose commercial façades and graced by some of high society's most elegant watering holes.

A revolutionary destiny was established for the street in 1917. The Moscow Soviet of Working People's Deputies, or Mossovet, chose as its headquarters Matvei Kazakov's Residence of the Governor General (1782). The Neoclassical urban palace fronted Skobelev Square, renamed Sovetskaya in 1918. Intersected by Tverskaya Street, the square became an important staging ground for mass processions celebrating May Day and the anniversary of the October Revolu-

tion. For these festivities the Mossovet was decked in garlands and agitprop placards, while banners and temporary murals adorned the length of Tverskaya's descent toward Red Square (fig. 3). The iconographic significance of this span of the street was reinforced through the construction of Sergei Cherneyshev's Institute for Marxism-Leninism directly across from the Mossovet. It was completed in time for the revolution's tenth anniversary in 1927.

The task of devising Moscow's redevelopment plan was entrusted to the Mossovet's Architecture and Planning Department in 1932. The Party's Central Committee had resolved the previous year that the city's "socialist reconstruction" would be based on the existing urban pattern, killing once and for all a wide array of avant-garde proposals to raze the city and to rebuild *ex nihilo*.[7] In July 1935, the new plan was approved in its final form.

Twenty-three design brigades, assembled from the ranks of the All-Union Academy of Architecture, were placed under the guidance of individual architects to work on specific projects. The remodeling of Tverskaya fell to the group headed by Mordvinov. Having begun his career as a Modernist, Mordvinov soon evinced a Pauline conversion to the classicist forms endorsed by Socialist Realism, as was typical for the period.

Although the Party's Central Committee had supported the preservation of the city's radial street layout, the 1935 plan reveals the legacy of the repudiated avant garde in a taste for demolition as a means of re-creating the city as a harmonious entity. The aerial perspectives that accompanied the plan suggested that virtually every structure outside the Kremlin walls would be obliterated (fig. 4). Unlike Modernist visions of the city as a collection of towers set in a naturalistic landscape, the Socialist Realist counterpart portrayed a new capital of solidly

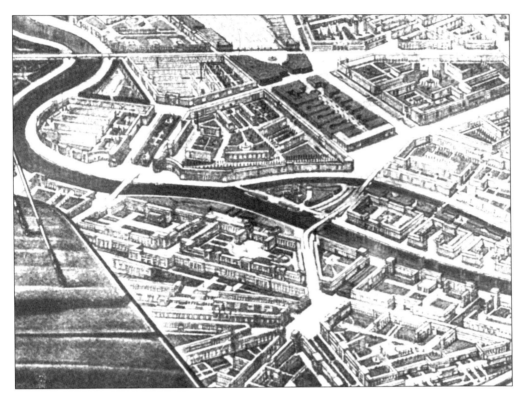

Figure 4. This detail of an aerial view from Moscow's 1935 Stalin Plan looks southwest, toward the Bolshoi Krasnokholmski Bridge and the Moscow River. A reconfigured Taganskaya Square—unrealized, as was most of the Plan—appears just to the right of the biplane wing at lower left. Those familiar with the area will search in vain for the Church of the Assumption, the Novospasski Monastery, or indeed any other orienting landmark. The image is that of a city re-created *ab ovo*.

framed street corridors and symmetrical building ensembles configured in huge open-court blocks. Hidden behind the elegant crust of apartment façades there were to be green park sanctuaries. If the rhetoric of the plan is to be believed, this cosmopolitan idyll was to be fully realized by 1946.

Mordvinov's vertiginous social mobility can be taken as a good indicator of the enthusiasm for his assignment, with its implausible timetable, and his knack for negotiating the jumbled mess of the Stalinist construction industry. His particular genius was an ability quickly to realize a simulacrum of the plan's goals through a series of brilliant improvisations, both technological and aesthetic.

Work began on Gorki Street in 1937. Its importance as a primary urban artery demanded

a tripling of the breadth of old Tverskaya Street. Formerly fifty to sixty feet wide, the new boulevard, 160 to 200 feet wide, would be the equal even of those in "advanced capitalist cities."[8] But the planned broadening of the street was complicated by its route. It traversed an area scattered with serviceable buildings now earmarked for preservation, including Ivan Rerberg's 1927 Central Telegraph building and the Mossovet. The solution to this dilemma revived a street-widening technique developed in Paris a century earlier by Haussmann's more cautious predecessor, Claude Berthelot de Rambuteau. Mordvinov demolished only the east-facing frontages along the north half of the route, and only the west-facing frontages of the last downhill blocks as the street approached the Kremlin (fig. 5). This also removed the street's gentle curve and provided

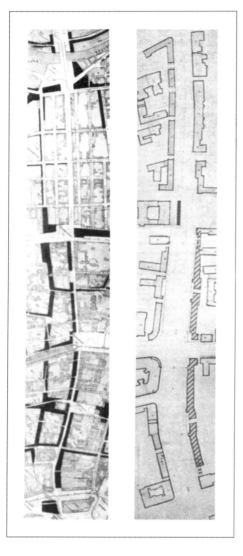

Figure 5. Gorki Street, plans of demolitions (left, in black) and new construction (right). Gorki's southern terminus into Manezhnaya Square, at the foot of the Kremlin, is at the bottom of both plans. On the demolitions plan, Gorki Street is to the right; a parallel thoroughfare planned to the west was not realized. The construction plan shows a close-up of the southernmost portion of the street. Mordvinov's A and B Blocks are shown in a darker tone; the lines protruding into the street further north indicate the original alignment of the Mossovet.

continuous use during the move, connected to street services through flexible coupling. During the building of Gorki Street, over fifty buildings were transported to new positions. These feats were publicized as socialist triumphs, with moves often scheduled for completion on important holidays. For the 1941 May Day celebrations, reporters described the delight of workers upon discovering that a protruding building had been rolled back overnight, so that their parade formations along Gorki Street could proceed intact all the way to Red Square.[9] Newspaper articles described buildings—from apartments to hospital surgery units—continuing to be used while on the move. Gorki Street's construction-site spectacles celebrated superhuman accomplishments in the service of the State, through the mastery of technology: marvels perfectly tailored to the publicity needs of the emerging Stakhanovite movement and its promotion of on-the-job heroism (fig. 6).

Two elongated apartments blocks designed for the ultimate five-hundred-yard approach to the Kremlin clinched Mordvinov's position in the Soviet architectural establishment. Known prosaically as Blocks A and B, they demonstrate Socialist Realism's proclaimed synthesis of up-to-date technology and timeless culture (see figs. 1, 2). Classical gestures include an unvarying pattern of fenestration, bas-relief sculptural panels of Pompeian delicacy, and an ashlar-faced two-story base. Triumphal arches pierce both blocks at secondary street intersections—an element borrowed from Carlo Rossi's Main Staff Building of 1819–29 in St. Petersburg. Block A's cornice band of industrially made decorative panels is continued on Block B as a Neorenaissance loggia, a favorite motif of Moscow architects of the late 1930s.[10] In plan, however, traditional monumentality disappears. The apparent mountain of masonry is revealed to be an eight-story screen only two rooms deep.

the *magestrale*'s mandatory axial emphasis, here provided by a distant view of the Kremlin wall's spires.

Along the conserved but ragged street edge, structures to be retained were raised off their foundations, mounted on girders, and rolled across a battery of steel cylinders to create a uniform street line. Water supply, sewage lines, electricity, and telephone cables were all in

Here, the slender apartment-block format of Ernst May's social housing for the Neue Frankfurt of the Weimar Republic seems a closer analogy than anything reclaimed from the nineteenth century.

Mordvinov's decorated slabs were the first products of an experimental building method called "assembly-line," or "conveyor-belt," construction, terms that reflect the Stalinist fetish for labor-speeding techniques imported from America during the first five-year plan.[11] This procedure slashed completion schedules in an industry infamous for strewing the city with unfinished construction sites. The decision to broaden Gorki by pushing back only one street edge moved the new street line far enough behind previous frontages to convert the cleared space of their courtyards to the new building zone. Demolition and construction thus proceeded simultaneously, rather than in phases. Building crews started from one or more points along the site and proceeded in a linear fashion. In theory, basements at one end could still be under construction while interiors were being finished at the other. By thus avoiding the successive surges of demand created by conventional building methods, Mordvinov employed his precious allotment of heavy equipment more efficiently. Precast ceilings, interior walls, decorative panels, and factory-loaded containers of bricks were hoisted by crane to the spot where they were needed, dispensing with the laborers who usually unloaded and moved materials around the site.[12] Mordvinov also struggled to minimize seasonal fluctuations in construction, no easy task in Moscow, where punishing winters traditionally shut down building sites.

Technical accomplishments, no matter how brilliant, did not fully satisfy the Socialist Realist architect's responsibilities. Party edicts called for his work to "strive for realistic criteria—for clarity and precision in its images, which must be

easily comprehensible and accessible to the masses."[13] For the builders of Gorki Street, this brief was critical. Their charge was to reconstruct "the celebratory highway of the capital," a pilgrimage route that led to a transformed Red Square. A permanent Lenin Mausoleum with flanking reviewing stands for ten thousand dignitaries had been completed in October 1930. Mass processions now culminated with a glimpse of Stalin on the reviewing stand atop Lenin's tomb, a transcendent instant that compressed the Revolution's past and future in a fleeting tableau. In newspaper articles and interviews, Stakhanovite worker-heroes cast this encounter with Stalin as a dazzling epiphany. The previous decade's carnivals of revolutionary fervor, marked by "asiatic chaos, lack of discipline and contagious disorder," had become unthinkable on this newly hallowed turf.[14]

By the mid-1930s, socialist celebration had taken a dramatic turn toward sobriety and conformity. Architectural ornament on Gorki Street reflected this change. Bas-relief panels featuring sheaves of grain, clusters of grapes,

Figure 6. Moscow's program of building relocations captured the attention of the press and the public in the 1930s. Seeming impossible technical accomplishments were publicized as the fulfillment of Stalin's maxim, "There are no fortresses that Bolsheviks cannot conquer." The caption of this Soviet cartoon reads: "Weightlifter Ambarzumyan offers his services to the Mossovet."

and fleshy vegetables—a staid paean to the fictive successes of agricultural collectivization—decorated Mordvinov's Blocks A and B. A literally stately sculptural theme was also adopted for the home of the Mossovet, remodeled beyond recognition by Dmitri Chechulin in the early 1940s (fig. 7). Kazakov's palace was clipped of its wings and porch and moved back fourteen meters to a new street alignment. There it received two additional stories and an imposing façade embellished with engaged columns. A bas-relief emblazoned with clusters of Soviet banners surrounded by laurel and oak leaves framed a new triumphal portal.[15]

The tony classicism of the façades on Gorki Street was anything but skin deep. Blocks A and B set the pattern for subsequent apartment buildings on the street, all of which offered a promenade of opulent restaurants, cafés, and shops at sidewalk level. Neoclassical plaster trim graced the ceilings of residences above. The average apartment consisted of just three rooms—drawing, dining, and bedroom—plus a small kitchen, bath, and entry. To say that these were (at least by Western standards) modest in size is an understatement: most of the social-housing units built by Ernst May in Frankfurt a decade earlier were more spacious.[16] But by contemporary Soviet standards, governed by the one-family-per-room formula of collective housing, these apartments represented the acme of comfort.

This luxury was a conscious element in Mordvinov's reconstruction efforts, but was not original to them. The gilding of Gorki had begun in earnest by the end of the first five-year plan. Stalin's open endorsement of wage differentials in 1931 had set the stage for the cultivation of an affluent elite. His 1935 pronouncement that "life has become better, life has become more joyful" authorized this elite to make its presence known. The gutting of

Bolshevik sumptuary standards showed itself early on in the rebuilding of Gorki Street. In 1933 construction began on Andrei Burov's eight-story Renaissance-style apartment block for Narkomlesprom, the People's Commissariat of the Timber Industry. A year later, the prerevolutionary provisioner to the rich, Yeliseev's, reopened as Gastronom No. 1, just down the street. Glass tanks stocked with live carp and special sausages and cheeses, available nowhere else, were among the twelve hundred different items that lined the shelves. Hothouse strawberries could be found there too, at 100 rubles a kilo — one or two weeks' wages for an average worker.[17]

Gorki Street's affluent socialist milieu was invariably presented to foreigners as that of the proletariat, a claim most found incredible. This was clearly an environment designed for a fresh cohort of prosperous Communists. They were called *vydvizhentsy*, or "promotees," a new class of white-collar managers who, in Stalin's words, "radically changed the contours of the intelligentsia, remaking it in their own image."[18] This privileged new cadre was headed by young men of working-class background. Most had moved up from the factory floor or the military via technical-school education. They owed their careers to Stalin's decision to arm a new intelligentsia with managerial, rather than doctrinal, skills in an effort to end reliance on foreign talent to fulfill technical needs. Gorki Street was not only created for members of the "New Class" (to use the term coined by Milovan Djilas), it was created largely *by* them as well.[19] The architect Chechulin, who entered the VKHUTEMAS design school directly from the ranks of the Red Army, was one of them; Nikita Khrushchev, a graduate of Moscow's Academy of Heavy Industry who managed construction of the new subway line running beneath Gorki Street, was another.

Hard work and achievement were the cornerstones of the New Man's work ethic; decorum

Figure 7. The Mossovet, as remodeled by Chechulin, has a cornice line carefully matched to those of the apartments on either side. To the left, the dark granite facing at the base of the apartment block by A. Zhukov, built 1948–50, is rumored originally to have been intended for a Nazi victory monument. To the right of the Mossovet, looking north, this stretch of the street is terminated by two more Neoclassical blocks by Mordvinov, dating from 1940.

and good taste were the standard aspirations. The assimilation of technical know-how and culture now superseded a command of Leninist ideology as a hallmark of social status. For the *vydvizhentsy*, Gorki Street's amalgam of engineering gymnastics and classicist discipline made it the perfect manifestation of *kul'turnost'*, an untranslatable term fusing the notions of "educated" and "cultured." It was embodied in the comfort of the street's apartments, the sophisticated goods displayed in its boutiques, the permanent waves and crêpe-de-chine dresses of its shoppers. A world away from ration coupons and crowded communal apartments, this new urban environment suggested that Homo Sovieticus had entered an age of prosperity.

A previous generation of Communists saw in these upstarts a betrayal of class origins; by the promotee's own reckoning, he had merely transcended them. But in any case the reproach of the old guard was, for the New Class, more a matter of speculation than anything else. During the late 1930s, the ideal of Bolshevik asceticism was simply vanishing, as indeed were its ideologues. The Great Purge of 1936–38 decimated the ranks of the State's previous elites at precisely the time when the new cohort of Red specialists was arriving on the scene. Dizzying production schedules, invoked in Stalin's campaign of industrial development, ensured a plentiful supply of managerial openings. In this time of precipitous social mobility, there was no lack of cash-rich promotees to populate the boutiques and cafés of Gorki Street. It was an urban ensemble built to pamper the beneficiaries of the Purge.

Why would a self-proclaimed worker's state not just tolerate, but actively cultivate Gorki Street's landscape of privilege? One explanation can be found in the writings of the Soviet mental-health movement of the late 1920s. Psychiatric studies had demonstrated that years of

Figure 8. The monumental façades fronting Gorki Street conceal another city, composed of modest nineteenth-century structures. A mix of low row buildings and freestanding wooden houses, interspersed with onion-domed churches, characterized pre-Stalinist Moscow. This townscape was slated for obliteration in the 1935 plan, but the scope of the task defied the state's resources. The two timescapes now co-exist, connected by a series of monumental portals that open onto the city's *magestrale*s.

war, famine, poverty, and upheaval had taxed Party activists to their limit. They had been found to suffer from a high incidence of neuroses, nervous breakdowns, hypertension, and other cardiovascular disorders, a collection of symptoms psychiatrists labeled "Soviet exhaustion." The most serious threat to mental health was said to be overcrowded housing. Ad hoc communal living arrangements stripped the Party activist of space in which to work, study, relax quietly, or have a normal sex life.[20] Although the preventive mental-health movement was formally suppressed in 1931 as a reactionary response to the five-year plan's revolutionary work tempos, its campaign to foster proper care of the upper stratum, that group now called upon to synchronize a centralized command economy, was duly incorporated into State housing policy.

By the time of Gorki Street's refurbishing, membership in this entitled elite had expanded beyond the ranks of managers to include other distinguished servants of the State as well. The Mossovet was responsible for selecting residents for the street's State-built flats. Apartments were also built by cooperative building enterprises organized around industrial ministries or specialist's unions: examples include Burov's 1933 Narkomlesprom block. Housing cooperatives were in turn required to turn over 10 percent of their units to the Mossovet. Those who made it to the top of the waiting list included military officers, well-trained technical specialists, prominent artists and writers, and (as representatives of the working class) celebrated Stakhanovite worker-heroes.[21] Mossovet responsibility for the design of Gorki Street was thus demographic as well as architectural, the finished product echoing that lexicon of ideal human types pervading heroic Socialist Realist sculpture.[22]

The presence of these elite enclaves posed thorny contradictions for a self-proclaimed state of workers and peasants. Beyond the margins of

Mordvinov's urban improvements was a city utterly at odds with the glamor of Gorki Street. The doctrine of Socialist Realism attempted to reconcile this juxtaposition of perquisites and penury. It prescribed a way of seeing the world that Sheila Fitzpatrick has called "the superimposition of a better 'soon' on an imperfect 'now.'"[23] In accordance with the canon, Gorki Street was exhibited as a representative Moscow thoroughfare. The comfortable apartments, well-stocked stores and well-heeled residents all typified Soviet life, bearing in mind that the "typical," as defined by the Party ideologue Georgii Malenkov, "is not that which is encountered most often, but that which most persuasively expresses the essence of a given social force."[24] Residents understood the correct explanation for their special status: as the most ardent builders of socialism, they had earned the privilege of living the way everyone else soon would.

This ideological trope, fundamental to Socialist Realism, is spatially manifested in Mordvinov's urban design as well. Although only a fraction of the demolition and reconstruction called for in the 1935 plan had been carried out, a ride down Gorki Street gave the impression that it had been scrupulously fulfilled. Here the slender curtain of majestic, street-defining buildings encased not the park oases called for by the plan, but the inconsistent remains of "the big village," as prerevolutionary Moscow was known (fig. 8). This sleight of hand created streetscapes that vividly portrayed the capital "as it will be." It also explains why, by 1939, more than half of all apartment buildings under construction in the city lined its main avenues.[25]

Catering to the needs of a materially favored minority was an innovation of the Stalin Revolution, but was not limited to its Socialist Realist guise. What was original to Socialist Realism was the unapologetic display of this lifestyle along an urban street. Modernist environments for a socialist gentry first appeared during the late 1920s—a phase of Stalin's rule characterized by avant-garde enthusiasms in every discipline, including architecture.[26] Early housing complexes for the elite were inward-turning, concealing by design the landscape of privilege within: examples include Boris Iofan's Government House of 1928–31 and the Constructivist apartments of 1928–30 for Narkomfin, the People's Commissariat of finance, by Moisei Ginzburg and Ignaty Milinis.[27] The streetscapes of Socialist Realism turned these environments inside out, advertising their comforts and patterns of consumption through sheet-glass windows arrayed along the sidewalk. Access was now limited primarily by extravagant prices, or possession of hard currency vouchers, available to a select minority. For the first time, the regime's class inconsistencies were in the open, legitimized (albeit unconvincingly) by a doctrine that championed a system of rewards commensurate with individual performance and utility to the State.

In a self-effacing mood, Lenin once claimed to have found power lying in the street, and to have picked it up. Stalin seized that power as his inheritance, purged it of the impurities of foreign influence and local doubt, and projected it back into the street in a self-conscious program of architectural and social design.

Like other disenfranchised radicals, the exiled Trotsky presumed that Stalin's caste-building project was perceived back in the homeland simply as capitalist recidivism: "Limousines for the 'activists,' fine perfumes for 'our women,' margarine for the workers, stores 'de luxe' for the gentry, a look at the delicacies through the store windows for the plebs—such socialism cannot but seem to the masses a new refacing of capitalism, and they are not far wrong."[28]

The notion of an unconditional retreat to

bourgeois life seduced not only Trotsky's follow-ers, but another group of discouraged true be-lievers as well: those for whom socialism and a Modernist built environment were synony-mous. The West's architectural vanguard had invested high hopes in the Soviet experiment. From their perspective, Socialist Realism was a heretical violation of the twentieth-century *Zeit-geist*. Canonical architectural histories record the West's response to this postmodern phase of Soviet cultural development: in the 1930s, we are told, the future moved suddenly elsewhere.

But the Socialist Realist street in general, and Gorki Street in particular, are repositories of meaning far richer than this dismissal would suggest. Access to Gorki Street's multiple read-ings as an artifact of High Stalinism requires a point of view planted firmly within the street's original context. As the expression of a culture hermetically isolated from outside influences, these readings, as one would expect, bear little in common with those forged in the West.

By way of explanation, let us jump to 1950, fifteen years after the Stalin Plan for Moscow's reconstruction was initiated. The capital's pro-gram of myths has ripened to maturity. Military valor is reflected in Moscow's official designa-tion as a "hero city" of World War II. A postwar campaign waged against "cosmopolitanism" has driven home the "fact" that Russian culture is, frankly speaking, more advanced than that of the West. The streets and squares of the capital are echoed in postwar reconstruction across an entire hemisphere. Moscow is now the cultural hearth not only of the Soviet Union, but of the world's largest empire as well.

Mordvinov's program for Gorki Street is complete, and its finishing touches exude this postwar euphoria. Across from Block B, new apartment blocks complete the street ensemble with triumphal pomp. Appropriately enough, the quarry-faced stone of their lower stories is reputed originally to have been carted into Moscow by the enemy for an intended Nazi victory monument (see fig. 7). Moscow's urban signature is now a skyline studded with sky-scrapers, and Gorki Street is graced with a miniature version of its own: the ornate new spire of Chechulin's Peking Hotel.

As a corridor leading to the symbolic heart of communism, Gorki Street is at the zenith of its prestige. For the masses who process along its pavements during important political holidays, it is a promised land, the unattainable preserve of "those who have given us such a happy life," as a Stalin-era toast puts it. It is also a source of pride. It is the culmination of the 1935 plan, a document that contains the solemn vow: "Un-der the masterly leadership of the great architect of socialist society, Stalin, Moscow, the capital of the land of the Soviets, will become the best city in the world in all its facilities, its culture and its appearance."[29] Gorki Street is a measure of the fulfillment of that promise, and, by ex-tension, a grander one. Set in a city in which housing standards have been in a thirty-year free fall, this hard-won fragment of utopia com-memorates the Bolshevik pledge to pluck a backward nation from its peripheral orbit and put it at the gravitational core of history.

Inextricably intertwined in this reading of Gorki Street are two conflicting messages: one of promises fulfilled, the other of promises abandoned. This double helix constitutes the genotype of subsequent generations of socialist *magestrale*s, reproduced from Berlin to Beijing during the postwar efflorescence of Stalinist urbanism. Replicas of Gorki Street, transplanted to the empire's periphery, were unequivocal referents to Moscow's proclaimed hearth of socialist culture. A fuller understanding of Stalinist urban form and its reception in these new colonial contexts awaits a more complete chronicle of the Socialist Realist street. ■

Notes

1 Daniel Burnham's plans for Chicago and Washington, D.C., were studied as valid design prototypes by a later generation of Socialist Realist designers in Eastern Europe. See W. Lenikowski, "Learning from Classicism: An Investigation of the Grand Urbanism Practiced by Haussmann, Burnham, and the Soviet Government," *Inland Architect* 6 (1987): 43.

2 A. Ikonnikov, *Russian Architecture of the Soviet Period* (Moscow, 1988), 182.

3 See G. Castillo, "Cities of the Stalinist Empire," in Nezar AlSayyad, ed., *Forms of Dominance: On the Architecture and Urbanism of the Colonial Enterprise* (Aldershot, 1992), 261–88.

4 L. Trotsky, *The Revolution Betrayed* (New York, 1937), 117–18.

5 Kopp dedicated his career to the rehabilitation of Russian Modernism as the "true" tradition of Soviet architecture. In his *L'Architecture de la période stalinienne* (Grenoble, 1978), Socialist Realism is assigned the role of architecture's Judas Iscariot and played against a Constructivist savior. M. Tafuri and F. Dal Co, *Modern Architecture*, 2 vols. (New York, 1986), vol. 1, 188. C. Jencks, *The Language of Post-Modern Architecture* (New York, 1977), 91.

6 Quoted in *Blue Guide to Moscow and Leningrad* (London, 1991), 155.

7 The best known of these proposals is Le Corbusier's. He recommended replacing "the old carcass of an Asiatic village" with "a great modern city," the plan of which was later known as the Ville Radiuse. See J.-L. Cohen, *Le Corbusier and the Mystique of the U.S.S.R.: Theories and Projects for Moscow 1928–1936* (Princeton, 1992).

8 L. Perchik, *The Reconstruction of Moscow* (Moscow, 1936), 67.

9 A. Ling, "Moving Buildings in the U.S.S.R.," *Architects' Journal* 2 (1944): 155.

10 See S. Boldirev and P. Goldenberg, "Ulitsa Gorkogo V Proshlom I Nastoyashchyem," *Arkhitektura SSSR* 4 (1938): 14–24.

11 The cult of technology associated with Stalinist industrialization prompted a fad for the term "conveyor belt." So named were the Soviet functionalist street prototype displaced by the Socialist Realist *magestrale;* a novel, Ilin's *Bol'shoi konveier,* 1934, comparing Soviet society to a perfectly organized factory; and the technique of round-the-clock interrogation employed by the NKVD to obtain confessions.

12 See A. Koslovski, "Organizatsiya Stroitel'ykh Rabot Po Ul. Gorkogo," *Arkhitektura SSSR* 4 (1938): 26–30. Mordvinov later credited himself with having eliminated piecework wages on the site, a claim that contradicts the universal trends in Soviet labor policy of this period. See "Soviet City Planning," *Landscape* 1 (1953): 20.

13 *Arkhitektura SSSR* 1 (1933), quoted in A. Tarkhanov and S. Kavtaradze, *Stalinist Architecture* (London, 1992), 49.

14 *Pravda* 253 (November 9, 1922), quoted in V. Tolstoy, I. Bibikova, and C. Cooke, *Street Art of the Revolution* (London, 1990), 143.

15 Critics later accused Chechulin of defacing, rather than remodeling. But in terms of Stalinist urbanism, this architectural escalation was a necessary correlate of ensemble planning. If left unchanged, embedded among the looming frontages of Gorki Street, Kazakov's landmark would have been lost against its newly monumentalized backdrop. The vertical increase and theatrical façade reclaimed the Mossovet's former place in the street's hierarchy of scale.

16 The published plan of a floor in Mordvinov's Block A shows five-room flats to be 104 square meters in area, four-room flats as 85 square meters, three-room flats as 57 square meters, and two designs for two-room flats at 39 and 35 square meters. Compare these floor areas to those of the flats in May's project at Niederrad, built for the city of Frankfurt in 1926–27: four-room flats are 105–15 square meters; three-room, 65 square meters; two-room, 56 square meters. It should also be noted that the latter are functionally more spacious as well, since they eliminate the formal entry

spaces that consume from four to eight square meters of floor space in every one of Mordvinov's flats.

17 *Vecherniaia Moskva* (October 4, 1934), quoted in S. Fitzpatrick, *The Cultural Front: Power and Culture in Revolutionary Russia* (Ithaca, 1992), 224.

18 Fitzpatrick, *Cultural Front*, 177.

19 M. Djilas, *The New Class: An Analysis of the Communist System* (New York, 1957).

20 D. Joravsky, "The Construction of the Stalinist Psyche," in S. Fitzpatrick, ed., *Cultural Revolution in Russia, 1928–1931* (Bloomington, 1978), 113.

21 Interview with Isaak Y. Aigel, July 29, 1993. Aigel was the personal assistant to Boris Iofan on the Palace of Soviets project and was in charge of procuring accommodations for its specialists.

22 Especially well represented among Gorki Street's residents was the creative branch of the intelligentsia. One of the residents was the painter Pyotr Vasil'yev, Lenin's portraitist. Nicholas Ostrovsky, whose novel *How the Steel Is Tempered* helped define Socialist Realist fiction, lived at No. 14; the long-time chief of the All-Soviet Union of Writers, A. A. Fadeyev, spent the last years of his life at No. 27. N. D. Kolli, construction super-visor of Le Corbusier's Tsentrosoyuz Building, lived on Gorki Street as well, in an apartment stocked with antiques.

23 Fitzpatrick, *Cultural Front*, 217.

24 In B. Groys, *The Total Art of Stalinism: Avant-Garde, Aesthetic Dictatorship, and Beyond* (Princeton, 1992), 50.

25 P. Hall, *Cities of Tomorrow* (Cambridge, Mass., 1988), 202. One of the street's great pleasures for the pedestrian, now that ideologically correct modes of perception can be dispensed with, is the discovery of these modest time-landscapes, framed behind the *magestrale*'s multistory triumphal arches.

26 The classic work on the period is S. Fitzpatrick, ed., *Cultural Revolution in Russia* (Bloomington, 1978).

27 The Constructivist Narkomfin block, built for the immense People's Commissariat of Finance, was designed to offer less than fifty employees, and their families, not only a private apartment, but a nursery school, catered dining facility, gymnasium, library, and roof garden. As with Burov's Neorenaissance Narkomlesprom block, these extravagances were explained as the preview of a new way of life that would ultimately be available to all citizens. That the former building is continually offered up as a prime example of Soviet social housing, while the latter evokes condemnation as an example of corrupt elitism, is one of the more blatant distortions of architecture's stylistically partisan historiography.

28 Trotsky, *Revolution Betrayed*, 120.

29 Perchik, *Reconstruction of Moscow*, 72.

5

CAIRO

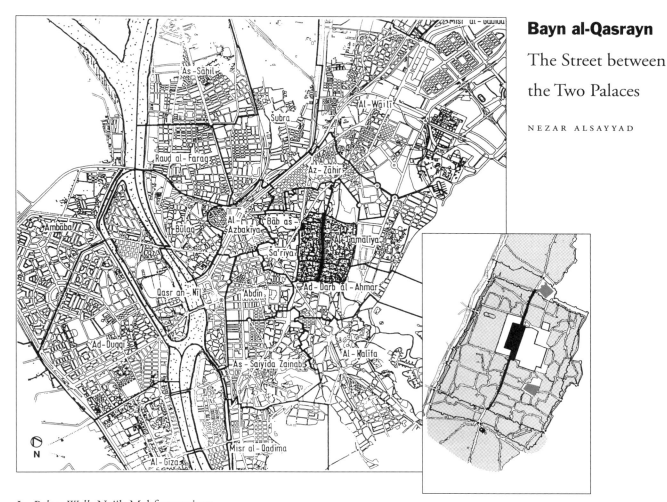

Bayn al-Qasrayn

The Street between the Two Palaces

NEZAR ALSAYYAD

In *Palace Walk,* Najib Mahfouz writes:

> This roof, with its inhabitants of chickens and pigeons and its arbor garden, was her beautiful, beloved world and her favorite place for relaxation out of the whole universe, about which she knew nothing. . . . She was awed by the minarets which shot up, making a profound impression on her. Some were near enough for her to see their lamps and crescent distinctly, like those of Qala'un and Barquq. Others appeared to her as complete wholes, lacking details, like the minarets of the mosques of al-Husayn, al-Ghuri, and al-Azhar. Still other minarets were at the far horizon and seemed phantoms, like those of the Citadel and Rifa'i mosques. She turned her face toward them with devotion, fascination, thanksgiving, and hope. Her spirit soared over their tops, as close as possible to the heavens. Then her eyes would fix on the minaret of the mosque of al-Husayn, the dearest one to her because of her love for its namesake. She looked at it affectionately, and her yearnings mingled with the sorrow that pervaded her every time she remembered she was not allowed to visit the son of the Prophet of God's daughter, even though she lived only minutes away from his shrine.

Figure 1. Plan of Fatimid Cairo. Bayn al-Qasrayn is marked and shown in black in the inset.

71

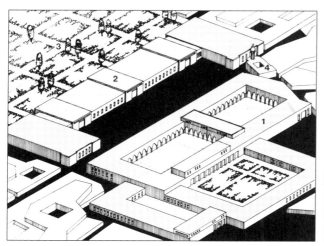
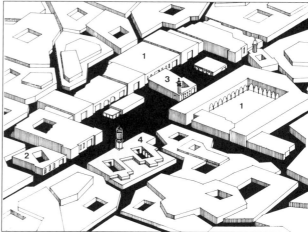

(left) Figure 2. Bayn al-
Qasrayn at the end of the
Fatimid era, showing, 1, the
Great (or eastern) Palace;
2, the Qasr al-Bahr; 3, the
caliphal gardens; and 4,
the al-Aqmar Mosque.

(right) Figure 3. Bayn al-
Qasrayn at the end of the
Ayyubid era, showing, 1,
remains of the eastern and
western palaces and the
*madrasah*s; 2, al-Siyufiyyah;
3, al-Kamiliyyah; and 4,
al-Salihiyyah.

In 1956, Najib Mahfouz, Egypt's most distinguished novelist, published *Bayn al-Qasrayn.* Translated in English as *Palace Walk,* the novel was the first volume in a trilogy that won its author the Nobel Prize in literature in 1989.[1] Is Mahfouz's title for the book incidental? No place or space in Cairo is as revealing of the city's long history as Bayn al-Qasrayn.

In 969 C.E., the Fatimid dynasty came from North Africa (especially Tunisia), established itself in Egypt, and founded a new state. Soon after their arrival, the Fatimid caliphs began to build Cairo, or al-Qahirah, "the city victorious," near the town of al-Fustat, at the northernmost single crossing of the Nile (fig. 1). In one of his first acts, Jawhar, the Fatimid general in charge of building the new capital, laid out the foundations of the caliphal palace at the center of the community. Some fifty years later, a second, smaller palace was built to the west of this palace. Together, the two palaces bracketed a huge open space, which quickly acquired the title "Bayn al-Qasrayn," or "between the two palaces." More than a thousand years later, while no longer a square, the space still carries that name.

Al-Maqrizi, the renowned fifteenth-century historian of Cairo, relates in his seminal work, *Al-Khutat wa al-Athar,* that Jawhar shunned the existing city of al-Fustat, choosing instead to build the 340-acre royal compound to its north. The settlement was designed from the inside out, beginning with the palace.[2] It was inaugurated when the first Fatimid caliph, al-Mu'izz, took up his residence there. Intent on giving his new imperial capital an instant sense of history, he brought with him from Tunis coffins containing the remains of some of his ancestors, which he buried in a space in front of the palace.[3] Al-Maqrizi's description of the city during this early period is quite detailed. The space in front of the palace, by then referred to as a *maydan,* or square, was used as an assembly ground for the more than ten thousand soldiers of the Fatimid army. To the west of the square was a large garden, called al-Bustan al-Kafuri, which was connected by underground tunnels to the palace, and was reserved for the caliph's private use.[4]

The image that we get of the original city of al-Mu'izz, around the end of the tenth century, is of a simple form with a palace at its center, connected directly to a garden and the nearby al-Azhar mosque, and surrounded by quarters housing the army. It was the subsequent building programs of al-Muʿizz's son al-ʿAziz and, a century later, the vizier Badr al-Jamali that gave Cairo its full Fatimid image. To the west of the main palace, al-ʿAziz built the small palace known as Qasr al-Bahr. Al-Maqrizi relates that it was intended as a prospective residence for the exiled Abbasid caliph, but ended up serving as a home for one of al-ʿAziz's daughters. This structure defined the central *maydan,* and separated it from the caliphal gardens. It is at this point that the title of Bayn al-Qasrayn was probably adopted as a new name for the redefined, enclosed urban square (fig. 2).[5]

In its heyday, the Cairo of Badr al-Jamali was an impressive city that had quickly developed into a full-scale urban center. The Persian traveler Nasiri Khusraw, who resided in the city from 1047 to 1050 C.E., describes its more than twenty thousand shops that sold all kinds of goods. All were owned by the caliph and rented to commercial tenants, who commuted from al-Fustat; no one was allowed to own property in the city except the royal family.[6] Khusraw gives special attention to Bayn al-Qasrayn, singling it out as the most impressive *maydan* in all Egypt:

The Caliph's palace lies in the middle of al-Qahirah. It is a freestanding structure detached from all its surroundings. It is guarded at night by a hundred guards who circle it all the time. You can see the palace from outside the city because of its high walls. . . . These also help define the different gates of the palace, many of which lead to the great space, *Biyn al-Qasriyn.*[7]

According to Khusraw, that great space accommodated thousands of troops on parade on major occasions and festivals, while other buildings and spaces around the palace served other functions. Specifically mentioned are the al-Aqmar mosque on the northeastern corner of Bayn al-Qasrayn, and Qasr al-Shawq, an important space at the southeastern corner of the palace. In different forms, both survive to this day, the former as one of the few well-preserved Fatimid mosques in Cairo; the latter as a small street, which lends its name to the title of the second novel in Mahfouz's trilogy, *Qasr al-Shawq*—literally, *Palace of Desire.*

When the Ayyubid Salah al-Din came to power as governor of Egypt in 1169, he unified al-Fustat and al-Qahirah through the construction of Cairo's massive walls. He opened the former princely precinct of al-Qahirah to the masses, who began building in its spaces and gardens, changing the old functions of the city. The citadel that he and his successors built on the southern hills as the new seat of Ayyubid government drew urban development with it in that direction.[8]

The pattern of narrow streets that characterized Ayyubid Cairo probably first developed during the reign of Salah al-Din (1169–93). When Abd al-Latif al-Baghdadi, an Iraqi traveler and scientist, visited Cairo in 1193, he described it as a city characterized by palaces, detached tall buildings, and wide streets. Al-Baghdadi tells us that Bayn al-Qasrayn was a "large space whose surrounding palaces were now occupied by members of the Ayyubid family." He speaks of it as a "pleasant spot where notables and other important people would stroll at night."[9] Indeed, the space was at that time a daily market, where meat, pastries, and fruits were sold, and a site for public performances, including biographical and historical recitations.[10]

The Moroccan traveler Muhammad Ibn Saʿid visited Cairo in 1243 and reported, in contrast, that its streets were very narrow and its buildings mostly attached. He described frequent bottlenecks and traffic jams along these alleys, and attributed many of the city's problems to its mixed functions and irregular streets:

The place in Cairo known as Bayn al-Qasrayn is of royal arrangement. It is a space which accommodates both troops and spectators. If all of al-Qahirah was like it, it would have been a great royal creation. But you walk through the space and then you find yourself in a dark alleyway with shops, people and horses, making your breathing heavy and your eyes hot. . . . Most of the streets of the city are narrow, dirty, and dark surrounded by mud brick houses with little air and light. I have never seen in the Maghreb anything as bad as this and the only way to escape this is to go out to Bayn al-Qasrayn.[11]

Both al-Baghdadi and Ibn Saʿid agree on the paramount importance of Bayn al-Qasrayn in Ayyubid Cairo. But the striking differences between their two descriptions of the rest of the city require careful examination. One may argue, for example, that the two travelers, each of whom had a credible reputation, simply perceived the city differently. Their descriptions may accordingly each be a reflection of their own varied visual experiences and notions of scale, rather than an accurate representation of the city. However, since descriptions by al-Baghdadi and Ibn Saʿid of Alexandria and Damascus show little or no disparity, this is a dubious assumption. One is left to conclude that al-Qahirah underwent enormous physical change during the fifty years between the two writers' visits.

Major events, including the great fire of al-Fustat and the Ayyubids' nationalization of Fatimid property, resulted in a massive resettlement of what had originally been the royal city. It is likely that, as the masses moved in and began to erect temporary structures wherever they could, their haphazard buildings encroached on the wide streets of the city, and its large gardens and open spaces gradually disappeared. The narrow streets of Islamic Cairo were probably the result of this unorganized process during the years of Ayyubid rule.[12] The Fatimid palaces were quickly taken over. Some were used as government buildings, residences for the Ayyubid entourage, apartment blocks, and shops. Bayn al-Qasrayn must have grown a little narrower during this period, as the Ayyubid rulers built the three important *madrasah*s, or schools—al-Siyufiyyah, al-Kamiliyyah, and al-Salihiyyah—in or around it. Although it no longer served the function of a space in which to display political or military power, Bayn al-Qasrayn remained an important visual node in the city (fig. 3). When Ayyubid rule finally came to an end, it was in Bayn al-Qasrayn that the conspiracy to assassinate the last Ayyubid ruler was carried out.

It was during the period roughly corresponding to the rule of the Bahri Mamluks (1250–1382) that Cairo experienced its greatest growth in the medieval era. Development in the north of the walled city was overshadowed by that occurring to the west and south, and indeed, the majority of new spaces and streets were developed outside of the walled city.[13] The hierarchy of street patterns connecting the walled city and its exterior surroundings seems to have evolved in response to strict laws regulating urban activities.[14]

The trend of building in Bayn al-Qasrayn, started by the Ayyubids, continued during Bahri Mamluk times. Again, three *madrasah*s—al-Nasiriyyah, al-Zahiriyyah, and al-Mansuriyyah—were built in the space adjoining what remained of the western and eastern palaces (fig. 4). The construction activity in Bayn al-Qasrayn at this time followed a conscious policy of the Bahri Mamluk sultans, who wished to create a building legacy that could compete with the architectural achievements of earlier

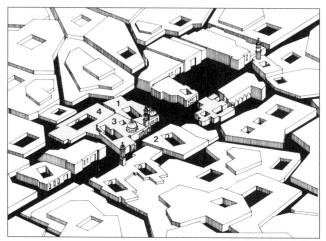

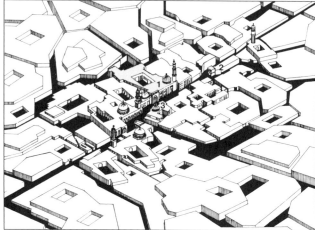

Fatimid and Ayyubid dynasties.[15] The building of the Qalawun complex, with its *madrasah* (al-Mansuriyyah), *dharih*, or tomb, and *bimaristan*, or hospital, is a testament to this effort. As if to underscore their point, the Bahri Mamluks built part of the *bimaristan* on the foundations of the earlier western palace. Because of its central location and immense size, this hospital served the entire population of Egypt. Although the choice of its location may have been incidental, the symbolism imbedded in that choice cannot be ignored. For this was the time when the sultanate of Egypt under Qalawun reached its peak. Egypt, the welfare state, was now reclaiming Bayn al-Qasrayn as a space and place that reflected the evolution of a social consciousness and the development of a system of government able to cater to the needs of a civil society.

On seeing the space of Bayn al-Qasrayn, the great traveler Ibn Batutah, who visited Cairo in 1326, commented: "The Biyn al Qasriyn where the tomb of Qalawun and his hospital lie is beyond one's ability to describe. People come to the hospital from all over because they find great medical care. One may see many people going in and going out of the many structures around the space."[16] Ibn Batutah's observations were confirmed by the Andalusian judge Khaled al-Balawi, who toured Cairo in 1335. He described Bayn al-Qasrayn as a very busy street, "where thousands of camels and mules pass by [and] where hundreds of water carriers serve passers-by with cups." Al-Balawi too singles out the Qalawun *bimaristan* as the most impressive and beautiful edifice overlooking Bayn al-Qasrayn.[17]

These chroniclers did not spend much time discussing the individual mosques that surround Bayn al-Qasrayn. Left out of those descriptions is the elaborate mosque and *madrasah* of al-Nasir Muhammad, with its Gothic entrance and Frankish door, brought from Palestine after a war. Also ignored were the nearby arms market, where bows and arrows were sold, and the jewelers' market, where rings, seals, and bracelets were on display. Both had mushroomed out of Bayn al-Qasrayn: the former due north, the latter due south. Further growing out from Bayn al-Qasrayn, and clearly forming the Qasabah, or main spine of al-Qahirah, were the tracts where book dealers, spice and nut suppliers, saddle makers, and cloth merchants sold their goods.[18] Indeed, it was during the Bahri

(left) Figure 4. Bayn al-Qasrayn at the end of the Bahri Mamluk era, showing the *madrasah*s: 1, al-Nasiriyyah; 2, al-Zahiriyyah; 3, al-Mansuriyyah; and 4, the *bimaristan* Qalawun.

(right) Figure 5. Bayn al-Qasrayn during Ottoman rule, showing Burji Mamluk and Ottoman structures: 1, al-Barquqiyyah *madrasah*; 2, *sabil/kuttab* Katkhuda; and 3, Sabil al-Nahhasin.

Figure 6. The space of al-Ghuri, or al-Ghuriyyah, as depicted by David Roberts in an 1843 painting under the title, *The Silk Mercers' Bazaar*. This view, facing south, shows the *madrasah* of al-Ghuri to the right and the tomb of al-Ghuri to the left.

Mamluk era that Bayn al-Qasrayn as a street became totally integrated with the Qasabah of Cairo, the city's principal, mile-long street. This extended from the southern gate, Bab Zuwaylah, to the northern gate, Bab al-Futuh. Long forgotten was the original Bayn al-Qasrayn of Fatimid military display and the space where the obsequies of the last Ayyubid ruler had been celebrated a century earlier.

Before the end of the fourteenth century, Cairo suffered several years of famine and plague and most of its open spaces fell into disuse. It was not until the beginning of the fifteenth century that a recovery started. Building activity picked up later in the century, much of it concentrated within the walled city. The Burji Mamluks, who ruled from 1382 to 1517, developed their own approach to building in and around the numerous monuments commissioned by earlier dynasties. To take these buildings into account became a distinctive Burji Mamluk trademark. This is very clear in the way new buildings were inserted along the Qasabah of Cairo, which by now had totally encompassed the old Bayn al-Qasrayn quarter, with the square in its center. Among the few new buildings added were the *madrasah* al-Barquqiyyah, which was squeezed in between two early Bahri Mamluk buildings, in effect closing off the Bayn al-Qasrayn space on the western side (fig. 5).[19]

Buildings with other commercial functions started to appear long the street. The most important of these were the al-Nahhasin, or coppersmiths' bazaar, which developed at the northern end of the Bayn al-Qasrayn, and the goldsmiths' bazaar, which evolved around its southern end.[20] Gaston Wiet reminds us that while al-Maqrizi wrote at great length of the prospects of the artisan markets of Cairo, he mourned the rapid disappearance of some of these crafts, particularly enameled glass and inlaid copper.[21] The traveler Leo Africanus, who saw the city near the beginning of the sixteenth century, speaks of Bayn al-Qasrayn:

The city is well provided with artisans and merchants. They are especially found in a street which goes from Bab al-Nasr to the Zuweila gate. . . . There are in this street several schools which are admired because of their size, their height, and their decorations. There are also to be seen several spacious and very beautiful temples. . . .

A section called Bain al-Qasreyn contains shops where cooked meat is sold; there are about sixty of them in all supplied with tin dishes. In others water is prepared with all kinds of ffiowers. This water has a very fine taste; therefore, the nobles drink it. Those who sell it keep it in glass bottles or in tin ones which are very artistically decorated. After that there are other shops where are sold very nicely presented sweets, different from those usually sold in Europe. There are two kinds: those made of honey and those made of sugar. Then come the fruit dealers who sell the fruits of Syria, such as pears, quinces and pomegranates, which do not grow in Egypt. Further along is the new school built by Sultan A. Ghuri.[22]

The Burji Mamluks successfully shifted the visual climax of the street from Bayn al-Qasrayn to the al-Ghuri complex and space to the south (fig. 6). But Bayn al-Qasrayn remained a very important space in the newly enlarged city. Its appearance was further articulated by dozens of well-placed, elegantly proportioned, and carefully shaped minor innovative urban elements, such as the *sabil/kuttab* structures, which served the double function of a water fountain on the ground floor and a Qur'anic school on the top floor. Several of these were added along the street in very sensitive locations. The skyline of Cairo was enriched by a great number of minarets that sprang up around the area.

With the Ottoman invasion of Egypt, Cairo

Figure 7. Bayn al-Qasrayn as depicted by Pascal Coste in 1838. This scene, looking north, shows the Qalawun complex and the *madrasah* al-Barquqiyyah to the left.

all the houses of Cairo have been built without any plan for the town; each one takes all the space that he wants to build without considering whether he blocks the street or not."[23] Although de Thevenot's understanding of the city and its streets was quite simplistic, he nevertheless presented an accurate portrait of the stillness of the urban fabric.

This stillness was shattered by the Napoleonic expedition into Egypt (1798–1801). Much of the fighting between the French and the Egyptians occurred outside of the walled city. But to quell pockets of resistance, the French demolished several structures both inside and outside al-Qahirah proper.[24] And although the French left Cairo in a shambles, their documentation of the city in the massive publication *Description de l'Egypte* was a major contribution to our understanding of its structural history.[25] However, the space of Bayn al-Qasrayn received little attention in this extensive document.

Following the departure of the French in 1801, Bayn al-Qasrayn witnessed one of its last important events. Mamluk forces, attempting to regain control of the city, entered it from both Bab al-Futuh and Bab Zuwaylah. Meeting in the middle of the city at Bayn al-Qasrayn, they were stunned by the forces of Muhammad ʿAli, the newly appointed and locally popular governor of Egypt. This event literally consolidated the power of Muhammad ʿAli's family, which ruled Egypt from 1805 to 1952.[26]

The era of Muhammad ʿAli and his immediate successors has left us some of the best visual documentation of Bayn al-Qasrayn (fig. 7). Hordes of European painters and travelers descended upon Cairo in those years. The paintings of the Scottish artist David Roberts, done between 1838 and 1849, record the richness of Cairo's Islamic heritage.[27] It is significant, however, that most of these painters were

experienced a period of relative stagnation. A few well-formed small mosques and *sabil/kuttab*s were added on the Bayn al-Qasrayn. Among these were the *sabil/kuttab* of Katkhuda at the northern end of Bayn al-Qasrayn and the *sabil/kuttab* of Khusraw Pasha at the southern end. During the era of Ottoman rule (1517–1805), little mention of Bayn al-Qasrayn may be found in the accounts of the many travelers who passed through the city. Instead, most of these writers concentrated on describing developments and spaces outside the walled city.

The Frenchman Jean de Thevenot, seeing the city in 1686, commented: "There is no handsome street in Cairo, but a great many little ones that are round about; it is well known that

Figure 8. Bayn al-Qasrayn,
or al-Nahhasin, as depicted
by David Roberts in an
1843 painting, under the
title, *The Bazaar of the
Coppersmiths, Cairo.* This
view, facing south, shows
part of the Qalawun
complex to the right. To
the left are part of the al-
Zahiriyyah (which no longer
exists), the *sabil/kuttab* of
Khusraw Pasha, and, hiding
behind it, the minaret of
al-Salihiyyah.

Figure 9. Al-Sukkariyyah,
or the area inside the gate
of Bab Zuwaylah, as
depicted by David Roberts
in 1843. To the right is the
Mosque of al-Mu'ayyad,
to the left is an Ottoman
wikalah (a type of bazaar),
and in the center are the
minarets of al-Mu'ayyad,
built on top of the
Fatimid gate.

now referring to the space as al-Nahhasin, the coppersmiths' bazaar (fig. 8). In his great twenty-volume study, *Al-Khutat al-Tawfiqiyyah,* the nineteenth-century biographer of Cairo ʿAli Mubarak refers to Bayn al-Qasrayn as neither a street nor a space. Instead, Mubarak, who was also Egypt's first minister of public works (1867) and the first planner of modern Cairo, gives only a historical overview of the old space of Bayn al-Qasrayn, under the category "al-Nahhasin Street," within which Bayn al-Qasrayn is labeled a *khatt,* or line.[28] Long gone are the days in which the space was called a "splendid place."

For more than a thousand years, Bayn al-Qasrayn had served as the city's ever-changing symbol. In its early Fatimid years, it stood at the middle of a new royal settlement, symbolizing the unity of state and religion and reflecting the unchallenged power of the caliph. The Ayyubids' building activity in it was a conscious attempt by the new rulers to erase the remnants of the Fatimid caliphate and to facilitate the transformation of Egypt from a Shiite to a Sunni state. The Mamluks perfected the art of building in Cairo, and nowhere is this better manifested than in the very fine *madrasah*s that were elegantly and carefully placed to redefine Bayn al-Qasrayn as the hub of the city in its social-welfare era. All of these monuments of different periods, styles, and functions stand in full harmony, side by side.

One of the things which so strikes the imagination here is the way in which names have survived; this street, the Qasabat el-Qahira, the High Street of Cairo, is still known in this part by its original name Bein el-Qasrein, though the palaces and their glory vanished eight hundred years ago. But the history of Cairo can be read in the names of the streets by one who knows.[29]

Najib Mahfouz's trilogy is a commentary on modern Egypt, presented through the life and times of three generations of the Abd al-Jawad family. Mahfouz brilliantly documents Egypt's coming of age by tracing the changing social relations in this extended family. He moves us very carefully from the emptiness of inherited tradition to the challenges facing a new generation in revolt. It is important to note that Mahfouz wrote these novels in the years immediately following the Egyptian Revolution of 1952, which gave Egyptians the power to govern themselves after centuries of foreign domination. It is significant that Mahfouz titled the first of the three *Bayn al-Qasrayn,* after the first, oldest, and most basic square on the Qasabah of Fatimid Cairo. It is equally significant that the two novels that followed, *Qasr al-Shawq* and *Al-Sukkariyyah,* or *Sugar Street,* were both titled after other streets and spaces directly connected with later Ayyubid and Mamluk developments on the Qasabah (fig. 9).[30]

The three historic periods in the development of the city are metaphorically reflected in the three generations of the Abd al-Jawad family and their struggles to cope with change. Mahfouz grew up in this medieval section of Cairo and was obviously very familiar with its history. Several of his other novels are also named after Cairene streets. His choices could not be more opportune. In the mid-1940s, the governorate of Cairo officially renamed the Qasabah Al-Muʿizz li Din Allah Street. Traditional names such as Bayn al-Qasrayn and al-Sukkariyyah are starting to disappear from the official maps and are seldom used, except by the older residents of the area. Maybe *Bayn al-Qasrayn,* a history turned into fiction in the hands of a great novelist, can preserve for future generations the memory of what once was. ■

Notes

1 N. Mahfouz, *Palace Walk,* W. Hutchins and O. Kenny, trans. (New York, 1990). The epigraph is from pp. 35–36.

2 A. al-Maqrizi, *Al-Mawa'idh wa al-'I'tibar fi Dhikr al-Khutat wa al-Athar* (1442), vol. 2 (Cairo, 1855), 179.

3 Ibid., 275.

4 A. Mubarak, *Al-Khutat al-Tawfiqiyyah Al Jadidah* 1 (Cairo, 1969), 36.

5 N. AlSayyad, *Cities and Caliphs* (New York, 1991), 144.

6 N. Khusraw, *Safar Nameh* (1047), Y. Khashab, trans. (Cairo, 1945), 48.

7 Ibid., 52.

8 N. AlSayyad, *The Streets of Islamic Cairo* (Cambridge, Mass., 1981), 24.

9 A. al-Baghdadi, *Al-Ifadah wa al-'I'tibar* (1204) (Cairo, 1946), 142.

10 G. Wiet, *Cairo: City of Art and Commerce* (Norman, 1964), 98.

11 M. Ibn Sa'id, *Kitab al-Maghrib fi Hula al-Maghrib* (1243) (Cairo, 1950), 45.

12 N. AlSayyad, "Urban Space in an Islamic City," in *Journal of Architecture and Planning Research* (Chicago) 4, no. 12 (June 1987).

13 J. Abu-Lughod, *Cairo: 1001 Years of the City Victorious* (Princeton, 1971), 27.

14 AlSayyad, *Streets of Cairo,* 36.

15 Ibid., 38.

16 M. ibn Batutah, *The Travels of Ibn Batutah* (1326), H. A. R. Gibb, trans., vol. 1 (Cambridge, 1958), 4.

17 K. al-Balawi, *Taj al-Mafraq fi Tahliyat 'Ulama 'al-Mashriq* (1336) (Cairo, 1960), 339.

18 Wiet, *Cairo,* 99.

19 AlSayyad, *Streets of Cairo,* 44.

20 Ibid., 46.

21 Wiet, *Cairo,* 102.

22 L. Africanus, *Description de l'Afrique* (1525) (Paris, 1956), as cited in Wiet, *Cairo,* 103.

23 J. de Thevenot, *The Travels of Monsieur de Thevenot* (1686), A. Lowell, trans., vol. 2 (London: M. Clark), 128.

24 A. Rahman Zaki, *Al-Qahirah, 969–1825* (Cairo, 1966), 280.

25 *Description de l'Egypte,* 20 vols. (Paris, 1818–28).

26 Rahman Zaki, *Al-Qahirah,* 289.

27 D. Roberts, *The Holy Land, Syria, Idumea, Arabia, Egypt and Nubia,* 6 vols.: 1, 1842; 2, 1843; and 3, 1949; and *Egypt and Nubia,* 1, 1846; 2, 3, 1849.

28 Mubarak, *Al-Khutat al-Tawfiqiyyah,* 89.

29 D. Russell, *Medieval Cairo* (London, 1962), 147.

30 Mahfouz published the second and third novels a year after the first, in 1957. All three novels were originally written in the early 1950s.

6

ISTANBUL

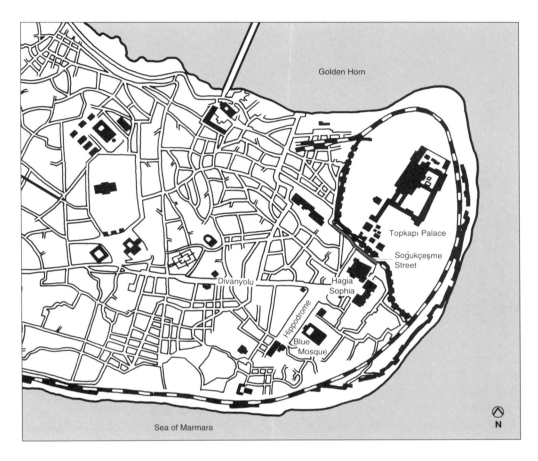

Golden Horn

Topkapı Palace

Soğukçeşme
Street

Divanyolu

Hagia
Sophia

Hippodrome

Blue
Mosque

Sea of Marmara

N

Urban Preservation as Theme Park

The Case of Soğukçeşme Street

ZEYNEP ÇELIK

Figure 1. Partial plan of Istanbul's historic peninsula, c. 1900. Soğukçeşme Street is marked in gray. To its north is the Topkapı Palace and to its south Hagia Sophia.

The dramatic interventions that transformed several historic neighborhoods in Istanbul in the 1980s were largely shaped by European definitions of "Oriental" cultures—a nineteenth-century legacy. The brazen urban-design operations followed two contrasting trends in the treatment of urban fabric and architectural heritage: wholesale demolition and authenticizing restoration. The former was the dominant policy; the latter process resulted in the remaking of Soğukçeşme Street, a picturesque thoroughfare adjacent to Hagia Sophia (fig. 1).

The residents of Istanbul will most likely remember their city during the 1980s as a demolition site, due to large-scale municipal projects that erased much of the nineteenth-century fabric of Tarlabaşı, across from the historic peninsula to the north of the Golden Horn, and cleared the banks of this waterway on both sides. Tarlabaşı was a dense settlement to the north of Pera's renowned central avenue, Istiklal Caddesi, formerly the Grande Rue. The quarter had taken its definitive form in the nineteenth century, paralleling the rise of Pera as the center of European-style living in the Ottoman capital.[1] The narrow streets of Tarlabaşı adhered to the complexity of the topography and formed a meandering network; they were lined with four- to five-story buildings adorned with sparse Neoclassical details. Then a residential neighborhood inhabited

Figure 2. Banks of the
Golden Horn, 1990.

largely by ethnic minorities, it had decayed substantially in the recent past, turning into a slum area with many small-scale commercial establishments, workshops, and dens of marginal and illegal activities. In the 1980s the city wished to cut large arteries to ease the congested motor circulation from the northern part of greater Istanbul to the historic peninsula; this urge coalesced with the desire to "clean up" the neighborhood and resulted in indiscriminate demolitions. Counter-proposals to preserve the urban fabric were overruled by the city administration, whose underlying philosophy was that the nineteenth century was not historically important for Istanbul and that unglamorous residential neighborhoods (especially those historically associated with minorities) were not worthy of architectural rehabilitation. In its essence, the attitude harks back to the Napoleonic urban-reform legacy: *nettoyer par le vide*—applied on a monumental scale in the Paris of Napoleon III and Baron Haussmann

and viewed as an ultimate model for Istanbul since the 1860s.[2]

The city administration followed a similar logic and once again revived an unrealized nineteenth-century policy when it cleared the Golden Horn's banks of the innumerable workshops and warehouses that had crowded the shoreline since Byzantine days, and replaced them with parks (fig. 2). While the functional, sanitary, and aesthetic problems caused by decrepit conditions here had called for a radical intervention for about two centuries, the abruptness of the recent gesture that erased uniform strips on two sides of the waterway disrupted the integrity of the urban structure. The scale and the bareness of the new parks, planted with uninterrupted lawns, establish an awkward relationship with the density of the built form. Consequently, the city seems to have lost its edge on the waterfront; it no longer presents a façade to the Golden Horn.

While municipal policies deleted chunks of

history from the urban fabric of Istanbul, simultaneously there arose an opposing tendency to restore entire streets and neighborhoods, in order to create a nostalgic aura of authenticity. This trend emerged in a semiprivate venture. Under the energetic leadership of its director, Çelik Gülersoy, the Turkish Touring and Automobile Association (TTAA) purchased and restored several historic urban "fragments." The prominent location of Soğukçeşme Street and its radical transformation make it the most visible achievement of the TTAA.[3] In its self-conscious architectural imagery, deemed to represent a "typical" Istanbul fabric, the new Soğukçeşme Street also reflects dilemmas pertinent to architectural symbolism, knowledge, and comprehension of history, as well as the durability of received cultural definitions.

To understand the rupture with the past and the meanings behind the restoration philosophy manifested in the TTAA's project, it is helpful to situate the practice in a historic context. In the Ottoman system, preservation and restoration were carried out through two agencies: the *vakıf* system and the Organization of Royal Architects (Hassa Mimarları Teşkilatı). A *vakıf* is a permanent endowment of land or real estate made by an individual and secured by a deed of restraint.[4] Through this act, the owner stipulated that the property be used for good purposes. The principles to be followed were regulated in detail: the purpose had to be compatible with Islam and pleasing to God; the object of the endowment had to be of a permanent nature and made in perpetuity.[5] *Vakıf*s varied from religious buildings to educational ones, to all kinds of public works (roads, aquaducts, bridges), to charitable institutions (hospitals, hostels, laundries, kitchens). Every *vakıf* had a manager, usually appointed by the founder, in addition to a number of technically skilled people on salary, responsible for its repair or restoration. These could include an architect, a plumber, a handiman, a roofer, a guard, a horticulturist, and an accountant. Depending upon the scale, function, and importance of the *vakıf*, the staff size varied. A local *kadı*, or judge, supervised its maintenance.[6] The system applied not only to major architectural monuments, but also, and more importantly, to every religious and public building, regardless of scale and architectural ambition.

The Organization of Royal Architects was responsible for the continuous supervision of the palace buildings and the establishment and maintenance of all major *vakıf*s. The architects of this organization also determined urban policies and building regulations—for example, regulations to prevent fires and limit construction on streets, and around and inside monuments. Construction was not permitted within eleven feet of the inner and outer façades of city walls. Likewise, Hagia Sophia was to maintain a vacant band of eighty-six feet around its major façades and six and one-half feet along its *medrese* façade.[7]

Even a broad-brush survey indicates that under the auspices of the *vakıf* system and the Organization of Royal Architects, the scope of conservation and restoration in the Ottoman capital was impressive during the classical age.[8] Furthermore, these efforts were distributed throughout the city quite evenly—a phenomenon that was reversed in the nineteenth and twentieth centuries, when major monuments were given definitive priority. In the nineteenth century the Ottoman administration underwent radical reforms that centralized its former decentralized apparatus, which had allowed the *vakıf* system to function efficiently. As part of the Tanzimat program, a Ministry of Vakıfs was founded in 1840, rendering the dispersed, neighborhood-scale *vakıf* obsolete.[9]

The practice of urban preservation in the post-Tanzimat era is significant for the persistance of its principles. Istanbul's urban fabric was

Figure 3. Divanyolu,
c. 1900. To the right are
the Çemberlitaş Bath,
sliced obliquely during the
enlargement of the street;
Constantine's column;
and the Mosque of Atik
Ali Paşa.

transformed in the 1860s according to an agenda
of regularization. Cutting long and orthogonal
streets through the dense quarters inevitably
led to a consideration of the historic patrimony. The widening of Divanyolu, the Byzantine *mese*, or middle street, is indicative,
because it is lined with major monuments
from all periods of the city's history (fig. 3). At
this time, a decision was made to clear the area
around Constantine's column, formerly cluttered with houses. Here, a small triangular plaza was opened. Simultaneously, the residential
area adjacent to Hagia Sophia was demolished
to make room for a square, and the entrances
to the Hippodrome and Beyazit Square (the
former Forum Tauri) cleared. The enlarged
street now connected these foci and privileged
the Byzantine heritage of the city.

The mentality that isolated the important
monuments and enhanced their connection to

each other ignored other architecture deemed
secondary. These less-esteemed buildings were
either torn down or liberally sliced. An example
is the Atik Ali Paşa complex (built in 1496),
consisting of a mosque, a *tekke* (Sufi convent),
an *imaret* (public kitchen), and a *medrese* (theo-
logical school). The *imaret* and the *tekke* that
obstructed the directionality of the street were
demolished completely, whereas only half of
the *medrese* was taken down, leaving the remaining building divided from the mosque by the
road. Çemberlitaş Bath, nearby, was also chopped
off to enable the enlargement of Divanyolu.[10]

The Haussmannian focus on major monuments as objects without context dominated
urban-planning activities in Istanbul until the
1970s. Residential fabrics and smaller public
buildings, such as neighborhood mosques,
*mescid*s, *tekke*s, and baths, were not considered
worthy of preservation and were indiscriminately demolished to make way for new roads—
a practice that reached its peak during the
"rebuilding" of the city in the 1950s. The mentality extended well beyond the technocratic
corps of the municipal administration. Even a
history-conscious architect such as Sedad Hakkı Eldem had no commitment to contextuality;
his study of historic structures concentrated on
"types," rather than their relation to their environment.[11] The Western rediscovery of vernacular architecture in the 1970s, however, found a
sympathetic milieu in Turkey and architectural
historians began to study urban fabrics and
vernacular buildings, engaging in long debates
on the value of history and its documentation.
Under the leadership of the High Council of
Monuments and Sites (Yüksek Anıtlar ve Sitler
Kurumu), preservation and restoration codes
were revised, now aiming to salvage humbler
buildings and contexts.[12]

The council classified residential buildings
according to their historic value. Type I com-

prised houses whose interiors as well as exteriors were historically meaningful: they were to be restored to their original state both on the inside and the outside. A house classified as Type II did not have an important interior, but contributed to the overall urban fabric because of its exterior: it could be rebuilt in modern materials (concrete frame, brick infill), with a totally new interior organization. While the façades of such houses were covered with wood and painted, even modifications in scale and exterior form were allowed in this category.[13] The remaking of Soğukçeşme Street is an outcome of the enthusiastic acceptance of contextualism and vernacular architecture, supported by the provisions of the new regulations.

Soğukçeşme Street is located at the core of Istanbul's monumental center, between the north façade of Hagia Sophia and the outer walls of the Topkapı Palace; it connects the city's first hill—its most important tourist center—to the historic commercial area toward Eminönü (fig. 4). As documented in engravings and early photographs, at least in the nineteenth century it demonstrated an atypical pattern as a residential strip: only one side of the street was lined with houses, while the other was defined by the garden walls of Hagia Sophia.[14] The houses, built against the high palace walls, had rather long façades on the street and relatively narrow depths. They afforded direct views of Hagia Sophia. The prominence of the street is enhanced at its eastern end by the Rococo-style northeastern gate to Hagia Sophia and, a little farther down, the Imperial Gate (Bab-ı Hümayun) of the Topkapı Palace. The eighteenth-century Baroque Fountain of Ahmed III sits in the large open space in front of the palace to the west of the Royal Gate, giving further definition to the beginning of Soğukçeşme Street. The street's western end is marked by the polygonal Alay Köşkü, a pavilion in the Ottoman Baroque style

Figure 4. Soğukçeşme Street, c. 1900. To the left is the northeastern gate to the Hagia Sophia precinct.

from which the sultans reviewed official parades (fig. 5).[15] Nearby, the Soğukçeşme Fountain, or Fountain of Cold Waters, dating from 1800, gives the street its name. Recent excavations have revealed a Byzantine cistern close to the south end of the street, possibly as old as Hagia Sophia itself.[16] Naziki Tekkesi, a Sufi residence sheltered in the structure facing the northeast gate of Hagia Sophia, contributed to the sociocultural significance of Soğukçeşme Street.

The historic value of Soğukçeşme Street was recognized by the High Council of Monuments and Sites even before the TTAA expressed interest in restoring it. In a 1975 decree the council agreed in principle that the houses on this street should be demolished and reconstructed in conformity with their original designs and that they should be adapted to tourist use. In 1982 the Council of Ministers declared Soğukçeşme Street a tourist center and a year later issued a third decree calling for the rebuilding of Naziki Tekkesi.[17] In 1977 the Ministry of Culture commissioned the Faculty of Architecture at Istanbul Technical University to study the area and

Figure 5. Soğukçeşme
Street, c. 1970. The back
façades of the houses on
the street face the outer
walls of the Topkapı
Palace. To the left is the
garden of Hagia Sophia.
The polygonal structure
marking the end of the
street is the Alay Köşkü.
The Golden Horn
is in the background.

submit a restoration proposal that would transform the houses on Soğukçeşme Street into tourist accommodations. TTAA's realization is based on this study.[18]

At the time when the tourist potential of Soğukçeşme Street was recognized, it was lined with modest houses in dilapidated condition. While ten of these houses were in wood, six others were modern structures in concrete and brick. Several were used as workshops; living conditions were crowded and poor. Yet the short strip had a romantic old flavor that made it a favorite stage set for movies dealing with historic topics (fig. 6).

By the mid-1980s the TTAA had acquired a reputation as the champion of restoration and conservation in Istanbul. The inauguration of the Yeşil Ev, the Green House, a restored mansion in the vicinity of the Sultan Ahmed Mosque converted into a hotel, established the Association as the ultimate protector of Istanbul's architectural heritage and facilitated Çelik Gülersoy's negotiations with the municipality over Soğukçeşme Street. It took the TTAA two years to bargain for and purchase the properties on the strip. According to the director, it was necessary to acquire the entire property and thereby "prevent its future use for purposes that would have harmed its touristic potential."[19]

Then, between 1985 and 1986, "with one sweep of a brush over an ancient canvas . . . a lovely old picture" was created.[20] The entire built fabric between Hagia Sophia and the walls of Topkapı Palace was torn down, rebuilt according to new designs, "correcting" the contemporary eyesores and filling the gaps between the houses with buildings of uniform appearance (fig. 7).[21] In accordance with legislative provisions, the new constructions are concrete frame with brick infill, but clad in wood paneling and painted in pastel colors, inspired by nineteenth-century accounts by European travelers. They

Figure 6. Soğukçeşme Street used as a stage set, c. 1960.

now shelter guest houses, complete with restaurants, cafés, and nightclubs. The Naziki Tekkesi, the largest, is a ten-room facility; the eight others have 120 rooms in total. Every house is named after a flower: the Jasmine House, the Honeysuckle House, the Morning-Glory House, the Lilac House, the Wisteria House, and so forth. Their interior decoration and furnishings derive from the turn-of-the century tastes of the Ottoman upper classes. The effect is described by Gülersoy:

On opening his door, the visitor will find himself in the warm atmosphere of a room furnished in the nineteenth-century Ottoman style with silks and velvets in delicate pastel shades. Every room is characterized by a particular color: the yellow room, the pink room, etc.[22]

The Byzantine cistern has been converted into a "Roman taverna" and furnished with "great solid wood refectory tables in the medieval style, wrought-iron chandeliers, massive candlesticks and wine-casks." It is perceived as "a synthesis of the Roman and the Ottoman adapted

Figure 7. Soğukçeşme
Street, 1990.

to modern tourism." Next to it, "a building
with the charming appearance of an old Anatolian house" shelters a library that specializes
in Western publications on Istanbul.[23] The tourist repertoire has been completed by the conversion of a nearby *medrese*, the Soğuk Kuyu
Medresesi, into a crafts center; aside from its
commercial function, this building provides a
stage where artisans producing "traditional"
arts and crafts can be watched by tourists.

This major intervention resulted in a scenographic fragment within the urban fabric of
Istanbul. Soğukçeşme Street stands out as a
curiosity in its pronounced difference from the
rest of the city. But perhaps more profound
than its formal and visual alienation is the
social impact caused by the displacement of
former residents and the wholesale dedication

of the area to the use of tourists. For the residents of late-twentieth-century Istanbul, the
new Soğukçeşme Street is a sightseeing object
that presents a fictional authenticity.

The legacy of constructing abstracted ur-
ban-scale fragments to represent cultures and
societies goes back to nineteenth-century universal expositions, the ancestors of today's theme
parks. Indeed, the rues de Caire, de Constantinople, and d'Alger built temporarily on the
exhibition grounds of European and American
cities bear striking similarities to the new
Soğukçeşme Street (fig. 8). Placed on the out-
skirts of the more serious, technologically and
artistically advanced, main displays, these streets
provided entertainment zones for fairgoers.[24]
They also created a prefabricated and idealized
tourism, a tourism *en place*. To walk through the

Figure 8. Rue du Caire,
Exposition Universelle,
Paris, 1889.

Islamic quarters of the world's fairs, often situated next to each other, was to simulate a miniature tour of the world. As one French writer, Hippolyte Gautier, noted in 1867, it was no longer necessary to take the boat from Marseille to go to the Orient: the Orient had come to Paris.[25]

The Islamic streets of the expositions were designed with much concern for authenticity, often meticulously duplicating famous monuments. For example, the "Ottoman quarter" in Paris in 1867 consisted of a replica of the Green Mosque of Bursa, a residential structure called the Pavillon du Bosphore, modeled after Çinili Köşk in the Topkapı Palace gardens, and a small-scale copy of Sinan's Hürrem Sultan Baths in Istanbul. In 1889, the rue du Caire in Paris was made up of twenty-five houses that recycled architectural fragments from recently demolished buildings in Cairo. According to its financier and organizer, Delort de Gleon, this street represented different periods and styles of Cairene residential architecture. A reduced copy of the Qaytbay Complex added to the picturesqueness of perspective views. De Gleon argued that the rue du Caire on the Champs de Mars was more authentic than any street in late-nineteenth-century Cairo, because it was impossible to find an untouched street in Cairo any more; the old houses with beautiful *musharabiyya*s, wooden window screens, no longer abutted each other, but were "separated, alas, by modern houses in bad taste."[26]

The concern for authenticity went beyond architectural imagery in exposition settings. The atmosphere was enriched by representatives from different cultures, dressed in their most colorful clothes and engaged in "traditional" activities (such as craftsmanship) and performances (among them the popular belly dancing). The parallels to tourist performances in Soğukçeşme Street are obvious: in the crafts center and the nightclubs, the same patterns that represented "Oriental culture" to Western audiences in the nineteenth century have been reassembled.

Nineteenth-century legacies thus determine at large the urban preservation ventures in contemporary Istanbul. As Edward Said has argued, reducing cultures to easily readable signs results not only in the creation of durable stereotypes, but, more significantly, in the "construction" of cultures: post-Enlightenment Europe produced an "Orient" and defined its sociocultural characteristics.[27] Nevertheless, this hegemonic phenomenon benefited from the contribution of "Orientals" themselves—a development commonly overlooked by critics of the West's Orientalism. Once the sociocultural signs were designated and the representations gained the authority of "authenticity," they were adopted and disseminated by the "insiders." The intervention at Soğukçeşme Street is a prime example of this process.

Europe's construction of the Orient has depended on binary oppositions. A major issue is the notion of history. The world has been divided into two types of societies: those with and those without history. The latter are characterized by their "traditions," which remain constant throughout time. Deemed incapable of change and dynamism, non-Western societies have thus been "fixed" in history. In architectural imagery, this has translated into the recycling of historically ambiguous, but "traditional," forms as summaries to represent cultures and societies. The essential issue, therefore, is the complicated link of a culture to history. An analysis of the historicist reinvention of Soğukçeşme Street in the context of what appears to be its diametric opposite, the wholesale demolitions of historic fabric, reveals how much Istanbul remains embedded in Orientalist mentalities. ∎

Notes

1 See Z. Çelik, *The Remaking of Istanbul,* 2d ed. (Berkeley, 1993), ch. 6.

2 For the impact of the Parisian model on nineteenth-century Istanbul, see Çelik, *Remaking of Istanbul,* especially chs. 4 and 5.

3 The other major example is the neighborhood around the Church of St. Savior in Chora (Kariye Camii).

4 H. A. R. Gibb and H. Bowen, *Islamic Society and the West,* vol. 1 (New York, 1957), 2, 164.

5 *Encyclopedia of Islam* (Leiden, 1960), 1096–97.

6 H. B. Kunter, "Türk Vakıfları ve Vakfiyeleri," *Vakıflar Dergisi* vol. 1, 115–16.

7 Ş. Turan, "Osmanlı Teşkilatında Hassa Mimarları," *Ankara Üniversitesi Tarih Araştırmaları Dergisi* 1 (1964): 169–71.

8 The classical period of the Ottoman Empire is acknowledged as the fifteenth and sixteenth centuries. The efficiency of both systems naturally depended on the economic well-being of the Empire.

9 *Encyclopedia of Islam,* 1101. The Tanzimat Charter, signed in 1839, made reformation according to European models official policy. Literature on Tanzimat reforms is extensive. See, for example, N. Berkes, *The Development of Secularism in Turkey* (Montreal, 1964); B. Lewis, *The Emergence of Modern Turkey* (London, 1961); and S. Shaw, "Some Aspects of the Aims and Achievements of the Nineteenth-Century Ottoman Reformers" in W. Polk and R. Chambers, eds., *Beginnings of Modernization in the Middle East—The Nineteenth Century* (Chicago, 1968), 32–33.

10 Çelik, *Remaking of Istanbul,* 57–62.

11 Sedad Hakkı Eldem was a prominent Turkish architect who practiced from the 1930s to the 1980s, and taught, wrote, and conducted research on architecture. For his housing typology, see S. H. Eldem, *Türk Evi Plan Tipleri* (Istanbul, 1954), and S. Bozdoğan, S. Özkan, and E. Yenal, *Sedad Eldem* (Singapore, 1987), 45.

12 While established in 1951, the Council gained considerable power after the 1973 legislation on "historic works." A threshold in preservation, this legislation extended the definition of "historic" from single buildings to environmental compounds. The responsibilities of the council are similar to those of a landmarks commission, and include devising principles for the preservation, maintenance, and restoration of historic buildings and sites. A significant number of its members are chosen from among university professors who specialize in archaeology, history, art history, architectural history, urban studies, or restoration. See T. Gök, *Kent Planlama ile İlgili Yasal Kurallardan Seçmeler* (Ankara, 1980), 75–76. In the 1970s and 1980s, leading Turkish architectural historians such as Doğan Kuban and Abdullah Kuran, as well as the architect Sedad Eldem, served on this council. By then, Eldem had revised his own views on contextuality, as may be seen in his Social Security Agency Complex in Zeyrek, a historic neighborhood in Istanbul. The building complex relates to the fabric behind it by means of fragmented volumes that do not overwhelm the context.

13 Type I houses are described as "monumental works" (*anıt eser*), whereas those of Type II are "old works that must be preserved as examples of civil architecture" (*sivil mimarlık örneği olarak korunması gereken eski eser*). See E. Apter, "Istanbul ve Tarihi Çekirdeği," *Bildiriler,* Proceedings of the Conference on the Preservation of Architectural Heritage of Islamic Cities (Istanbul, 1987), 196. To enable preservation on a large scale, a regulation was passed on March 30, 1979, that provided for financial and technical assistance to owners of buildings classified as "historic." See Gök, *Kent Planlama,* 286.

14 Although the houses were continually built and rebuilt, Gülersoy argues, on the basis of his research on title deeds, engravings, and the date on the Soğukçeşme Fountain, that the street must have been lined with houses for at least 250 years. See Ç. Gülersoy, *Soğukçeşme Street* (Istanbul, 1989), 9.

15 The current building dates from 1819; nevertheless, there has been an Alay Köşkü here since much earlier.

16 Gülersoy, *Soğukçeşme Street*, 18.

17 Ibid., 13. The first decree is dated August 2, 1975; the second June 9, 1982; the third October 10, 1983.

18 N. Eldem, M. Kamil, and A. Yücel, "A Plan for Istanbul's Sultanahmet-Ayasofya Area," *Conservation as Cultural Survival*, ed. Renata Holod, The Aga Khan Awards in Architecture, Proceedings of Seminar 2 (1980), 53–56.

19 Gülersoy, *Soğukçeşme Street*, 10.

20 Ibid., 15.

21 The association is currently negotiating to purchase the lower part of the street, in order to extend the tourist strip down to the Alay Köşkü.

22 Gülersoy, *Soğukçeşme Street*, 17. The name of the Wisteria House comes from the resemblance of this house to the one in which the Turkish novelist Halide Edip spent her childhood (in another neighborhood) and which she described in her memoirs, *Mor Salkımlı Ev* (Istanbul, 1963).

23 Gülersoy, *Soğukçeşme Street*, 18–19.

24 For further discussion of the Islamic villages at the universal expositions, see Z. Çelik, *Displaying the Orient: Architecture of Islam at Nineteenth-Century World's Fairs* (Berkeley, 1992), ch. 2.

25 H. Gautier, *Les Curiosités de l'Exposition Universelle de 1867*, 2 vols. (Paris, 1867), 2:85–86.

26 D. de Gleon, *La Rue du Caire à l'Exposition Universelle de 1889* (Paris, 1889), 10.

27 E. Said, *Orientalism* (New York, 1979).

7

EPHESUS

The Street Experience of Ancient Ephesus

FIKRET K. YEGÜL

Figure 1. Plan of Ephesus. The main thoroughfare is marked in gray.

The institutions of the classical city—temples, stoas, basilicas, gymnasia, baths, and theaters—provided cultural and intellectual character, but it was the streets that provided the lifeblood of the system and gave these institutions visibility. Articulated by colonnades, arches, and gates; defined by bends, curves, and crossings; expanded by plazas and squares; celebrated by fountains and commemorative monuments, the street brought vitality and meaning to this interconnected urban tissue. In the words of William L. MacDonald, a prominent student of Roman architecture, it created an "armature" that "framed and facilitated much of the business of town life."[1]

If "armatures were sophisticated responses to the universal urban need for an architecture of connection and passage," as MacDonald observes, few cities of classical antiquity presented so rich and sophisticated an armature as did Ephesus of the Imperial Roman era.[2] A theoretical study of the city planning of ancient Ephesus may be attempted elsewhere; here, it is appropriate instead to re-create the experiential aspects of the major streets, and to respond to the architectonic whole created by the urban armature, rather than to the specific historical conditions that shaped its individual features. Although some of the elements common to most cities can be cited, such as gates, walls, waterways, highways traversing the city, and market streets, the growth of an armature is a practical, not a theoretical matter. Armatures were the result of cumulative acts of planning unique to each city. The primary value of their study lies in re-creating the street experience in antiquity.[3]

Located on the western coast of Asia Minor (modern Turkey), Ephesus interwove an intimate blend of public and private space with the unique natural features of its site (fig. 1).[4] Perhaps the most distinctive urban connector in the city was a thoroughfare stretching between the

Coressian Gate on the northeast and the Magnesian Gate on the southeast (fig. 2, 1, **48**). The course of this mile-and-a-half-long thoroughfare had already been determined during the Hellenistic period, as a part of an artery linking the new city to the ancient Sanctuary of Artemis, to the north of the town. It looped around a major hill with three peaks (the ancient Pion, modern Panayirdağı), and changed its name and character several times. No single ancient or modern name has been assigned to this remarkable street. The colonnaded stretch that occupied the bottom of a narrow valley between Panayirdağı and a larger mountain to the southeast, modern Bülbüldağı (Mount Lepre Akte), followed an ancient processional route and was known in late antiquity as the Embolos.[5] A broad, colonnaded avenue, the Arcadiane (10), joined the thoroughfare at midpoint, connecting the harbor with the city center. The curved arms of a magnificent theater (8), rising against the mountain slope toward the sea, punctuated the crossing (fig. 3). Architectural monuments, formal peristyle courts, intersecting secondary streets, and plazas defined, embellished, and energized the thoroughfare. The network created by this artery and its numerous tributaries was not the result of a single act of planning, but a spontaneous, though controlled, growth along a pattern shaped by the unique urban history and geography of the pre-Roman site. The street in turn shaped and controlled the Roman city's character and destiny.

Unlike some Roman cities, Ephesus never developed a traditional strict orthogonal plan with an emphasized pair of crossing streets. It is true, however, that the Embolos intersected diagonally a number of smaller streets, which created a loosely organized grid plan at least for the residential zone on both sides of the steeply sloping hills.[6] Yet the varying direction of individual houses on each block, built on overlapping

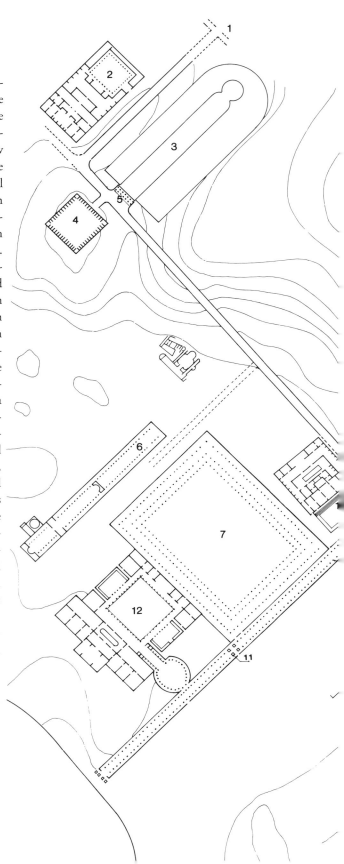

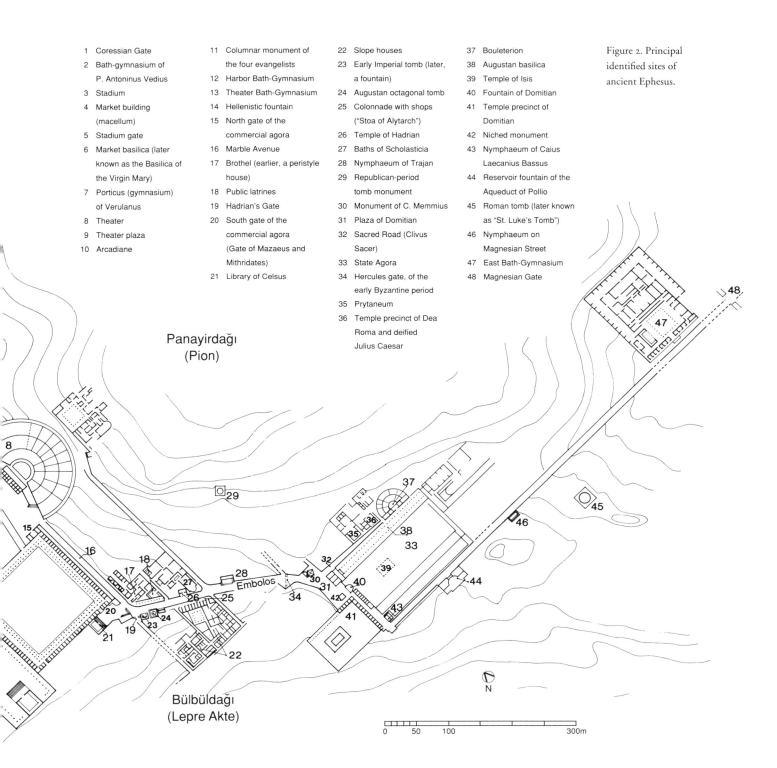

1 Coressian Gate
2 Bath-gymnasium of P. Antoninus Vedius
3 Stadium
4 Market building (macellum)
5 Stadium gate
6 Market basilica (later known as the Basilica of the Virgin Mary)
7 Porticus (gymnasium) of Verulanus
8 Theater
9 Theater plaza
10 Arcadiane

11 Columnar monument of the four evangelists
12 Harbor Bath-Gymnasium
13 Theater Bath-Gymnasium
14 Hellenistic fountain
15 North gate of the commercial agora
16 Marble Avenue
17 Brothel (earlier, a peristyle house)
18 Public latrines
19 Hadrian's Gate
20 South gate of the commercial agora (Gate of Mazaeus and Mithridates)
21 Library of Celsus

22 Slope houses
23 Early Imperial tomb (later, a fountain)
24 Augustan octagonal tomb
25 Colonnade with shops ("Stoa of Alytarch")
26 Temple of Hadrian
27 Baths of Scholasticia
28 Nymphaeum of Trajan
29 Republican-period tomb monument
30 Monument of C. Memmius
31 Plaza of Domitian
32 Sacred Road (Clivus Sacer)
33 State Agora
34 Hercules gate, of the early Byzantine period
35 Prytaneum
36 Temple precinct of Dea Roma and deified Julius Caesar

37 Bouleterion
38 Augustan basilica
39 Temple of Isis
40 Fountain of Domitian
41 Temple precinct of Domitian
42 Niched monument
43 Nymphaeum of Caius Laecanius Bassus
44 Reservoir fountain of the Aqueduct of Pollio
45 Roman tomb (later known as "St. Luke's Tomb")
46 Nymphaeum on Magnesian Street
47 East Bath-Gymnasium
48 Magnesian Gate

Figure 2. Principal identified sites of ancient Ephesus.

Panayirdağı (Pion)

Bülbüldağı (Lepre Akte)

Embolos

N

0   50   100   300m

Figure 3. The theater, theater plaza, and east end of the Arcadiane, looking east.

terraces to catch the view and the breeze, represents an individualized interpretation of the grid (22).[7] Order in the plan of Ephesus is imposed by a remarkable conformity in the alignment of all major buildings, but this does not express a desire for strict reticulation. This alignment (13.78 degrees east of true north) follows precisely the orientation of the archaic temple of Artemis, located nearly two kilometers to the northeast of the city.[8] A tightly integrated network of streets and colonnades, draped over blocks of differing sizes, shapes, and internal arrangements, bound the physical urban shape together. In its loose interpretation of an urban grid, Ephesus is typical of many coastal cities under the Roman Empire, as well as many inland, where Greek theories of urban planning met a native Anatolian preference for organic improvisation.[9] The existence of a binding order of orthogonal planning, reflecting Ionia's Hippodamian tradition, has been posited, but is very much a theoretical construct without real basis

or meaning in Asia Minor under the Empire. In fact, it is doubtful whether the "Hippodamian tradition" was ever a tradition at all.

A traveler approaching Ephesus from the direction of the famed Sanctuary of Artemis, near the early Greek settlement called Smyrna, could have entered the city from north–northwest, by way of the Coressian Gate (1).[10] Although the exact location of the Coressian Gate is unknown, it was clearly situated directly north of the stadium (3), aligned on the initial stretch of the thoroughfare (which, for convenience, may be named Coressus Street), between the bath-gymnasium complex of Vedius (2) and the stadium. Having passed through the formal entrance, the visitor was immediately absorbed into a world created by the signs and symbols of a monumental urban classicism befitting the Roman metropolis of Asia.[11]

Running between the rising walls of two massive structures—the steady rhythm of the arches and engaged columns of the stadium on

Figure 4. The Marble Avenue, looking south.

one side and the larger, plainer wall surfaces, lofty vaults, and broad gables of the baths on the other—the street cut through a deep, artificial valley. Vision was controlled, restricted. The rhythm of the ponderous architectural presences, like sentinels on either side of the straight street, created a tangible and formal sense of entrance, arrival, and reception. Only the gateway to the palaestra of the baths, on the right, arrested movement momentarily by offering a discrete visual focus. If a more powerful visual terminus existed at the end of this initial stretch of the thoroughfare, where it took a sharp right-angle turn to the south, no trace of it remains today. However, a square, porticoed building occupying the top of a small but conspicuous hillock opposite the stadium entrance must have served effectively in holding the vision and terminating the westward direction of movement (4). If this building was a macellum, as tentatively identified, it would have greeted the visitor with an emphatically urban cocktail of bustle, noise, and smell typical of any market town.

Across from the macellum, the west entrance gate to the stadium was one of the most magnificent landmarks of Ephesus (5). flanked by a pair of gigantic archways (marking the ends of the *vomitaria* vaults supporting the seats), an imposing but airy gate structure ran along the street and screened the open end of the horseshoe racetrack: between end piers, seven pairs of tall columns raised on podium bases were connected by graceful arches.[12] The visual contrast between the massively built and vaulted ends of the stadium and a light, elegant, and almost transparent gate of columns and arches must have been a memorable early impression of the city, whose mixed notion of classicism sought to integrate the architectural heritage of its Hellenistic past with its Roman present.

Between the stadium and the square, in front of the theater, the thoroughfare extended for a full six or seven hundred meters. At some point along this tract it must have bent or jogged westward for a length of about thirty meters, to negotiate the difference of alignment between the two structures. It must have been intersected by a number of smaller streets, some running uphill to Panayirdağı (probably to residential areas), others downward toward the flat ground of the valley. At least one major street leading to the harbor area passed across it and between the long market basilica (6, now called the Basilica of the Virgin Mary or the Cathedral of Ephesus) and the huge gymnastic establishment known as the Porticus of Verulanus (7). This part of the city and the street are largely unexplored.[13]

Also unexplored is the square in front of the theater. This is the place where the silversmith Demetrius raised a storm of citizens' protest against St. Paul, who had preached against the worship of devotional images of Artemis (Acts 19). Defined on the west by the massive stage wall of the theater, this open space (9, see fig. 3) was one of the most important hubs of Ephesus, connecting the harbor and the large public structures that occupied the flat northern quarters of the city with the public, commercial, and private institutions draped unevenly over the hilly terrain through which the valley of the Embolos cut southeast.[14]

The Arcadiane, a straight, broad, colonnaded avenue half a kilometer in length, connected the theater plaza with the harbor (10). Perhaps laid out during the last decade of the first century B.C.E., the Arcadiane received its name from Emperor Arcadius (r. 395–408), who repaired and widened the avenue with double porticoes and a row of shops. During the sixth century, a monument with four tall columns supporting the statues of the four evangelists was placed in the middle of the marble-paved Arcadiane (11), providing effective visual relief to the street's relentless formality.[15] Terminated at both ends by richly articulated gates, the Arcadiane was

both a ceremonial way between the busy harbor and the heart of the city and a majestic visual vector, leaping, as it were, from the taut bow of the theater to the shimmering expanse of the Aegean horizon. It was also a practical route of access to three of the largest and most popular educational and recreational institutions of Ephesus—the Harbor Bath-Gymnasium (12), the Porticus of Verulanus (7), and the Theater Bath-Gymnasium (13).[16] The small palaestra of the last opened to the theater square and was a popular corner for informal performances and athletic events.

A visitor walking through the theater square could take refreshment at the small, columnar Hellenistic fountain that stood against the terrace wall of the theater stage (14). One could then continue south, up the gently sloping street, passing by the classically composed north gate of the commercial agora on the right (15) and into a bottleneck leading to another colonnaded street. This broad, marble-paved street, named the Marble Avenue (16), followed the eastern perimeter of the commercial agora and connected the theater square with the west end of the Embolos (fig. 4).[17]

The transitional character of the Marble Avenue—transforming movement from the flat zone of rigidly composed large public structures to the more informal arrangement of organically interlinked, smaller buildings along the bottom and the sides of a narrow valley—is reflected in the distinctive design of its porticoes. The western portico is built partially over the east wing of the agora, atop a masonry podium rising 1.7 meters high, composed of exquisitely fitted marble blocks of convex profile. The austere Doric colonnade, of sturdy, unfluted columns, itself dates to Nero's reign. The colonnade on the opposite side was at street level and screened a row of shops and offices. The uneven heights of the two colonnades

defining the avenue and the powerful barrier created by the sculpted ashlar wall of the west side imparted to this stretch of the thoroughfare a sense of enclosure and a solemn grandeur unmistakable even today.

The simple, somber cadences of the Marble Avenue can be contrasted with the rich mixing of architectural elements grouped closely at the juncture where the street broadens, bends, and joins the Embolos. A popular brothel (17, originally a large peristyle villa) and a public latrine (18) located at this busy intersection attest to the range and diversity of urban life that existed on one long street.[18] Walking south on the avenue, a visitor's attention would have been arrested by a tall and ornate gate signaling the terminus of a street joining the Marble Avenue and the Embolos at their junction and leading south, uphill, toward residential districts (19, fig. 5).[19] The gate can be reconstructed on paper, based on its preserved foundations and some architectural fragments: a row of four

Figure 5. Junction of the Marble Avenue and the Embolos, looking west, reconstruction sketch. From left to right: Hadrian's Gate, the Library of Celsus, the south gate of the commercial agora, and the south end of the western portico of the Marble Avenue (partial).

double-engaged columns carry an attic and a second story crowned by a central pediment broken by an arch (called a Syrian pediment); the wider central bay of the first story is spanned by an arch. Tall, thin, and airy, the general scheme recalls Hadrian's Gate in Athens, and can be assigned to the same period. Like the famous gate at Athens, it related one part of the city to another.[20] While acting as a point of visual reference, the gate invited the eye and the mind to linger and assess the changing character of the urban scenography framed by its familiar elements. It also served as an effective visual reflector, redirecting the pedestrian's gaze from the gently rising Embolos, leading southeast, back to the rich ensemble of architectural façades dominating the junction.

On the west side of this junction, at a level lower than the street but linked to it by a ramp and stairs, a rectangular plaza formed a visual apron for two of the most imposing façades in Ephesus. On the right was the triple-arched, high-atticked south gate to the commercial agora (20), a magnificent specimen of the muscular but subdued classicism of the late Hellenistic and early Augustan periods, with its distinct triumphal-arch motif—perhaps more at home in Italy than in the East. Inscriptions on the attic declare that it was a gift to the city by Mazaeus and Mithridates, freedmen of Augustus.[21] Next to the gate and at right angles to it, atop a bold, broad flight of steps, stood the sumptuous, two-storied aedicular façade of the Library of Celsus (21). Allegorical statues, women representing Wisdom, Virtue, Reason, and Knowledge, appropriate for a library, adorned the undulating columnar composition in the style loosely referred to as "Roman Baroque" and typical of the many nymphaea façades in the same city and on the same street.[22] These two adjacent monuments, one commercial, the other cultural, shared the same space and the same audience. Their façades, one reserved and restrained, the other dynamic and flamboyant, were proper expressions of their times. Like the Doric portico, the urban villa, the public latrine, and the brothel, they attest to the richness of urban experience accumulated over time.

As one looked east from the plaza, the long view from one end of the Embolos to the other must have been memorable, a colorful and messy mosaic occasionally called to order by the classicizing accents of a familiar architectural monument (fig. 6). On the hills on either side of the street houses, mainly of the courtyard type, rose over terraces and overlapped each other in tight, picturesque groups; streets, transformed into long flights of stairs, crossed the marble-paved Embolos obliquely (22). The course of the Embolos has only a very gentle curve, but this must have been enough to give it a tense energy emphasized by slight variations and shifts in the orientations of individual building façades. An uneven and subtly undulating colonnade on both sides of the street must have provided a sense of cohesiveness and continuity, while allowing certain individual elements, such as a temple front, a tomb, a fountain group, to accent the overall scene with moments of visual privilege.

The Hadrianic arch mentioned above and two tomb monuments that follow it immediately form just such a sequence. The first tomb, of the late first century C.E., has a roughly horseshoe-shaped plan (23); it was converted into a fountain reservoir during the Byzantine era, with a basin projecting into the street. The second was a tall, octagonal tomb monument of Augustan date (24). A peristyle of Corinthian columns, carrying a tall pyramidal roof, rose above a three-meter-high marble podium. Two late-fourth-century inscriptions carved on the base mention financial measures taken to relieve and restore the city, which had recently suffered from catastrophic earthquakes.[23] Joining this group further up was a colonnade (rebuilt in the fifth century by a city official) masking a row of shops and a restaurant (25).

A little further up, across the street, are the eye-catching façade and porch of the so-called Temple of Hadrian (26, see fig. 6). This small, elegant building, possibly a shrine to the Imperial Cult, consisted of four Corinthian columns, raised on pedestals, carrying an exceptionally ornate Syrian pediment. The frieze, a late-antique replacement, depicts the foundation legend of Ephesus; the keystone of the pediment arch prominently displays a handsomely carved head of Tyche, the city goddess.[24] The Temple of Hadrian is façade architecture at its most emphatic; the minuscule cella is simply carved out of the larger volume of the Baths of Scholasticia (27), which occupy the entire block. One imagines that its jewellike elegance was set effectively against the large, planar walls, arched windows, and broad projecting apse of the baths. The visual contrast presented by these juxtaposed institutions was heightened by the conceptual contrast inherent in their nature and function: a temple and a bath, a neighborhood of the spiritual and the physical that enhanced the meaning of each in the integrated life of the Roman street.

Past the Temple of Hadrian, the next columnar display of Baroque splendor was the Nymphaeum of Trajan (28). A fine example of the marble façade architecture of Asia Minor, the U-shaped, double-storied structure combined lavish ornament, statuary, and the play of water.[25] A colossal statue of Trajan dominated the central bay. The image, the rich architectural backdrop, and the multiple sources of cascading water were mirrored in a large pool and a smaller, utilitarian basin in front of it. The open, projecting arms of the monument embraced the street and reflected its fast-moving pace in the alternating, contrapuntal

rhythms of its architecture. Looking above Trajan's Nymphaeum, on the upper slopes of Panayirdağı, the visitor could see a fine round building composed of a double-storied colonnade over a square ashlar podium base—possibly a tomb or a heröon dating from the Republican period (29).[26] In pristine and lofty isolation, such a monument recalled the city's heroic past and effectively linked it with the opulent present below.

The straight view up the Embolos focused on another funerary monument related to the city's Republican history (30). Built under Augustus by Caius Memmius, the grandson of the dictator Sulla, it occupied an exceptionally prominent position at the point where the Embolos forked: the right branch curved south and opened into the so-called Plaza of Domitian (31); the left, also known as the Sacred Road (Clivus Sacer, 32), proceeded uphill to connect with the great flat plane of the State Agora (33). The monument, now partially restored, was a tall, square tower on a stepped base (fig. 7).

Figure 6. The Embolos, looking east. The façade of the so-called Temple of Hadrian is at center left; the Nymphaeum of Trajan is to its right, in the distance.

Figure 7. The eastern end of the Embolos and the Plaza of Domitian, with the Monument of C. Memmius and the Hydreion at center; substructures of the Augustan basilica and the Domitianic fountain (with a reconstructed arch) are at right.

Four-way arches separated by corner pilasters carried a high attic decorated with reliefs of solemnly standing togate members of the Memmius family.[27] The arches framed deep rectangular niches facing the street. At a later date a public fountain, called the Hydreion, was built adjacent to the Memmius monument, facing the Embolos. Statues of the Tetrarchs placed in front of the four columns of this fountain joined those of Memmius's ancestors above.[28] The whole visual ensemble, with its remarkable layering of urban history, was viewed through a monumental arch set at the top of the Embolos sometime in the fifth century. The gate opening appears to have been flanked by a pair of pillars, or herms, sculpted with images of Hercules—pieces reused here from an earlier structure (34, fig. 8).[29]

A visitor continuing eastward, uphill beyond the Memmius monument, would have walked along the massive substructures of the basilica (opening to the State Agora above) on the right, passed through a small gate decorated with the image of Hermes, and entered the narrow lane called the Sacred Road, which appropriately gave direct access to several of the city's most important religious and civic institutions (32).[30] On the left, the uphill side, was the Prytaneum (35), the meeting place of the executive council and the official guesthouse, its imposing pedimented façade carried by six massive Doric columns between antae. In an inner chamber approached by a peristyle court, the sacred fire of Hestia Boulaea was kept alive perpetually. Next came the precinct of the temples of Dea Roma and deified Julius Caesar, an official acknowledgment of Imperial presence and its cult (36). The Clivus Sacer terminated at the Bouleterion (shaped like a traditional Odeion and formerly identified as one), where the council of the city held its meetings (37). Across from these buildings, a long, three-aisled stoa, or rather a basilica, originally dedicated to Augustus and Livia, extended along the entire north side of the State Agora (38). The flat expanse of the State Agora was like a great forecourt to the administrative center of the city. Lined with marble benches and official monuments, and with the small Temple of Isis (39) in the middle, it served as the premier political meeting place of Ephesus.[31]

The clearing at the east end of the Embolos, dubbed the Plaza of Domitian, represents a very different kind of space and a different kind of experience from the open space of the State Agora above (31, figs. 7, 9). The area is relatively low. In antiquity it was closed in by the towering terrace of the Temple of Domitian (41, see fig. 9) on the south and west, and the rising embankment of the agora terrace on the east. The advancing visitor's glance, skirting past the south flank of the Memmius monument and the Hydreion, would have been arrested by the projecting bulk of the rusticated ashlar substructure supporting the west end of the basilica. Close to it and more dramatic was the deep, cavelike opening of a fountain monument of Domitianic date carved into the mass of the agora terrace (40, see fig. 7).[32] A great semidomed apse, framed by an arch and tall pilasters, housed a semicircular pool. Around the water's edge, in half-darkness, were grouped the white marble statues representing the familiar theme of the blinding of the Cyclops by Odysseus and his companions. The sound of the falling water, echoing in the shadowy depths of the artificial cavern, the cool spray filling the air, and the shimmering and distorted reflections of the statuary on the water's surface must have left an impression on a hot summer day, inviting every citizen into this memorable theater of the street.

The south end of the plaza, across from the State Agora, was dominated by the terrace of the Temple of Domitian. The northeast end of this terrace, some ten meters high, was designed as a two-story façade, whose lower story of engaged Doric columns supported piers carved with

figures of male and female captives in Eastern dress. This ornate façade concealed an impressive array of shops and storage units built into the vaulted substructures of the terrace.[33]

The plaza had an irregular and richly articulated periphery. Roughly at the geometric center of this space, across from the arched entrance of the grand staircase leading up to the temple platform, was a tall, freestanding monument with four-way niches—or rather, four back-to-back concave walls supporting, possibly, a round, open, templelike structure (42). The sweeping curves of this niched monument provided a visual accent to the open space and became a pivot around which movement was organized and channeled southward.[34] Compressed by the aggressively textured and lofty masses of the two artificial terraces facing each other, the southern continuation of the Embolos must have felt like an urban canyon. Looking up, one could catch a glimpse of the great pediment of the Flavian Temple, outlined against the mountain and the blue sky. This was a space dominated by heights.

Figure 8. The Byzantine gate with herms of Hercules, at the eastern end of the Embolos, looking east. The Monument of C. Memmius can be seen in the distance, between the herms.

Figure 9. The Plaza of
Domitian and the
substructures of the
Temple of Domitian,
looking southwest. Ashlar
substructures of the
west end of the Augustan
basilica are in the
foreground.

At the southeast corner of the State Agora the
street took a sharp left turn and suddenly and
dramatically assumed flat, open ground.[35] It
continued for a way along the south edge of the
agora as a straight, colonnaded way, leading
eventually to the Magnesian Gate.

The corner, marking this dramatic transition, was punctuated by a lavishly decorated
nymphaeum whose two-storied aedicular façade was a typical but early example of the
"Baroque" architecture popular in Asia Minor
after the early second century (43). An inscription found nearby indicates that this sumptuous water monument was a gift of C. Laecanius
Bassus, a city administrator of the late first
century.[36] A rectangular basin filled the entire
area between the projecting arms of the U-
shaped nymphaeum, comparable to the ar-

rangement of the Nymphaeum of Trajan. Also
similar was a smaller, lower basin in front, easily
accessible from the street. Combining convenience with delight, it was for the daily use of
citizens, who refreshed themselves at the fountain
or carried the water home in buckets. Between the
columns, inside the niches, under the aediculae, a
rich display of marble statuary depicting marine
themes offered another urban theater for the
enjoyment of the Ephesians.

The long, straight stretch of this street for a
distance of about six hundred meters, leading to
the Magnesian Gate (48), has been only sketchily
explored.[37] A round tomb monument of the first
century C.E. (45), conspicuous on the south side of
the road, suggests that this area, near the eastern
city gate, may have had many more tombs and
funerary monuments, making it comparable to

Via Appia Antica in Rome. On the same side of the street was a another nymphaeum of Trajanic date, decorated in sumptuous aedicular style, a last civic display of visual splendor (46). Close to the gate, this attractive fountain no doubt also served the thirsty travelers entering or leaving the city from the east.[38]

Like the bath-gymnasium complex of Vedius Antoninus, the first building a visitor encountered on approaching Ephesus from the northeast by the Coressian Gate, the East Bath-Gymnasium (47) was the last to be seen as one left the city by the Magnesian Gate.[39] These two monumental way stations, embracing the thoroughfare back to back like a pair of bookends, offered the traveler entering or leaving the urban zone a chance for washing and refreshment. Both incorporated gymnastic and cultural facilities. At the edge of the rude and rugged countryside, tied to each other by a thread of urban life a mile and a half long, they were emphatic reminders of what a city was and what it stood for.

Along the course of this long urban artery and its complex network of tributaries, a visitor was offered a wide variety of visual, physical, and symbolic amenities to enjoy. From the simple Hellenistic fountain opening into the Theater Plaza to the Magnesian Gate, an Ephesian was never completely out of reach of water. As the sights and sounds of one water monument faded, another along the same course, equally sumptuous, equally refreshing, almost miraculously appeared and served to delight the eyes and satisfy the needs of the pedestrian. The civilizing presence of water was one of several master themes that bound together all other institutions along this thoroughfare. Plazas and courtyards inspired large political and social gatherings. Porticoes set along the street provided protection from the elements and fostered smaller groups for more intimate commerce. Porches of prominent buildings, exedrae, marble seats inspired quiet conversation. Arches and gates emphasized passage and gave a sense of place to the urban elements they ushered and framed. Commemorative and funerary monuments, statuary, inscriptions, public decrees carved in marble—all linked the city's important past with its auspicious future. Monuments belonging to different periods in time, layered and connected along the thoroughfare, helped to create feelings of collective consciousness, pride, and historic perspective in which all individuals could share. Through relation and passage, both the monument and the individual were celebrated.

In sketching an Existentialist philosophy of personal conduct, Jean-Paul Sartre observed that life, in its long and seemingly unintelligible and undifferentiated course, held out "privileged situations" capable of being developed into "perfect moments." To recognize these required skill and sensitivity; to transform them, once recognized, to their optimum potential was not a mere matter of choice but a moral obligation.[40]

Cities, like people, are organic creations. A city's physical setting and particular history together create a situation capable of being developed into a "perfect moment" of urban form. Perhaps the most important and unique aspect of the urban network of Ephesus, especially the long street that formed its backbone, was in the degree of skill and sensitivity with which the historical and natural potential of the place was recognized and exploited. Its idiosyncrasies; its cultural and religious traditions; economic and geographic realities; the natural characteristics of its site—hills, valleys, harbors, waterways—were the "situation" that inspired its physical form. Roman Ephesus was successful in transforming its privileged situation into a perfect moment of urban experience, both civilized and delightful. ■

Notes

1 W. L. MacDonald, *The Architecture of the Roman Empire: An Urban Appraisal*, vol. 2 (New Haven, 1986), 29.

2 Ibid., 30.

3 For ideas on the nontheoretical nature of armatures, see MacDonald, *Architecture of the Roman Empire*, vol. 2, 17–31, esp. 17–18.

4 For a general survey of planning and architecture of Roman Ephesus, see W. Alzinger, "Ephesos," in *Paulys Real-Encyclopädie der classischen Altertumswissenschaft*, ed. G. Wissowa, E. Kroll, et al., suppl. 12 (1970), 1588–1704; idem, *Ephesos: Ein Rundgang durch die Ruinen* (Vienna, 1972); J. Keil, *Führer durch Ephesos* (Vienna, 1955); F. Miltner, *Ephesos: Stadt der Artemis und des Johannes* (Vienna, 1958); A. Bammer, *Ephesos: Stadt an fluss und Meer* (Graz, 1989); E. Lessing and W. Oberleitner, *Ephesos: Weltstadt der Antike* (Vienna, 1978). An excellent description of the architectural remains of the late-antique and Byzantine city along the course of the main streets is found in C. Foss, *Ephesus after Antiquity: A Late Antique, Byzantine, and Turkish City* (Cambridge, Mass., 1979), 46–99.

5 This is the only section of the long, continuous artery whose name is based on ancient authority. In some of the early and popular publications, the excavators referred to it as "Curetes Street" (*Kuretenstrasse*); in recent, more scholarly work, "Embolos" is commonly used. *Embolos* is a widely used designation for a colonnaded street in late antiquity; the Embolos of Ephesus is mentioned in three inscriptions, the earliest of these Domitianic. For a discussion of the term and its application in Ephesus, see Foss, *Ephesus*, 65–66, n. 39, and idem, *Byzantine and Turkish Sardis* (Cambridge, Mass., 1976), 44f., 115.

6 A. Bammer, "Zur Topographie und städtebaulichen Entwicklung von Ephesos," *Jahreshefte des österreichischen archäologischen Institutes in Wien* 46, 1961–63, 136–57, esp., 143–49; Alzinger, "Ephesos," 1595f.; F. Brein, "Zur ephesischen Topographie," *Jahreshefte des österreichischen archäologischen Institutes in Wien, Beiblatt* 51 (1976–77), 64–75.

7 H. Vetters, "Die Hanghäuser an der Kuretenstrasse," *Jahreshefte des archäologischen Institutes, Beiblatt* 50

(1972–75, 331–79). See also V. M. Strocka, "Die Wandmalereien der Hanghäuser," *Forschungen in Ephesos* 8, no. 1 (Vienna, 1977).

8 Bammer, "Topographie," 145–46.

9 F. K. Yegül, "Roman Architecture at Sardis," *Sardis: Twenty-seven Years of Discovery*, ed. E. Guralnick (Chicago, 1987), 46–61, esp., 48.

10 The Greek city is believed to have been founded in the vicinity of the Sanctuary of Artemis. During the third century B.C.E., the settlement moved south, into the valley between Panayirdağı and Bülbüldağı. The main street of the Hellenistic city followed the course of the ancient processional way at the bottom of the valley (the Embolos). The lower end of this artery terminated in a marketplace and commercial square serving the harbor. The Harbor Avenue, called the Arcadiane, may have existed during this early period partly as a pier extending into the sea. See Bammer, "Topographie," 156–57; Keil, *Führer*, 17–21. For the harbor district in the Roman period, see W. Wilberg, "Die Agora," *Forschungen in Ephesos* 3 (Vienna, 1923). For the Coressian Gate, see Alzinger, *Ephesos: Ein Rundgang*, 48; Keil, *Führer*, 50.

11 For the bath-gymnasium complex of Vedius, see Keil, *Führer*, 46–50; Miltner, *Ephesos*, 58–69; F. K. Yegül, *Baths and Bathing in Classical Antiquity* (New York, 1992), 282–84. For the stadium, see Keil, *Führer*, 50–52; idem, *Jahreshefte des archäologischen Institutes, Beiblatt* 15 (1913), 181; Miltner, *Ephesos*, 32–34.

It is assumed that the visitor is following the course of the thoroughfare from the Coressian Gate to the Magnesian Gate sometime during the second century. However, information on urban features from the early Byzantine period (c. fourth to sixth centuries) is provided on occasion, where such information explicates the development of the street and enhances a sense of the street experience.

12 Alzinger, *Ephesos: Ein Rundgang*, 46; Keil, *Führer*, 51.

13 For the basilica, see Alzinger, *Ephesos: Ein Rundgang*, 44; idem, "Ephesos," 1636f., 1678f.; Keil, *Führer*, 54–57; Miltner, *Ephesos*, 91–95; Foss, *Ephesus*, 51–53; E. Reisch, et al., "Die Marienkirche," *Forschungen in Ephesos* 4, no. 1 (Vienna, 1932).

14 Keil, *Führer*, 72–75; Miltner, *Ephesos*, 30–32; Alzinger, *Ephesos: Ein Rundgang*, 35–36; R. Heberdey, et al., "Das Theater," *Forschungen in Ephesos* 2 (Vienna, 1912).

15 Keil, *Führer*, 57–61; Alzinger, *Ephesos: Ein Rundgang*, 43–44; Foss, *Ephesus*, 56–60; W. Wilberg and R. Heberdey, "Die Viersäulenbau auf dem Arkadian-estrasse," *Forschungen in Ephesos* 1 (Vienna, 1906), 55f., 133–42.

16 For the Harbor Bath-Gymnasium, see Keil, *Führer*, 61–65; Miltner, *Ephesos*, 43–50; Yegül, *Baths and Bathing*, 272–73. For the Porticus of Verulanus, see Keil, *Führer*, 66–68; Alzinger, *Ephesos: Ein Rundgang*, 44. For the Theater Bath-Gymnasium, see Keil, *Führer*, 69–70; Miltner, *Ephesos*, 70; Yegül, *Baths and Bathing*, 279–82, 307.

17 Keil, *Führer*, 79–80; Miltner, *Ephesos*, 34–37; Alzinger, *Ephesos: Ein Rundgang*, 32. The Marble Avenue (also referred to as the "Doric Portico" in early publications) was rebuilt by Eutropius, a fifth-century proconsul of Ephesus. Foss, *Ephesus*, 61–62; *Jahreshefte des archäologischen Institutes, Beiblatt* 10 (1907), 71–73.

18 W. Jobst, "Das 'öffentliche Freudenhaus' in Ephesos," *Jahreshefte des archäologischen Institutes, Beiblatt* 51 (1976–77), 64–75.

19 Keil, *Führer*, 91–92; Miltner, *Ephesos*, 53–54; Alzinger, *Ephesos: Ein Rundgang*, 29; H. Thür, "Das Hadriansstor in Ephesos," *Forschungen in Ephesos* 11, no. 1 (Vienna, 1989).

20 J. Travlos, *Pictorial Dictionary of Ancient Athens* (London, 1971), 253–57. Poised at the western edge of the Severan Plaza, where a winding route joins the public space, the Caracallan arch at Djemila (Cuicul, Algeria) is another tall signpost between the urban center and a hilly, suburban neighborhood.

21 W. Alzinger, *Augusteische Architektur in Ephesus*, 2 vols. Österreichischen Archäologischen Institutes in Wien, *Sonderschriften* 16 (Vienna, 1974), 9–16; idem, *Ephesos: Ein Rundgang*, 33–34; Miltner, *Ephesos*, 23–24.

22 Alzinger, "Ephesos," 1630–33; Keil, *Führer*, 87–90; Miltner, *Ephesos*, 55–58; F. Eichler, "Die Bibliothek," *Forschungen in Ephesos* 5, no. 1 (Vienna, 1944).

23 For the first tomb, see Keil, *Führer*, 92; Miltner, *Ephesos*, 29–30; Alzinger, *Ephesos: Ein Rundgang*, 28–29. For the second tomb, see Keil, *Führer*, 92–94; Alzinger, *Augusteische Architektur*, 40–43; H. Thür, "Arsinoe IV, Grabinhaberin des Oktogons von Ephesos?" *Jahreshefte des archäologischen Institutes* 60 (1990), 43–56.

24 Miltner, *Ephesos*, 52–54; Alzinger, "Ephesos," 1650–52; idem, *Jahreshefte des archäologischen Institutes, Beiblatt* 44 (1959), 267–73; B. Brenk, "Die Datierung der Relief am Hadrianstempel in Ephesos und das Problem der tetrarchischen Skulptur des Ostens," *Istanbuler Mitteilungen* 18 (1968): 238–58; R. fleischer, "Der Fries des Hadrianstempels in Ephesos," *Festschrift Eichler* (Vienna, 1967), 23–71.

25 Miltner, *Ephesos*, 50–52; Alzinger, *Ephesos: Ein Rundgang*, 25; *Jahreshefte des archäologischen Institutes, Beiblatt* 44 (1959), 339f. For Asiatic façades, see G. M. A. Hanfmann, *From Croesus to Constantine* (Ann Arbor, 1975), 52–53.

26 Keil, *Führer*, 94–97; Miltner, *Ephesos*, 15–17; Alzinger, *Augusteische Architektur*, 37–40; G. Niemann and R. Heberdey, "Der Rundbau auf dem Panajirdagh," *Forschungen in Ephesos*, vol. 1 (Vienna, 1909).

27 Alzinger, *Augusteische Architektur*, 16–20; Miltner, *Jahreshefte des archäologischen Institutes* 44 (1959), 355f.; A. Bammer, "Ein Rundfries mit Bukranien und Girlanden," *Jahreshefte des archäologischen Institutes* 49 (1968–71), 23–40, esp. 33–36; W. Alzinger and A. Bammer, "Das Monument des C. Memmius," *Forschungen in Ephesos* 7 (Vienna, 1970); U. Outschar, "Zum Monument des C. Memmius," *Jahreshefte des archäologischen Institutes* 60 (1990), 57–85.

28 Foss, *Ephesus*, 78; *Jahreshefte des archäologischen Institutes, Beiblatt* 45 (1960), 25f.

29 That the road was narrowed by the building of steps across it indicates that the Embolos was closed to vehicular traffic during late antiquity. A. Bammer, "Römische und byzantinische Architektur,"

Jahreshefte des archäologischen Institutes, Beiblatt 50 (1972–75), 383–94; idem, "Ein spätantiker Torbau aus Ephesos," *Jahreshefte des archäologischen Institutes, Beiblatt* 51 (1976–77), 92–126.

30 Alzinger, *Augusteische Architektur*, 51–55; idem, "Grabungen in Ephesos von 1960–1970: Das Regierungsviertel," *Jahreshefte des archäologischen Institutes, Beiblatt* 50 (1972–75), 230–58; Foss, *Ephesus*, 80–81; E. Fossel, "Zum sogennanten Odeion in Ephesos," *Festschrift Eichler* (Vienna, 1967), 72–81.

31 Statues of Augustus and Livia, found inside the building, may have been displayed at its east end. Alzinger, *Augusteische Architektur*, 26–37; idem, "Das Regierungsviertel," 258–94; E. A. Fossel, *Das Basilika am Staatsmarkt in Ephesos* (Graz, 1982). For the State Agora, see Foss, *Ephesus*, 82; Alzinger, *Augusteische Architektur*, 49–51; idem, "Das Regierungsviertel," 295–99; E. A. Fossel, "Zum Tempel auf dem Staatsmarkt in Ephesos," *Jahreshefte des archäologischen Institutes* 50 (1972–75), 212–19.

32 Alzinger, *Ephesos: Ein Rundgang*, 17; Lessing and Oberleitner, *Ephesos*, 145, 210; Bammer, "Römische Architektur," 386; idem, "Das Denkmal des C. Sextilius Pollio in Ephesos," *Jahreshefte des archäologischen Institutes* 51 (1976–77), 76–91; B. Andreae, "Rekonstruksionsvorschlag für die Polyphemgruppe aus dem Pollio-Nymphaeum in Ephesos," *Festschrift für F. Brommer*, ed. U. Hockmann and A. Krug (Mainz, 1977), 1–11; R. fleischer, "Späthellenistische Gruppe vom Pollionymphaeum in Ephesos mit dem Polyphemabenteuer des Odysseus," *Jahreshefte des archäologischen Institutes, Beiblatt* 49 (1971), 137–64.

33 Miltner, *Ephesos*, 38–40; Bammer, "Römische Architektur," 383–87; idem, "Elemente flavisch-trajanischer Architekturfassaden aus Ephesos," *Jahreshefte des archäologischen Institutes* 52 (1978–80), 67–90; H. Vetters, "Domitianterrasse und Domitiangasse, *Jahreshefte des archäologischen Institutes, Beiblatt* 50 (1972–75), 311–30.

34 Alzinger, *Augusteische Architektur*, 44–45; Bammer, "Rundfries," 36–40, esp. 39f.

35 A broad gate articulated with Doric columns appears to have provided a station of reference at this corner. A. Bammer has proposed a major street crossing here, as extensions of the Embolos continuing south and west. According to Bammer, the major north–south street, the *cardo* of Ephesus, follows the line of the old terrace wall of the Domitianic temple, while the east–west street, the *decumanus*, is the straight street leading to the Magnesian Gate. However, there is little hard evidence to support this theory. In either direction the rising slopes would make large streets unlikely; smaller secondary roads, or "stairs," would be more realistic expectations. Bammer, "Topographie," 149– 50, fig. 98.

36 Alzinger, *Ephesos: Ein Rundgang*, 15–16; E. Fossel and G. Langmann, "Nymphaeum des C. Laekanius Bassus," *Jahreshefte des archäologischen Institutes, Beiblatt* 50 (1972–75), 300–310.

37 The next prominent visual station along the colonnaded eastern continuation of the "Magnesian Street" was another public fountain located on the right (south) side, some one hundred meters from the corner of the agora. This was an imposing urban presence, a large apsidal building with wings added on in the second century (44). It combined a capacious city cistern—the terminus of an Augustan aqueduct partially built by Caius Sextius Pollio—with a decorative nymphaeum. See Keil, *Führer*, 102–4; W. Wilberg, "Die Agora," *Forschungen in Ephesos* 3 (Vienna, 1923), 256.

38 During the Christian era the round pagan tomb was incorporated into a church and remembered as St. Luke's Tomb. See Keil, *Führer*, 105–6; idem, *Jahre-shefte des archäologischen Institutes, Beiblatt* 23 (1926), 278f.; Foss, *Ephesus*, 83. For the nymphaeum, see Keil, *Führer*, 106–7; idem, *Jahreshefte des archäologischen Institutes, Beiblatt* 23 (1926), 271–74, and 28 (1933), 12f.; Bammer, "Architektur-fassaden," 86–90.

39 Keil, *Führer*, 108–10; idem, *Jahreshefte des archäologischen Institutes, Beiblatt* 27 (1931), 25–51, and 28 (1933), 5–12; Miltner, *Ephesos*, 74–78; Yegül, *Baths and Bathing*, 279–82.

40 J.-P. Sartre, *Nausea*, trans. L. Alexander (New York, 1964), 195–99.

8

ATHENS

Etching Images on the Street
Planning and National Aspirations

ELENI BASTÉA

Figure 1. Plan of Athens, 1877, detail. The old town, clustered around the north side of the Acropolis, retained the irregular street pattern of ancient times. The nineteenth-century plans for the first time imposed a geometric order on many streets. Of the three that are the focus of this discussion, Athinas and Panepistimiou are broad and straight, while Mitropoleos Street is closer in character to the streets of old Athens.

> Belonging is a privilege, and has its price. All this is determined by an arbitrary line. What is the nature of this line?
>
> —Spiro Kostof, *The City Assembled*

Arbitrary and not-so-arbitrary lines are put up not only around a city but within it. Shifting lines claim provinces of political, cultural, and popular influence within a city. With real and imaginary lines, modern Greece constructed a web of historical belonging stretching from Pericles and Alexander the Great to Napoleon and Lord Byron, creating a political niche for itself. We can identify three major fields that describe the country's cultural and intellectual orientation in the nineteenth century, as directed by the government at the time and by the intellectual elite: yearning for acceptance in the family of civilized, modern European nations; yearning for internal political and cultural unity and national definition; and yearning for a strong connection—if not identification—with the classical past. An analysis of three streets in Athens, Panepistimiou (University), Mitropoleos (Cathedral), and Athinas (Athena) Streets, reveals how planning and civic architecture in modern Athens addressed these seemingly incompatible national aspirations and how the public responded to these efforts (fig. 1).

Athens had been perpetually under construction since 1833, the date of the establishment of an independent Greek nation.[1] By the turn of the twentieth century it was transformed from a provincial Ottoman village of four thousand into a bustling capital of 128 thousand.[2] In 1866, the general in charge of public works, Emmanuel Manitaky, proudly recorded the country's reconstruction: "Greece," he wrote, "when it came out of the War of Independence was literally a pile of ruins." After the liberation and within the first thirty years, "23 old cities were rebuilt and 10 new ones founded." The general reminded the reader of Chateaubriand's description of Turkish Athens in the 1800s: "A skeleton of a city with winding, narrow streets." Compare this, he continued, with modern Athens, "with [its] large and well-aligned streets, with beautiful houses built according to Italian taste, the oldest of which date only to 1834, and among which one notices the numerous public structures." All one had to do was compare "the sedentary and gloomy population of the former [city] with the tenfold population of the latter, which, in its manner of dressing, living, and thinking is so well identified with the great family of the civilized nations of Europe."[3] It was the new buildings, the well-aligned streets, and the "manner of dressing, living, and thinking" that championed national progress. Indeed, the streets became not only the locus but also the testing ground of the city's culture. Internal cohesion and the creation of a national identity were dependent on the cultural and social production originating within the new state.

Comparing maps and images of prerevolutionary Athens with ones from the end of the nineteenth century, we can clearly see the dramatic physical changes brought about in a relatively short period. The new city plan, based on an 1833 design by the German-trained architects Stamatios Kleanthes and Eduard Schaubert, and later altered by Leo von Klenze and subsequent planning committees, embodied the image, if not the soul, of the new state (figs. 2, 3). So did the new official civic architecture that was carried out between 1834 and the turn of the century in the palace, the university, the cathedral, the Academy of Arts and Sciences, the archaeological museum, the polytechnic school, and the national library, as well as the many private residences of wealthy newcomers. From the very beginning, the planning of Athens focused far beyond the borders and needs of the small state to the expanses of the prominent Greek residents in Europe, Russia, and the Ottoman Empire. "The capital of Greece, Athens," proclaimed an 1861 report, "is the focal point and center of light and culture for two . . . concentric nations, the nation of liberated Greece, and the larger nation of greater Hellenism, which is still under foreign rule."[4] While the first one was already inscribed, the second was almost infinite in its borders.

The guidelines for the rebuilding of the new capital were set by a royal decree in 1836. A year later, a second decree further defined and elaborated critical issues of building methods and

ΣΧΕΔΙΟΝ ΤΗΣ ΝΕΑΣ ΠΟΛΕΩΣ ΤΩΝ ΑΘΗΝΩΝ

ΕΠΙΚΥΡΩΜΕΝΟΝ ΑΠΟ ΤΗΝ ΕΛΛΗΝΙΚΗΝ ΚΥΒΕΡΝΗΣΙΝ

ΤΩΙ 1833 ΙΟΥΛΙΟΥ Ϟ

compensation.[5] Both decrees on the planning of Athens were specific and prescriptive. It was established that all new buildings were to respect both alignment with the street and a fixed building height. Properties on the three primary streets that cut through the fabric of the old city—Ermou, Athinas, and Eolou Streets—and on all the streets of the new, northern extension of the city were to meet the street at right angles. To that effect, owners were obligated to alter the borders of their lots, cooperating with each other, so that each would receive a street façade proportionate to the size of his property. Neighbors were also required to compensate the owner whose property suffered after the realignment. In cases of disagreement, the city architect had the final word. Buildings erected contrary to these regulations were to be torn down at the expense of the owner.

Thus, the burden of compensating those affected by the opening of new streets was placed on the owners of surrounding lots, in proportion to their gain. The city undertook to pay part of the cost of opening Athinas Street, which was especially wide, and of public squares. The evaluation of the lots in question was deter-

Figure 2. Stamatios Kleanthes and Eduard Schaubert, plan for New Athens, 1833. The plan was approved by the Greek government, but altered significantly in the process of its implementation (see fig. 1).

Figure 3. General view of the city, with the royal palace at center right and Syntagma Square in front of it. Mount Lycabettos is at left.

mined by two experts, one representing the owner, and one the city council; and in case of continued disagreement, the value was established by the court.[6] It is important to note that the focus of planning legislation was on new building. While the language of the law made it clear that sanctions would be imposed on the owners and architects of new buildings that did not conform with the plans, most decrees did not require the alteration of existing buildings. Once the older buildings reached a point beyond repair, they were to be replaced by new structures that followed the street alignment.

An important change in the city's fabric, effected by the 1836 decree, was the establishment of minimum-size building lots. Along the three major streets of the old town and all the streets of the new town lots were to have a minimum area of two hundred square *pique*s, or eighty square meters. They were also required to have a minimum façade length of eight *pique*s (five meters) and a depth of at least ten *pique*s (six meters). The rest of the lots in the old city had to be at least one hundred square *pique*s (forty square meters). Owners of smaller lots could either buy adjacent land, or sell to the neighboring owners.[7] This established a social and economic homogeneity of the wealthy along the main streets. The smaller landowners who did not have the means to purchase adjacent land were displaced.

By the turn of the century, Athens boasted

several paved, straight, wide streets, some with trees planted along the sidewalks, lit at night, and even sprinkled with water on very hot summer days. The new streets that were opened through the old city terminated at the palace (Ermou Street) and the Acropolis (Athinas Street), connected old and new landmarks, the palace and the cathedral (Mitropoleos Street), or led to the surrounding countryside, where Athenians took day trips on Sundays.[8] The nation's political and cultural aspirations—to become part of Europe, to achieve cultural unity and national definition, and to connect modern Greece with classical antiquity—were physically manifested on three major avenues: Panepistimiou, Mitropoleos, and Athinas Streets.

Through both their design and their symbolic, programmatic impact, the buildings of the so-called Athenian Trilogy on Panepistimiou Street—the university, the academy, and the national library—contributed to the first national aspiration: the architectural transformation of Athens into a European-style capital, intended to hasten the political incorporation of Greece into modern Europe. Becoming part of Europe was, in fact, a cultural as much as a political feat. The creation of these institutions was intended to address not so much the country's practical needs at the time, but rather its projected image as the cultural beacon of the Balkans and the Middle East.

The university was founded in 1837, four years after the establishment of the new nation. The building, an elegant and restrained Neoclassical structure, was completed in 1864. Designed by the Danish architect Christian Hansen, who had also worked on the restoration of the Temple of Nike on the Acropolis, it betrays an admiration for and familiarity with ancient Greek architecture (fig. 4). The design also shows knowledge of the Neoclassical architecture of northern Europe, for example, that of Copenhagen, Berlin, and Munich. Although the erection of the university did not address the most pressing educational problems of the time, namely the lack of elementary schools, it helped to fix Athens as the cultural focus of Greece, increasing its stature in the Balkans. "The establishment of the university was one of the most important events in the history of modern Athens," wrote a Greek historian at the turn of the century.[9] Thus were revived "the ancient times, when those who desired higher education came from all over to the country of Plato . . . and Aristotle. . . . Serbians, Bulgarians, Romanians began to come to Athens, and to take the literature, science, and culture of Athens back to their own countries." According to the modern historian C. Th. Dimaras, this was indeed the lofty, albeit political, mission of the university in particular and of Greece in general during the nineteenth century: to act as a conduit, receiving the light of Western civilization and transmitting it to the East.[10] Embodying these ideals, Hansen's design provided a most fitting envelope for the university's political task.

The erection of the academy and the national library, begun in 1859 and 1887 respectively, and designed by Hansen's brother Theophil, further established Panepistimiou Street as the official cultural axis of the new capital.[11] Questions about the need for such extravagant structures and institutions notwithstanding, their impact on the city was unmistakable. Discussing the appropriateness of the new academy building, for example, the city council argued that "the academy, to be erected on University Square, will become an agent of the greatest ethical and material value for the municipality and the nation, contributing furthermore to the beautification of the city. Believing that it is for the profit of the municipality to support any work that

Figure 4. The university building, facing Panepistimiou Street, was designed by Christian Hansen.

contributes to the ethical and material development of the nation [the city council] has decided unanimously to donate the lot" (fig. 5).[12] Similar arguments supported the erection of the national library, which completed the Athenian Trilogy. Terminating at Syntagma (Constitution) Square, the elegant, tree-planted plaza fronting the palace, Panepistimiou Street symbolically and literally etched the line connecting official cultural production with the monarch's residence (fig. 6).[13]

The Greek state's second political aspiration—to create political and cultural nationhood—found expression in the erection of the new cathedral on Mitropoleos Street, next to the modest twelfth-century church of Panagia Gorgoepekoos, which had served the Athenian populace during Ottoman rule. While the royal palace, designed by Friedrich von Gaertner in 1836, signified the newly established political independence of Greece, the building of the cathedral church in Athens symbolized a cultural and religious continuity with a Greek past (though not with classical antiquity) that was necessary for the majority of the population. "Although the city of Athens has theaters, palaces, etc., it does not even have one church appropriate for celebrations for the whole city," wrote the liberal newspaper *Athena* in 1840.[14] The widespread demand for a new cathedral had both historical and political roots: it reflected the country's continued attachment to Orthodoxy, the only tradition that had united the population during the long years of Ottoman domination, and the Greeks' most articulate and continuous cultural heritage. Although some Greeks disagreed with the conservative and provincial views of the clergy, most wholeheartedly supported their church in its fight against the imposed Bavarian government. finally, for the small group of Westernized Greeks who supported a secular state, the building of the cathedral, like the building of the university, came to symbolize the cultural independence of Athens in the Greek-speaking world, gradually supplanting the position that Constantinople had once held.

Originally, the commission for the design of the cathedral was given to Theophil Hansen, but his proposal, a mixture of Byzantine and Gothic details dominated by a large dome, was not carried out. After Hansen left Athens in 1846, an architectural competition was held for the revision of his design using a "Greek Byzantine" order. This was one of the first open architectural competitions held in Greece. The architectural definition of this order was not clear; its inspiration was manifestly intended to come from the Byzantine and not from the classical Greek period. The espousal of a Greek Byzantine style was indicative of a general intellectual anxiety to establish the unbroken continuity of the Greek nation from antiquity through Byzantium and the Ottoman years to the post-liberation period. Thus, while the architectural pluralism introduced by the cathedral's final design challenged the earlier formal harmony of the palace and the university, the resulting image of the city reflected more accurately the antithetical forces that stirred Greek society at the time: ancient Athens on the one hand, Byzantium on the other (see fig. 6).[15] The short stretch of Mitropoleos Street that connected the palace with the new cathedral became a very important thoroughfare during the nineteenth century. The king and his entourage would progress down it to arrive ceremoniously at the cathedral not only on religious holidays, but also on all major national holidays, which tradi-

tionally began with a special mass. Thus Mitropoleos Street etched another line on the cultural map of Athens, this one firmly connecting church and state.

The last and perhaps most important national aspiration, to claim the classical past for modern Greece, manifested itself in a multitude of ways: in the restoration of the Acropolis and the removal of all post-Roman structures from it; in the ambitious excavation plans, which continue to the present day; in the design of most civic and governmental buildings in the Neoclassical style; and even in the adoption of the German educational model, which favored a classical curriculum. This explicit orientation toward antiquity was evident not only in the architecture, but also in the planning of the modern city. When the provisional Greek government commissioned Kleanthes and Schaubert to design the capital, it asked for "a new plan *equal with the ancient fame and glory of the city and worthy of the century in which we live*" (emphasis in the original).[16] In their 1833 plan for New Athens, Athinas Street, which cut through the fabric of the old town, established a north–south axis in the city, stretching

Figure 5. Next to the university, the academy building is shown here under construction, c. 1880. Designed by Theophil Hansen, it was financed by the Sina family.

between the royal palace and the foothills of the Acropolis (see fig. 2).

Although the palace was finally built at the eastern point of the imposed triangle, Athinas Street continued to be a fashionable and heavily trafficked thoroughfare, now anchored by Omonia (Concord) Square at the northern node. By the turn of the century, Omonia Square, smartly landscaped and surrounded by elegant hotels, had become the first stop for many upon their arrival in Athens, since it was located near the new train station. From Omonia Square, Athinas Street, with its generous dimensions and imposing buildings, its thriving shops and businesses, had indeed a markedly modern, European look (fig. 7). As it neared the Acropolis, however, it expired unceremoniously amid a web of narrow, preliberation alleys. Since the original plan had designated a wide zone around the Acropolis to be set aside for future archaeological excavations, no new streets could be cut there, nor permits issued for new buildings. As a result, the Plaka, the area around the Acropolis, has to a large extent preserved its early-nineteenth-century character. Islanders who had come to Athens for work had erected small dwelling for themselves and their families around the ancient hill. Though originally illegal, these houses, with their distinct Aegean vernacular architecture, were allowed to remain, challenging, as they do to this day, the nineteenth-century vision of an orderly, Neoclassical capital. Taken in its totality, then, Athinas Street, a modern avenue under the shadow of the Acropolis, etched and calibrated the distance between the classical and the modern city.

Just as the development of major avenues reflected contemporary national aspirations, so did the architecture of the new civic and government buildings. Adhering for the most part to Neoclassical prototypes, it set a stamp of permanence not only on the newly established political and cultural institutions but also on the city itself. The new buildings along the major streets were orderly and imposing, their tall, symmetrical façades and regular floor plans defining the newly opened boulevards. Neoclassical architecture, introduced first by the Bavarians, found fertile ground in the period of reconstruction. Since European culture saw itself as based on the ancient Greek heritage, and since modern Greece, eager to forget the Ottoman legacy, oriented its policy toward Europe, the adoption of the Neoclassical style was doubly justified: it strengthened ties to the classical tradition and demonstrated the country's Western orientation. Most of the major post-liberation buildings, of which a representative few have been discussed here, bespeak the cultural image that Athens sought to establish, for reasons both economic and political. Since money for most major buildings came from private donors, cultural institutions were arguably more glamorous benefactions than prisons, markets, or elementary schools. Furthermore, focus on the cultural achievements of modern Athens strengthened the city's ties with ancient Athens and connected, in still another way, the present with the past.

Even when the general outlines of Neoclassicism were taken for granted, the details of its interpretation were often contested among architects. A case in point is the design of the Arsakeion School for Girls on Panepistimiou Street, across from the national library. The Society for Education, which had originally commissioned Kleanthes to design the school, later invited Lysandros Kaftanzoglou, an Italian-trained architect, to submit his own proposal. Kaftanzoglou's design was finally chosen, setting off a stream of bitter attacks by Kleanthes. Both proposals were executed in the classical idiom, their symmetrical, monumental façades fronting Panepistimiou Street. Yet Kleanthes,

himself trained under Karl Friedrich Schinkel in the Berlin Bauakademie, decided to attack his rival's Italian affiliations, writing in a pamphlet he circulated: "None of the four façades [designed by Kaftanzoglou] appropriately characterizes the idea of the Parthenon; it would be highly desirable if this national Parthenon were built more according to the Greek style, because it does no honor to us Greeks to erect Parthenons in Athens imitating Tuscan architecture, while all the rest of the countries in Europe are zealously imitating Greek architecture in all of their buildings."[17] What the heated duel demonstrates, beyond the obvious professional rivalries, is the importance of defining

an appropriate Greek architecture at a time when Greece, a young nation with an unstable government, was trying to define itself as a political entity. By the turn of the twentieth century, the architecture and urban design of the new capital were, in fact, addressing the national yearning to belong to the present, through a modern plan worthy of the country's Western orientation; to the classical past, through the focus on cultural institutions and the adherence to Neoclassicism; and to itself, through the construction of a modern Greek national image.

Looking at images of Athens at the turn of the century, it becomes clear that buildings are much easier to tame than the street. While the

Figure 6. View of the southwest corner of Syntagma Square, 1865. The new cathedral is featured prominently in the background, flanked by the new houses on Mitropoleos Street.

ture—persistent, untamed, vulgar, provincial. The opposition to the forces of change is particularly interesting, since that opposition was expressed physically in the fabric of the city and verbally in the contemporary press. Although on one level the mercurial urban polity supported the metamorphosis of Athens, and appeared to fall in love with the beauty of its new buildings, on another level it hated and resisted such change, and indeed is still resisting.

Like the streets of Athens, with their skin-deep European façades and indigenous backs, Greek society was characterized by a duality, embracing modernity on the one hand, while holding to earlier ways of life on the other. Becoming part of Europe was clearly the aim of Greek reconstruction. There was no other choice. At a time when national consciousness was still considered synonymous with being anti-Turkish, the new buildings and roads that marked a tangible departure from the Ottoman past were considered to forge a de facto national Greek identity.[19] Repeatedly, the inhabitants expressed their pride in the impressive new structures that were going up, in the restoration of antiquities, and in the return of classical architecture to the country of its birth. Athenian architecture would soon surpass that of Turkey and the Ionian islands together, argued a magazine article in 1853, because "our buildings were designed by Europeans or European-trained Greek architects, not by practical builders, who have no concept of line or symmetry."[20] Since the country lacked a proper architecture school until the last third of the nineteenth century, all its major buildings until then were designed by foreign-trained architects and executed under the direction of Bavarian contractors and master builders. Local builders, who often apprenticed under the foreigners, gradually became familiar with the particular brand of Neoclassicism that flourished in Athens,

main boulevards, notably Panepistimiou and Athinas Streets, had indeed acquired the sought-after European look, the back roads and even the backs of major buildings remained decidedly unglamorous. Even the Neoclassicism of the major civic structures—the palace, the Athenian Trilogy, and the Arsakeion School, among others—was not uniformly applied. Private residences, especially when located far from the center, displayed a rather eclectic stylistic blend. Uneven streets were a perpetual problem, since the planning of Athens was carried out in a piecemeal fashion that addressed each new street opening individually, and lacked an overall leveling program. While the new buildings made a concerted effort at the front to meet the street at a ninety-degree angle, their backs often remembered the street patterns and property lines of ancient, Byzantine, and Ottoman Athens (fig. 8).[18]

In order better to understand the urban and social changes in nineteenth-century Athens, it is necessary to see clearly the relationship between civic architecture—state-sanctioned, internationalist, highbrow—and popular cul-

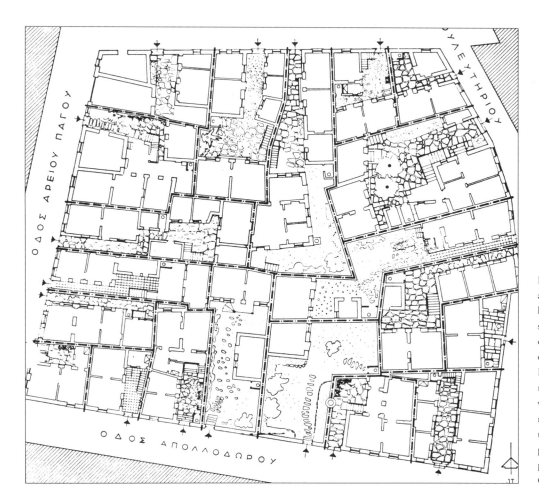

Figure 8. Plans of houses of a complete building block, located on the northern side of Areios Pagos, and demolished for the excavations of the Roman Forum. While a relative regularity of alignment with the street was maintained on the façades, the interior of the block preserved an intricate property-line pattern of the Ottoman years.

imitating it and adapting it to the needs of the lesser residential structures.[21]

Despite a certain sense of civic pride, criticism of the new government, its policies, and its building programs was widespread, often outstripping any show of support. This had in part to do with the various affiliations of the critics themselves. Each of the numerous newspapers that circulated in Athens during the last century had a definite political agenda that colored its editorials and articles. This alone, however, does not explain the strength of opposition to the cultural aspirations of the young state. It

was not that the Greeks resisted the ideas themselves; it was their implementation that provoked heated editorials.

To the average citizen of Greece, except for the Orthodox religion, nothing was sacred, least of all the ancient theaters and temples so revered by European visitors. "Of what use are they to me, the glorious ruins of immortal antiquity, among which I live as a stranger?" complained the resident of a small town, in an 1833 issue of the newspaper *Athena*. "Of what use is it to me that I am neighbor of Agamemnon . . . and that my village is only an hour from the capital, when I have no idea of what is happening in the world? . . . It is true that so-called travelers often come through my village . . . but what can I learn from these strange gentlemen, who, when you ask them about people, question you about piles of stones; and when you talk to them about the living, ask for information on the dead?" And we read in an 1834 issue: "[The plans] for future excavations, which Greece, because of its poverty, will not be able to undertake for a century, prevent many from building on the ruins, where the stone is available, and which the poorest people do not have the means to transport; it is the general opinion that the government could allow the building of houses within the excavation line, at least for twenty years, upon the agreement that if, after that time, the government wants to excavate, the owner will tear his house down at his own expense."[22] Of course, no such proposal could be sanctioned by the government.

The plan of the city, hailed at first for its modern, European character, was soon enough ridiculed by the press, which, by attacking the architects, was indirectly attacking the government: "Messrs. Kleanthes and Schaubert have been ordered to make a plan that resembles rather the plan of a garden, than of a city. . . . In designing the streets, they did not leave out any geometric shape; . . . they drew triangles, squares, hexagons, polygons, trapezoids, rhomboids, etc., so that the professor of mathematics, Mr. Negres, when he teaches geometry, does not need [to draw] geometric shapes, having the plan of our city [to refer to]." The extravagance of the academy building was another frequent target of the press. We read in an 1858 newspaper, as the building

was under construction: "We have no ships, no army, no roads, but soon we will have an Academy. Turkey, beware!"[23]

The people of Athens often challenged and resisted the official pro-European position of the government, not only through words but also through actions. Family photographs from the mid and late nineteenth century more often than not include some members in European clothes, while others proudly wear their elaborate, traditional regional garb. Old customs die hard. Despite the influx of Greeks from other European states, and their economic and political prominence, the local population remained greatly attached to its provincial, preliberation ways of life. A contemporary observed in 1875 that Greece was no longer Greece, but neither was it yet Europe.[24]

The opening of new boulevards, notably Panepistimiou and Athinas Streets; the widening of existing ones such as Mitropoleos Street; and the design of major new structures such as the Athenian Trilogy and the cathedral etched an image of Athens that reflected the nation's aspirations: modernity, cultural unity, and connection with antiquity. This image, however, came to coexist with, rather than replace, that of the earlier city, with its ancient, Byzantine, and Ottoman roots. Although the nineteenth-century literature implied that it was only a matter of time before New Athens completely superseded its predecessor, it is clear that the legacy of the earlier city, its culture, its way of living, its spatial claims, and its own architectural order endured; they are still evident today. Etched on the buildings and the streets of Athens are the lines of belonging to both the East and the West, with the privilege and the price that brings. ■

Notes

I would like to acknowledge the generous support of an American Council of Learned Societies Grant-in-Aid, which allowed me to carry out part of the research on which this essay is based. I remain especially indebted to Vilma Hastaoglou-Martinidis, at the Aristotle University of Thessaloniki, and Dimitri Philippides, at the National Technical University of Athens, for their suggestions, criticisms, and inspiration, and for their unfailing support, technical and otherwise.

In transliterating the Greek words and passages in the text, I have followed the Library of Congress system. Street names, however, follow the phonetic transliteration adopted by most cartographers today. All translations are mine. In the nineteenth century there was a twelve-day difference between the Julian calendar, which the Greeks used, and the Gregorian calendar, used in western Europe. I have maintained the dating of the original sources in the Julian calendar, unless otherwise noted. Government publications usually included both dates, with a solidus, as below. Government legislation was published in the *Ephemeris tes kyverneseos* (Government Gazette), abbreviated *FEK*.

1 The conquest of Constantinople by the Ottoman Turks in 1453 had marked the fall of the Byzantine Empire. By the end of the fifteenth century, most Greek-speaking territories were subordinated to Ottoman rule. Following the Greek War of Independence (1821–27), diplomatic negotiations among the major European powers, France, England, and Russia, finally established an independent Greek nation in 1833, under the leadership of seventeen-year-old Prince Otto of Bavaria. Otto brought to Greece his own court and an army of thirty-five hundred Bavarian troops. Internal instability, however, coupled with a general dissatisfaction with Otto's autocratic ruling manner and frequent disregard for local religious traditions, led to his abdication in 1862. The Danish-born King George I ascended the throne in 1863, initiating a period of true constitutional government that carried the country into the twentieth century.

2 The population figures are approximate. For Ottoman Athens, see D. Karydis, "Poleodomika ton Athenon tes Tourkokratias," Ph.D. diss., National Technical University, Athens, 1981. For a compre- hensive treatment of the city, see J. Travlos, *Poleodomike exelixis ton Athenon* (Athens, 1960), where the figure of four thousand is cited on p. 235. For the twentieth-century city, see, among others, G. Burgel, *Croissance urbaine et développement capitaliste, le "miracle athénien"* (Paris, 1981), and L. Leontidou, *Poleis tes siopes* (Athens, 1989), where the figure of 128 thousand is cited on p. 304.

3 E. Manitaky, *Aperçu sur les progrès matériels de la Grèce*, 2d ed. (Athens, 1869), 15–17.

4 *Athena*, November 11, 1861. Cited in E. Skopetea, *To "protypo vasileio" kai he Megale Idea* (Athens, 1988), 291.

5 See "On additions to the decree on the plan of Athens," November 12/24, 1836, *FEK*, no. 91, 1836. The 1836 decree of April 9/21, "On the Execution of the Plan of Athens," *FEK*, no. 20, 1836, also appeared in the newspaper *Athena*, May 27, 1836.

6 The articles on compensation can be found in the decree of November 12/24, 1836. See also the September 28/October 10, 1837 decree, "On a change of the November 12/24, 1836 Royal Decree about pieces of lots of the city of Athens," *FEK*, no. 35, 1837: "Because Article 25 of our 12 (24) November 1836 decree, which was misunderstood by the municipal authority of Athens, was applied wrongly . . . we have decided [that] the lot pieces that, according to Article 13 of the same decree, were transferred immediately and without the intervention of the city of Athens to the ownership of the adjacent landowners will be appraised by two arbitrators appointed by both parties."

7 See Decree of November 12/24, 1836, *FEK*, no. 91, 1836. A *pique*, or *peche*, the length of the forearm, is about twenty-five inches, or 63.5 centimeters.

8 See M. Skaltsa, *Koinonike zoe kai demosioi choroi koinonikon synathroiseon sten Athena tou 19ou aiona* (Thessaloniki, 1983), for a detailed discussion of the use of the streets.

9 A. Argyros, *Historia ton Athenon* (Athens, 1896?), 193. The cornerstone of the first elementary school in Athens was placed in the Plaka, the oldest extant quarter of the city, in 1836.

10 C. Th. Dimaras, *Hellenikos romantismos* (Athens, 1982), 349–50.

11 Theophil Hansen is perhaps best known for his work in Vienna, notably the design of the Austrian parliament building, 1874–83, which bears a marked resemblance to his earlier academy building in Athens. See C. E. Schorske, *Fin-de-siècle Vienna: Politics and Culture* (New York, 1979), for an exemplary analysis of the architecture and political symbolism of the parliament and the other new civic buildings erected on the Ringstrasse in Vienna.

12 Archive of the City of Athens, Proceedings of the City Council, no. 67/29, July, 1859, cited in G. Laios, *Simos Sinas* (Athens, 1972), 143–44.

13 The royal palace now houses the Greek parliament. The original linear connection between official culture and the monarchy has thus shifted to a broader-based and multiparty network that still links politics and culture.

14 *Athena*, April 6, 1840.

15 The architects of the cathedral's final design were Dimitri Zezos, F.-L.-F. Boulanger, and Panagiotes Kalkos.

16 General State Archives, Ministry of the Interior, Otto's Archive, f220, document dated July 10, 1836, and signed "S. Kleanthes."

17 S. Kleanthes, *Ekthesis . . .* (Athens, 1845), 16.

18 This is a common phenomenon in many nineteenth-century cities that underwent similar transformations. In London terrace houses, for example, it was referred to as a "Queen Anne front and Mary Anne back"; it should probably here be called a "Pericles front and Kararghiozes back."

19 See V. Kremmydas, *Historia tes hellenikes koinonias (1700–1821)* (Athens, 1976), 205.

20 *Pandora* 3, no. 67 (January 1, 1853).

21 One should not assume that all building before the liberation was carried out by local Greeks. Wealthy individuals often hired traveling builders, or even European-trained architects and builders to construct their mansions. For a discussion of "traditional" Greek architecture before 1830 and a review of the current literature, see E. Bastéa, "The Sweet Deceit of Tradition: National Ideology and Greek Architecture," in *Twentieth-Century Art and Culture* 1, no. 2 (Spring 1990).

22 Letter signed "The Old Man of Dalamanara," *Athena*, May 13, 1833; *Athena*, November 21, 1834.

23 Ibid., March 11, 1839; *Aion*, March 27, 1858, cited in Skopetea, *To "protypo vasileio,"* 76.

24 *Asmodaios*, January 26, 1875, cited in Skopetea, *To "protypo vasileio,"* 162. On pro-Europeanism, see Skopetea, 45, 55. The best analysis, to my mind, of the Westernizing forces in modern Greece has been provided by C. Th. Dimaras. See, for example, *Hellenikos romantismos*, passim.

9

NOTO

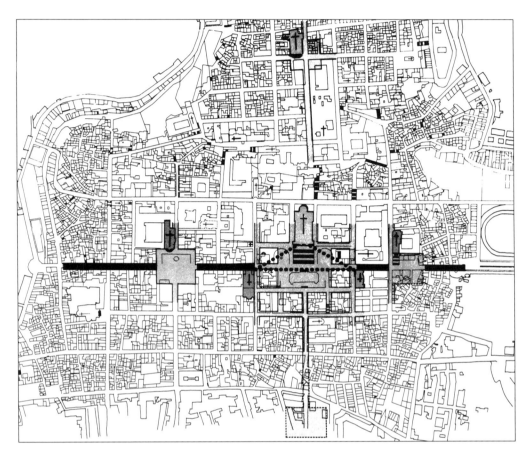

Noto's Corso Remembered, 1693–1993

S T E P H E N   T O B R I N E R

Figure 1. Composite map of Noto, uniting the plan of the city as it exists with that proposed by Fra Angelo Italia. The smaller, northern grid on the Pianazzo (at top) contrasts with the grid on the slope of the Meti. The Corso, marked in black, runs east–west, transversally across the grid, joining three piazzas, each with a church at its northern perimeter. Fra Italia's incomplete plan was to unite the upper grid with the lower through building placement. The southernmost piazza (the dotted square at lower center) was never built.

They call it Noto *puntellata* (shored up), a city whose lovely Baroque façades of golden limestone are braced by "temporary" diagonal timbers, cables, and steel trusses. With many of its major buildings threatening collapse, Noto's Corso Vittorio Emanuele, the former Cassaro, is a statement of the city's continuing metamorphosis (fig. 1). Noto Antica, some seven kilometers northwest, was destroyed in the earthquake of 1693 and the city was moved to its present site. The main street of the new Noto was intended to embody the wisdom, world view, and elegance of eighteenth-century Sicily: a safe, enduring, up-to-date thoroughfare that would symbolize the resurgence of Noto as a cultural and economic center in southeastern Sicily. The year 1993 marked the three-hundredth anniversary of the earthquake and the reconstruction of the town. The current state of the once-proud Corso, however, with its bandaged façades, declining commercial life, and diminished traffic, records changes that could not have been anticipated by the application of urban design (fig. 2).

Noto Antica, like forty other cities in southeastern Sicily, was seriously damaged by earthquakes on January 9 and 11, 1693.[1] These were not the first earthquakes to strike the area, which is prone to seismic disturbances, but the previous series of tremors, accompanying Mt. Etna's eruption in 1669, were a distant memory. The

Figure 2. Noto, looking westward up Corso Vittorio Emanuele, from the Piano di S. Francesco toward the braced façade of SS. Salvatore, 1992.

Spanish viceregal government faced the disaster with surprising efficiency, dispatching several officials to assess the damage and oversee reconstruction, and establishing a governing body for conducting recovery operations.[2] No stated policy or established procedure for the vast reconstruction that ensued has been discovered, but the work done by numerous town councils and individual administrators, following *ad hoc* decisions, was surprisingly similar. If a city was partially damaged, individual structures were rebuilt within it. If a city had been razed but was on a flat site, its street plan was changed from organic and curvilinear to straight and gridded.[3] If badly enough dam-

aged, a city was moved away from a tortuous mountaintop to a flat site, or from an inland to a coastal position, and a grid plan was developed.

Noto's neighbors Syracuse, Catania, and Avola represent the three variants. Of the three, the least damaged was the coastal fortress of Syracuse, which was reconstructed *in situ* on its former plan.[4] The port city of Catania, which was razed by the earthquake so that the remaining ruins were, according to a Spanish report, "as flat as the palm of your hand," was rebuilt in the same location but on a rectilinear plan, with new, straight streets.[5] Avola, a small baronial fortress town on a mountaintop with a curvilinear plan, was moved to a plain close to the coast and given a hexagonal plan with straight streets and large piazzas.[6]

In both Catania and Avola safety considerations played a significant role in the new city location and plan. According to a contemporary report, medieval Avola had been constricted by the crown of the hill and the steep slopes on which it was built.[7] Houses had been set close together, terraced down the slopes, not unlike those in present-day Ragusa Ibla. Thus, when one house fell, as the report continues, it pulled down its neighbors. Avola's new flat location eliminated the dangers of steep slopes; the wide, straight streets and hexagonal plan organized and distributed structures, and the large piazzas provided refuge in time of earthquakes. The citizens of Catania, choosing not to move their city, focused instead on the narrow, twisting medieval streets of the old town as its most hazardous feature. The city council condemned these streets because they were so easily closed by rubble. The wide, straight streets they proposed were designed to enable people to leave their houses even if city streets and piazzas were clogged with debris from another earthquake. The council further designated the large piazzas as places of refuge after a quake, open for camping, so that people could remain near their possessions even if they were unable to reenter their dwellings.

While Catania and Avola represent relatively unified preventive strategies, Noto's story is more complex, a complexity that is preserved in Noto as it appears today.[8] The Netinese, like the Avolese, transferred their city to a new location, but not all the citizens wanted to move. For nine years a dispute raged between those who supported the new town and those who wanted to return to the old. Simultaneously, another dispute erupted between the Spanish planners, who had intended the summit of a hill called the Meti to be the center of

the town, and most of the local population, who settled on the southwest slope of the hill. The top of the hill, because of its flatness, was called the Pianazzo. It could be fortified and had a spectacular view but lacked the water which could be found lower on the slope in wells and at the bottom of the hill where the Asinaro River flowed. Two distinct grid plans developed, the first up on the Pianazzo, the second below it, on the slope. The architect Fra Angelo Italia linked these two grids together in the unified plan we see today (see fig. 1). In it the four major squares in Noto balance one another: one lies on the summit and three on the slope below.

The Corso is the east–west spine (actually running southeast to northwest) that joins three squares on the slope and establishes the center of the city. In the eighteenth century the Netinese called their main street the Cassaro, emulating Palermo's famous Cassaro, a straight street that ran northeast, from the shores of the Mediterranean, southeast to the Viceroy's palace.[9] The name "Cassaro" may derive from an Arabic word meaning "to the fort," but for the Netinese it meant something close to "main street." During the Risorgimento, in the throes of patriotism, the Cassaro in Noto, like that in Palermo and indeed most main streets in Italy, became Corso Vittorio Emanuele, in honor of the king who unified the nation.

Noto was always a small town, and the Corso is a short, straight street of 468 meters, bisecting the populous lower portion of the city. As one looks down the street to the west, it is nearly impossible to distinguish it from the three open spaces it links (fig. 3). From the east, an arch commemorating the entry of Ferdinand II in 1838 marks the beginning of the Corso, which then continues uphill for 72 meters to a small piazza called the Piano di S. Francesco (see fig. 2). Passing through this piazza, it resumes for the length of one short block (90 meters),

bordered to the south by the monastery of Sta. Chiara and to the north by the monastery of SS. Salvatore. It then continues through the Piazza Maggiore (fig. 4) to resume as a street at the former Jesuit church of S. Carlo (fig. 5). The Corso continues for 126 meters, past the Jesuit church and college to the third open space, Piazza S. Domenico, now called Piazza XVI Maggio. At the west end of this piazza it becomes a street again and descends at a gradual grade for 180 meters, until it exits the city.

Noto's architects were conscious of seismic problems, although little in the design of the Corso reflects their concern. True enough, it is a straight street, but not as wide as the streets proposed for Catania, while the gracious two- and three-story Baroque monasteries that tower above it make the Corso dangerous in earthquakes.[10] The buildings themselves are made of unreinforced masonry and are therefore extremely hazardous. Rosario Gagliardi (c. 1698–1762), the most prominent architect in the reconstruction of Noto, explains in a proposal for the construction of a church in the southeastern Sicilian town of Scicli that wood and plaster vaults withstand earthquakes better than stone vaults.[11] This is, in fact, correct, and may have led to the wooden vault proposed for the church of Sta. Chiara, but otherwise little antiseismic technology can be seen along the Corso.[12] Paolo Labisi (c. 1720–98), an architect born in Noto, suggests that piazzas should be used as refuges in earthquakes. The Corso, being a short street sectioned into four even shorter lengths, may indeed facilitate escape to open urban spaces, but otherwise, this main street is probably no safer than its antecedent in Noto Antica.[13]

Because of the Corso's position on the slope of the Meti it had surprisingly poor drainage. Indeed, all the streets on the Meti were designed improperly. Only twenty years after the

major monuments of the city were completed, citizens complained of excessive dust in the summer and mud in the winter. Water cascaded down the slope, destabilizing the Corso. To solve the problem, Paolo Labisi's son, Bernardo (b. 1747), proposed in 1787 to install subterranean drains and to level the street throughout its length. His project was rethought and actually completed only in 1887.[14] The nineteenth-century engineers were far more radical than Labisi, removing all loose earth from the Corso and taking the entire roadbed down to bedrock. To achieve this, they had to clear the roadbed to a level far below the cellars of buildings fronting on the street. Soon, the entrance to the monastery of Sta. Chiara was three meters higher than street level. Fountains attached to the façade of SS. Salvatore were isolated in midair, high above the pedestrians and horses they were supposed to serve. Since the excavations exposed the foundations of buildings to erosion, the Netinese responded by shoring them up with new stone façades covering what had formerly been their basements and sub-basements. In stabilizing the Corso, the Netinese destabilized the buildings along its frontage.

The aristocrats of Noto had designs on the Corso from the beginning. A majority of them built their palaces on the street or on the three piazzas it linked.[15] They vied among themselves for prominent lots and fought protracted legal battles with the church over property rights. In order to stimulate Noto's growth, the Senate or University of Noto was empowered to give sites to those who wanted to build.[16] These recipients were required to erect a structure or forfeit their lot.

Each religious institution jealously guarded its cramped position, often regarding its neighbor, or proposed neighbor, with suspicion and misgivings.[17] On one occasion, when the

(opposite) Figure 3. Aerial view of Noto from the south, 1969. Corso Vittorio Emanuele cuts diagonally from the arch of Ferdinand II, on the right, through Piazza Maggiore, to Piazza XVI Maggio, on the left.

Figure 4. Corso Vittorio Emanuele at Piazza Maggiore, looking west, toward the shrouded façade of S. Carlo. The Palazzo della Città is at left.

Crociferi fathers wanted to build their house on a street that adjoined the monastery of S. Domenico, the Domenican fathers objected that the newcomers were too close.[18] Paolo Labisi, then the city architect, testified that there was plenty of room, quoting the distances between each church and monastery in Noto. To modern eyes, Labisi's defense seems nearly an indictment: the small town of Noto seems crowded with religious institutions.

The earthquake had not disturbed the endowments and property that sustained the churches, monasteries, and convents of Noto. The fortunes of the aristocrats who sponsored

them endured as well. But small businessmen, discouraged by the protracted indecision about the site of the new city, left. Noto rose as an incarnation of Sicily's almost feudal agrarian society: a city of palaces, churches, monasteries, and convents, not of commerce. As a French traveler wrote in the 1780s, the city looked "as if it were only meant to accommodate a population of mostly priests and nuns; their only object seems to have been to build churches and convents, which are so wide and numerous that there appears to be nothing else."[19]

Despite the loss of commercial enterprises, the small core of extremely rich aristocrats who lived in Noto guaranteed its livelihood. Their palaces, with private libraries, museums, and collections of art, added enormous prestige. They banded together to sponsor musical events. Their sons and daughters, brothers and sisters administered the monasteries and convents of the city, took refuge in them, or were educated by them. Aristocrats controlled the committee of streets and water, which oversaw the maintenance of city streets such as the Corso.[20] Their tastes influenced every structure in Noto. When they commissioned the new Palazzo della Città, or city hall, the plan was based on an eighteenth-century French concept of an Italian palace, a *maison à l'italienne*—the same model Frederick II used for Sanssouci in Potsdam. This building of the French Enlightenment stands sentinel between two Sicilian Baroque churches. Next door, the Jesuit church of S. Carlo, with its somber basilica plan and Vignolan capitals, is decorated with *chinoiserie* stuccos.[21]

The nobility and clergy knew what they wanted. The Corso and its buildings were to remind them of Baroque Rome. The architects, first Rosario Gagliardi and later Vincenzo Sinatra and Paolo Labisi, made Angelo Italia's abstract plan experiential by playing walls, façades, and decorative details against the topography of Noto. They took maximum advantage of placement to dramatize their structures. The buildings, though quite different from one another, are united by the golden stone that adorns them, their common style, and their shared motifs. Whether intentionally or not, the buildings along the Corso seem to have been designed by a group of architects concerned to create a cohesive whole.[22]

Noto endured as an aristocratic center until as late as 1865.[23] It proved so loyal to the Bourbons that they transferred the administration of the entire province there from Syra-

cuse in 1837. For almost thirty years more the city thrived because of the administrative functions it housed. The triumphal arch on the Corso, erected for the visit of the Bourbon king Ferdinand II in the mid-nineteenth century, testifies to the renewed vigor of this period and the continuance of Noto's past pretensions.

With the end of the monarchy, aristocrats embedded in Sicilian culture saw their world crumble. The Risorgimento ate at the twin foundations of Noto's existence: the aristocracy

Figure 5. Façade of the church of S. Carlo on the Corso, with scaffolding, 1992.

Figure 6. The façade of the Liceo Classico, part of the former Jesuit College, Piazza XVI Maggio, 1992. The upper part of the façade collapsed in 1985 and was reconstructed, and the rest of the façade was braced.

and the church. The nobles who controlled the city government gradually lost their influence, their interest in civic affairs, and their fortunes. When the national parliament of Florence transferred the capital of the province back to Syracuse in 1865, the prestige of Noto was much reduced; the loss of governmental offices sealed its fate. Now dependent upon a largely agricultural economy, and with practically no commerce, Noto began a steady decline.

In spite of the citizens who valiantly raised the national tricolor on Piazza S. Domenico in 1860, and changed its name to Piazza XVI Maggio in memory of the event; in spite of the enthusiasm with which they changed the name of their main street from the Cassaro to Corso Vittorio Emanuele, Noto was doomed by the

unification of Italy and the consequent abrupt change of government and gradual change of cultural values.

No new lifeblood came to the city, despite nineteenth-century improvements. With the lowering of the Corso, former cellars and basements became tiny shops and each piazza, because of the radical grade change, had room for new, half-buried shops on its northern side. Convents and monasteries, dissolved by the new, anticlerical government, became schools, courthouses, and even penitentiaries. The maintenance of monumental buildings declined markedly. After all, the number of Noto's religious structures and its isolated position in Sicily made outside help unlikely. The house of the Crociferi, for example, subsequently became low-cost housing, a primary school, and a law court. Grass was allowed to grow in the gutters and the roof, dislodging masonry and tiles. With twentieth-century sanitation requirements, sewer pipes laced their way from the toilets, through mouldings and cornices and entablatures, to the ground. Still, the archdiocese retained some of its strength, erecting an enormous seminary in the former Benedictine monastery of SS. Salvatore after a fire in the 1930s, and repairing several churches in the 1950s and early 1960s. But intermittent restoration did not halt Noto's downward spiral, which seems not to have been slowed by the generally better economic conditions in Sicily in the 1960s and 1970s.

The present provincial authorities, as well as Noto's citizens, have neglected to repair many buildings, leaving them vulnerable to water and seismic damage. The upper part of the façade of the Liceo Classico collapsed into Piazza XVI Maggio in 1985 (fig. 6), and by 1986 experts had advised that nearly all of Noto's major buildings were at risk.[24] They were proven correct by the earthquake of 1990, which cracked walls and threw down a few more façades in the city. Without maintenance and seismic retrofitting, all of Noto's major structures are in danger of collapse.

In its latest transformation, Noto's Corso is dying. With the aristocrats and their urban culture gone, the buildings have become badly kept museum pieces, waiting to be unmade by the very earthquakes that caused them to be built. Although the eighteenth-century architects did their best, they created buildings whose rubble construction will not survive a shock similar in magnitude to that of 1693. Poor maintenance decreases their chances still more. The Corso is a fragile artifact containing Noto's lifespan in microcosm: its troubled but exuberant Baroque birth, its brief period of prosperity, and its impending ruin. Rarely does urban history present us with so eloquent a *memento mori*. ∎

Notes

1 S. Tobriner, *Genesis of Noto, an Eighteenth-Century Sicilian City* (London and Berkeley, 1982), 25.

2 Ibid., 27.

3 For a discussion of the term "organic," see S. Kostof, *The City Shaped: Urban Patterns and Meanings through History* (London, 1991), 43–45.

4 For Syracuse, see L. Trigilia, *Siracusa: Distruzioni e trasformazioni urbane dal 1693 al 1942* (Rome, 1983), 17–32.

5 Tobriner, *Genesis of Noto*, 25–26, 103–4.

6 S. Tobriner, "Angelo Italia and the Post-Earthquake Reconstruction of Avola in 1693," *Le Arti in Sicilia del settecento: Studi in memoria di Maria Accascina* (Palermo, 1985), 73–86; and L. Dufour and H. Raymond, "La Riedificazione di Avola, Noto e Lentini: Fra Angelo Italia, maestro architetto," *Il Barocco in Sicilia*, ed. M. Fagiolo and L. Trigilia (Palermo, 1987), 11–31.

7 Tobriner, "Angelo Italia," 85–86.

8 Tobriner, *Genesis of Noto*, 41–65.

9 Ibid., 75.

10 Ibid., 75, 214–15, n. 48.

11 P. Nifosi, *Scicli: Una vita tardobarocca* (Scicli, n.d.), 32, 37. Gagliardi's report for S. Michele Archangelo in Scicli quotes his opinion: "Esso Ingegniere relate di doversi fare finto con l'ossatura di legname e virgoni col gisso di sotto e sopra e non già reale, e ciò unica-mente per più facilmente resistere alle scosse del terremoto che suole più offendere alli dambusi reali che a quelli finti." Gagliardi also calls for "catene di ferro," iron chains, to run from one side of the church to the other.

12 Tobriner, *Genesis of Noto*, 220. For illustrations and discussion of the wooden vault for Sta. Chiara, see C. Fianchino, "Caratteri tecnologici della rico-struzione settecentesca nella Sicilia sud-orientale," *Documenti dell'istituto dipartimentale di architet-tura e urbanistica dell'Università di Catania* 7 (Catania, 1983): 74–75.

13 Tobriner, *Genesis of Noto*, 97.

14 For Bernardo Labisi's report of 1787, see Tobriner, *Genesis of Noto*, 218; for resumption of his work, 1873–77, ibid., 240.

15 Tobriner, *Genesis of Noto*, 17–18.

16 For the university's dispensing of land, ibid., 46.

17 Tobriner, *Genesis of Noto*, 51.

18 L. DiBlasi, *Noto barocca, tra controriforma e illumi-nismo: L'utopia* (Noto, 1981), appendix 4, nn. 2–4.

19 Tobriner, *Genesis of Noto*, 110.

20 Ibid., 238.

21 Ibid., 172–80, 134–35, 221, n. 54.

22 Ibid., 140.

23 Ibid., 200–202; F. Balsamo, *A Visit to Noto, the Golden City* (Noto, 1980), 12–13.

24 Members of a seminar held at Noto, entitled "Vulnerabilità ai terremoti e metodi per la riduzione del rischio sismico," September 1984, warned the city of impending danger. Noto's mayor in the late 1980s, Corrado Passarello, responded to these warn-ings by advertising the plight of the city and valiantly trying to rally support for extensive renovation. When he was voted out of office, his program was discontinued and the subsequent local government was entirely dissolved in 1992, leaving the town in political chaos. For recent events in Noto, see the extensive newspaper clippings compiled in "Noto e il barocco siciliano, le capitali del barocco," *Ras-segna stampa beni culturali* 1, Syracuse, 1990.

10

TRIPOLI

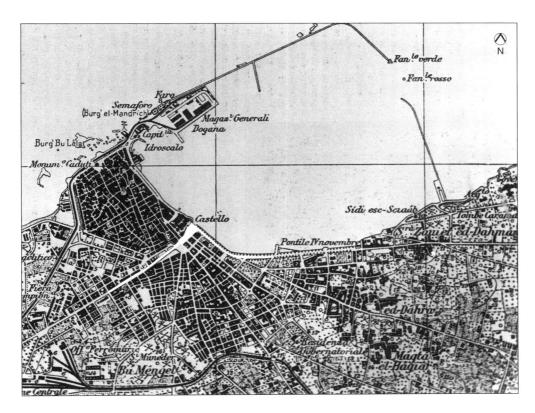

Piazza Castello and the Making of a Fascist Colonial Capital

KRYSTYNA
VON HENNEBERG

Figure 1. Tripoli in the
1930s. The old town is to
the west of the castle and is
surrounded by the new
town. Note the radiating
streets converging on the
castle, including the seafront
Lungomare Conte Volpi,
running east from Piazza
Castello, and Corso Sicilia,
cutting southwest into the
new town.

In a rare departure from its traditionally sanguine prose, the November 1911 issue of the *National Geographic* magazine published an article under the skeptical title "Tripoli: A Land of Little Promise." Tripoli and its hinterland, the author wrote, constituted little more than a "forlorn province of the Ottoman Empire," whose climate and geography had frustrated the reformist energies of even the ablest Turkish administrators.[1] Once a flourishing colony of the Roman Empire, Tripoli's decline had introduced its inhabitants to the twin evils of crop failure and tribal lawlessness. "It was a pitiful sight," remarked a traveler on a journey south to the Sahara, "to see a hungry-looking crowd of fanatics under the ruins of the Roman gateway bearing the inscription, 'Pro Afr. Ill.' (Provincia Africa Illustris)."[2]

Such gloomy visions were common fare in European travel accounts in the early part of the century.[3] The capital of a largely neglected province of the Ottoman Empire, Tripoli was, however, soon to undergo enormous changes. In the fall of 1911, the Italian government, under the Liberal leadership of Prime Minister Giovanni Giolitti, launched an invasion of Libya's coastal cities. Interrupted by World War I, the Italian state went on to pursue a campaign of military conquest lasting some twenty years, facing bitter resistance on the part of tribal groups, particularly in the eastern province of Cyrenaica. Following the Fascist seizure of power in 1922, local resistance was crushed, and the colony subjected to a twenty-year period of often brutal direct rule. From the 1930s onward, Libya became the target of a massive campaign of what the Fascists termed "demographic colonization," as tens of thousands of Italian peasants were settled on confiscated land. Under the leadership of Governor General Italo Balbo (1934–40), the colony was held up as a model of Fascist organizational brilliance, rivaling the achievements of the French and British empires. Tripoli became the colony's cultural and administrative capital, and a symbol of what the Fascists saw as Rome's imperial resurgence.

The Fascist state's cultural and political appropriation of Libya is best seen in its efforts to transform precolonial urban space. Faced with the skepticism of critics both at home and abroad, the Fascists embarked on a series of interventions in the city of Tripoli designed to carve out a new—and thoroughly Italian—civic center along the edge of what was seen as an inaccessibly unmodern and "disorderly" city. The area came to be known as Piazza Castello, after the historic castle located on its northwestern corner (fig. 1). In the days before the Italian invasion, the square was considered a marginal area, occupying a stretch of the waterfront just east of the city walls, and serving as a transit route to open-air markets located east of, and outside the old city, or medina (fig. 2). Over the next two decades, its status was to change dramatically. By the late 1930s, Piazza Castello became a symbol of Fascist architectural grandeur and a forum for the kinds of swaggering political displays that so typified the Duce's quest for recognition and ascendancy.

Like many other urban areas designed to meet Fascism's aesthetic and political standards (including those in Italy), the square was gradually refitted to suit the regime's vision of history, and of its own role in shaping the destiny of the region. Colonization thus involved more than a simply physical or military appropriation of a foreign space. In the case of

Piazza Castello, it meant investing such spaces with new and serviceable meanings designed to demonstrate both the benevolence and the inevitability of Italian rule. As a political stage, the creation of Tripoli's new center reflected the regime's uncanny grasp of the political potentials of urban space and of the powerful link between architecture and public ceremony.

Fascist efforts to model Piazza Castello into an Italian civic space reflected several important aspects of Italian policy in Libya. Chief among these was the regime's often complex attempt to pacify Libya's Muslim population culturally, at a time when Islam served as one of the principal vehicles of indigenous opposition to European rule. In an effort to deflate such opposition, Italian authorities pursued a policy of religious tolerance. Mussolini actively wooed international Muslim opinion in an effort to undermine British and French primacy in the Muslim world. The regime launched a program of mosque construction and restoration, and curtailed Catholic missionary activities. Italy's tolerance for Islam was, however, largely confined to the cultural sphere. Islam as an independent political force was severely repressed. Co-optation was thus the principal directive of Fascist direct rule: Islam the quietist and picturesque was supported over Islam the militant or reformist.

In an effort to assert Italian hegemony, the regime resorted to other strategies as well. Tripoli, like Rome, was a convenient locus for resuscitating tales of Roman and Christian glory. Archaeology was put at the service of Fascist policy. Monuments were unearthed and museums established with the goal of scientifically demonstrating Rome's historical superiority in the art of colonial rule. Lest one perceive Fascism as a merely derivative or backward-looking phenomenon, Tripoli's new rulers also placed great emphasis on innovation. A new town was built east and south of the medina to house the growing influx of Italian administrators, merchants, soldiers, and craftsmen. The chaotic and haphazard building programs of the Ottoman and Liberal periods were superseded by modern planning and design projects that reflected the newest trends in Italian Rationalist architecture.

Fascist efforts to institutionalize architecturally this unstable blend of traditions posed obvious problems in matters of building and preservation. In the case of Piazza Castello, the propagation of new historical myths or newly construed traditions often required the destruction or modification of other, sometimes cherished, historical markers—a dilemma familiar to the architects of Mussolini's Third Rome. Such policies also produced an unusual brand of eclecticism in the fabric of the city: widely disparate traditions and styles were cultivated or resurrected side by side, producing a diversity that came to stand as a conscious metaphor for the peaceful cultural coexistence supposedly inaugurated under Fascist rule. Like visitors to Europe's colonial expositions, tourists in the Tripoli of the 1930s thus discovered a city replete with vistas both modern and ancient, planned and organic, Muslim and Christian, domesticated and exotic. This contrived diversity was Fascism's most useful—and revealing—fiction. The architectural transformation of Tripoli was, at best, a tangible expression of the regime's often confused quest for symbolic and political primacy over its Italian and Libyan subjects.

Set against the eastern wall of Tripoli's old castle, the Piazza Castello of the 1920s and 1930s marked the boundary between the Arab medina to the west and the modern city of Tripoli to the east and south (figs. 1, 3). To the north, the square opened onto the port. To the south, it formed an extended apex to a set of seven radiating streets running along the waterfront, through the new city, and along the castle's

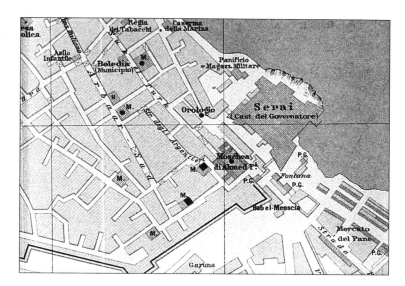

Figure 2. The castle (*Serai*) and its surrounding area under Ottoman rule, c. 1910. The city walls are still intact. "P.G." indicates *posto di guardia*, or sentry station; the fountain is labeled *fontana*.

southwestern edge. Shaped like an elongated rectangle, the piazza was obliquely joined to the former market area of Piazza Italia, located at its southern end. Together, the two squares formed the representational and administrative center of the new Tripoli, embracing those elements that most defined the capital: the castle, the port, the old town, and the new. It was here that the colony's governors, Balbo especially, chose to celebrate the achievements of Italian rule in a number of carefully orchestrated public ceremonies designed to affirm the regime's ever-contradictory tenets of tolerance, strength, tradition, and innovation.

The modern history of Piazza Castello is as variegated as the history of Tripoli itself, and requires a note of introduction. Long before the arrival of the Italians, the square had been shaped by centuries of political struggle, as power passed from the Spaniards to the Knights of St. John and finally to the Turks in the sixteenth century; to the partly native Karamanli dynasty in the eighteenth century; and again into Ottoman hands from 1835 to 1911. The Italians were hardly the first to reconstitute the

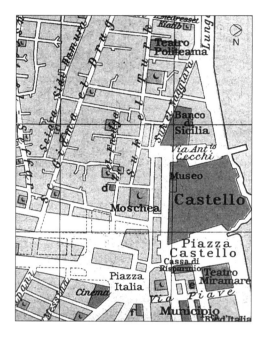

Figure 3. The castle area in the late 1920s, including the mosque (*moschea*) and theater (*teatro*). The dotted lines prefigure the changes to the square carried out in the 1930s. The Cassa di Risparmio, a bank, was subsequently replaced by the Istituto Nazionale delle Assicurazioni (INA).

serve as a military bastion, soldiers' barracks, base for pirates, arms depot, princely residence, governors' headquarters, prison, and torture chamber, variously sheltering a church, crypt, mosque, and mint.[5] The area flanking the castle underwent a nearly equivalent number of changes. As late as the seventeenth century, the castle was surrounded by a moat, and was sealed off from the sparsely settled area that encircled the town, as well as from the medina itself. By the nineteenth century, the moat had been filled in and a wall erected that joined a neighboring fortified door with the castle's protruding southeastern corner, the Bastion of Saint George (see fig. 2). Henceforth, one entered the medina through an arched opening leading directly into a marketplace, the Suq al-Mushir, and to the eighteenth-century Karamanli Mosque complex. In the course of the late nineteenth century, the area that was later to become Piazza Castello was gradually filled in and widened, a fountain built, and a curving stone balustrade and sentry stations supplied at water's edge.

As a formalized square, Piazza Castello owed its existence to the gradual dismantling of the city's traditional defenses, on the one hand, and growth of the modern European city on the other. Both processes were enormously accelerated by the arrival of the Italians. Italy's victory over the Ottoman Empire effectively demilitarized the area. By abolishing the threat of invasion from the sea, the Italians eliminated the castle's historic function as the defensive bastion of the city, opening the area up to the kind of architectural and archaeological speculation that is only conceivable in peacetime. Henceforth, the castle was "no longer a citadel, but a relic," as one visitor shrewdly observed in 1925.[6] The same can be said of the city's fortifications. Tripoli's first master plan, drawn up by colonial urban planners in 1912 and amended in 1914, called for the destruction of a large part of the

area in their own image. Nor were they the first to engage in major demolitions and modifications, a number of which were carried out under Ottoman rule to make room for the several mosques, marketplaces, squares, and thoroughfares located inside the walled medina.[4] Though contrived, the architectural eclecticism of Fascist Tripoli was also nothing new. The alternating presence of Christian and Muslim overlords, and the city's history as a trading port and center of piracy, gave the city a religious and ethnic diversity best reflected in the existence of segregated Arab, Jewish, and Christian quarters, each with their respective houses of prayer, shops, schools, and cemeteries.

The transformation of the area of Piazza Castello at the hands of its mostly foreign occupiers is best seen in the history of the castle, the centerpiece of the square and the city's most imposing structure. Originally built in the years of the Muslim invasion (642–43) over the site of a Roman fort, the castle went on to

city's old walls (at which time the fountain was also destroyed), opening up the liminal area between the medina and the new town to European construction.[7]

Even more important, the establishment of Italian military control made it possible for the city's center to shift to an area that would once have been considered exposed and unsafe or, at best, a mere thoroughfare. That a square, and a central one at that, came to be located outside the medina was in turn testimony to the growing Italian presence in Tripoli. European settlement certainly existed east and south of the old town prior to the Italian conquest. After 1911, however, the growth of the Italian urban population was substantial, outstripped only by the growth in the number of Libyans, as those deprived of their land clustered to the capital in search of work. On the eve of Giolitti's conquest, Tripoli counted 29,869 inhabitants, of whom a mere 819 were Italians. By 1931, the number of Italians had reached 21,756 out of a total population of 81,438, increasing to 39,098 out of a total population of 108,157 by 1938.[8] Virtually the entire Italian population settled outside the medina, in a mixture of mostly single-story middle-class residences, low-rise state employee apartments, and worker housing. Government offices, services, and industry were also established outside the old city. Barring a few interventions in the 1930s, the medina was left largely untouched, a symbol of the "genuine orient" and an incentive to European tourism. The preservation of the old city as a cultural artifact, combined with the regime's purported tolerance of Libyan traditions, militated against trying to situate the city's new center within the medina. As an unclaimed space, the area outside the walls could simply be appropriated with greater ease and less controversy.

With the expansion of the new town, Piazza Castello thus became a central focus of architectural and archaeological activity designed to attract public life and increase its status as a civic center. For the most part, such modifications reflected the colonial state's hybrid agenda, combining patronage of local traditions with a desire to affirm Italian hegemony. The edge of the square facing the water was transformed into a ceremonial docking area (regular maritime traffic approached the city west of the medina, at the site of the customs and health offices). Seen from the water, the entrance to the square was framed by two square columns topped by sculptures of the Roman she-wolf on one side and a boat representing the city of Tripoli on the other—symbols of Rome and Tripoli's intertwined glory (fig. 4). Though nowhere explicitly stated, the new vista was a clear reference to the Piazzetta San Marco in Venice, a city whose own history was thus deftly mobilized to suggest the idea of Italy's historic supremacy over the East.[9] The adjacent waterfront area was refashioned into a grand, palm-lined boulevard reminiscent of nineteenth-century Italian and French sea resorts. Named the Lungomare Conte Volpi, after Tripolitania's governor from 1921 to 1925, and built under the direction of the architect Armando Brasini, the road opened up a broad eastward sweep that linked the castle to several of the new city's most important hotels, bank buildings, state offices, and parks built along the waterfront.

Of these buildings, the Miramare Theater was the one situated closest to the castle. Located on the square's eastern edge (fig. 5), the building was erected in 1928 in flamboyant Moorish style, with a central dome, stucco façade, windows with pointed arches, and an enclosed courtyard along its northern side. This style was nothing unusual. While scorned by avant-garde Rationalists in Italy (the theater was in fact not deemed fit for review in the

Figure 4. Piazza Castello
in the 1930s, during a visit
from the Italian king.
Note the waterside pillars
and the bas-relief of St.
George and the dragon,
visible at top left.

leading architecture journals of the period), Libya's modern Moorish architecture reflected a common desire to soften Italy's image as a conquering power in the eyes of the resident population with the help of local—if often fanciful—stylistic references. The exotic appeal to Europeans of Moorish structures was similarly not discounted, as such buildings provided a sanitized but seemingly authentic impression of life in the medina to tourists too timid to appreciate the real thing.

The theater was not the only Moorish structure to be built along the perimeter of the square. Bolder still in its appeal to local Muslim and Italian exoticist sensibilities was the Sidi Hammuda Mosque, located just off the square's southeast edge. Rebuilt by the Italians on the site of an existing mosque in 1926, the building was a classic example of early-twentieth-century Moorish pastiche, of the sort commonly erected at colonial fairs. Divided into three sections, the

building sported a central dome topped with a crescent moon, doorways with pointed arches in alternating dark and white bands, decorative stalactite motifs, elaborate crenellations, and an interior carefully rendered in what the Italians believed to be the traditional Muslim style by a Turinese engineering firm. The mosque itself occupied only the central part of the structure. The building's two lateral wings were mere façades for shops and apartments, designed to integrate the central mass into a street front that included other Moorish-style European structures.

The same kind of stylistic invention came to grace the square's northwest corner, at the entrance to the medina. In the mid-1930s, a plan was drawn up to reconstruct the Suq al-Mushir marketplace, situated just west of the arched entrance to the medina, next to the Karamanli Mosque (fig. 6). The work was carried out in 1935 under the direction of Florestano di Fausto, one of new Tripoli's principal architects and a master

Figure 5. Aerial view of Piazza Castello, with the Miramare Theater and INA building in the left foreground.

at achieving syncretic styles combining Rationalist and local elements. Construction of the new marketplace was part of the regime's broader effort to "rationalize" artisanal and market activity within the city, usually by shifting it to new locations or buildings. In the case of di Fausto's work, the result was to replace the traditional warren of workshops with a complex of modern, Moorish-style courtyards, covered walkways, and porticoes, including an Arab café featuring "fanciful dances by oriental ballerinas," and destined to become one of Tripoli's principal tourist attractions.[10] Known as the *Quartiere dell'Artigianato*, or artisan's neighborhood, the new market area included special "indigenous schools" in carpet weaving, goldsmithry, and ceramics, established to rescue local craftwork from what the Italians termed "indubitable symptoms of decadence," with the help of Italian instructors. Di Fausto, one report concluded, had thereby introduced the

principles of "order, hygiene and dignity" into what had once been a "decadent" and undignified environment. A tribute to the Fascist state's patronizing embrace of local traditions, the new souk was deemed one of part of Italy's *opera rinnovatrice e risanatrice* that both domesticated and highlighted Tripoli's exotic character.[11]

An even more important target of renovation was the castle itself. Starting in 1922, the complex underwent major modifications under Brasini's direction, with further changes inaugurated during the period of Balbo's rule. The arched entrance leading through the city wall into the medina and the Suq al-Mushir was restored and the street south of the castle (renamed the Corso Vittorio Emanuele III) cleared of a number of nineteenth-century buildings that had served as barracks under Turkish rule (fig. 7). A bronze statue of the Libyan-born Roman emperor Septimius Severus was erected at the entrance to the medina, a reminder of

Figure 6. A view into the Suq al-Mushir and Karamanli mosque area through the archway into the medina.

Meteorological Observatory for Tripolitania, and the police headquarters. Both the castle's mosque and its sixteenth-century Christian crypt were restored, while its numerous court-yards, gardens, and walkways were embellished with an eclectic selection of archaeological fragments drawn from Libya's newly excavated Roman sites.

Balancing this panoply of historical symbols were a number of new buildings along the square's eastern edge. Built in the mid-1930s, these were the product of a series of demolitions carried out in keeping with the city's new 1933 master plan. The overall effect of these changes was to move the edge of Piazza Castello further south, merging it with Piazza Italia (whose eastern corner was transformed into a traffic rotary) and linking it with the opening of the new city's major northwest–southeast artery, the Corso Sicilia.[12] As far as the buildings were concerned, the square's eastern and southern sides were remade in the Rationalist image, providing a stark contrast to the Moorish structures they abutted. Their inclusion signaled a shift in the government's attitude away from the architectural eclecticism of earlier days, to the more imperial image that later came to be associated with Italy's conquest of Ethiopia and her declaration of empire in 1936. Indeed, the 1933 master plan, drawn up by the architects Alberto Alpago Novello, Ottavio Cabiati, and Guido Ferrazza, was the first to impose stylistic restrictions on new buildings in the city, designed to "prevent shamelessly exotic or pretentious types of construction and to en-courage a much more harmonious modernity and simplicity" than had characterized earlier structures.[13] No doubt, a stylistic division of labor may also have been at work, with Moor-ish design reserved for the square's cultural and representational structures (theaters, mosques, marketplaces, museums, the seat of

Italy's and Libya's common history and of Rome's renewed imperial mission. Overlooking the statue was a bas-relief depicting St. George and the dragon. Placed along the top edge of the bastion of St. George, the image was a striking reminder of the sixteenth-century rule of the knightly orders, reaffirming the historical pre-cedent for Christian rule in a setting where Christianity per se could not be openly extolled.

The structure of the castle itself was also modified. Inside, it was remodeled to accom-modate a number of important administrative and cultural functions, including the offices of the governor general, the Royal Archaeological Museum, the head of the Monuments and fine Arts Service, the historical archive, the Central

government), and Rationalist design reserved for buildings housing more prosaic, bureaucratic activities.

The first such building, standing directly across from the castle, was the state National Insurance Institute (INA), designed by the architect Luigi Rossi (see fig. 5). Located on the site of a former bank, the building occupied an entire city block, facing the Miramare Theater to the north and the Sidi Hammuda Mosque to the south. A few decorative details betrayed the architect's concern for the setting; these included a row of oversized latticework windows reminiscent of the local *mashrabiyyah*, each inset with a small image of boats or fish. Aside from these references, however, the build-

ing was unmitigatedly Rationalist, with travertine and stucco porticoes topped by a set of unadorned horizontal bands of overhangs and windows.[14] The same was true of a neighboring office building erected just south of the INA complex. This building seems to have almost intentionally dwarfed the mosque, towering over its dome and concealing it from the view of the square—as if to mask an earlier "indigenist" indulgence. A third building, visible from the square, though not actually part of it, produced a similar modernizing effect. Standing at the opening of the Corso Sicilia, the Bank of Rome was defined by a central clock tower adorned with a bas-relief of the Roman she-wolf. Its style and shape were directly reminiscent of the type

Figure 7. The eastern flank of the castle in the 1930s, with a view into the Corso Vittorio Emanuele III. The statue of Septimius Severus is at bottom left.

of Rationalist *Case del Fascio* being erected in many Italian towns and cities at the time (fig. 8).[15]

The same kind of studied modernization, with its ensuing contrasts, could be seen in the development of the streets leading into the area around Piazza Castello. The master plan of 1933 was primarily concerned with rendering the area accessible to traffic, linking the city's new center to several key points (the hospital, trade-fair grounds, stadium, train station, governor's residence, etc.) located in the city's southern and eastern reaches. Piazza Castello, and the adjoining area of Piazza Italia, were thus transformed into a sort of representational hub, from which residents could fan out to residential, industrial, or recreational zones situated along any of the seven major axial streets that converged on the castle area. The streets, some of which merely retraced the steps of existing roads, were conceived as wide, rectilinear thoroughfares, tree-lined, paved, illuminated, and connected by gridlike networks of secondary roads. Virtually all boasted entrances framed by imposing institutional buildings, as in the case of Corso Sicilia and the Lungomare Conte Volpi, and were named after Italian provinces, cities, leaders, and luminaries. Overall, the modernization and extension of Tripoli's street network signaled the colonial government's desire to open the city to European commercial activity, reflecting the state's almost obsessive concern with transparency, accessibility, and order in the urban fabric. Circulation and viability became metaphors for governability. So too, the creation of large vistas and squares represented the triumph of the state and master plan over the forces of speculation, improvisation, and crowding. The joining together of Piazza Castello and Piazza Italia, with its attendant demolitions and addition of large representational and institutional buildings, was in this sense a willful violation of the more intimate scale preserved in the master plan of the Liberal era. The resulting area constituted by far the largest open space anywhere in the city, introducing the notion of a public arena in which citizens could convene, see, and be seen.

Set off by little more than an arched entrance, Tripoli's new civic center stood in stark contrast to the more reclusive spatial arrangements of the neighboring medina. Though mostly straight, the streets of the medina were narrow and sometimes covered, letting in limited light; their function was not so much to open the medina to the outsider as to negotiate the passage between enclosed spaces located inside private dwellings, shops, or houses of prayer. Civic squares as such did not exist: what collective life there was took place in the market areas (some of them covered), public baths, mosques, temples, and churches. To the Italians, torn between feelings of repulsion and fascination, the old city represented all that was inaccessible, mysterious, and archaic. The medina, one traveler wrote, is full of "narrow and meandering streets." There is "no light, but . . . plenty of filth. Walking along the streets is like proceeding under an uninterrupted vault. The houses, which are almost leaning up against each other, are joined by a series of arches that are anything but triumphal: they do for [the houses] what crutches do for the lame."[16] Others instead celebrated the medina for its so-called primitive, Cubist volumes, simplicity, and sense of intimacy. Despite an increase in the numbers of Libyans settling there during the Italian occupation, the medina remained an object of romantic admiration on the part of many European visitors, drawn by its supposedly timeless and unchanging nature.

Straddling preservationist and reformist impulses, city officials under Balbo embarked on projects to "reclaim" (*risanare*) certain areas considered decrepit and overbuilt, to supply water and sewage facilities, and, in one cele-

Figure 8. Piazza Castello seen from the north, with the Bank of Rome in the background. To the right is a statue of Mussolini waving the "Sword of Islam," commemorating his visit to the city in 1937. Here, thousands of Italian peasant colonists salute the newly inaugurated statue during Balbo's massive welcoming ceremony in 1938.

brated case, to isolate a Roman arch dating from the time of Marcus Aurelius. For the most part, however, the medina was preserved, the purported inaccessibility of its streets providing what the Italians saw as an instructive contrast with the expansive and monumental spaces of the new city's boulevards. With the growth of the Italian population, the contrast became even more extreme: successive plans of the city show a medina increasingly encircled by broad thoroughfares, as the Italians claimed the waterfront area north and west of the old town for traffic leading in and out of the port, and along the coast. The medina came to resemble an island, impenetrable to the romantic European imagination, and yet surrounded. In a telling gesture, the 1933 master plan depicts the streets of the new town in broad white strokes, while the streets of the medina are shaded in gray, labeled simply as "neighborhoods reserved for the indigenous inhabitants."[17] In the Italian literature of the period, this dichotomy between dark and light, narrow and broad, reclusive and civic—drawn from studies of the urban fabric—was elevated to a symbol of all that differentiated Italian from Libyan traditions, with a clear emphasis on the superiority of the colonizing culture.

By the late 1930s, the area around Piazza Castello had thus undergone a major physical transformation. Guidebooks and architectural reviews from the period heralded its renovation, and concurred in recognizing its new character as the official center of Fascist Tripoli. From a peripheral space, the square had become host to the colonial administration's government offices, a theater, mosque, market, insurance, bank, and office building—a balanced arrangement that spoke to the city's principal activities, from the political and commercial to the cultural and religious. From a peripheral and transitional area, Piazza Castello had become a major point of arrival and departure, opening onto the Lungomare Volpi, Corso Sicilia, and Corso Vittorio Emanuele III, among others. Its main monument, the castle, was reincarnated as a cultural and administrative site, rather than a military seat of power. The former market area of Piazza Italia was similarly made over into an extended civic space. Finally, Piazza Castello was no longer a disorderly parenthesis between the two disparate worlds of the medina and the new town. The inauguration of the market and mosque, on the one hand, and the construction of the National Insurance Institute and its neighboring office and bank buildings, on the other, produced a kind of visual integration of the two cultures that sought to go beyond mere juxtaposition. The two simply offset each other. Any jarring disjunctures between the old and the new had been eliminated, one critic reported, thanks to the square's "harmonious" and "artful" conception.[18] Architecturally, Piazza Castello had become a kind of modified colonial fairground, co-opting and reinventing the Moorish, the Italian, the old, the eclectic, and the modern in the name of Fascism's liberality and tolerance.

Even more important than the square's new configuration, however, were the public uses to which it was put. Political ceremony and ritual played a critical role in the Fascists' symbolic appropriation of Piazza Castello, expressing the regime's confidence in its own position as colonizer, and asserting its leadership of both its Libyan and Italian subjects. Two events in particular mark the high point of what Fascist propaganda of the time termed the *conquista morale* of Libya and its capital. The first, held in March 1937, was a major political demonstration held in honor of Mussolini's visit to the colony. The second, held one year later, heralded the arrival of a mass convoy of twenty thousand Italian settlers destined to colonize Libya's hinterland. Organized by Balbo, the two events were masterful feats of propaganda, alternating the cult of the leader with a populist celebration of the masses, and exhibiting Italy's respect for Islam while arrogating the right to lead and interpret it.

In both cases, Piazza Castello served as the principal setting for the events. With its rich symbolic backdrop, it fulfilled a role not unlike that of Piazza Venezia in Rome, a central locus for Fascist gatherings that embraced Italy's greatest historical monuments, from the Colosseum to the Forum to the Campidoglio and the Vittoriano, as well as Mussolini's offices and his famous balcony. The analogies between the two squares are not to be dismissed. Both have as a backdrop the selective restoration of suitably ennobling monuments and the destruction of others. Historical theme parks in the best sense of the term, both squares lent themselves to the kind of oceanic political demonstrations so crucial to the regime's domestic and foreign pretensions. The analogy may not have escaped Libya's governor general. One of the original leaders of the March on Rome, Balbo had been sent to Libya by Mussolini out of jealousy over his growing popularity. The posting was considered a demotion. During his years in Tripoli, Balbo sought to capitalize on what he perceived as his virtual exile by vigorously promoting Libya's modernization, using his substantial rhetorical and political skills to draw international attention to the work of the colony.

Mussolini's visit to Libya in 1937 was a perfect occasion for such display. His first tour of the colony since 1926, the event sparked feverish preparations. The Duce was returning to affirm Italy's role as a newly constituted empire, as well as her continuing commitment to Islam. Roads were repaved, buildings demolished and refaced, and ornamental gardens laid down virtually overnight. Reporting on the event, the British consul in Tripoli described the construction in Piazza Castello of "a steel scaffolding, 106 meters in height, and steel frames for benches for spectators," next to which "a very powerful search-light, visible some 20 or 30 miles inland, played from the top of a specially erected steel tower" in the square. A second scaffolding, bearing the illuminated letters DUX, was erected near the port, while "the motto of the Militia 'Credere, Obbedire, Combattere' shone in letters which must have been at least 12 feet high from the roofs of the Customs warehouses." Owners of buildings located along the route Mussolini was to travel were instructed to repaint their buildings, while "all shops in Tripoli, large and small, showed not only the Italian flag, but also one or more large photographs of the Head of the Italian Government."[19] With accommodations in Tripoli's hotels insufficient to hold the incoming crowds, ships were stationed in the harbor to serve as floating hotels.

On his first evening in the city, Mussolini was escorted into Piazza Castello in a procession headed by Italian and Arab cavalrymen. On his way, he was met by some sixteen thousand Arabs carrying lighted torches and the standards of their religious orders; many of these were brought in from neighboring villages to celebrate the Duce's arrival. The stands of the square were filled with ticket holders, who stood quietly for the duration of a "very brief and completely inaudible" address delivered by a Tripoli notable.[20] The next day, following an official reception and a tour of the city, Mussolini was escorted outside Tripoli for a ceremony in which he was presented with one of the regime's most colorful concoctions: a Sword of Islam. Manufactured in Florence, and handed to him by a local dignitary, the sword was a symbolic tribute to Mussolini's self-proclaimed role as steward of the Muslim world. Sitting astride a white horse, "Signor Mussolini un-

leashed the sword, and holding it aloft gave the Arab cry of ʿUled,'" a witness reported. Entering Piazza Castello with the sword hanging from his black saddlecloth, he rode his horse to the top of a specially prepared three-foot mound and, waving the weapon three times, delivered a speech from the saddle celebrating Italy's role in the Muslim world.[21] Thousands gathered to hear him, with the central part of the square ostentatiously reserved for Arab horsemen. With Balbo at his side, Mussolini retreated into the castle, appearing on the balcony overlooking the square to receive the "prolonged and vociferous demonstrations of enthusiasm from all sections of the large crowd."[22]

"The Italian authorities generally can be congratulated on the arrangements made in connection with the Duce's visit," the British consul wryly noted. The numerous rehearsals for Mussolini's entrance had served the regime well. "Even in such trifling matters as teaching the Arabs to cry 'Duce, Duce' when Signor Mussolini passed, teaching the young Arabs of the Lictor [a Fascist youth group] to say 'We are the little soldiers of Benito Mussolini' and to sing 'Giovinezza' in Italian, and providing the Arab gentleman who broadcast a description of Mussolini's triumphal arrival with a manuscript from which he read his eye-witness account of the proceedings had not been overlooked."[23] Other viewers did more than merely register the event's evident irony. Arab leaders in the Middle East and exiled members of the Libyan resistance expressed indignation at the show. In an open letter to the Duce published in Iraq, the Mufti of Mosul pointed to what he called the "disgusting and hatred-breeding means [Mussolini] has used to pursue Moslem friendship." Reviewing the day's events, he decried the participation of pacified Arabs in the granting of the sword. "Their present," he wrote, "amounts only to handing back to you the sword with which you have been ruling them."[24] Others went on to note that Mussolini's patronage of Libyan Islam came on the heels of years of brutal repression of local opposition movements, a policy exemplified in his twenty-year campaign against the rebel Sanusi Brotherhood of Cyrenaica.[25]

One year later, Balbo's scenographic skills were again put to the test. Capitalizing on his promise to turn Libya into Italy's "Fourth Shore," Balbo orchestrated the arrival of a mass convoy of twenty thousand peasants (the first of a projected one hundred thousand) destined for settlement on newly constructed homesteads in the colony's hinterland. Handpicked by Fascist administrators, the peasants were widely heralded as a symbol of Italian tenacity and hard work, sent to fertilize fallow lands "abandoned" since ancient times to the careless and unproductive Libyans. As part of the regime's campaign for demographic colonization, each male peasant was accompanied by his entire family to ensure the stability and future growth of each homesteading unit. Never before had Fascist propaganda found a more promising target. The colonists' arrival spawned thousands of articles, reports, and photographs, striking a strong populist note that came to typify Balbo's administration.

Landing in Tripoli, the colonists were escorted to Piazza Castello to participate in a massive welcoming celebration. "Arabs and Sudanese fought to see the ceremony," an attending journalist wrote. "Puccini's beautiful Hymn to Rome was played by massed bands as a solemn interlude between the various Fascist anthems in marching strain dedicated to every branch of Fascist life and activity." In what must have struck amazement into the hearts of the colonists, many of whom had never before left home, "free food, cigarettes, visits to the theatres and cinemas were provided," while

soldiers, priests, party leaders, and members of Fascist youth groups thronged below newly painted, massive portraits of the Duce.[26] Piazza Castello, with its regimented crowds and flags, was once again the center of the celebration and a symbolic port of arrival into the peasants' new world. All along the perimeter of the square, people lined the rooftops of the buildings to witness the fray. As a culmination of the day's events, Balbo appeared on the scene to unveil a statue of Mussolini astride a horse, waving the Sword of Islam. The statue, cast especially for the occasion, was placed at the eastern entrance to the castle, atop a large white pedestal (see fig. 8). Just what the colonists may have felt in the midst of such a display, beyond perhaps complete bewilderment, has unfortunately gone unrecorded. Unrecorded also are the voices of local Libyans: critical musings on the regime's policies could not be easily or safely recorded during the Fascist era. Architecturally speaking, the statue—the regime's last addition to the square in the years before World War II—signaled the completion of a long process of Fascistization of Tripoli's new political center.

Looking back on the interwar period, historians today have labeled Italy's colonization of Libya a failure. The state's loudly touted colonization campaign, though massive and original, fell far short of the goals of either reducing Italian peasant landlessness or achieving agricultural miracles in the desert. Mussolini's bombastic pretensions to leadership of the Islamic world were also predictably fruitless. With the onset of World War II, the Libyan experiment came to an end. More important than Fascism's practical gains in Libya, however, was its architectural and ritual redefinition of the fabric of modern Tripoli. The former Turkish outpost had been transformed by a joint process of social and architectural engineering into a radically different city. Its monuments and buildings had undergone a selective restoration that spoke to the regime's complex appropriation of local and Modernist traditions. In the case of Piazza Castello, Rationalist concepts of planning and design turned away from the militant ahistoricism of much European Modernism, toward a more malleable and inclusive approach that reflected the state's quest for primacy in Italy and the Muslim world. Ritual and procession were part and parcel of this symbolic war, turning a once undefined space into an important setting for the public, theatrically consensual consumption of official propaganda. More than a social space, Piazza Castello came to stand for the centrality of the state. More than a civic center, it became a stage for the enactment of mass politics. Such ritual celebrations were unknown to the Tripoli of Ottoman times, reflecting a vastly different conception of space, power, and the relation between them. In hindsight, this may have been one of Fascism's most enduring colonial exports.

Renamed Maydan al-Saraya in the years following Libya's achievement of self-rule in 1951, Piazza Castello was eventually shorn of its most visible tributes to Fascist rule. Nevertheless, it remained the center of the new Tripoli. Political demonstrations carried out under the banner of an independent state signaled the reappropriation of the square's heritage by new, local elites. An official government guide to Libya, published during the reign of King Idris, offers a photograph of uniformed members of an official women's group lined up alongside the castle's eastern entrance, banners and loudspeakers aloft, marching under the purview of assembled officials.[27] However different their content, such displays nevertheless signaled an implicit acknowledgment of the changes wrought by Italian rule, recasting Piazza Castello as a backdrop for the invention of new political traditions. ∎

Notes

1   A. L. Vischer, "Tripoli: A Land of Little Promise," *National Geographic* 22, no. 11 (November 1911): 1042.

2   Ibid., 1044.

3   See, for example, C. W. Furlong, *The Gateway to the Sahara: Observations and Experiences in Tripoli* (New York, 1909); A. Ghisleri, *Tripolitania e Cirenaica dal mediterraneo al Sahara: Monografia storico-geografica* (Milan, Bergamo, 1912), 196–68; and M. Loomis Todd, *Tripoli the Mysterious* (Boston, 1912).

4   E. Rossi, *Storia di Tripoli e della Tripolitania dalla conquista araba al 1911* (Rome, 1968), 193 and *passim*.

5   The history of the castle is described in L. V. Bertarelli, *Guida d'Italia del Touring Club Italiano: Possedimenti e colonie, isole egee, Tripolitania, Cirenaica, Eritrea, Somalia* (Milan, 1929), 281–85; and idem., *Guida d'Italia del Touring Club Italiano: Libia* (Milan, 1937), 153–57. I draw extensively on these two guidebooks for descriptions of the square.

6   G. Casserly, "Tripolitania, Where Rome Resumes Sway," *National Geographic* 48, no. 2 (August 1925): 131. While the Ottomans used the building as a military barracks, the Italians could afford to post their soldiers one mile or more south of the medina, see Geographical Section of the Naval Intelligence Division, Naval Staff, Admiralty, *A Handbook of Libya* (London, c. 1916), 136.

7   O. Sangiovanni, "La Medina di Tripoli: Dal piano regolatore del 1912 ai lavori del 1936–37," *Islam: Storia e civiltà* 9, no. 1 (January–March 1990): 48–58. At the same time as they destroyed the old walls, the Italians erected their own line of defense in the form of walls some ten kilometers in length and four meters in height, built in the period from 1912 to 1915. Known as the *Mura nuove*, they appear to have served primarily as a defense against the interior, probably against rebel attacks by land. By the late 1920s, they were already obsolete, and are mentioned for their historical interest in Bertarelli, *Guida* (1929), 294–96.

8   C. G. Segrè, *Fourth Shore: The Italian Colonization of Libya* (Chicago, 1974), 41; R. de Felice, *Jews in an Arab Land: Libya, 1835–1970* (Austin, 1985), 351. The figures cited by de Felice are from the Ministry of Italian Africa, 1942.

9   The square in Venice similarly has two columns placed at water's edge, surmounted by sculptures representing San Marco and San Todaro. The use of such columns was common in the Italian colonial architecture of the 1930s, at least as far as Italy's Mediterranean possessions were concerned. Two columns, bearing the she-wolf and winged lion, were built along the Benghazi *lungomare;* in Rhodes, the Mandraki harbor was framed by columns bearing a deer and a stag.

10 The market traditionally held in Piazza Italia was suppressed in the 1930s, and shifted to a large new building in Via Manzoni, along the medina's southeast flank. *Viaggio del Duce in Libia per l'inaugurazione della Litoranea, Anno XV: Cenni sull'attività municipale di Tripoli, Orientamenti e note ad uso dei giornalisti* (1938), 6. Di Fausto's work is described in E. Bonfiglio, "A Tripoli dopo undici anni," *L'Italia d'oltremare* 2, no. 5 (March 5, 1937): 20–21.

11 Spectator Libycus, *Due anni di governo del Maresciallo Balbo in Libia* (Tripoli, 1936), 41. For the "indigenous schools," see Notiziario per radio-diffusione, "Scuole artigiane a Tripoli," Archivio Storico del Ministero dell'Africa Italiana, II: Libia. Varie (1926–43), pos. 150/35, 1926–37, fol. 157. Broadcast August 12, 1936. On di Fausto, see *Notiziario corporativo della Libia* (September 1938), 47.

12 Ministero delle Colonie, Consiglio Superiore Coloniale (*CSC*), n. 158, Relazione ministeriale n. 7789 del 19 ottobre 1928, Direzione Generale Africa Settentrionale, Variante al piano regolatore di Tripoli, Archivio Storico del Ministero degli Affari Esteri, *CSC*, pacco 6, 1928.

13 M. de Rege, "Il Nuovo piano regolatore di Tripoli," *Urbanistica* 3, no. 3 (May–June 1934): 128.

14 B. M. Apollonj, "L'Attuale momento edilizio della Libia," *Architettura italiana* 16 (1937): 806. The building's porticoed façade and the presence of a large central courtyard may also have been intended as references to the nearby Karamanli Mosque.

15 See D. Ghirardo, *Building New Communities: New Deal America and Fascist Italy* (Princeton, 1989), 24–109.

16 Ghisleri, *Tripolitania*, 196. Ghisleri here cites the voice of a visitor to Tripoli in the years prior to the Italian invasion.

17 De Rege, "Nuovo piano regolatore," map of 1933 master plan, n.p.

18 Bonfiglio, "A Tripoli dopo undici anni," 21.

19 Public Records Office (*PRO*), Foreign Office (*FO*) 371/21158/fol. 54 (R2515), Eric Drummond to Anthony Eden, n. 296, April 8, 1937, cites Despatch no. 10 from Hugh McClelland to E. Drummond, April 1, 1937.

20 Ibid., fol. 57.

21 "La Remise de l'Epée de l'Islam à Mussolini," *Eclair du Nord* (Aleppo), March 23, 1937.

22 *PRO*, Drummond to Eden, fol. 62.

23 Ibid., fol. 68A.

24 *PRO, FO* 371/2081/fol. 231 (E2614/84/93), Clark Kerr, Baghdad, to G. W. Rendell, n. 92/18/13, publication in Iraq of a letter from the Mufti of Mosul to Signor Mussolini, encloses translation of an article appearing in *Al Bilad*, April 19, 1937.

25 The Italo-Sanusi war is brilliantly analyzed in E. E. Evans-Pritchard's classic work, *The Sanusi of Cyrenaica* (London, 1949).

26 H. Bailey, "The Colonization of Libya," *Fortnightly* 866 (February 1939): 199.

27 Libyan Ministry of Information and Culture, *This is Libya* (Tripoli, c. 1969), 167.

11

ROME

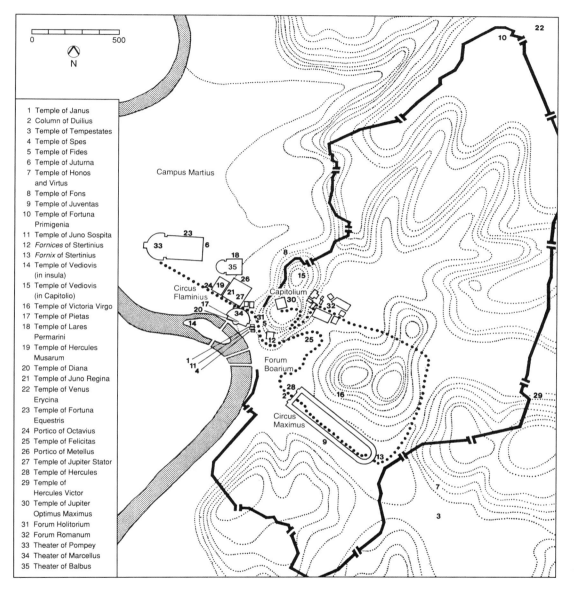

The Street Triumphant

The Urban Impact of Roman Triumphal Parades

DIANE FAVRO

Legend

1 Temple of Janus
2 Column of Duilius
3 Temple of Tempestates
4 Temple of Spes
5 Temple of Fides
6 Temple of Juturna
7 Temple of Honos and Virtus
8 Temple of Fons
9 Temple of Juventas
10 Temple of Fortuna Primigenia
11 Temple of Juno Sospita
12 *Fornices* of Stertinius
13 *Fornix* of Stertinius
14 Temple of Vediovis (in insula)
15 Temple of Vediovis (in Capitolio)
16 Temple of Victoria Virgo
17 Temple of Pietas
18 Temple of Lares Permarini
19 Temple of Hercules Musarum
20 Temple of Diana
21 Temple of Juno Regina
22 Temple of Venus Erycina
23 Temple of Fortuna Equestris
24 Portico of Octavius
25 Temple of Felicitas
26 Portico of Metellus
27 Temple of Jupiter Stator
28 Temple of Hercules
29 Temple of Hercules Victor
30 Temple of Jupiter Optimus Maximus
31 Forum Holitorium
32 Forum Romanum
33 Theater of Pompey
34 Theater of Marcellus
35 Theater of Balbus

Campus Martius

Circus Flaminius

Capitolium

Forum Boarium

Circus Maximus

Figure 1. Plan of first-century B.C.E. Rome, with triumphal architectural monuments. The triumphal route is a heavy dotted line.

The people [of Rome] erected scaffolding in the theaters . . . and round the Forum, occupied the other parts of the city which afforded a view of the procession, and witnessed the spectacle arrayed in white garments. Every temple was open and filled with garlands and incense, while numerous servitors and lictors restrained the thronging and scurrying crowds and kept the streets open and clear. Three days were assigned for the triumphal procession.

Triumph of Aemilius Paullus, 167 B.C.E.
Plutarch, *Aemilius* 32

Figure 2. The porticoed elevation of the Villa Publica, depicted on a *denarius* of 61 B.C.E.

A parade prescribes a distinct pathway through a city. In the case of ancient Rome, triumphal military parades had lasting implications for the city's plan. Delimited by human action, rather than flanking buildings, unifying paving, or set limits, a processional path creates a distinct urban route. A well-attended, lengthy parade transforms a series of interconnected thoroughfares into a new, independent processional street, with its own superseding identity. The triumphal route through ancient Rome is a premier example (fig. 1). Triumphal processions repeatedly energized the city during the period of the Republic, from 508 to 44 B.C.E. Lasting several days, each occasion elicited a powerful triumphal itinerary, defined by temporary seating, jostling crowds, and fluttering decorations.

Roman processions honoring successful generals have a long history, which Plutarch traces all the way back to Romulus.[1] The triumph was the highest attainable honor for a male citizen of the Republic. The Senate awarded a triumph based on complex criteria. The victor had to be a magistrate holding *imperium* who had been proclaimed triumphator in the field by his troops. The war whose victory was celebrated had to be a just, concluded confrontation involving the death of at least five thousand foes.[2] Since tradition forbade the discussion of war-related topics within the city proper, senators deliberated petitions for triumphs outside the *pomerium*, or sacred urban boundary. If all requirements were met, the Senate proclaimed the general a triumphator, acclaimed his troops as well, formally declared a holiday, and granted public resources to fund a parade and other festivities. At first, triumphs were infrequent and simple. Gradually, under the influence of extravagant Hellenistic celebrations and with an expanding power base, Rome developed impressive and numerous triumphs. Between 220 and 70 B.C.E., ceremonies occurred approximately once every year and a half.[3]

The triumph was trenchantly bound to the city as a cosmological and political necessity. No matter how far Roman authority extended, the city on the Tiber remained the focal point of power. Rome was the wellspring of *romanitas* and the home of Jupiter Optimus Maximus, to whom all triumphs were dedicated.[4] As a result, all communal ceremonies had to occur amid the seven hills. When Marcus Antonius celebrated a triumph in Alexandria, Romans reacted violently, considering this act a sacrilegious insult to the gods, the city, and the people.[5]

Descriptions of triumphs appear repeatedly in ancient literature; visual depictions are found in ancient art. Throughout, however, the emphasis is on the parade's participants and elaborate displays. Similarly, scholarly research on the Roman triumph focuses on the pageant as ritual. To date, the procession's considerable impact on the city's physical form has not been thoroughly considered.[6] Clearly, the relationship between the triumphal parade and the urban form was reciprocal. The temporary triumphal route drew strength from the power of place—that is, from the city locales through which it passed and from the historical moment in which it existed. At the same time, the processional practice affected building typologies, patronage, and siting.

The Roman triumph served three primary purposes, each associated with a select activity and a select sector of the city.[7] First, and probably oldest, was the ceremonial culmination of a successful military campaign, serving ritually to purify both the troops and the citizenry contaminated by war. Celebratory preparations began in the Campus Martius, northwest of the city center. Named after the war god Mars, this extrapomerial flood plain had a long military history. In the years before the creation of a standing army, the Romans had conducted military maneuvers and worshiped the war gods Bellona and Mars here. The Campus also accommodated foreign ambassadors, who resided in the Villa Publica while awaiting permission to enter the city (fig. 2).[8] A general petitioning for a triumph found ample room in the plain for his troops and appropriate shelter for himself in the porticoed public villa. There he waited anxiously for the decision of the Senate, convened in the Temple of Bellona. An affirmative vote resulted in raucous celebrations by the troops, along with solemn purification rituals, award ceremonies, and speeches by the new triumphator.[9] Immediately, preparations began for the triumphal procession into Rome.

During the Republic, the exact starting point of the triumphal parade varied greatly. Staging occurred throughout the southeastern Campus Martius. In particular, the unencumbered area known as the Circus Flaminius was conveniently located and large enough to be used for speeches, displays of captured goods, and the orchestration of the triumphal parade.[10] The procession gained definition as it left the Campus Martius and passed through the Porta Triumphalis. After years of study, this structure remains enigmatic,

Figure 3. A drawing of a lost relief in the *Codex Corburgensis*, 1500–1554, possibly representing the Porta Triumphalis.

its precise date, form, and location hotly debated. The earliest literary references come from the late Republic. The term *porta* indicates a door or gatelike form. Located in the area of the Forum Holitorium, the Porta Triumphalis has been identified as either a gate in the Republican wall or a freestanding structure. Closed during most days of the year, the Porta was specifically opened for triumphal processions. Passage through the Porta Triumphalis both signified a symbolic purification and was a celebration of entry into the city (fig. 3).[11]

Conceptually, this choreography mimed Rome's topographical and functional realities. At its southern edge, the vast, flat Campus Martius gave way to the cramped hills and valleys of the city; in parallel, the free movement of masses possible in the plain gave way to the restricted activities allowed within the city's sacral and official boundaries. The teeming crowds of soldiers, prisoners, displays, and

Figure 4. A small clay relief depicting a triumphator.

carts that swarmed over the Campus likewise were restrained within the city; there, an amorphous crowd became a visible and controlled urban line: the triumphal street.

The second aim of the triumph was to justify military campaigns to the Senate and populace who had remained at Rome. Wending through the dense city center, the procession had a large audience. At its head were Roman magistrates and senators, visible manifestations of State sanction. Behind them lumbered cartloads of booty, sacrificial animals, and captives, collectively vindicating the cost of war. Next came the triumphator in all his glory. Wrapped in a richly embroidered purple toga, he stood high in a gleaming chariot drawn by four white horses. Above his head a slave held a victory wreath, while whispering, "Look behind you [i.e., look to the future] and remember that you are a man," a cautionary reminder that the general acted on behalf of Rome (fig. 4). After the triumphator came his military officers, Roman citizens rescued from slavery, and the cheering (and jeering) troops.[12]

The parade formed the body of the triumph. Hour after hour over several days, spectators watched the flowing course of the pageant. The endlessly diverse triumphal extravaganzas drew enormous crowds from both Rome and throughout Italy.[13] Triumphal parades were as much didactic as celebratory. Through the exhibition of spoils, Rome's citizens learned not only about the prowess of their armies and generals, but also about the people, art, architecture, and fauna of their conquered foes. Along with the general and his rowdy troops came a panoply of exhibitions. The parade of Lucius Scipio in 189 B.C.E., for example, included 224 captured military standards, 134 *simulacra*, 231 ivory tusks, 234 gold crowns, 137,420 pounds of silver, and equally impressive quantities of gold, metal vases, coins, and prisoners. Particularly interesting are the *simulacra*, believed to be models of captured buildings, cities, or regions (fig. 5). In addition, large painted or woven panoramas several stories high tottered past the spectators; by depicting battles and related events, these allowed observers vicariously to experience being in the field. Often, the panels were later placed on permanent public display in Rome. Exhibits of captured exotica, ranging from jewel-encrusted furniture to elephants and other wild beasts, instructed the crowd about life and art in foreign lands.[14]

Moving with measured slowness, the pageant passed through the Forum Holitorium, the Velabrum, and the Forum Boarium, then circled around the base of the Palatine Hill, through the valley of the Circus Maximus, and into the Forum Romanum. Originally, spectators selected good viewing spots on the grassy hillsides. Later, as the slopes became densely built, they watched from porticoes, balconies, roofs, and windows. The poet Propertius describes lying in the arms of a paramour while gazing out an upper-story window at the banners of a passing triumphal parade.[15] At the base of the Capitoline Hill, the triumphal procession halted, and the chief captives were led off and killed, while the triumphator prepared for

Figure 5. Andrea Andreani, after Andrea Mantegna, *The Standard-Bearers*, from *The Triumphs of Caesar*, woodcut, 1599.

his ascent to the temple on the crown of the hill.

The route of the triumphal parade clearly followed Rome's earliest trails along the floors of connected valleys. In fact, each step drew upon the city's topographic history. For example, the loop through the Velabrum preserved the memory of the swamp that once had occupied the area northeast of the Forum Boarium (see fig. 1). The encirclement of the Palatine brought to mind the limits of early Rome under Romulus.[16] At the same time, the path of the procession exhorted all observers

to "look behind" to the future. Each procession was part of an urban continuum, a street connected in time as well as in space with the past and future of the Roman state, the triumph ritual, and the topography of Rome.

The third purpose of the triumphal ceremony was to appease and honor the gods—in particular, Jupiter, guarantor of the Roman state. The expiatory nature of the event was evident in each phase. Religious sacrifices began with the offerings of the troops in the Campus Martius. In the city proper, the pro-

Figure 6. Reconstructed view of the Temple of Jupiter Optimus Maximus, top center, as seen from the area of the Porticus Octaviae and Theater of Marcellus in the southern Campus Martius.

cession made an irregular loop; the counter-clockwise direction emulated the choreography of other rituals and may have been apotropaic. A similar protective power may have been associated with the Sacra Via, the Sacred Highway in the Forum Romanum, traversed by the triumphal parade. Activities on the Capitoline hill focused on the triumph's religious purpose. The triumphator proceeded on foot up the steep Clivus Capitolinus to the Temple of Jupiter Optimus Maximus.[17] Once at the huge temple, he solemnly sacrificed a white ox and laid a laurel branch and wreaths in the lap of Jupiter's statue; nearby, he offered selected spoils of war at the smaller shrine to Jupiter Feretrius. The ceremonies closed with the triumphator and Senate feasting in Jupiter's great temple.[18]

The *locus* on the Capitoline marked the end both of the improvised street and of an arduous military journey. Before leaving Rome on his campaign, the general had sacrificed to Jupiter on this same site; returning victorious, he came full circle. The procession drew upon the city's topography to recall his journey and prepare the triumphator for this potent terminus. Literally and figuratively, the parade left behind the field of Mars and passed through the civilizing urban zone. All along the way, participants caught glimpses of the Temple of Jupiter Optimus Maximus, hovering above the worldly realm of the city (fig. 6). Only a few, led by the triumphator, were allowed to ascend and face the god atop the Capitoline.

The triumphal street was powerful and enduring, yet it did not have a fixed itinerary. Three broad topographical components remained constant in all processions: the sorting out in the Campus Martius, the loop around the Palatine, and the terminus at the Capitoline.

Within these areas, however, the route could vary. Each triumphator designed his parade to provide the greatest propagandistic benefit for his personal agenda. For example, he might direct the parade to pass by a monument erected by his family or himself. Due to this variability, the improvised street formed by the triumphal parade remained always new and vital, redefined periodically with each ceremonial event.

Celebration of a triumph transformed the urban realities of Rome. For a few hours or days, the parade route became the city's major thoroughfare, yet it was a street closed to use by urban residents. Lictors and other official attendants kept citizens off the processional path.[19] Made up of a series of connected thoroughfares, the triumphal street was recognizable as a conceptual whole through the ephemeral trappings added to define its edges and length. Scaffolding for temporary seating and a solid wall of spectators formed the contours of the street at ground level. The gleaming white garb of the spectators contrasted greatly with the colorful dress of the figures in the parade, visually distinguishing the two groups.[20] Above the heads of the crowd, temporary decorations graced the buildings along the route, setting them apart from other structures in Rome. In addition to the usual floral garlands added to major structures on holidays, urban buildings received militaristic ornaments, the so-called *spolia*, commemorating battles (see fig. 3). For example, in 308 B.C.E., the triumphator Papirius Cursor proudly displayed gilt shields on the shops of the silversmiths in the Forum Romanum.[21] Such ornaments visually and programmatically linked urban buildings associated with military victory.

The rituals of a triumph redefined the use of key buildings in Rome. For most of the year, the Porta Triumphalis stood as a mute billboard, its passageway blocked; on the days of a triumph, the barrier was torn away and the parade poured through. Thus, during the few hours of the ceremony, the monument actually functioned as an urban doorway. The celebration also transformed Rome's entertainment structures. To keep large audiences comfortable throughout the lengthy event, triumphators diverted processions directly into and through spectator buildings such as theaters and circuses.[22] The public perception of these structures thus changed temporarily from having a centralized focus to having a linear one. Theater orchestras and circus tracts became segments of the triumphal street, with the stone seating acting as a solid version of the temporary grandstands defining the processional route elsewhere in the city.

Significantly, Rome first acquired large permanent theaters in the first century B.C.E., a period when triumphs proliferated at an astonishing rate. The three that were built in the Campus Martius were all associated with triumphs.[23] In fact, the orientation of one of these, the Theater of Marcellus, may have directly responded to processional dictates. When clearing room for a stone theater near the Circus Flaminius in 44 B.C.E., Julius Caesar cavalierly destroyed temples erected by earlier triumphators. Dedicated by his heir as the Theater of Marcellus, this structure was not aligned on a east–west axis like other permanent theaters in the Republican city. Its skewed southwest–northeast orientation may have been chosen to facilitate the movement of triumphal processions from the Circus Flaminius, through the theater, and into the Forum Holitorium (fig. 7).[24]

Spectator events were an integral part of Roman life. Thus it is not surprising that they had a significant impact on building design. In the late first century B.C.E., Vitruvius explained the layout of the Roman fora as responding to the requirements of gladiatorial contests by including spacious colonnades, with balconies above for spectators.[25] All along the parade

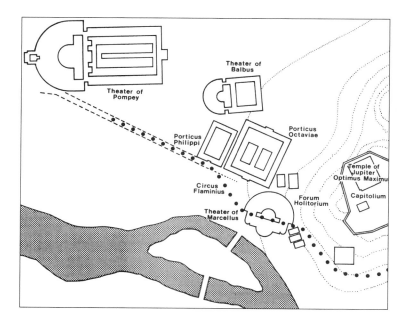

Figure 7. Plan of the
southern Campus Martius,
with the theaters of Pompey,
Balbus, and Marcellus.
The triumphal route is a
heavy dotted line.

routes of Rome, buildings responded to spectators' needs. Thus, the open external arcades of theaters and circuses let light into interior galleries and simultaneously acted as platforms from which to view processions in the public streets below. Shady porticoes, high temple podia, balconies, and large upper-story windows likewise served parade watchers. The elevation of important Roman buildings upon podia may in part have been an attempt to keep façades visible above standing crowds.

The triumphal ceremony also promoted certain building types. The form most directly associated with the event is the commemorative arch. During the Republic, memorials took many forms in addition to buildings: single ornamented columns, statues atop viaducts, free standing sculptures, and *fornices*. Formed by freestanding piers connected by an arched lintel supporting sculpture, the *fornix* held special appeal for triumphators (see fig. 3).[26] Like city gates or doorways, *fornices* compelled movement *through*, an act associated with purification. Victorious generals carefully sited their arches so that later triumphal parades would be compelled to pass through them and thus under their sculpted images, an effective means of demonstrating their linkage, if not superiority, to subsequent triumphators. Commemorating his Spanish victories in the early second century B.C.E., L. Stertinius shrewdly erected a *fornix* as the eastern gateway of the Circus Maximus, even though he had not formally been awarded a triumph.[27] All later triumphal processions had to exit the Circus through the Fornix Stertinii. Commemorative arches are valuable urban-design components; they divide one area from another, frame views, and mark shifts in street directions.[28] Yet without the persistence of the triumphal parade, this architectural form of street articulation might not have proliferated in Rome.

The requirements of triumphal ceremonies may also have strengthened the public resolve to maintain open areas within the city. Long after troops ceased to practice maneuvers in the Campus Martius, they mustered there for victory parades, along with captives, animals, and carts. This important activity called for ample open space, and thus promoted the preservation of unbuilt areas in the field of Mars. Elsewhere along the triumphal route, open urban land was continuously preserved for temporary seating, as well as post-parade events. Whenever possible, commemorative games and enormous feasts occupied facilities along the route. After his multiple triumph in 47 B.C.E., Caesar gave a great public banquet on twenty thousand dining couches. These must have occupied every open space in the Campus Martius, Forum Romanum, Circus Maximus, and Capitoline; maybe some couches also stood in Julius's new forum, then under construction, tangent to the triumphal path.[29] The needs of the triumph of course did not prevent the inexorable densification of Rome, yet they may have helped preserve open urban space as a planning priority.

Triumphal parades stimulated urban construction in other ways as well. During the Republic, the Romans felt culturally inferior to the Hellenistic world in all areas, including architecture and urban appearance. This feeling increased as triumphators displayed booty from conquests in the East, during the second and first centuries B.C.E. In a few instances, victorious generals carried back parts of Greek buildings for reuse in Rome.[30] The *simulacra* displayed in victory parades provided even more provocative exemplars of Hellenistic architecture and urban design. In his triumphal parade of 47 B.C.E., Julius Caesar included a model depicting one of the seven wonders of the ancient world, the enormous Pharos (lighthouse) of Alexandria, complete with the flames of its beacon. This display not only inspired architects, it also helped to justify Caesar's plans to erect similar extravagances in Rome.[31]

Every triumphator was expected to spend a portion of his booty on a public building in Rome. Thus, many of the city's magnificent structures, especially the temples, were windfalls of the triumphal ceremony. Furthermore, ambitious nontriumphators likewise sought permission to erect public buildings advertising their own successes. For maximum exposure and association, patrons of both kinds located their projects as closely as possible to the procession way (see fig. 1). Since the exact parade route varied, such monuments clustered near the nodal points of the route, rather than along a specific urban line. During the Republic, a number of victory monuments appeared in the southwestern Campus Martius and the vicinity of the Circus Maximus.[32] For example, in the Forum Holitorium stood numerous statues, the *fornices* of Stertinius, and the temples of Janus, Juno Sospita, and Spes; near the Circus Maximus triumphators erected the column of Duilius and the temples of Juventas and Hercules.

Individuals were not the only patrons of triumph-related constructions. The Senate and People of Rome funded hundreds of triumphal commemoratives. After all, triumphs were a reaffirmation of the collective power of Rome. Memorials sponsored by individual victors provided exemplars for all Romans, but especially for participants in the parades. Passing monument after monument, the troops were reminded of their place within a victorious continuum. Simultaneously, the hundreds of captives were made aware of the overwhelming might of their conquerors—a memory that freed prisoners carried back to their homelands.[33] As a result, the State naturally took an active role in embellishing the ritual street. Most of the state-sponsored triumphal monuments stood in the areas of greatest public meaning and involvement, namely, the Forum Romanum and Capitoline, where they would reach the largest audience. In fact, the State exercised close control over these areas and periodically had to remove old commemoratives to make space for new ones.[34]

The concentration of memorial buildings, in turn, gradually shaped the choreography of the triumphal procession and of the city. For example, victorious generals erected several temples across from the Circus Flaminius, defining an impressive, straight street. The addition of surrounding porticoes by later triumphators further clarified the street edge and provided ground and rooftop space for spectators.[35] The street thus shaped by these buildings cut a straight line through the southwestern Campus. Here, a large segment of the parade could be orchestrated and viewed at one time. From the arcaded cavea of Pompey's theater, located to the north, observers, or even the triumphator himself, could look down and evaluate the relationships among various parts of the choreographed pageant before it moved through the Porta Triumphalis.[36]

At the end of an ephemeral event such as a Roman triumphal parade, much more remained than the detritus of marching troops, lumbering animals, and an immense crowd. The parade left an enduring imprint upon both urban structure and urban existence. After the last trumpet had sounded, residents found their understanding of the city's topography and history once more strengthened. They carried home a sense of security tangibly evidenced by the active presence of their impressive army and by the manifest power of the place where they lived. Those with the means and status to erect major structures in Rome noted the important rhetorical role buildings played in the triumph, and determined which sites, building types, and *simulacra* would have the greatest impact upon both spectators and participants. Throughout the rest of the year, concrete reminders kept the ritual alive. The impact of the procession remained clearly evident in the clustering of grand buildings, architectural forms accommodating spectators, militaristic ornamentation, and a thousand other symbolic reverberations. Collectively, the triumphal intervention clarified Roman urban imperatives: planning did not follow absolutist formal ideas, but was implemented in sympathy with the potent experience of a changing ritual. ∎

Notes

1 Plutarch, *Romulus* 16. The origins and history of the pre-Imperial triumph are covered in greater depth by L. Bonfante Warren, "Roman Triumphs and Etruscan Kings," *Journal of Roman Studies* 60 (1970): 49–66; R. Payne, *The Roman Triumph* (London, 1962), and H. S. Versnel, *Triumphus: An Inquiry into the Origin, Development, and Meaning of the Roman Triumph* (Leiden, 1970). Those of the Imperial triumph are handled by C. Barini, *Triumphalia: Imprese ed onori militari durante l'impero romano* (Turin, 1952); S. G. MacCormack, *Art and Ceremony in Late Antiquity* (Berkeley, 1981); and, most recently, E. Kunzl, *Der römische Triumph: Siegesfeiern im antiken Rom* (Munich, 1988). The best sources for the heady experience of a Roman triumph remain literary and cinematic recreations; for example, see L. Davis, *Silver Pigs* (New York, 1989), 200–206; and the 1951 MGM film "Quo Vadis."

2 These are but the most significant of many requirements to be met before the Senate would allow an armed force into the city. Exceptions were not infrequent and the criteria changed over time. In a few cases, the people overrode the Senate's decision and awarded triumphs themselves. Other options also existed. A few generals paid for victory celebrations at Monte Albano, thirteen miles southeast of Rome. A larger number accepted the *ovatio*, often called a lesser triumph. Awarded by the Senate and held in Rome, this event lacked the accoutrements and significance of the triumph; Versnel, *Triumphus*, 165–68; H. H. Scullard, *Festivals and Ceremonies of the Roman Republic* (London, 1981), 213–18.

3 Regarding Republican triumphs and their frequency, see J. S. Richardson, "The Triumph, the Praetors and the Senate in the Early Second Century B.C.," *Journal of Roman Studies* 65 (1975): 50–63; and L. Pietila-Castren, *Magnificentia Publica: The Victory Monuments of the Roman Generals in the Era of the Punic Wars* (Helsinki, 1987). Even in years when no triumph was awarded, the triumphal parade resonated in Republican Rome. Parades were a major component of many Roman rituals in addition to triumphs. Other *pompa* often followed a route very close to that of the triumph and likewise drew large crowds; Versnel, *Triumphus*, 94–131. The funeral processions of important citizens included figures

in triumphal regalia, representing the ancestors of the deceased who had triumphed; these parades followed a route similar to that of a triumph, but in reverse, moving from the city center to tombs in the Campus Martius; Versnel, *Triumphus*, 115–29.

4 Regarding the complex relationship between the triumphator and Jupiter, see Versnel, *Triumphus*, 66–93; and Bonfante Warren, "Roman Triumphs," 53–63.

5 Plutarch, *Antonius* 50.2. A few foreign rulers staged their own triumphs, including Antiochus IV in Antioch; Polybius, *Histories* 30.25. Though grand, such imitative events remained inferior to those in Rome, for they could not draw upon the same power of place or cultural history.

6 A. Plattus deals with the triumphal parade's relationship to the city's image, rather than its physical form: "Passages into the City: The Interpretive Function of the Roman Triumph," *Princeton Journal* 1 (1983): 93–115.

7 This tripartite conceptualization of the city in relation to the ritual is especially clear in the writings of Josephus from the Imperial period; Josephus, *Jewish War* 7, 118–62.

8 Troops and foreign ambassadors approaching Rome from the south had to circle the city's *pomerium* to reach the approved waiting place in the Campus Martius. The form and functions of the Villa Publica are discussed by E. Makin, "The Triumphal Route, with Particular Reference to the Flavian Triumph," *Journal of Roman Studies* 11 (1921), 26–30.

9 One of the purificatory rituals may have involved walking one mile. Two Imperial inscriptions refer to a Porticus Triumphi, giving its length and the number of circumambulations necessary to complete a mile. In the late Republic, Caesar likewise built a marble portico one mile in length as part of the new Saepta, or voting enclosure, in the central Campus Martius; Cicero, *Ad Atticus* 4.16.14; Makin, "Triumphal Route," 28–29.

10 T. P. Wiseman has convincingly argued that the Circus Flaminius was not a built circus with perma-

nent seats, but an open area defined by a low enclosure wall. Over the years, new buildings (many erected by triumphators) encroached upon this space. By the first century, the large Circus Flaminius area was reduced to a plaza; T. P. Wiseman, "The Circus Flaminius," *Papers of the British School at Rome* 42 (1974): 3–26; F. Coarelli, "Il Campo Marzio occidentale: Storia e topografia," *Mélanges de l'Ecole Française de Rome* 89 (1977): 807–46.

11 Originally, the Porta Triumphalis may have stood on Rome's pomerial line. Its role in purification is underscored by the fact that the *porta* was apparently opened only for triumphal parades; Cicero, *In Pisonem* 23.55; Festus, *Latin Glossary, Epitome* 104 L (117 M); Versnel, *Triumphus*, 135, 152, 394–96. For a contrasting interpretation of the Porta Triumphalis as a gate in daily use, see L. Richardson, Jr., *A New Topographical Dictionary of Ancient Rome* (Baltimore, 1992), 301. On the debates over the Porta Triumphalis, see the extensive research by F. Coarelli, "La Porta Trionfale e la Via dei Trionfi," *Dialoghi di Archeologia* 2 (1968): 55–103, and *Il Foro Boario dalle origini alla fine della repubblica* (Rome, 1988), 363–414; as well as Versnel, *Triumphus*, 132–63, and the analytical review by F. S. Kleiner, "The Study of Roman Triumphal and Honorary Arches fifty Years after Kähler," *Journal of Roman Archaeology* 2 (1989): 201–4.

12 Zonaras, *Epitome* 7.21; cf. Tertullian, *Apologeticum* 33.4. In contrast to the modern linear, progressive view of time, some Romans perceived the future as coming from behind, rather than lying ahead; Seneca, *Ad Lucilium* 1.1–3; M. Bettini, *Kinship, Time, Images of the Soul* (Baltimore, 1991), 124–33. On Roman conceptions of cyclical time, see P. Holliday, "Time, History, and Ritual on the Ara Pacis Augustae," *Art Bulletin* 72 (1990): 542–57.

By shouting insults, the troops demonstrated their faith in the triumphator and his reliance upon them; Suetonius, *Caesar* 49. The sequence of components in triumphal parades varied slightly over time; that cited here is the one most commonly followed in the Republic. Naturally, the order had powerful implications. To demonstrate his superior standing, the first emperor, Augustus, placed himself, rather than the magistrates, at the head of his parade in 27 B.C.E.; Dio Cassius, *Roman History* 51.21.

13 Hundreds thronged to Rome in 47 B.C.E. to see Caesar's extravagant triumphal parade and entertainments. Since the city did not have enough available lodgings, visitors pitched tents on the streets, highways, and rooftops; two senators and several other individuals died in the press of the crowd; Suetonius, *Caesar* 39.

14 For Scipio's parade, see Livy, *From the Founding of the City* 37.59. For his triumph of 61 B.C.E., Pompey had gathered so much material that he could not show it all in the two days allotted; at an earlier triumph he had wanted elephants to draw his chariot, but the huge beasts would not fit through the city gate; Plutarch, *Pompey* 14.45.

    The exact meaning of *simulacra* is still under debate; generally it is assumed to mean three-dimensional representations. Regarding the depiction of architectural images in triumphal parades, see Appian, *Punic Wars* 66; Livy, *From the Founding of the City* 37.59. Triumphal parades also included statues of personifications representing cities and regions. In 264 B.C.E., M. Valerius Maximus Messala displayed a painting of his victory over the Carthaginians on a side wall of the Curia Hostilia in the Forum; Scipio, in 190 B.C.E., placed a picture of his Asiatic victory on the Capitoline; Pliny, *Natural History* 35.22–25. Pictures of actual triumphal celebrations appeared in the temples of Vertumnus and Consus as early as the fourth century B.C.E.; Festus, *Latin Glossary, Epitome* 228. The most detailed descriptions of the towering panoramas carried in triumphal parades come from the Imperial period; Josephus, *Jewish War* 5.123–60. In describing the triumphal parade of 275 B.C.E., Florus gives a sympathetic portrait of the elephants and carefully lists the diverse peoples included among the captives; *Vergilius orator* 1.13. In the Imperial period, Domitian allegedly hired actors in blond wigs to represent Germans in his triumph of 84 C.E.; Tacitus, *Agricola* 39; Dio Cassius, *Roman History* 67.8; Payne, *Roman Triumph*, 172.

15 Propertius, *Elegies* 3.4.15–18.

16 The route around the Palatine Hill essentially followed the presumed pomerial line of Rome's earliest settlement; Dionysius of Halicarnassus, *Roman Antiquities* 1.56. The counterclockwise movement of

the procession may have been a kind of lustration; similar choreography occurred in a number of other Roman *pompa*, or processions; Scullard, *Festivals and Ceremonies*, 77; Coarelli, "Porta Trionfale," 59–66; Bonfante Warren, "Roman Triumphs," 54–55.

17 The triumphator did not go directly to Jupiter's temple, but instead apparently first went to the Arx, the northeastern mound of the Capitoline Hill; Bonfante Warren, "Roman Triumphs," 55. Julius Caesar added greater drama to his passage by climbing up the hill on his knees, accompanied by forty elephants bearing lamps; Suetonius, *Caesar* 37. For the Sacra Via, see Horace, *Epodes* 7.8; Ovid, *Tristia* 3.126–27.

18 The two consuls did not attend the feast atop the Capitoline, so that they would not draw attention away from the triumphator.

19 The triumphal pathway was technically a street, yet its inaccessibility led ancient observers to find alternative descriptors. For example, Josephus referred to the procession as a river running through Rome; Josephus, *Jewish War* 7.140. Triumphators also received permission to impose upon other urban streets throughout the year; Pliny notes that they were allowed to have the doors of their houses open outward onto the public thoroughfares; *Natural History* 36.112.

20 The Romans considered white the appropriate color for celebrations and formal occasions. This color coding possibly had social implications as well, since not every resident in Rome could afford a bleached toga; see Plutarch, *Aemilius* 32 ;Suetonius, *Augustus* 40; Juvenal, *Satires* 10.44–47.

21 Livy, *From the Founding of the City* 9.40.16. Not far from the Tabernae Veteres, the speakers' platform had earlier been decorated with captured ships' beaks or *rostra*; thereafter it became known by that name. *Rostra* also decorated a nearby column commemorating a naval victory over the Carthaginians in 260 B.C.E.; Pliny, *Natural History* 34.20; Livy, *From the Founding of the City* 8.14. When denied a triumph in 66 B.C.E. for political reasons, Lucullus displayed heaps of his booty in the Circus Flaminius; Plutarch, *Lucullus* 37.2.

22 Both the Circus Flaminius and the huge Circus Maximus (capacity 150 thousand) accommodated triumphal rituals at an early date; Livy, *From the Founding of the City* 39.5; Dionysius of Halicarnassus, *Roman Antiquities* 3.68. Before the construction of permanent theaters, temporary structures provided additional seating; Plutarch, *Aemilius* 32.

23 Pompey erected Rome's first permanent theater in 55 B.C.E. Although he was not triumphator that year, the huge stone complex had significant triumphal associations: it included a temple to Venus Victrix (Venus the Conqueror), statues representing the fourteen nations subdued by Pompey, and a hall where the Senate could meet to make extrapomerial decisions, such as the awarding of triumphs. The triumphator Caesar laid the foundations for a theater, dedicated by Augustus as the Theater of Marcellus in 13/11 B.C.E. Around the same time, L. Cornelius Balbus dedicated his own theater, commemorating his victories in Africa. Josephus describes an Imperial triumph of 70 C.E. as moving through several theaters, presumably those listed above; *Jewish War* 7.113. In addition to these permanent structures, Marcus Aemilius Scaurus erected a temporary theater when aedile in 58 B.C.E., in part to commemorate his eastern campaign; it remained standing for several years; Pliny, *Natural History* 34.36; 36.113–15.

24 The skewed angle may also be explained by the desire to present a dramatic façade to the river. Caesar's destruction of temples caused great consternation among Rome's highly religious citizenry; Dio Cassius, *Roman History* 43.49.

25 Vitruvius indicates that good seats in the balconies (*maeniana*) of fora could be sold to generate public revenue; *On Architecture* 5.1.1–2. The Forum Romanum in Rome was frequently the site of the gladiatorial games and other spectator events presented after triumphal parades.

26 Despite the popular misconception, not all Roman arches were associated with triumphs, nor did all straddle thoroughfares. For an overview of recent literature on the subject, see Kleiner, "Roman Triumphal and Honorary Arches," 195–98. Regarding the change in terminology from *fornix* to *arcus* in the first century B.C.E., see G. A. Mansuelli, "Fornix e arcus: Note di terminologia," *Studi sull'arco onorario romano* (Rome, 1979), 15–18.

27 Since he was not an office holder at the time of his victory, Stertinius was not eligible for a triumph. His *fornix* in the Circus Maximus was later replaced by one commemorating the victories of the emperor Titus. Stertinius also erected two other *fornices* in the Forum Boarium; Livy, *From the Founding of the City* 33.27. Coarelli located these near the temples to Fortuna and Mater Matuta; Coarelli, "La Porta Trionfale," 91; Pietila-Castren, *Magnificentia publica*, 72–74.

28 D. Scagliarini Corlàita, "La Situazione urbanistica degli archi onorari nella prima età imperiale," *Studi sull'arco onorario romano*, 29–72.

29 Adjacent to the Forum Romanum, the crisply defined open space of the Forum Iulium readily accommodated triumph-related events. Caesar ended his triumphal celebrations there and then proceeded home, accompanied by the entire populace of Rome, with elephants carrying torches; Dio Cassius, *Roman History* 43.22.

30 To celebrate his campaigns in Spain, in 173 B.C.E. Quintus Fulvius Flaccus, as censor, stripped the marble roof tiles off a temple in Croton in southern Italy; he was severely reprimanded by the Senate; Livy, *From the Founding of the City* 43.3. Marcus Antonius, triumphator in 100 B.C.E., used *spolia* on his victory monument, the so-called Ara Domitii Ahenobarbi; A. Kuttner, "Some New Grounds for Narrative: The 'Ara Domitii Ahenobarbi' and Other Republican Commemorative Bases," in P. Holliday, ed., *Narrative and Event in Ancient Art* (New York, 1993). Similarly, the triumphator Sulla took Corinthian columns from the Olympeion in Athens for reuse on the great Temple of Jupiter Optimus Maximus on the Capitoline in Rome; Pliny, *Natural History* 36.45.

31 Florus 2.13.88. In the first century C.E., the emperor Claudius modeled his lighthouse at Ostia after the Pharos of Alexandria; Suetonius, *Claudius* 20.3. Hellenistic items displayed in triumphs

influenced Roman aesthetics in many fields, including painting and furniture design; J. J. Pollitt, *The Art of Rome c. 753 B.C.–337 A.D.* (Englewood Cliffs, 1966), 29–53. Conversely, in the high Empire, the architectural and artistic images displayed in triumphs frequently demonstrated Roman cultural superiority, since the victories were over tribal societies in the West; for example, see the images on Trajan's Column.

32 The few projects not directly related to the triumphal route were built outside the Servian Wall, along major roadways into the city; Pietila-Castren, *Magnificentia publica*, 154–58; Coarelli,"Il Campo Marzio occidentale," 807–46.

33 In the triumph of Pompey alone there marched nearly three hundred important prisoners, including kings and other royalty, many of whom were later sent back to their homes; Appian, *Mithridates* 117. In the early Empire, Augustus put on permanent display in the Forum Romanum the impressive list of all triumphators in Rome's history.

34 In particular, the Rostra or speakers' platform in the Forum became a magnet for State triumphal memorials, including individual statues, columns, weapons, and of course *rostra*. The censors of 158 B.C.E. eliminated all statues in the Forum not authorized by decree of the People or Senate of Rome; Pliny, *Natural History* 34.30–31. Earlier, the censor Aemilius Lepidus removed statues from the Capitoline Hill; Livy, *From the Found-*

ing of the City 40.51. The Senate apparently carefully controlled building in the Forum Romanum, since Roman generals did not erect structures there as triumphators, but as censors; Pietila-Castren, *Magnificentia publica*, 155–56.

35 Long, straight streets were rare in ancient Rome, and practically nonexistent inside the Servian Wall. The straight, lengthy edge of the Circus Flaminius was paralleled by the temples of Hercules Musarum (189 B.C.E.), Juno Regina (187 B.C.E.), and Jupiter Stator (148 B.C.E.); Pietila-Castren, *Magnificentia publica*, 154–56.

Both Republican porticoes commemorate victories over Macedonia. That of Gnaeus Octavius celebrated his triumph of 168 B.C.E.; that of Q. Caecilius Metellus honored a triumph of 146 B.C.E., and surrounded the temples of Juno Regina and Jupiter Stator; B. Olinder, *Porticus Octavia in Circo Flaminio* (Stockholm, 1984), 83–124. The Porticus Triumphi may also have been in this area; Makin, "Triumphal Route," 28–29. Two more porticoes were added in the Augustan Age: the Porticus Philippi and the Porticus Octaviae. Due to their location, these structures were adopted for use during subsequent triumphs; Josephus, *Jewish War* 7.

36 A similar view could be had northward, once the Theater of Marcellus was completed in 13/11 B.C.E. In effect, the curving cavea of the two stone theaters framed this straight road.

12

ROME

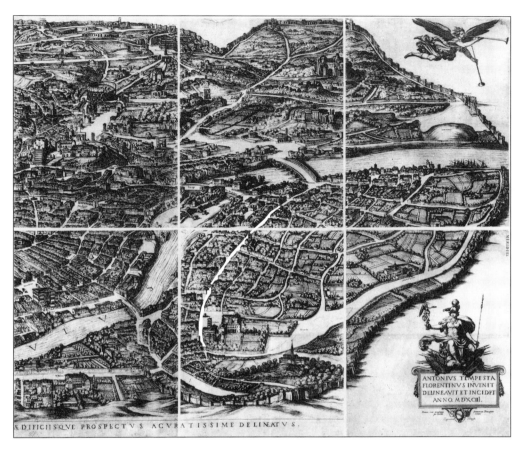

ÆDIFICIISQVE PROSPECTVS ACVRATISSIME DELINATVS.

Via della Lungaretta
The Making of a Medieval Street

DEBORAH ROBBINS

Figure 1. Antonio Tempesta, *View of Rome*, 1593. Detail showing the Tiber River, with Trastevere below it. Via della Lungaretta is marked in white.

The medieval Via della Lungaretta in Rome's Trastevere district is a typical example of urban process (fig. 1).[1] Its development during this period, in which there were few urban controls and no formal city planning, reflects both natural and artificial topography, a limited degree of regulation, a long tradition of local building styles and materials, and the powerful socioeconomic and religious forces that defined the daily life of the city.

Medieval Trastevere clung tightly to the winding bank of the Tiber River, which defined its identity as the city's *other* bank and its economy as the site of medieval Rome's main port.[2] The densest settlement was in a narrow *abitato* be-

tween the river and Via della Lungaretta. More than any other artificial construct, Via della Lungaretta determined the fabric of Rome's other bank, and joined with the Tiber River and the Janiculum hill to define its topography. The origins of the street date back to Rome's earliest centuries; it was the backbone of the Trastevere district from Republican times onward. Until the nineteenth century and the intrusion of Viale Trastevere and the Lungotevere boulevard, running along the riverbank, this street remained the largest and busiest thoroughfare in the area. The homes of the most powerful Trasteverine families stood along Via della Lungaretta; it was the path for important religious processions and connected the economic center of Trastevere, the Ripa Romea port, with the district's northernmost gate and St. Peter's.

Via della Lungaretta began as an imperial highway, the ancient Via Aurelia Vetus. By the early fifteenth century it was called Via Transtiberina.[3] The ancient street followed a straight line from the Ponte Sta. Maria (the ancient Pons Aemilius, whose present remains are called the Ponte Rotto) to the base of the Janiculum hill. It curved only slightly to climb the steep slope up the hill to Porta S. Pancrazio, the ancient Porta Aurelia. The medieval street followed the ancient course with only minor deviations, caused by the encroachment of houses, porticoes, and other medieval constructions. These accretions broke the straight edge of the ancient route, creating a more medieval street outline—slightly curving, with frazzled edges.

Urban transformations such as that of Via della Lungaretta were common in medieval cities of ancient origin. The dissipation of a once-rigorous structure is obvious in Roman colonial cities such as Florence, where the break-up of a *castrum* grid is easily observable. As progenitor rather than product of empire, Rome possessed a more organic urban fabric. The great imperial fora were pockets of disciplined architectural order inserted into tight, organic patterns. Several wide, straight avenues, such as Via Flaminia/Via Lata (now Via del Corso), marched through the otherwise disorderly network. Via della Lungaretta in Trastevere was one of these avenues, still remarkably intact in the Middle Ages because it continued to serve the communication needs of the city, despite its reconfiguration.

As the intraurban extension of Via Aurelia, the pre-Republican highway that connected central Rome to western territories across the Tiber, the ancient Via della Lungaretta established its importance early. Indeed, this street was for centuries the only major construction in the Trastevere basin below the Janiculum hill. The area was originally marshy and low-lying, and thus virtually uninhabited in early Republican times. By the late Republic, the marshy conditions became impossible and a viaduct was constructed for the increasing traffic, perhaps in conjunction with the Pons Aemilius (and possibly an aqueduct) in the middle of the second century B.C.E. Remains of this viaduct were found in the late nineteenth century under Via della Lungaretta and affirm the correspondence of the ancient and the medieval street. Within two centuries, however, the viaduct's function was rendered obsolete by the filling-in of the low-lying areas.[4] Though the extent of this landfill is unknown, it probably occurred during the first two centuries of the Empire, a period of increasing population and economic expansion in Trastevere.

The viaduct became an Imperial roadway, maintaining the straight path from the bridge-head of the Pons Aemilius to the Janiculum hill. The connection between the two banks of Rome by way of the Pons Aemilius became increasingly important; first, in order to continue the great highway, Via Aurelia, into the heart of the city, and then, as Trastevere developed, to link its population and industry with the main bank.

While Trastevere may have been sparsely populated throughout much of the Republican era, by the height of the Empire it was a densely built and lively region, populated largely by workers and artisans, many of whom were of distant origins and unorthodox religions. The Imperial government patronized Trastevere primarily with essential amenities, such as water and police services, while creating there a recreational center for all Romans in a "suburban" zone at the base of the Janiculum hill and on its slopes.[5] Although the region seems to have been considered a part of Rome as early as the second century B.C.E.—when the Aqua Marcia may have entered Trastevere—it remained a semi-suburban edge of the city, even after its inclusion as the fourteenth Augustan municipal region. The peculiar, ambiguous identity of Trastevere as a part of the city and yet an independent community continued well into the medieval period, along with the remnants of its street pattern and a port district on its southern bank.

After the decline of the Empire in the fourth and fifth centuries, a greatly reduced population became concentrated along Rome's river banks. In Trastevere, this settlement was densest near the bridgeheads at the island and the Ponte Sta. Maria, while it extended inland toward the major churches of Sta. Maria in Trastevere, S. Crisogono, and Sta. Cecilia.[6] The gradual transformation of this urban fabric in response to historical events and conditions is typical of the evolutionary character of urban process.

Phases of urban process also include the continuation of previous patterns. The morphology of early-medieval Trastevere was much affected by the remains of the ancient region in its street pattern and its centers of activity. Via della Lungaretta remained the main thoroughfare of the region, though its function as a link to the extramural highway had certainly declined.[7] Its importance in the Middle Ages was due largely to its connection with the most frequently used Roman bridge, Ponte Sta. Maria, linking Trastevere to the other side of the river at one end and to the church of Sta. Maria in Trastevere at the other. The street was also the most significant ceremonial route in early medieval Trastevere.[8] Its importance was further enhanced by its connection with Via dei Vascellari, which led to Rome's port at the Ripa Romea, as well as with Via della Scala, which linked Via della Lungaretta with a pilgrimage route to St. Peter's.[9] As the population and economy expanded, many of Trastevere's wealthiest

Figure 2. Via della Lungaretta, view westward toward Piazza Sta. Maria in Trastevere.

families settled on or near Via della Lungaretta, taking advantage of and contributing to its prestige and grandeur.

The church of Sta. Maria in Trastevere was the most important basilican church in Trastevere and one of the earliest titular churches in Rome. It had been the seat of a cardinal priest since the fourth century and was closely tied to the papacy and the Lateran. It was also a minor pilgrimage stop on the city circuit, as the second oldest Roman church dedicated to the Virgin and as the site of the legendary *fons olei*, the fountain of oil that miraculously foretold the coming of Christ.[10]

The importance of the church was celebrated urbanistically by a spacious piazza before it, and a dramatic approach to it. Although medieval in date, this entrance to the piazza resembled a Baroque stage set in its sequence of features. As one moved west along Via della Lungaretta from Ponte Sta. Maria (fig. 2), a "triumphal" arch came into view, framing the entrance to the piazza. This arch, the Arco dei Cavalieri, was shown in several views before its destruction in 1603 (fig. 3). Although its appearance in Renaissance *vedute* recalls the form of a triumphal arch, it was probably a rather grand version of a common type of medieval arch: a structure built between two buildings to buttress them and create a passageway over a street.[11]

Passing under the Arco dei Cavalieri, one's pathway was suddenly restricted. Continuing along Via della Lungaretta a few meters past the arch, the confined space expanded with the opening of a small piazza to the north (see fig. 3). Beyond this piazza, one's path constricted again into a short tunnel, until suddenly Piazza Sta. Maria opened up dramatically on the diagonal.

The use of diagonal axes and the contrast of constricting and expanding space were typical devices used later in Baroque architecture and urban design. The Baroque scenography of the medieval approach to Sta. Maria in Trastevere may have been accidental, but its drama was well-suited to the site's importance. The Roman or pilgrim traversing this ancient pathway was rewarded by the sight of this church dedicated to the Virgin Mary, its grand mosaic façade dominating the piazza, the largest open space in the Trasteverine *abitato*. The experience would have been particularly heightened on special feast days, when many hundreds, perhaps thousands, proceeded along Via della Lungaretta to the basilica. Thus the religious life of the region was integral to its urban process and form.

While great churches and public piazzas often determined the pathways of medieval streets, the house was the principal generating element of the medieval city. The house of the period was not only a residence, of course; it was also a place of business, commerce, and storage. The traditional medieval house type, with ground-floor shop and family quarters above, was common all over Europe. But the architectural form of the house, its scale, its materials and decoration, and its relationship to the street, varied from country to country, even from city to city. In medieval Rome there was no single dominant house type, but instead many variations, creating great architectural richness in the cityscape.[12]

Within the quarter itself there was little socioeconomic distinction between one area and another, and this was generally true of most medieval cities. There were not the kind of clear social and economic divisions in the physical form of the city that are common in the modern city, since the home and workplace were not usually separate. Rome was nonetheless unique, since it did not have the strong guild organization that often divided other medieval European cities into distinct neighborhoods. The lack of substantial industry and trade in Rome affected its form by attrition, at least in contrast to the situation in such cities as Florence and Ghent.[13]

The only suggestion of class division in the housing stock of Trastevere was on its major thoroughfares, especially on Via della Lungaretta, where many grand houses stood out among the more typical smaller dwellings. Among the great families located there were the Alberteschi, the Mattei, the Anguillara, the Romani, and possibly the Stefaneschi. The Alberteschi and Mattei dominated the eastern end of the street. Renaissance *vedute* and nineteenth-century drawings and photographs depict a tower of the Alberteschi compound that was destroyed during the construction of the Lungotevere in the late nineteenth century (fig. 4). The nineteenth-century

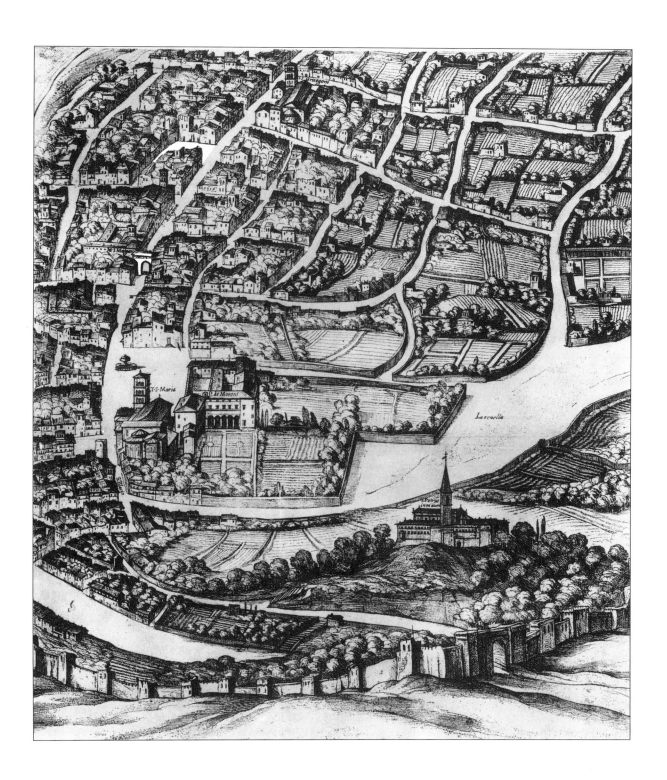

Figure 4. The Tower
of the Alberteschi, in a
photograph of 1864–66.

masonry, punctuated by a corner portico and irregularly placed, exquisitely designed biforate windows. Its piecemeal construction resulted in a surprisingly unified ensemble that is a microcosm of urban process at work.

Further west, Palazzo Anguillara dominates Via della Lungaretta, near the church of S. Crisogono.[15] Most of the existing palace is a restored version of its mid-fifteenth-century condition. A great mass of wall with few openings now faces the street, though a column inserted in one corner is a remnant of an earlier medieval portico. The remains of the portico and a truncated medieval tower suggest an earlier, more complex and open façade.

Just down the street the immense compound of the Romani dominated a central section of Via della Lungaretta, as well as Piazza di Bucio Romani, named for an early patriarch of this wealthy family. The piazza seems to have been generated by the presence of the Romani and their great *accasamenta,* and is an excellent example of the interaction of private and public realms. Documents from the fourteenth century onward indicate a very large extended family in the Piazza di Bucio Romani, which would have required a palace at least as large as any of those described above.[16] The piazza itself can be seen in most Renaissance and Baroque *vedute* and plans, and the Tempesta map of 1593 depicts three towers at the site, which were probably part of the family compound (see fig. 3).

In these examples it is clear that the private dwelling interacted with, and sometimes actually generated, nearby public spaces. The portico was a common feature of both upper- and middle-class homes that effectively linked public and private realms, mediating between the residence and the street. It often provided a place of ritual, where family ceremonies might take place or important documents be

archaeologist Rodolfo Lanciani also recorded a plan of the complex, showing an immense compound that extended across Via della Lungaretta and included four towers and at least two porticoes, elements typical of a Roman nobleman's house.[14]

Just west of the Alberteschi site, much of the nearby Casa Mattei still stands intact, its beautiful biforate windows, a façade and corner portico, and fine medieval brickwork attesting to this family's importance (fig. 5). The Mattei *accasamenta,* or compound, wraps around an irregular interior courtyard, like many of the larger medieval houses. The brickwork and various window designs of the façade reveal several different phases of construction, typical of the accretive building process of such extended family compounds. The mural façade on the Lungaretta side was originally composed of a varied pattern of brick and *tufelli*

Figure 5. Casa Mattei, the south façade from the southwest corner of Piazza in Piscinula.

signed.[17] In many cases the portico was also a place of commerce, with counters and stalls extending out from an interior shop.

Architecturally, the portico is inherently a contrast between void and solid, between the solid of columns and the void of the spaces between them. Similarly, loggias carried this contrast to the upper reaches of houses. Balconies jutting out over the street added to the volumetric variety, as did buttressing arches stretched between buildings. The external staircases of middle- and lower-class houses often pushed out from their façades, and onto the side streets of Trastevere. The looming presence of a nobleman's fortified tower added its own vertical volume to the scene. The effect is powerfully re-created from a distance in a fifteenth-century drawing by the Escurialensis draftsman (fig. 6).

The complexity of the street façade was enriched by the juxtaposition of various build-

ing materials. The combination of brick, *tufelli,* tile, thatch, ancient Roman sculptural spoils and marble, all made for a unique and subtle palette of color and texture that complemented the powerful architectural effect of solid and void.

The heterogeneity of the architecture, and the fluidity between public and private space along Via della Lungaretta created a complex and integrative urban experience. While the location of the church of Sta. Maria may have assured the continued presence of Via della Lungaretta from antiquity on, domestic architecture defined its edges and determined its architectural quality.

Traditionally, the medieval city has been considered an organic formation that developed in response to the exigencies of daily and ceremonial life.[18] Urban process, however, almost always includes some degree of planning and regulation. While there are no medieval regulatory or city-planning records referring specifically to

Figure 6. Trastevere and, in the background at right, the left bank of Rome, seen from the Aventine, 1495. A typical portico is at lower left.

Via della Lungaretta, documents do exist for unnamed Trasteverine streets that suggest how Via della Lungaretta may have been influenced by legal controls.

The state of urban planning and regulation in Rome resembled that of other Italian cities, although the complex and mutable state of Rome's political life led to a much more limited exercise of urban regulation than in such relatively stable and wealthy communes as Florence or Siena. Nonetheless, communal statutes existed from at least the late fourteenth century, and the office of the *magistri aedificorum*, the building magistrates, may have been established as early as the thirteenth century.

The earliest extant statute of the *magistri aedificorum* of 1410 emphasized practical con-cerns—safety and convenience—rather than aesthetics. It focused primarily on the use of public property, but private property was also subject to regulation when it interfered with the public good. There were, for example, laws against the obstruction of free movement along public thoroughfares and established punish-ments for heedless trash and waste disposal that endangered the public environment.[19]

The *magistri aedificorum* were not the the only citizens involved in the control and main-tenance of the city fabric. Both private citizens and the institution of the church supple-mented the activities of that public office. Two documents from the archive of Sta. Maria in Trastevere record the first examples of such private intervention to be noted among the remains of medieval legal documents in Rome, and they refer specifically to streets in Trastevere.

In the first document, of October 1250, the canons of Sta. Maria in Trastevere attest that new construction on properties held by one Giovanni Silvestri will not adversely affect adjacent public thoroughfares.[20] Specifically, the street width will be maintained at "eight palms" and passage to the river will remain unimpeded. Further, any construction between buildings (such as the Arco dei Cavalieri, described above) will be high enough to allow a woman with a bushel on her head to pass safely underneath. Giovanni is to comply under pain of a ten-*libra* fine. Very likely, the church owned one or both properties and had leased them to Giovanni and therefore maintained some control over the lessee's modifications. However, this document is more concerned with the impact of potential construction upon the surrounding urban fabric than with changes to the property itself. In other words, the church's focus is on public property and its maintenance.

The second document is a 1455 lease of land and buildings to the Florentine Cipriano Magnonibus by the canons of Sta. Maria in Trastevere.[21] Again, the church is concerned with maintaining public property in case of future construction on private land. The document states that if the new lessee should undertake any building, or repair the nearby bridge ("ponte rocto," the ancient Pons Aurelius), he is required to maintain a public right of way through the property, a *vicus* running through the property clear or straight ("recta"), as far as a nearby public street ("strata publica").[22] This document, while distinguishing between public and private streets, makes clear that nongovernmental institutions and private parties, such as the church and the leaseholder, consider it their responsibility to maintain the public function of private property, and that they see such property in a larger context (specifically, the relationship of the *vicus* to the *strata publica*).[23] In both documents, the church of Sta. Maria is overseeing its own properties leased to other parties, while assuring the maintenance of public thoroughfares and property. Private property is thus controlled by private parties in the interests of public space.

While neither of these documents refers specifically to Via della Lungaretta, so far as we know, they both indicate the kind of regulation that no doubt affected it. We have noted already the construction of one archway over the street; very likely there were others. Presumably, their relationship to the street was determined either indirectly, by the existence of the statute's regulations, or directly, by controls similar to those we have seen exercised by the church of Sta. Maria. In addition, other constructions along Via della Lungaretta—towers, porticoes, shop counters, external staircases—may well have been regulated to maintain this important public thoroughfare.[24]

While government regulation did not dominate medieval urban development, it played a significant and generally underestimated role. Florence and Siena may have had more carefully articulated urban environments, but less developed medieval governments, such as Rome's, nonetheless directly and indirectly influenced their urban morphologies. The formation of the medieval Via della Lungaretta comprised a complex urban process, affected by very limited urban regulation.[25] While urban planning may have played a more important role in other periods or places, in Rome it has always been one element in a much larger scenario. It is important to recognize that a fully developed urban process neither excludes the metabolic behavior of private building, nor the intention of legal procedures. ■

Notes

1 Spiro Kostof refers to "urban process" in his un-published Columbia University Mathews Lectures of 1976, "The Seat of Peter: The Medievalizing of Rome." The term describes a gradual definition of urban fabric through a variety of socioeconomic, political, and other factors, including city planning or regulation. Sir John Summerson uses the term "process" in a paper published in 1963, though he never refers specifically to urban process. J. Summerson, "Urban Forms," *The Historian and the City* (Cambridge, 1963), 165–76. The geographer James Vance uses the term "urban morphogenesis" to describe the phenomenon of urban process, and Wolfgang Braunfels describes it as "urban development." J. Vance, *This Scene of Man* (New York, 1977), vii; W. Braunfels, *Urban Design in Western Europe: Regime and Architecture, 900–1900* (Chicago, 1988), 6.

2 Since antiquity there had been a major port district in Rome on the Tiber's southern banks. It served as the arrival point and repository for most goods ferried upstream from the seaport at Porto, at the mouth of the river. During the Empire, an extensive port facility was constructed at the Marmorata, on the left bank, with a smaller warehouse district and loading banks on the Trastevere side. By the ninth century, the main intramural port may have crossed the river to the Trasteverine site later called the Ripa Romea. R. Krautheimer, *Rome: Profile of a City, 312–1308* (Princeton, 1980), 239. A lease document of 1074 refers conclusively to the Ripa Romea in Trastevere. D. Robbins, "A Case Study of Medieval Urban Process: Rome's Trastevere (1250–1450)," Ph.D. diss., University of California, Berkeley, 1989, 169. For a detailed study of Rome's medieval port, see ibid., 150–95.

3 The name Via Transtiberina first appears in the Liber Pontificalis in 1404–6. L. Duchesne, *Le Liber Pontificalis*, vol. II (Paris, 1903), 552. Most likely, the street had been called that for some time before this reference, since street names were rarely given in written documents in the Middle Ages. It will be referred to here as Via della Lungaretta.

4 Archaeologists have suggested that the Pons Aemilius and the viaduct over Via Aurelia Vetus may have carried the Aqua Marcia (and perhaps the Aqua Claudia) into Trastevere. G. Gatti, "Il Viadotto della Via Aurelia nel Trastevere," *Bullettino della Commissione Archeologica Comunale di Roma* 1–3 (1940): 129–41.

Remains of the elevated roadway were found in 1889, 3.5 meters under the modern Via della Lungaretta, near an Imperial police and fire station and the medieval church of S. Crisogono. The viaduct arcade and the ancient building façades flanking it to the south correspond to the path and approximate width of Via della Lungaretta. The original length of the viaduct is unknown, since only seventy meters of it have been uncovered. Gatti, "Il Viadotto," 129–41.

5 The recreational zone included extensive gardens and a *naumachia* for mock naval battles.

6 Rome's population plummeted from one million at the height of the Empire to perhaps only a few hundred during the most violent period of the Gothic wars. P. Llewellyn, *Rome in the Dark Ages* (London, 1971), 3. On the left bank the population expanded inland to areas served by the remaining aqueducts, including the southern Campus Martius and the areas around the Palatine and Celian hills and the Lateran. Trastevere had never been well-served by the Imperial aqueduct system, and had relied more heavily on local sources, such as wells. The polluted river water was rarely drunk, but it provided water and power for washing, milling grain, and other semi-industrial needs. The proximity of the river meant that whatever safe water there was to drink, from aqueducts and wells, would not be wasted on other needs.

The Pons Aemilius first appears as the Ponte Sta. Maria in a papal document of 1018 or 1019, confirming the territory of the bishop of Porto, in which it is mentioned as a topographical landmark. It was named for a small chapel on the bridge dedicated to the Virgin. It was also called the Ponte dei Senatori (Pons Senatorum), as in the Mirabilia guidebooks of the mid-twelfth century. The early-medieval Einsiedeln itinerary called it the Pons Maior (Ponte Maggiore) in the mid-eighth century, indicating the importance of this crossing. C. D'Onofrio, *Il Tevere* (Rome, 1980), 142–44; and E. Amadei, *I Ponti di Roma* (Rome, 1948), 13–14.

7 According to Peter Partner, the highway of Via Aure-

lia from Rome to Civitavecchia was "definitely in decline" at the end of the fourteenth century, indicating a long period of disuse. P. Partner, *The Lands of St. Peter* (Berkeley, 1972), 423.

8 In addition to its connection with the bridge of Sta. Maria, the medieval Via della Lungaretta was also linked to the island bridges by a short street with ancient origins.

9 Via dei Vascellari and Via della Scala are the modern street names. The latter was called Via Sancta in the late Middle Ages and Renaissance; the medieval name of the former is unknown.

10 In 1230 and in a second appointment between 1244 and 1251, the cardinal priest of Sta. Maria in Trastevere, Stefano de Comitibus, became the papal vicar, representative of the pope in city affairs and in the administration of the local church, confirming the importance of the titular seat. Stefano was one of only six titular cardinals appointed as papal vicar through the year 1500 (in 1350 the cardinal priests of S. Crisogono and Sta. Cecilia, both Trasteverine basilicas, were also appointed papal vicars). The majority of papal vicars were bishops. P. Crostarosa, *Dei Titoli della chiesa romana* (Rome, 1893), 7–22, 73–85.

For the most thorough study of Sta. Maria in Trastevere, see D. Kinney, "S. Maria in Trastevere from its Founding to 1215," Ph.D. diss., New York University, 1975.

11 Usually, such an arch was built between two houses owned or held by one party or family. This arch was named after the Cavalieri, the Trasteverine family that had once owned it. The arch was sold, along with some houses in the area, to the church of Sta. Margherita in 1564. L. Gigli, *Rione XIII: Trastevere,* vol. 2 (Rome, 1980), 150.

The arch is seen in many other views, including the Mario Cartaro map of 1576, the Du Pérac-Lafréry view of 1577, a view of 1523–24 edited by Francesco di Paolo, and the 1593 version of Antonio Tempesta's *veduta* (it seems to have been erased or torn off the page in the 1606 version).

The Arco di S. Callisto, which still stands nearby, on Via di Arco di S. Callisto, is an extant example of this type of construction; many nineteenth-century

photographs showed the last of these arch structures across the river, especially in the Ghetto district.

12 The most thorough discussion of the medieval Roman house is H. Broise and J.-C. Maire-Vigueur, "Strutture familiari, spazio domestico, e architettura civile a Roma alla fine del Medio Evo," *Storia dell'arte italiana,* pt. 3, *Momenti di architettura* (Turin, 1983), 99–160. See also D. Wilde, "Housing and Urban Development in Sixteenth Century Rome: The Properties of the Arciconfraternità della SS.ma Annunziata," Ph.D. diss., New York University, 1989, which includes a discussion of medieval houses still extant in the sixteenth century.

13 The Trastevere district has long been associated with the proletariat of Rome. While this may have been true in recent centuries, all evidence suggests that it was not the case during the Middle Ages, when there were few social and economic distinctions between the two banks of Rome. The housing stock of medieval Trastevere was not notably different from that of the rest of Rome. For a discussion of this theory of socioeconomic and architectural parity, see Robbins, "Trastevere," 258–358. For Florence, see G. Fanelli, *Firenze: Architettura e città,* 2 vols. (Florence, 1973); for Ghent, see D. Nicholas, The *Metamorphosis of a Medieval City: Ghent in the Age of the Arteveldes, 1302–1390* (Lincoln, 1987).

14 Lanciani's plan of the Alberteschi compound is in his notebooks (*schede*) in the Archive of the Vatican Library (Vat. Lat. 13044), and is reproduced in Robbins, "Trastevere," 586.

15 Throughout the medieval period the Anguillara family was one of the wealthiest and most powerful landowners in the Roman *campagna*. See L. de Gregori, "La Torre Anguillara e la casa di Dante," *Bollettino del Reale Istituto di Archeologia e Storia dell'Arte* 2 (1928): 11–116; and V. Sora, "Conti di Anguillara dalla loro origine al 1465," *Archivio della Società Romana di Storia Patria* 29 (1906): 397–442, and 30 (1907): 53–118.

16 Robbins, "Trastevere," 318–23.

17 Broise and Maire-Vigueur, "Strutture familiari," 152–53; and R. Brentano, *Rome before Avignon* (New York, 1974), 33.

18 The nineteenth-century theorist Camillo Sitte idealized the urban form of the generic medieval city, as if its aesthetic coherence and charm had sprung from the unconscious minds of medieval city dwellers and rulers. It is true that the early-medieval city developed with little organizing activity on the part of its inhabitants, and that this city form provided the foundation for the development of many great cities of the late Middle Ages. But it has become increasingly clear in the last few decades that medieval city governments were greatly interested in the form and symbolic value of their city, and that in many cases they consciously sought to control that form and its subsequent meanings. This line of research has as yet received relatively little attention. The focus is largely on the Italian and especially the Tuscan situation—certainly the most advanced, as described so well by Wolfgang Braunfels in *Mittelalterische Stadtbaukunst in der Toskana* (Berlin, 1952).

19 The *magistri* were in charge of the maintenance of the city's buildings, houses, thoroughfares and highways, fountains, bridges, and the riverbank. For a detailed discussion of the 1410 statute, including the possibility of a much earlier version, see E. Re, *Statuti della città di Roma* (Rome, 1880–83); and L. Schiaparelli, "Alcuni documenti dei 'magistri aedificorum urbis' (secolo XIII e XIV)," *Archivio della Società Romana di Storia Patria* 50 (1927): 239–308.

20 This is precisely the type of potentially dangerous construction that could impede public traffic, expressly forbidden by chapter 21 of the 1410 statute of the *magistri aedificorum*. For a partial transcription and translation of the 1250 document, see Robbins, "Trastevere," 414–15. An earlier and more complete transcription is Vat. Lat. 8051.I, fol. 41, in the Vatican Library Archive. The original document no longer exists.

21 See Robbins, "Trastevere," 455–57. An earlier transcription of the document is Vat. Lat. 8051.II, fols. 33–38, in the Vatican Library Archive. The original document is in the Archives of Sta. Maria in Trastevere at the Vicariato at the Lateran, box 532, perg. 73.

22 A *vicus* was a small-scale neighborhood street, or even an alley.

23 The church, of course, was not strictly speaking a private institution. Still, this is the first suggestion that legal bodies—private or public—other than the *magistri aedificorum* as an arm of the Roman commune, affected the physical welfare of the city. Notably, in both cases the regulation of private property follows the example set by the statute of the *magistri*. Obstructions of private and public thoroughfares are the main concern of each document, and follow the intent of the statute's twenty-first chapter. The second document was recorded after the first statute was implemented in 1410—and even after the expanded version of 1452—while the earlier document of 1250 predates the statute but not the office of the *magistri aedificorum*. Unless an original statute appeared earlier than anyone has determined thus far, the regulation of the urban fabric was already a concern of the Roman community long before legal codes were created or enforced. The office of the *magistri* and perhaps its predecessor, the city prefect, affected indirectly the regulation of the cityscape from early on in Rome's medieval history. And the concept of public property as distinct from private appears as early in Rome as in any other Italian city of the period.

24 Via della Lungaretta remained unpaved in the medieval period, as did major streets throughout the city. Street paving began in Rome around the middle of the fifteenth century. In the statute of 1452 a new ordinance appears regarding the paving of streets. This was to be the responsibility of the *maestri di strada,* but was to be paid for by the homeowners along each street. Re, *Statuti*, 96–97. As late as 1588 Via della Lungaretta was being paved, along with several other Trasteverine streets, presumably for the first time since antiquity. F. Cerasoli, "Notizie circa la sistemazione di molte strade di Roma nel secolo XVI," *Bullettino della Commissione Archeologica Comunale di Roma* 28 (1900): 342–43, 361–62.

25 Italo Insolera offers an unusual but unconvincing argument for the Renaissance reconstruction of Via della Lungaretta. I. Insolera, *Roma: Imagini e realtà dal X al XX secolo* (Bari, 1981), 55–60. For an analysis and critique of his hypothesis, see Robbins, "Trastevere," 89–93.

13

ROME

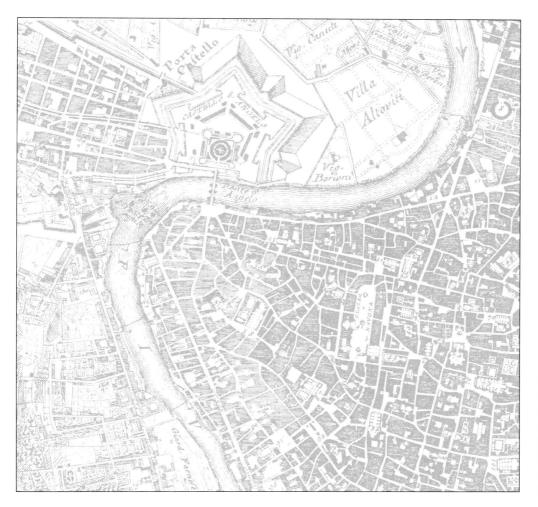

Figure 1. Detail from Gian Battista Nolli's 1748 map of Rome, showing Piazza di Ponte and radiating from it the streets of Via Paola (left), Via de' Banchi (center), and Via di Panico (right), marked in black.

Piazzi di Ponte and the Military Origins of Panopticism

RICHARD INGERSOLL

Piazza di Ponte, which disappeared with the construction of the Lungotevere river embankments in the 1880s, was the center point for a system of radiating streets in the heart of Renaissance Rome (fig. 1). The axis of the ancient bridge of Castel Sant'Angelo and the course of the existing road along the river were intersected by a trident of new streets that reached their architectural completion during the reign of Pope Paul III Farnese (1534–49). The bridge, which served as a hinge between the papal enclave of the Vatican Borgo and the vital commercial areas of the *abitato*, was a significant site in the ceremonial life and mythos of Rome. It marked the passage from secular to sacred space for official visitors, pilgrims, and papal processions. The sixteenth-century improvements to the piazza at the bridgehead accommodated a variety of rituals, but in particular became the scenic backdrop for the papal theater of terror as the site of frequent public executions.

The geometric purity of the trident at Piazza di Ponte and the resulting star-shaped pattern have a formal architectural power that antici-

Figure 2. View of Castel
Sant'Angelo.

The Panopticon was a radially planned car-
cerial building with all the cells visible from the
central core; the architecture allowed the person representing authority in the center to be
all-seeing, or "panoptic." For Michel Foucault
this liberal punative technology became a con-
ceit for modern power relations. Rather than
exercise direct control over the body in the
form of a public execution, the agents of power
could use architecture to establish psychological control over prisoners, and thus appear to
be more humane.[1] The eventual uses of Piazza
di Ponte combined the pre-Enlightenment
mandate to demonstrate control over the body
of the wrongdoer with the more psychological
aspects of panopticism.

The bridge and the piazza are physically
dominated by the impressive bulk of Castel
Sant'Angelo across the river (fig. 2). Originally
built as the tumulus mausoleum for Emperor
Hadrian in the second century, Castel Sant'Angelo was over the centuries transformed into
an impenetrable fortress. The bridge, known in
antiquity as Pons Aelius, was constructed as
part of the mausoleum complex and has survived, with many restorations and additions,
to the present. Castel Sant'Angelo became the
key to Roman defense, as well as a major icon
of papal power and a frequent papal residence.
Placed at the apex of the castle, the sculpture of
the Archangel Michael gave the building its
post-classical name and stood as a reminder of
the alleged power of popes to summon divine
intervention on behalf of the city. According
to legend, in 590 the angel appeared to Pope
Gregory the Great on the roof of the mausoleum, after he had led a series of processions
calling for the end of a devastating plague. The
angel returned his sword to its sheath to signal
the end of the crisis.[2] This same statue was
inadvertently an excellent lightning rod, and
was destroyed and replaced many times. The

pated the more celebrated trident at the gate of
Piazza del Popolo, planned during the first two
decades of the sixteenth century and built some
time later. Renaissance artistic principles of
symmetry, axiality, and uniformity are often cited
to explain its design. But while art undoubtedly
had much to do with the formal results, it was
more than likely the art of war that was its chief
inspiration. Considering the time of trident's
final design, ten years after the Sack of Rome of
1527–28, and the provenance of its design—from
Antonio da Sangallo the Younger, the architect
responsible for the city's defenses—one may sup-
pose that more than just formal issues were involved in it. The radiating pattern of Piazza di
Ponte is probably the first built realization of the
theory of military city planning advocated by
Sangallo. In successive years the piazza was adapted
for the rituals of public punishment: the views
from five different perspectives provided a relentless view of the hangman's scaffold. A message
of control was thus transmitted through the city
fabric in a way quite similar to that envisioned for
the Panopticon invented by Jeremy Bentham in
the late eighteenth century.

most significant restorations of the statue in the context of the construction of Piazza di Ponte occurred under Nicholas V in the 1450s and Paul III in 1534.[3]

The redesign of the bridge district was contemporary with alterations made to Castel Sant'Angelo. Nicholas V, early in his papacy, ordered the construction of a set of square gate towers on the bridge and the three round bastions on the outer walls of the castle. After the bridge collapsed in 1450, and over two hundred pilgrims lost their lives, he began planning the enlargement of Piazza di Ponte. As an expiatory gesture, he sponsored the addition of twin octagonal votive chapels, seen in the Hartmann Schedel view of 1493 (fig. 3), and ordered the clearing of various jerry-rigged wooden structures from the bridge. With the local landowners, he initiated a process of eminent domain, which eventually came to be known in the city's planning legislation as the *gettito*. Buildings could now be condemned for the purpose of widening the piazza, and property owners were either taxed or credited according to an assessment of their frontage.[4]

The next significant alteration to the bridge and its area occurred under Alexander VI Borgia, who by 1495 had refortified Castel Sant'Angelo and replaced the square bridgetowers with a round gun tower, set back from the structure of the bridge and placed slightly off axis. A new, classically inspired gate to the Borgo was built as the terminus of the future Via Alessandrina, built for the Jubilee of 1500. Other new features included polygonal additions to the outer bastions, a restoration of the *passetto*, the escape route between the Vatican Palace and the castle that ran along the top of the Leonine walls, and new additions and decorations to the apartments in the upper part of the fortress. According to the diaries of Johannes Burchardus, papal master of ceremonies, in the year 1500 part of

Piazza di Ponte was widened and the embankment restored.[5]

In 1500 Alexander VI initiated the first *sventramenti* (disembowelments) of post-antique Rome, with the demolitions for the new straight street of Via Alessandrina (later known as the Borgo Nuovo and replaced in the late 1930s by Via della Conciliazione), which ran axially from the new gate of the castle to the portal of the Vatican Palace. Large-scale demolitions on the other side of the river, which were much more politically sensitive, began in 1508 with Julius II, whose projects included the new straight street of Via Giulia and the widening of Via de' Banchi, the street on axis with the bridge. For the latter renewal, the church of San Celso, which had an open portico that faced Piazza di Ponte, was demolished and replanned with a new orientation to Via de' Banchi. Other buildings on the north side of this street were also

Figure 3. Hartmann Schedel, view of the Vatican Borgo and Ponte Sant'Angelo, from the *Liber Chronicarum* [*Nuremberg Chronicle*], 1493.

Figure 4. Axial view on
Via Paola to San
Giovanni dei Fiorentini.

strongest influence of all the foreign communities on the financial and cultural affairs of the city. The presence of over thirty banks, or *banchi*, in the area, gave it its name. At the time of the construction of Via Giulia, the Florentines were granted permission to construct their national church, but plans for San Giovanni dei Fiorentini did not surface until the next decade, under the papacy of a Florentine, Leo X Medici. Though the construction of the church dragged on for over a century, and the façade was not in place until 1734, San Giovanni dei Fiorentini was from its inception an important urban goal and symbol of Florentine presence.[7] Via Paola, one of the three axes of the Ponte trident, uses it as a focal terminus (fig. 4).

Among the Florentine residents of the Banchi district was the architect Antonio da Sangallo the Younger, who had a prominent role in the design of the area. His career as an urbanist began in 1516 under Leo X, assisting Raphael with the planning of Via Leonina, one of the trident prongs leading from Piazza del Popolo. In 1520 he succeeded Jacopo Sansovino as architect of San Giovanni dei Fiorentini, and later, in 1535–42, he built his own palace next to the church. Sangallo was thus committed to this area as a Florentine, a designer, and a property owner.[8]

Before the addition of the new streets to Piazza di Ponte, the connections to Via Giulia were narrow capillary *vicoli*, as narrow as 2.5 meters wide. Günther has clarified in his study of the *gettito* tax records and in the related drawing by Sangallo from the Uffizi that in 1524 the planning of this area included Sangallo's concave triumphal façade for the Zecca, the widening of Via del Consolato, which connected the Zecca axially to San Giovanni dei Fiorentini, and the trace of a new straight street between the bridge and the church—

torn down. At the terminus of Via de' Banchi, Julius placed the papal mint, or Zecca. These changes have been charted in detail in Hubertus Günther's maps reconstructing this area of Piazza di Ponte before and after the time of Paul III's interventions.[6]

A significant factor in the development of the district around the bridge was its distinctive ethnic composition. At the end of the fifteenth century it was inhabited predominantly by Florentines, who on the whole did not have rights as citizens of Rome, but who exerted the

anticipating Via Paola. As the drawing can safely be attributed to Sangallo, so can the idea of this triangular street pattern.[9] Construction of the hypotenuse, however, was not implemented, due to the increasing bad fortune of the city, which culminated in the Sack of Rome in 1527. It goes without saying that the destruction, deaths, impoverishments, plagues, famines, and humiliations caused by the renegade imperial troops had a profound effect on the moral and cultural life of the city, and, naturally, on the future of urbanism. The ill-fated Clement VII Medici was unable to effect further urban changes during his pontificate, but one of his last acts of patronage in 1534 was to replace the damaged votive chapels at the mouth of the bridge, which had served to shelter attackers during the Sack, with two statues of Saints Peter and Paul. The significance of these will be discussed presently.

Clement's successor, Paul III Farnese, had accompanied him as a hostage in Castel Sant'Angelo for seven months during the Sack. Among his first acts as pope was the commissioning of a new angel to place atop the castle and the convocation of a group of military experts and architects to discuss the problem of the city's defenses. This group included generals, such as Giulio Orsini and Sforza Pallavicino; famous architects, such as Michelangelo and Sangallo; lesser architects, such as Jacopo Meleghino and Francesco Laparelli (both of whom later built parts of the Borgo defenses); and several younger architects, who became the first specialists in military architecture. From this latter group, Galasso Alghisi, Giacomo Castriotto, and Francesco de' Marchi produced illustrated treatises. Horst de la Croix has shown that these Roman meetings were the seminal moment of a new military and urbanistic theory that favored radial planning. Both Castriotto and de' Marchi composed treatises in the 1540s (published at

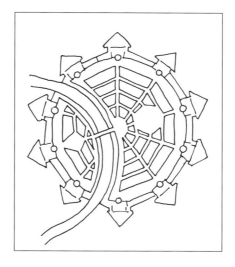

Figure 5. Francesco de' Marchi, plan for a radial river city. From his treatise *Della architettura militare*, drawn in the 1540s, but published in 1590. The plan is close to Antonio da Sangallo's reworking of Piazza di Ponte. De' Marchi mentions Sangallo as the great proponent of radial planning.

later dates) in which they paid homage to Sangallo as the leading theorist (fig. 5). De la Croix notes that none of the treatise writers claim authorship of the radial plan, but rather treat it as an *a priori* motif, conceivably passed on from Francesco di Giorgio to Baldassare Peruzzi and Sangallo—both of whom made drawings for radially planned compounds. We may assume, then, that Sangallo was a major proponent of the radial scheme.[10]

Sangallo, who was charged with the design of the new defenses after the 1534 meetings, produced two of the most technologically advanced bastions of his time for the southern flank of the city, at the Ardeatine and Aventine positions. The strategy of the period was to shrink the circumference of city walls to almost half that of the Aurelian walls.[11] In 1542, however, many of the same experts were reconvened, as the cost of the first two bastions proved prohibitively expensive, at forty-four thousand ducats, and a new, more economical plan was needed.[12] The revised strategy concentrated defenses at Castel Sant'Angelo. The Borgo was to be refortified with modern bastions, and the northern flank of the *abitato*

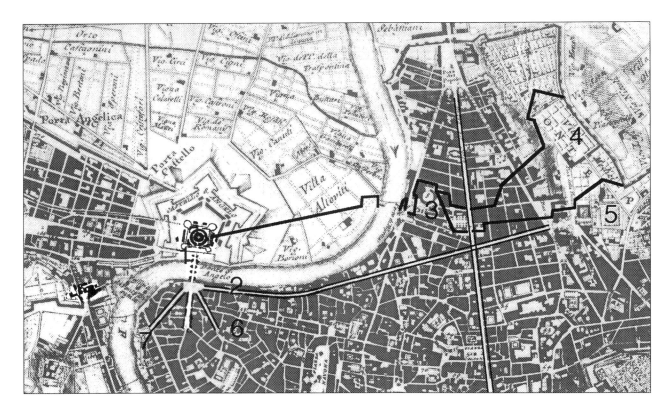

Figure 6. Heavy lines indicate the fortifications proposed by Antonio da Sangallo the Younger in 1542. Thinner lines show streets built during the reign of Paul III. 1, Castel Sant'Angelo; 2, Tor di Nona; 3, Mausoleum of Augustus; 4, Villa Ricci (now Medici); 5, Trinità de' Monti; 6, Monte Giordano; 7, San Giovanni dei Fiorentini.

was to be tightened by drawing the walls in to the erstwhile Port of Ripetta, making a bastionated fortress out of the nearby Mausoleum of Augustus. In addition, a new fortress was to be positioned on the Pincio hill, at the site of the present Villa Medici. This plan can be reconstructed from a Sangallo drawing in the Uffizi.[13] If one were to overlay the major new streets built during this period—Via Paola, Via di Panico, and Via Trinitatis (now Condotti)—on this plan for the fortifications, it is clear that a radial arrangement had been installed that allowed for direct paths leading from the fortress to the battle stations (fig. 6).

One further point that hints at the military intentions of the interventions at Piazza di Ponte was the excessive cost of the project. No

record of the cost of Via Paola, finished in 1543—the same year Sangallo began the bastions at Porta Santo Spirito in the Borgo—exists, but the extent of the twenty-nine demolitions is comparable to those of its sibling axis of Via di Panico. Via di Panico was begun in 1546, required thirty-nine demolitions, and cost 7,012 ducats—the greatest single expenditure in the *gettito* records.[14] Since there was no overwhelming dynastic reason for the new streets, as there had been for Via dei Baullari, an axis leading to Palazzo Farnese, it is tempting to assume that such a large expense was required for the other major urban consideration of the Farnese regime: defense. In 1544 work was begun to clear the path for Via Trinitatis, a third new axial street that fed into the river road at Tor di Nona. There are no records of its costs.

The straight axis pushed through the less developed part of the Campus Martius to the French convent at Trinità dei Monti and extended the fourth prong of the star.[15]

To claim that military considerations were the only intention governing the plan of these new straight streets would deny the multivalency of cultural decisions in sixteenth-century Rome; it would be equally erroneous, however, to ignore the connection of this radial system to military needs. Its proximity to the fortress, its authorship by the city's military architect, and the coincidence of its timing with major defense projects are all evidence in this direction.

As elements of urban design, these new axes conformed to the code of *ornatum*, or city beautification. They also fulfilled encomiastic functions by providing axes to monumental terminus points. That Via Paola points to San Giovanni dei Fiorentini is a clear legacy of a Medici pope's favoritism to Florentines. That Via di Panico points to the Orsini compound of Monte Giordano also makes sense in terms of Farnese politics, since both Paul III's sister and his son had married into the Orsini family, while in 1542 the papacy began a war against the Colonna family, the traditional enemies of the Orsini.[16] Much of the Monte Giordano compound was occupied by Cardinal Ippolito d'Este of Ferrara (on Bufalini's 1551 map, the site is labeled "PR C. Feraria"), son of Lucrezia Borgia and chief representative of French interests. Paul III's debt to the Borgia (Alexander VI had made him a cardinal) and his favoring of the French over the Spanish could thus be demonstrated.

Beyond these possible symbolic meanings, the space of Piazza di Ponte acquired new meaning as the setting for major urban rituals. It was initially one of the few legal marketplaces of the city. In 1450 the bridge was used by the visiting Holy Roman Emperor as a stage for knighting the young nobles of the city. By the early sixteenth century every documented official entry of regal guests, cardinals, and foreign ambassadors passed by this space to witness a characteristic display of fireworks and bombards, launched from the castle's parapets. The carnival parades also habitually passed here, and until 1566 the six yearly Carnival races used the bridge as the halfway mark on the route from Campo de' Fiori to the Piazza S. Pietro.

The foremost ritual, however, and the one that most characterized the space by the end of the 1500s, was that of public executions. During the first half of the sixteenth century, following the traditions of the previous century, Roman executions were carried out in a variety of places. The major courts and prisons at the Campidoglio and the Curia Savella (near Palazzo Farnese) served as sites. The largest prison, the Tor di Nona, located fifty meters upstream from the bridge, was also used, as was the public square of Campo de' Fiori. Knowledge of the location and frequency of executions from 1499 onward can be fairly accurately tallied from the scrupulously kept records of all executed prisoners compiled by the Florentine brotherhood of San Giovanni Decollato.[17] Their ledgers catalogue the number of yearly executions, the site, the name of each prisoner, and usually the method of execution. During the first half of the sixteenth century, Piazza di Ponte and Tor di Nona, while being the most frequent sites for executions, hosted only about one-third of their total. During the second half of the same century over 75 percent of the executions took place on or near the bridge, while only a tiny fraction occurred at the Campidoglio (in fifty years, a total of four);[18] this change clearly demonstrated the transfer of authority away from communal institutions to papal substitutes.

The inscriptions on the two statues placed

on the bridgehead in 1534 appear to be the first formal acknowledgment of the execution ritual. Under Peter, who is standing closest to the Vatican, reads: HINC HUMILIBUS VENIA (here the humble shall be pardoned); under Paul, who holds the sword of justice: HINC RETRIBU-TIO SUPERBIA (here the proud shall be punished).[19] Paul is standing closest to the prison of Tor di Nona, and directly to his left on the embankment is a small walled area called the *conforteria*, a partially screened area used for some of the executions (fig. 7). The more dreadful crimes were punished directly on the bridge and the remains, such as severed heads or dangling corpses, were left exposed for several days. The *conforteria* and a small chapel to its side were probably built between 1551 and 1565, since they do not appear in Bufalini's map but do in Du Pérac's views. They were most likely designed and funded by the confraternity of San Giovanni Decollato, but the evidence has not yet emerged.

This confraternity was dedicated to accompanying prisoners in their last hour, assisting them to prepare their souls, leading them in procession to the scaffold, and afterward burying them. Its members included some of the richest Florentine bankers, including Bindo Altoviti, whose palace facing the Piazza di Ponte had a corner lopped off to accommodate Via Paola. The confraternity also included some of the most prestigious artists, such as Michelangelo, although he appears not to have participated after 1514. Among the most active members in the 1530s and 1540s was Bastiano da Sangallo, brother and a frequent collaborator of Antonio.[20] In 1540 Paul III awarded the confraternity the special privilege (shared only by the confraternity of the Gonfalone) of freeing a prisoner of their choice on their annual feast day. It is for these reasons that one may suspect the confraternity's complicity

in planning the area and, by inversion, the connection of the plan to the interests of papal justice.

The brothers of San Giovanni Decollato became an essential component in the ritual of execution—their actions both moralized and sanitized the events. As Michel de Montaigne reports in 1581:

There are two of these brothers, or monks, dressed and masked the same way, who attend the criminal on the cart and preach to him; and one of them continually holds before his face a picture on which is the portrait of Our Lord, and has him kiss it incessantly; this makes it impossible to see the criminal's face until he is launched.[21]

In her study of the confraternity, Jean Weisz explains that thirty brothers were obliged to be available as the *trenta della sera*, to go in procession to the prison cell, take the prisoner in procession to the gallows, and later take the body in procession to be buried. The wooden panels mentioned by Montaigne were painted on both sides to communicate the redeeming message to criminal and crowd alike.[22] The bodies were left on display until nightfall, and sometimes for longer periods, as a visible example of justice in action. The papal government thus manifested its control of the bodies of miscreants.

Through their ceremonial participation, the brothers were agents of a cover-up; their good deeds glossed over the advance of an increasingly tyrannical and unaccountable course of justice. The number of executed prisoners in Rome far exceeded that of other major cities: during the years 1499 to 1549, there was a median of seventeen executions per year. Executions in Florence and Venice, which both had larger populations, rarely

(opposite) Figure 7. Detail from Antonio Tempesta, *View of Rome*, 1593. The statues of Saints Peter and Paul at Ponte Sant'Angelo, the *cortiletto* for displaying prisoners, and the prison of Tor di Nona are highlighted. Castel Sant'Angelo is at far left.

exceeded four or five.[23] From 1550 to 1600 the number of capital punishments rose dramatically—there were rarely fewer than twenty per year and usually between thirty-five and fifty. The first two years of Sixtus V's reign brought papal justice to the verge of genocide, with ninety-nine executions in 1585 and eighty-seven in 1586 (of these, seventy-five were executed at Piazza di Ponte the first year and seventy-three the next). The population at this time numbered about one hundred thousand, which suggests that one in every thousand was dispatched to the gallows. To blame this escalation of justice on the Counter-Reformation's persecution of heretics does not correspond to the data, as there was no significant increase in executions by fire, the conventional form for executing heretics. Instead we should consider the social situation in the city at this time. Rome was undergoing what in modern terms would be called a welfare crisis, with an uncontrollable growth in the population of poor and vagrants. Vincenzo Paglia has estimated from prison, hospice, and census data that there was evidence of at least 10 percent destitution—a figure that is well beyond the modern crisis point—and most of the crime at the time can be linked to this factor.[24]

The ever-increasing numbers of executions in sixteenth-century Rome had a minor role in the planning of Piazza di Ponte, but subsequently furnished the area's predominant characteristic. The convergence of so many sight lines served the repressive goal of papal justice to produce what one contemporary called this "*horrendo spettacolo*."[25] The source of the radial street pattern, attributable to the military agenda of Rome after the Sack, calls to mind what was clear to leading Renaissance intellectuals such as Alberti and Machiavelli, and probably seems even clearer from modern experience: military expenditure is usually a two-edged sword, and what is promoted as defense against the external may just as easily serve to control within. De' Marchi, in his treatise, specifically underlines the effect of fortifications: "Like the bridle in the mouth of wild horses . . . fortresses are dangerous to build in cities or places used to living free."[26] The eyes of Rome were funneled toward the executions at Piazzi di Ponte, but as with the Panopticon, the central eye of authority was looking back in all directions. It is in this way that the accommodation to a form supplied by military theory can be seen as the beginning of panopticism, promising a new technology of social control. ∎

Notes

1 M. Foucault, *Surveillir et Punir* (Paris, 1975); published in English as *Discipline and Punish* (New York, 1977). R. Evans, in *The Fabrication of Virtue: English Prison Architecture, 1750–1840* (Cambridge, 1982), 195–236, explains Jeremy Bentham's *Panopticon*, 1791.

2 C. d'Onofrio, *Castel Sant'Angelo e borgo, tra Roma e papato* (Rome, 1978), 148–72.

3 A. Ceen, "The Quartiere de' Banchi," Ph.D diss., University of Pennsylvania, 1977.

4 C. Burroughs, "Below the Angel: An Urbanistic Project in the Rome of Nicholas V," *Journal of the Warburg and Courtauld Institutes* 45 (1982): 94–124; E. Re, "Maestri di Strada," *Archivio della Società Romana di Storia Patria* 43 (1920): 5–105, is the definitive source on *gettito* laws.

5 D'Onofrio, *Castel Sant'Angelo*, 258–59, dates the Borgia additions between the 1492 inscription on the *passetto* and the 1495 inscription on the castle itself; L. von Pastor, *The History of the Popes*, ed. and trans. F. I. Antrobus, 5th ed. (St. Louis, 1950), 168–70, dates the castle works 1495–97. J. Burchardus, *Diarium, Sive Rerum Urbanarum*, ed. L. Thuasne, vol. 3 (Paris, 1985), 45. According to Burchardus, the buildings were torn down because they were damaged by a flood.

6 H. Günther, "Das Trivium vor Ponte S. Angelo: Ein Beitrag zur Urbanistik der Renaissance in Rom," *Römische Jahrbuch für Kunstgeschichte* 21 (1984): 209–13. For the restructuring, see B. Horrigan, "Imperial and Urban Ideology in a Renaissance Inscription," *Comitatus* 9 (1978): 73–85. On the project for San Celso, see A. Bruschi, *Bramante architetto* (Bari, 1969), 981.

7 P. Portoghesi, *Roma nel Rinascimento*, vol. 2 (Rome, 1974), 446–48. The competition for the church design was won by Jacopo Sansovino; the foundations were supervised by Antonio da Sangallo, the nave finished by Giacomo della Porta, 1583–1602, the dome erected by Carlo Maderno, 1614, and the façade was by Alessandro Galilei, 1734.

8 On Via Leonina, see G. Ciucci, *Piazza del Popolo* (Rome, 1974), 22; on Sangallo's palace, see C. L. Frommel, *Der römische Palastbau der Hochrenaissance*, vol. 2 (Tübingen, 1973), 315–20.

9 Günther, "Trivium," 178–86, cites *gettito* documents in the Archivio di Stato Romano (*ASR*), Presidenza delle Strade, Bd. 445 (*Taxae viarum*, 1514–83), fol. 81r–82r, for a December 1524 tax on Via del Consolato; and fol. 101r–v, for a tax for the Zecca façade. The Sangallo drawing in the Uffizi is UA 1013r.

10 H. de la Croix, "Military Architecture and the Radial City Plan in Sixteenth-Century Italy," *Art Bulletin* 42 (1960): 263–90. Although de la Croix convincingly traced the theory of radial planning and its propagation to Paul III's military advisers, he overlooked the appearance of the radial plan in Rome itself—with dates that coincide exactly with the construction of the new defenses. Likewise, Günther, who has made the definitive assessment of the urbanistic events at the Piazza di Ponte and established Sangallo's determining role, has not considered Sangallo's commission as the city's military architect as a factor in its design.

11 S. Pepper and N. Adams, *Firearms and Fortifications: Military Architecture and Siege Warfare in Sixteenth-Century Siena* (Chicago, 1986), 23–26.

12 Pastor, *History*, vol. 12, 556–58.

13 S. Pepper, "Planning vs. Fortification: Sangallo's Project for the Defence of Rome," *Architectural Review* (1976): 159–69.

14 On demolitions at Via Paola, see Ceen, "Quartiere de' Banchi," 198–200; on those in Via di Panico, Günther, "Trivium," 241–47, transcrip. of *ASR*, Presidenza delle Strade, Bd. 445 (*Taxae viarum*, 1514–83), fol. 206–18.

15 Pastor, *History*, vol. 12, 567.

16 Pastor, *History*, vol. 12, 17, 23, 224; in 1534 Paul III also appointed Virgilio Orsini commander of the papal fleet.

17 *ASR*, San Giovanni Decollato, "Indice dei Libri dei Giustiziati."

18 For a tabulation of the executions between 1499 and 1590, see R. Ingersoll, "The Ritual Use of Public Space in Renaissance Rome, 1450–1590," Ph.D. diss., University of California, Berkeley, 1985, 464.

19 A. Romano and P. Proia, *Roma nel Rinascimento,* vol. 3 (Rome, 1943), 26. M. Weil, *The Decoration and History of the Ponte Sant'Angelo* (University Park, 1974), 25, reports the inscriptions erroneously.

20 J. Weisz, "Pittura e misericordia: The Oratory of S. Giovanni Decollato in Rome," Ph.D diss., University of California, Los Angeles, 1982, 5–7.

21 M. de Montaigne, *Complete Works*, ed. D. Frame (London, 1955), 942.

22 Weisz, "Pittura e misericordia," 4–6; S. Edgerton, "A Little Known Purpose of Art in the Italian Renaissance," *Art History* 2 (1979): 47–48, draws on Weisz's research to examine the use of the painted panels.

23 G. Ruggero, *Violence in Early Renaissance Venice* (Trenton, 1980), 40–53.

24 V. Paglia, *La Pietà dei Carcerati: Confraternite e società nei secoli XVI–XVIII* (Rome, 1980), 46. In 1591 there were 3,666 registered in hospitals, 6,000 estimated in the prisons (Roman prisons held a maximum of 350 at a time, but there was a rapid turnover), and uncounted hundreds of beggars. In most modern societies, the number of destitutes rarely exceeds 3 percent.

25 Biblioteca Apostolica Vaticana, *Avvisi*, Urb. Lat. 1049, fol. 70: "Fu portato sopra una stora in Ponte al luoco dove si fa la giustitia con horrendo spettacolo di tutta Roma."

26 Pepper and Adams, *Firearms and Fortifications*, 28, from de' Marchi, *Della architettura militare*, vol. 1 (Brescia, 1599), 13, fol. 3v; 18, fol. 5r–v.

14

ROME

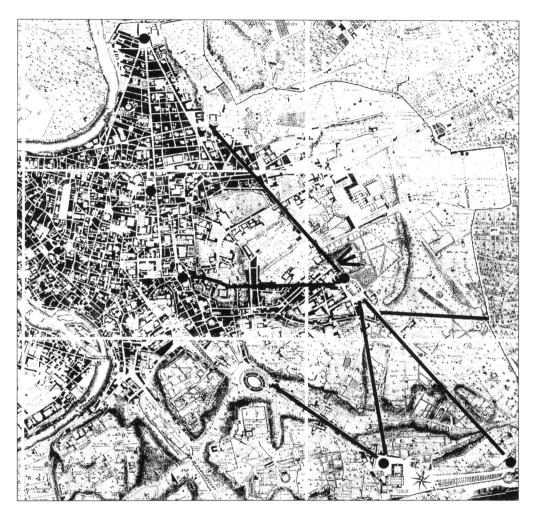

Absolutism and the Rhetoric of Topography

Streets in the Rome of Sixtus V

CHARLES BURROUGHS

Figure 1. Detail from Gian Battista Nolli's 1748 map of Rome. Black lines trace streets laid out or straightened by Sixtus V, converging on Sta. Maria Maggiore. Dots indicate the obelisks erected by Sixtus V at four locations and the two colossal columns of Trajan and Marcus Aurelius, dedicated by Sixtus to Saints Peter and Paul. A fifth obelisk is in Piazza S. Pietro, beyond the left edge of the image.

Few projects of urban remodeling are as celebrated as that of Pope Sixtus V (r. 1585–90) for Rome. In his short reign, Sixtus envisaged an ambitious street network to connect the city's farflung major shrines and encourage settlement in the extensive hilly terrain that, though within the ancient urban perimeter, had been largely destitute of population since the destruction of the aqueducts and other calamities of late antiquity (fig. 1). Much was realized: great, straight avenues were laid out or regularized; four immense obelisks, brought from Egypt in antiq-uity to commemorate the victory of Rome over Africa and the East, were re-erected in front of major shrines to terminate long urban vistas, to give visual prominence to sacred places, and to celebrate the triumph of the Roman church; new fountains improved the supply of water to strategic locations, notably in areas designated for new development; impressive new buildings catered to administrative needs and the spiritual or moral welfare of the population, as Sixtus conceived of it. The result was a transforma-tion of the spatial organization and scale of the

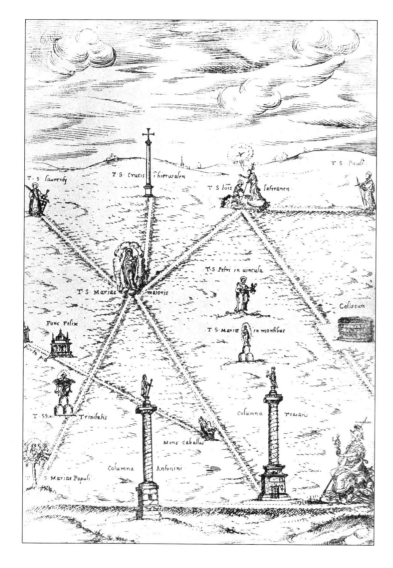

anticipated in the celebrated description of about 1455 of an unexecuted project for the Vatican Borgo, formulated under Pope Nicholas V.[2] Nicholas, like certain later popes, was clearly concerned with the condition and ordering of the city as a whole; more often, papal projects involved areas, even enclaves, associated with specific political or dynastic agendas and programs.

Sixtus V's urbanism, too, accommodated private interests. Just as his governmental innovations developed measures taken by predecessors, yet manifested a consistent reforming vision, so his urbanistic program exceeded existing models. Like many of his administrative reforms, Sixtus's infrastructural and architectural projects were primarily conceived as elements of a larger campaign of spiritual and moral purification and amelioration, as well as repression, in the social realm. His new streets, moreover, as sites of the circulation no less of information and injunctions than of persons and goods, served as instruments of an authoritarian, spatial semiosis of distinctive and novel character. This was intimately—and even, to a degree, consciously—related to habits of thought and representation fundamental in the evolving mental world of late Renaissance Italy.

Sixtus's implemented projects only suggest the full reach of his ambitions. For the first time in the history of Western urbanism, contemporary visual documentation exists of ideal city-wide planning projects. Two documents in particular have drawn the attention of scholars: one a schematic plan of Rome published by Gian Francesco Bordini in 1588 in a short, encomiastic book (fig. 2); the other a frescoed panorama of the city, one of a series of topographic representations in the great hall of the new Vatican Library erected under Sixtus (fig. 3).[3] For all their differences, both images clearly indicate the coherence and scale of the planned street network; both are, indeed, icons of a reformed urban totality.

Figure 2. Gian Francesco Bordini, *Rome as a Star-shaped City*, from *De rebus praeclaris gestis a Sixto V p.m.*, 1588.

city that in time supplied paradigms of monumental urbanism to cities throughout Europe and beyond.[1]

Sixtus's work culminated a long tradition of Renaissance papal urbanism, characterized especially by two motifs: the trident, or wedge of three straight streets meeting at a single point, and the street axially aligned with a prominent architectural element. These street types were

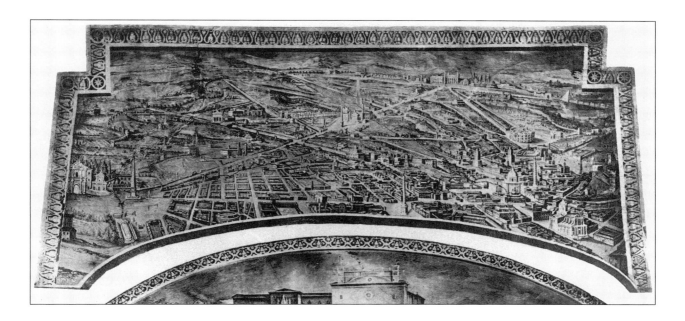

Bordini, despite all the attention paid to his Rome plan, remains obscure.[4] His book resulted from a collaboration with the well-known topographical artist Giovanni Maggi; it contains poetic and pictorial celebrations of Sixtus's achievements, not least in architectural patronage and urbanism. Divested of this context and even of the poem it accompanies and illustrates, Bordini's Rome plan turns up regularly not only in more specific studies of the period but also in general accounts of European urbanism, most conspicuously that of Sigfried Giedion.[5] It has never been seriously analyzed in terms of its own character and implications.

The Bordini plan is crudely schematic and bears a highly approximate relationship to topographical fact. The major shrines are indicated by symbols (the Virgin, for example, at Sta. Maria Maggiore, or the obviously exorcised poplar tree at Sta. Maria del Popolo); secular monuments ancient and modern, such as the Colosseum or Sixtus's Moses Fountain, are represented iconically. The various topographical

signs are set in an abstracted urban matrix organized by the famous Sistine network of thoroughfares, which takes the form of a star centered at the basilica of Sta. Maria Maggiore, as indicated in the accompanying poem.[6]

Sta. Maria Maggiore was an early object of veneration on the part of Sixtus. Long before his accession he had established nearby his suburban residence, the Villa Montalto, in a particularly lofty, thinly populated region near the city walls (fig. 4). The villa's name derived from his hometown, Montalto ("high mountain"), which appears in Sistine iconography as a paradigmatic holy city; this is surely related to the particular veneration of sacred mountains in the Franciscan order, to which Sixtus belonged.[7] Montalto was also the source of one of Sixtus's most ubiquitous heraldic motifs, a group of three stylized hills, or *monticuli*, surmounted by a star. These appear, for instance, at the foot of the ribs of St. Peter's dome and at the apex of each of Sixtus's famous obelisks, just beneath the triumphant cross (fig. 5).

Figure 3. *Rome Transformed by Sixtus V,* fresco in the Salone Sistino, Vatican Library.

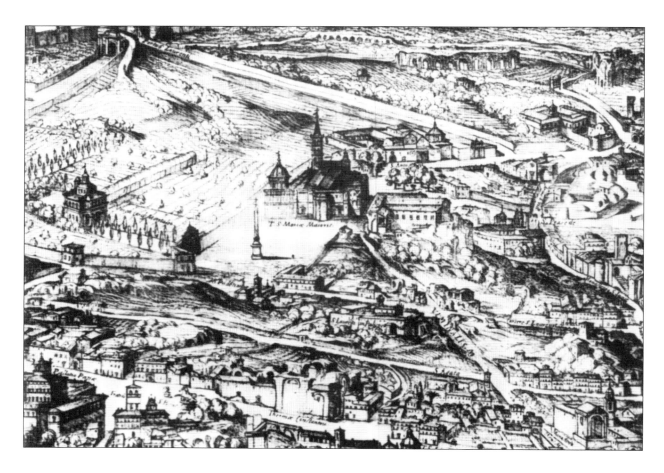

Figure 4. Villa Montalto, at left, with the obelisk and rear façade of Sta. Maria Maggiore. Detail from Antonio Tempesta, *View of Rome*, 1593.

On the Bordini plan, the motif of the *monticuli*, though without a star, marks the element "Monti" in the names of the churches of Sta. Trinità dei Monti and the Madonna dei Monti. Both churches predated Sixtus's accession and had become celebrated centers of Counter-Reformation spirituality. However, the *monticuli* device surely affirms the association of Sixtus with the district containing both the Villa Montalto and the magnificent funerary chapel, with a prominent dome (as we will see, a symbolic mountain), that he was constructing in the adjacent basilica of Sta. Maria Maggiore. The *monticuli* on the Bordini plan, therefore, assimilate the hilly Roman district of Monti to

Montalto, the Sistine sacred mountain and city, establishing it as the paradigmatic core of the reformed symbolic topography of the entire city, the place of the star of Bordini's poem.

In its abstractness, the Bordini plan recalls the ichnographic maps developed by Renaissance cartographers on the basis of exact surveying procedures.[8] Yet the star of streets that surmounts and organizes the city is not ichnographic; it is absent, for instance, from a schematic but relatively accurate topographical diagram of Monti on a contemporary medal of Sixtus V celebrating the improvement of the street system around Sta. Maria Maggiore. Bordini's star is a symbolic configuration saturating the lofty terrain of Monti with the presence of the Virgin, in her familiar manifestations as *stella maris* or *stella matutina*. It is associated, if not identified, with the familiar papal device of stylized hills surmounted by a star: emblem becomes topography. Yet the star is framed and made palpable within an undeniable ichnographic matrix, as if to claim transparency to topographic reality by dissembling the Bordini plan's status as symbol.[9]

This claim may have been reinforced by a further cartographic resonance, for the star motif itself echoes a characteristic motif of an important type of ichnographic plan, the portolan chart. From the fourteenth to the seventeenth centuries, portolans served as practical and highly accurate aids to navigation along the indented and often dangerous coastlines of the Mediterranean and, in time, across the Atlantic; in later charts practical concerns were combined with, or even gave way to, aesthetic ones (fig. 6).[10] The space represented in a portolan chart is articulated not—or not only—by graduation lines, but by networks of wind roses, so that the whole chart is covered with lines radiating from starlike points, in a system that is sometimes anchored in an image of the enthroned Virgin and Child.[11] Many sixteenth-century charts document the church's work of conversion and coercion throughout immense, newly accessible spaces. Just as in ancient Rome expansion of the Imperial boundaries was celebrated by expansion of those of the city, so Sixtus's conception of a new, greater Rome surely acknowledged the vastly expanded realm of the church's missionary and pastoral activity.[12] Certainly the twin storiated columns of ancient Rome, rededicated to Saints Peter and Paul by Sixtus and prominent on the Bordini plan, had long been associated, especially in Hapsburg emblems, with the Pillars of Hercules that marked the opening to the Atlantic world.

In the new lands, Europeans devised various ways to inscribe and legitimize their presence; along the African coast, for instance, the Portuguese erected four-sided stone pillars marked with heraldic crests and religious symbols and carrying the cross. Such *padrões* had both navigational and symbolic significance: reinforced by other markers—chapels, cairns, forts—they abstracted from indigenous cultural landscapes in the production of a rationally ordered colonial world, associating this with the saintly

Figure 5. The four faces of the obelisk of Piazza del Popolo and the colossal ancient columns of Trajan and Marcus Aurelius. Engraving by Natale Bonifacio da Sebenico, in Domenico Fontana, *Della trasportatione dell'obelisco vaticano et delle fabriche di nostro signore Papa Sisto V*, 1590.

cults and providential ideology of Christianity. Needless to say, the Madonna traveled with the voyagers (the first ship to reach America was Columbus's Santa Maria; the first gold from the New World was set in the ceiling of Sta. Maria Maggiore) and Marian cults were soon established overseas, part of a worldwide network of observances centered at the Madonna's great shrine in Rome.[13] If indeed Sistine Rome functioned as a microcosmic model for the wider world of Christian action, Sixtus's obelisks perhaps echoed the formally somewhat similar *padrões* and other markers erected by European voyagers and conquistadores in distant seas.[14]

The Renaissance developed diverse genres of city representation, from the abstract ichnographic plan to the realistic panoramic view. An example of the latter is prominent in the lavishly frescoed wing, the Salone Sistino, added by Sixtus to the Vatican Library. The best-known component of these decorations is the series of topographical views depicting, for the most part, buildings and urban spaces variously transformed, or designated for transformation, by Sixtus. The series includes, and is synoptically recapitulated by, an aerial perspective of the city as ideally transformed through the realization of all the pope's plans (see fig. 3).[15] In this panorama, the famous obelisks, absent from the Bordini plan, extend to the third dimension the newly explicit topographical relations of the city; the hub of the represented city is the great basilica of Sta. Maria Maggiore, marked by the dome of Sixtus's chapel, which is also conspicuous as the subject of some of the other topographical views. Neither the panorama nor any of the other views shows any trace of such schematic symbols as Bordini's star motif. On the other hand, the topographical views are spatially associated with, and formally related to, pictorial allegories involving Sixtus's emblems, especially his lion, pear tree,

and mountain.[16] In this hall, the symbolic and the pictorial are not opposed categories.

A further fresco in the series of topographical views depicts the basilica of St. Peter's as ideally completed (fig. 7). Two aspects of this image require comment: the basilica is not the building projected by Sixtus on a Roman-cross plan (to judge from the location of the Vatican obelisk), but the structure envisaged by Michelangelo on a Greek-cross plan; it stands in a vast piazza, backed by green mountains, that occupies much of the site of the Vatican Palace, which Sixtus himself greatly expanded.[17] Other Sistine imagery retains this superseded conception of St. Peter's, notably a medal presenting a schematic elevation of the basilica, with its three domes, that unmistakably assimilates it not only to the papal tiara, the triple crown that signified papal temporal authority, but also to the *monticuli* (fig. 8).[18] The Sistine images of St. Peter's dematerialize the basilica's architecture, reducing it to a mere sign, not unlike the obelisks, suitable for insertion into an emblematic topography such as that evident in the Bordini plan or—however differently—in the perspective of Rome in the library.[19]

The Roman urban environment as actually modified under Sixtus was saturated with symbols. Passage through the streets, especially that of procession or pilgrimage, was accompanied and given meaning by an array of texts and emblems on buildings, fountains, and obelisks. Two obelisks carry Egyptian hieroglyphic inscriptions that resonate with the modern "hieroglyphs" deployed by Sixtus.[20] The pope's interest in diverse modes of the legitimation, communication, and activation of his religious program and disciplinary regime is clearly expressed in the fresco decoration of the Salone Sistino in the Vatican Library. An image of the Council of Trent concludes a series of representations of major ecclesiastical councils in which church doctrine was formulated and heresies identified and censored; two frescoes show the destruction of offending books.[21] The topographic views illustrating Sixtus's building programs overlap with depictions of processions and ceremonies, a visual and thematic association that indicates the importance to Sixtus of public ritual and the coherent sanctification of urban space.[22] Such imagery makes of the library hall a microcosm of the reformed city.

The frescoes of the Salone Sistino include an unprecedented cycle illustrating the history of writing through portraits of the mythical inventors of different scripts, including the Egyptian divinity and protomagus Hermes Trismegistos as the inventor of hieroglyphics. This theme gives particular point to the heraldic and emblematic devices liberally scattered through the rich *alla grottesca* decoration of the vault and window embrasures of the Salone and brought to life in some of the narrative fields. This cycle clearly refers to the function of the library itself and of the Vatican printing press founded by Sixtus and intended for the lower floor of the library wing. Equally reflexive is the series of images of great libraries of history, culminating in the apostolic library itself.[23]

The library decoration firmly sets the pope's urbanism within a more general discourse of the production, communication, preservation, and censorship of learning. This is articulated in a contemporary description of the library and its frescoes, published in the year following Sixtus's death by Angelo Rocca, director of both the Vatican Library and the papal printing press under Sixtus.[24] Rocca lists the various cycles, appending a full account of Sixtus's urban interventions to his description of the topographical views. As a scholar and librarian, he pays particular attention to the images of libraries and the inventors of writing; he moves from historical narrative to theoretical considerations,

directing particular attention to the identification and elucidation of optimal forms of communication, especially that of angels with each other and with mortals, which, he claims, is both immediate and error-free.[25] Such concerns connect Rocca's discussions to the extensive Renaissance literature on the nature and operation of hieroglyphs and related forms, notably emblems. It anticipates, moreover, a later work in which Rocca's theoretical consid-

Figure 6. Detail of a portolan chart by Francisco de Oliva, 1603.

Figure 7. *St. Peter's as Ideally Completed*, fresco in the Salone Sistino, Vatican Library.

eration of privileged modes of communication merges far more thoroughly with a discourse concerning the city.

In 1612 Rocca published the first book on campanology.[26] This includes affectionate accounts of the venerable bells of Roman churches, but the author reserves particular praise for the peals of northern Europe, motivated in part by an aesthetic appreciation of their musicality and the prominence and beauty of the belfries. He notes the importation into Rome of northern bells for some of the leading institutions of the Counter-Reformation; the subject of bells is indeed, in Rocca's account, closely related to post-Tridentine concerns with the transmission and consolidation of religious principles. This function of bells is evidently in large part a matter of their magical properties: Rocca claims, for instance, that Muslims abhor bells because they dispel aerial demons, and Muslims resemble demons; he asserts in general that bells can exert influence over the "aerial powers" that cause violent storms, and he recounts his own experience of a terrible storm over the Vatican allayed by the sound of bells; he mentions the baptism of bells, as if they were human, and describes the custom of engraving on bells images and texts believed to be activated when the bells sound.[27]

Rocca's text conveys a striking visual image of northern cities dominated by high belfries that position and celebrate the cults of patron saints; one thinks of the silhouette views of city skylines especially popular in sixteenth-century northern Europe.[28] It is no less an aural than a visual image, involving the call of the bells (and, by extension, the saints often figured upon them) over the huddled roofs of the city in a contrapuntal barrage of sound. Rocca's enthusiasms echo contemporary practice in Rome itself, where belfries, sometimes paired, began to appear with some frequency in the late sixteenth century over churches associated with the reformist movements and institutions of the age.[29] Rocca articulates, therefore, a well-established Counter-Reformation interest in bells and belfries; he also develops a theme already present in his earlier book on the Vatican Library and, indeed, in Sixtus's urbanism.

To the rear of Sta. Maria Maggiore, in Piazza Esquilina, Sixtus erected an obelisk of particular importance in his city-wide array of symbols (see fig. 4).[30] The obelisk closed the view down the Strada Felice (now Via Sistina, Via delle Quattro Fontane, and Via de Pretis), the major street of the Sistine addition, which Sixtus proposed to extend, dead straight, as far as Piazza del Popolo and the obelisk set up there, at the northern entrance of the city. It was aligned also with other streets, notably Via Panisperna, approaching from the heart of the city, and with the portal of the Villa Montalto on Piazza Esquilina. The ancient inscriptions on its base referred to the Emperor Augustus, who had originally brought the obelisk to Rome and set it up as a trophy of his victory over Cleopatra. Inscriptions added by Sixtus, however, proclaimed that the triumph of Augustus and the pagan Empire had been

Figure 8. Converging images of St. Peter's basilica, Sixtus's heraldic *monticuli*, and the papal tiara. Reverse of a medal of Sixtus V, 1586.

surpassed and superseded by that of Christ, whose birth in the time of Augustus was commemorated by the great relic of Sta. Maria Maggiore: the very manger in which the Christ child had supposedly been laid, now the centerpiece of Sixtus's grand domed chapel. The iconography of the chapel's rich, marble-encrusted decoration is an elaborate agglomeration of narrative and emblematic elements. Its message is inscribed in a more condensed and emphatic version on the nearby obelisk—or rather, is imagined as proclaimed by the obelisk, speaking *in the first person* to the piazza, the radiating streets, and the city.[31]

We can now trace the common ground in Rocca's two books between the discourse of bells and that of visual and spatial markers and signs. Sixtus's images of Rome and his interventions therein alike project a conception of urban and social space as defined and ordered through a network of reciprocally allusive and responsive emblems and symbols. The obelisks especially, addressing each other over great distances, suggest a utopic collapsing of topographical relations into relations of signification. The city reveals itself as transparent to an emblematic discourse of which it is both the necessary matrix and a privileged sign; the act of mapping the city rehearses this transparency and prefigures the exercise of power that its implementation entails. Yet the play of visual signs characteristic of Sistine Rome must traverse a resistant medium, the urban environment. In Rocca's campanological discourse, the airborne sound of bells and the irresistible exchange of sacred, even magical messages from high belfries provide an auditory model for the Sistine exercise of the power of imagery in the streets and squares of a city in which, as it turned out, neither Sixtus's spatialized emblems nor his savage repression constituted an adequate response to the burgeoning crisis of social order and public welfare. ∎

Notes

I am grateful to Hilary Ballon and C. W. Westfall for the opportunity to present this material, and to Joseph Connors, Jesus Escobar, Irving Lavin, and Steven Ostrow for helpful readings of manuscript drafts.

1 For a fine account of the historical significance of Sixtus's urbanism, see S. Kostof, *The City Shaped: Urban Pattern and Meanings through History* (London, 1991), 218–22, 263–65. Important recent discussions of Sixtus's pontificate include M. Fagiolo, "La Roma di Sisto V: Le Matrici del policentrismo," *Psicon* 3 (1976): 24–39; D. Fontana, *Della trasportatione dell'obelisco vaticano*, ed. A. Carugo, with an introduction by P. Portoghesi, 2 vols. (Milan, 1978); H. Gamrath, *Roma sancta renovata: Studi sull'urbanistica di Roma nella seconda metà del secolo XVI, con particolare riferimento al pontificato di Sisto V (1585–1590)*, Analecta Romana Istituti Danici, suppl. 12 (Rome, 1987); R. Schiffmann, *Roma felix: Aspekte der städtebaulichen Gestaltung Roms unter Papst Sixtus V* (Bern and New York, 1985); L. Spezzaferro, "La Roma di Sisto V," in *Storia dell'arte in Italia* 12 (Turin, 1983): 363–405; L. Spezzaferro and M. E. Tittoni, eds., *Il Campidoglio e Sisto V* (Rome, 1991).

2 On these two motifs, see especially E. Guidoni, "Antonio da Sangallo e l'urbanistica del '500," in G. Spagnesi, ed., *Antonio da Sangallo: La Vita e l'opera* (Rome, 1986), 217–19.

For recent discussions of the extensive literature on the Borgo, see M. Tafuri, "'Cives esse non licere': The Rome of Nicholas V and Leon Battista Alberti, Elements towards a Historical Review," *Harvard Architectural Review* 6 (1984): 61–75; C. Burroughs, *From Signs to Design: Environmental Process and Reform in Early Renaissance Rome* (Cambridge, Mass., 1990), 9–16, 72–98.

3 G. F. Bordini, *De rebus praeclaris gestis a Sixto V p.m.* (Rome, 1588).

On the Library, see A. Dupront, "Les Fresques de la Bibliothèque de Sixte-Quint: Art et Contre-Reforme," *Mélanges d'archéologie et d'histoire* 48 (1931): 282–306; J. Bignami-Odier, *La Bibliothèque vaticane de Sixte V à Pie XI*, Studi e testi 272 (Vatican City, 1973); A. Böck, *Das Dekorationsprogramm des Lesesaals des Vatikanischen Bibliotheks* (Munich, 1988).

4 Bordini was a member of the Oratory of S. Filippo Neri, a highly disciplined organization of influential laymen that assumed a leading role in the development of Counter-Reformation piety in Rome; see Dupront, "Fresques," 294. No other works by Bordini have come to light.

5 S. Giedion, "Sixtus V and the Planning of Baroque Rome," in *Space, Time, and Architecture*, 3d ed. (Cambridge, Mass., 1953), 75–106, especially 82, fig. 28.

6 Bordini, *De rebus*, 48 (by an error of binding in the copy of the book that I consulted in the Metropolitan Museum of Art, New York, the plan does not appear opposite the engraving to which it obviously refers). The poem is entitled, "On the most ample streets which Sixtus V has opened and paved in the form of a star from the Esquiline hill to various places." It begins: "The star's radiance stationed on the *monti* shines forth over the city: brighter than a star shines the Virgin Mother . . ." The *pianta stellata* also appears in A. Rocca, *De biblioteca vaticana a Sixto V in splendidiorem commodioremque locum translata* (Rome, 1591), 27. This is evidence of its official status as published by Bordini.

7 St. Francis substituted mountainous places associated with his own most significant actions for the sacred mountains of Christian tradition; he received the stigmata at Monte La Verna, while the Umbrian hill town Greccia, site of a famous Christmas celebration, became a Franciscan New Bethlehem. See H. Feld, *Der Ikonoklasmus des Westens* (Leiden, 1990), 76–79. The cult at Greccia clearly relates to the presence of the *presepe* (the manger of Christ's birth) in Sta. Maria Maggiore, where it became the centerpiece of Sixtus's chapel. In Sistine imagery, Montalto and Loreto appear as sanctified hill towns, e.g., on a well-known engraving of Sixtus V surrounded by his Roman projects; see G. Pinadello, *Invicti quinarii numeri series quae . . . maxime a Sixto Quinto res praeclare gestas adnumerat . . .* (Rome, 1989), frontispiece. See also Gamrath, *Roma sancta*, 46, fig. 36.

8 J. Pinto, "The Renaissance City Image," in A. C. Crombie and N. Siraisi, eds., *The Rational Arts of Living*, Smith College Studies in History 50 (Northampton, Mass., 1987), 205–54.

9 For the medal of Sixtus V, see British Museum, Department of Coins and Medals, nos. 805, 849 (1586, 1597; CURIA PONTIFICIA); cf. no. 808 (1586; FIERI FECIT). See also A. Armand, *Les Médailleurs italiens des XV et XVI siècles,* vol. 1 (Bologna, 1883), 258, 293; Schiffmann, *Roma felix,* 66f, 73f.

The symbolism of Bordini's star is suggested by René Schiffmann in *Roma felix,* 124. On Marian symbolism, see M. Warner, *Alone of All Her Sex: The Myth and Cult of the Virgin Mary* (New York, 1976), 262f, 267.

For maps in and as emblems see H. Harms, "Die Karte als Emblem," in W. Schärfe, et al., eds., *Kartenhistorisches Colloquium, Bayreuth '82: Vorträge und Berichte* (Berlin, 1983), 79–90.

10 On early modern portolans, see R. V. Tooley, *Maps and Map Makers,* 6th ed. (New York, 1978), 15f; K. Kretschmer, *Die italienischen Portolane des Mittelalters: Ein Beitrag zur Geschichte der Kartographie und Nautik* (Hildesheim, 1962), 227f. For more general accounts, see T. Campbell, "Portolan Charts from the Late Thirteenth Century to 1500," in J. B. Harley and D. Woodward, eds., *The History of Cartography,* vol. 1 (Chicago, 1987), 371–463; M. Mollat du Jourdin and M. de la Roncière, eds., *Sea Charts of the Early Explorers, Thirteenth to Seventeenth Centuries* (New York, 1984); S. Sider, ed., *Maps, Charts, Globes: five Centuries of Exploration, Catalogue of the Exhibition and New Edition of E. L. Stevenson's Portolan Charts (1911)* (New York, 1992).

11 See, for example, Mollat du Jourdin and Roncière, *Sea Charts,* 236, no. 56; 246, no. 68. In these manuscript charts from 1563 and 1603 the Virgin appears on the neck of the vellum sheet, i.e., in the West, "indicating at one and the same time . . . both the head of the chart and the central axis of the rhumb-line network." Some charts carry wind roses ornamented with images of saints that recall the representation of the Madonna in the Bordini plan. See Sider, *Maps, Charts, Globes,* 45.

12 An important Roman cartographer, Bartolomeo Crescenzi, was closely associated with Sixtus's ad-

ministration and in 1602 published a *Nautica mediterranea* that included a chart of the Mediterranean region and lengthy disquisitions on cartographic method and navigational techniques; see Kretschmer, *Portolane*, 230, no. 9. A copy belonged to Paolo Maruscelli, architect of leading religious institutions in Rome around 1600; see J. Connors, *Borromini and the Roman Oratory: Style and Society* (Cambridge, Mass., 1980), 154; cf. app. 2, 107–12.

13 On *padrões* markers, see W. Pietz, "The Problem of the Fetish, 1," *RES: Anthropology and Aesthetics* 9 (1985): 15–17. Pietz mentions two *padrões* dedicated to specific saints. For the mapping of the African coast in portolan charts, see Campbell, "Portolan charts," 411f. An early-sixteenth-century map of the known world by a Genoese cartographer shows *padrões* studding the coast of subsaharan Africa; see Mollat du Jourdin and Roncière, *Sea Charts*, 216, no. 26.

Warner, in *Alone of All Her Sex*, 267, discusses the name of Columbus's ship; resonances of the Marian cult extended into the mariners' jargon: *stella maris* or its vernacular equivalents could mean "wind rose"; Mollat du Jourdin and Roncière, *Sea Charts*, 16.

For the ceiling of Sta. Maria Maggiore, see P. J. Jacks, "Alexander VI's Ceiling for Sta. Maria Maggiore in Rome," *Römisches Jahrbuch für Kunstgeschichte* 22 (1985), 63–83.

14 The obelisks also resemble ancient Roman spatial markers, at least as reconstructed in the sixteenth century. Thus, an image of an obelisklike milestone, inscribed with legal and commemorative texts and the indicator of scale, appears in the map of the Italian province flaminia in the Galleria delle Carte Geografiche, Vatican Palace; see E. R. Knauer, *Die Carta Marina des Olaus Magnus von 1539* (Göttingen, 1981), 72, with fig. 26. Knauer, 77, notes the merging of historical and spatial dimensions in the cartographic frescoes of the Galleria, as completed under Gregory XIII. Under Gregory's successor, Sixtus V, the same phenomenon occurs both in representations of the city and in the physical fabric of the city itself.

15 The Salone Sistino was begun in May 1587 and completed, as inscriptions record, in February 1588.

The fresco decorations were completed in November 1589, and the books installed in the following year. See Dupront, "Fresques," 282–306; Bignami-Odier, *Bibliothèque*, 70–74; Böck, *Dekorationsprogramm*, 15–17. The fullest contemporary published account of the library and its decorations is that of Angelo Rocca, in *De biblioteca;* see also Fontana, *Della trasportatione*, vol. 1, fol. 83f.

Giedion calls the aerial perspective view Sixtus's "master plan of Rome," *Space, Time,* 82; cf. 93f. See also Schiffmann, *Roma felix*, 60f.

16 Similar scenes had already appeared in the frescoes of the Lateran Palace; Rocca, *De biblioteca*, 12; Fontana, *Della trasportatione*, vol. 1, fol. 61r/v. See also the frontispiece to Pinadello, *Invicti quinarii numeri.* The *monticuli* and pears were derived from Sixtus's chosen hometown, Montalto, and surname, Peretti; the lion, his personal emblem, was deployed throughout Rome, notably on the Vatican obelisk as re-erected in the Piazza S. Pietro on the backs of four lions clutching *monticuli.* The obelisk carries on its eastern face an inscription referring to the apocalyptic lion, FUGITE PARTES ADVERSAE; VINCIT LEO DE TRIBU JUDA (Revelations 5). This surely equates Christ and Sixtus, *pace* C. D'Onofrio, *Gli Obelischi di Roma* (Rome, 1965), 102. For earlier appearances of the apocalyptic lion in the Vatican Palace, in Leo X's decorations in the Sala di Costantino, see R. Quednau, "Zeremonien und Festdekor: Ein Beispiel aus dem Pontifikat Leos X," in A. Buck, ed., *Europäische Hofkultur im 16. und 17. Jahrhundert,* vol. 9 (Hamburg, 1981), 355. Sixtus significantly altered this room, appropriating and modifying the existing imagery. Like Leo, he exploited the astrological connotations of the lion, linking it with the Golden Age; see C. Mandel, "'Starry Leo,' the Sun, and the Astrological Foundations of Sixtine Rome," *Racar* 17 (1990): 17–96.

17 On Sixtus's project, see D'Onofrio, *Obelischi di Roma*, 79f; G. Curcio and M. Manieri-Elia, *Storia e uso di modelli architettonici* (Bari, 1982), 246. Michelangelo claimed he had revived Bramante's conception of a Greek-cross project; this did not defuse opposition to his designs. See J. S. Ackerman, *The Architecture of Michelangelo*, rev. ed. (Chicago, 1981), 204–6; H. Hibbard, *Carlo Maderno and Roman Architecture 1580–1630* (London, 1971), 156; E.

Francia, *Storia della costruzione del nuovo S. Pietro, 1506–1606* (Rome, 1977), 32.

Contemporary accounts of Sixtus's projects emphasize the isolation of major buildings and the leveling and ordering of the surrounding or interjacent terrain. See Fontana, *Della trasportatione,* vol. 1, fol. 101v; Rocca, *De biblioteca,* 27. The often-reproduced Pinadello frontispiece of 1589 shows Sixtus's portrait surrounded by buildings represented as isolated structures. Kurt Schwäger, in "Zur Bautätigkeit Sixtus V an S. Maria Maggiore in Rom," *Miscellanea Bibliothecae Hertzianae* (Munich, 1961), 352, suggests a connection with Carlo Borromeo's precepts.

18 The medal is in the British Museum, Department of Coins and Medals, no. 842 (1586, SACRA PROPHANIS PRAEFERENDA); cf. Armand, *Médailleurs,* vol. 1, 293. The obelisk is correctly identified by A. Patrignani, "L'Obelisco vaticano in una presunta medaglia della Basilica Liberiana," *L'Illustrazione vaticana* 2 (1931): 15–20; his hypothesis that the building beyond the obelisk echoes a rejected project for St. Peter's is untenable. A striking example of the visual convergence on the medal is an engraving of an unexecuted project for a monumental fountain on the Piazza del Quirinale, incorporating the famous ancient statues known as the Dioscuri, or horse tamers; see T. Buddensieg, "Zum Statuenprogramm im Kapitolsplan Pauls III," *Zeitschrift für Kunstgeschichte* 31 (1969): 193, fig. 14; I am grateful to Joseph Connors for this reference. This links the tiara, *monticuli,* and star with the horse tamers and their familiar ideological overtones as privileged symbols of absolute authority.

19 On the medal and its imagery, see the excellent, though formalist, account of Schwäger, "Zur Bautätigkeit," 353 n. 138. On the Moses Fountain, the monumental outlet constructed by Sixtus for the Acqua Felice and designed on the model of an ancient triumphal arch, miniature obelisks appear along with the usual Sistine emblems; such an obelisk is not, even potentially, a carrier of hieroglyphs, but itself functions as a kind of hieroglyph. In the frontispiece of Pinadello's biography of Sixtus of 1589 (see n. 8, above), the pope's portrait appears surrounded by vignettes of his individual buildings and some allegorical images and scenes; the sign

character of Sixtus's buildings could not be more clearly indicated.

20 The obelisks at the Lateran and the Piazza del Popolo carry hieroglyphs; see D'Onofrio, *Obelischi di Roma,* 160f, 173f, 32.

21 Böck, *Dekorationsprogramm,* 43, 52, 58: Arian books are burned after the first Council of Nicaea; at the fourth Council of Constantinople the books of Photius and records of his council are destroyed.

22 See the excellent chapter in Gamrath, *Roma sancta,* 123–63.

23 On these images in the Salone, see Böck, *Dekorationsprogramm,* 27–35, 62; for a contemporary discussion of Hermes's importance, see Rocca, *De biblioteca,* 101–3; M. Mercati, *Gli Obelischi di Roma (1589),* ed. G. Cantelli (Bologna, 1981), 43f, 106f. In an engraving of the four hieroglyph-encrusted faces of the obelisk of Sta. Maria del Popolo (see fig. 4), the title "Trismegistos" is associated with Sixtus's triadic *monticuli;* see D'Onofrio, who incorrectly identifies the print as a representation of all four obelisks, *Obelischi di Roma,* fig. 89.

24 Rocca was an Augustinian monk, sacristan of the Vatican Palace, and founder of the Biblioteca Angelica in Rome; see N. A. Weber, "Angelo Rocca," *The Catholic Encyclopedia,* vol. 13 (New York, 1912), 100; Dupront, "Fresques," 300–303. He was a stout defender of papal supremacy and even of the Donation of Constantine, the venerable but forged legitimation of papal territorial claims; he denounced in print not only Lorenzo Valla's fifteenth-century exposure of the Donation (Dupront, op. cit., 302), but also, in his *Observationes in sex libros Elegantiarum Laurentii Vallae* (Venice, 1576), Valla's work on language. This convergence, long before Sixtus's accession, of literary, broadly theoretical, and political concerns, is particularly significant.

25 See the section "De dialectis" in Rocca, *De biblioteca,* 291–376.

26 A. Rocca, *De campanis commentarius* (Rome, 1612). The text is available in A. H. de Sallengre, ed., *Novus thesaurus antiquitatum Romanorum,* vol. 2 (Venice, 1735), 1232–1303.

27 The name Mary was often given to bells, especially at Rome; see Rocca, *De campanis*, 52.

28 Kostof, *City Shaped*, 284–87; C. Talbot, "Topography as Landscape in Early Printed Books," in S. Hindman, ed., *The Early Illustrated Book: Essays in Honor of Lessing J. Rosenwald* (Washington, D.C., 1982), 105–16; T. Colletta, *Atlanti di città del Cinquecento* (Naples, 1984), 68f, noting the persistence in Italy of images of cities in elevation, even after the advent of ichnographic mapping.

29 S. Atanasio dei Greci and SS. Trinità dei Monti have double belfries, in each case constructed in the early 1580s. The single belfries of Sta. Caterina dei Funari, with its Jesuit patronage, and the Madonna dei Monti are singled out by Rocca, *De campanis*, 15. The former was probably part of the construction campaign of the early 1560s, while the latter was not built until the 1580s. After 1577, the campanile of the Palazzo Senatorio was reconstructed and commemorative medals struck, one showing the belfry in front of the palace, another as if freestanding in space. This is clearly not a matter of alternative designs, as has been suggested by I. S. Weber, "The Significance of Papal Medals for the Architectural History of Rome," in G. Pollard, ed., *Italian Medals* (London, 1987), 288f; rather, it is a question of the emblematic character of belfries in late-Cinquecento culture.

30 D'Onofrio, *Obelischi di Roma*, 154f; Mercati, *Obelischi*, 374f.

31 I am grateful to Steven Ostrow for this observation. Two of the four Sistine inscriptions on the obelisk's base are in the first person, addressing the Strada Felice and the portal of Sixtus's villa, with its miniature trident of garden avenues; see D'Onofrio, *Obelischi di Roma*, 159. The obelisk "says": "With great joy I venerate the cradle of Christ, eternal God, I who performed a sad service at the tomb of dead Augustus." Bordini, *De rebus*, 23, also attributes the power of speech to the obelisk, as well as characteristic punning on the name of the pope; elsewhere, in an allusion to Virgil's *Eclogues*, he includes mountains among various inanimate landscape features that give praise (Bordini, op. cit., 13; cf. Rocca, *De biblioteca*, 24). The obelisk at Sta. Maria del Popolo is also represented as uttering the sentences inscribed upon it; indeed, in an engraving by Natale Bonifacio included by Fontana in *De trasportatione*, it is associated with trumpeting angels who dramatically embody the theme of the vocalization in urban space of Sistine messages (see fig. 5). See also D'Onofrio, op. cit., 173f.

15

LONDON

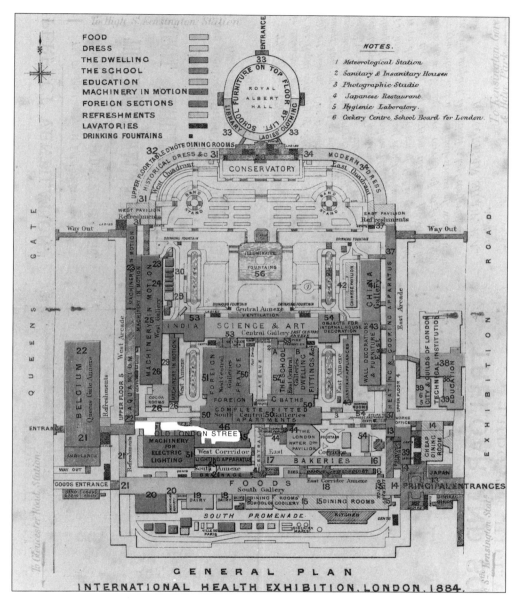

The Healthy Victorian City

The Old London Street at the International Health Exhibition of 1884

ANNMARIE ADAMS

Figure 1. General plan of the International Health Exhibition, London, 1884, from *The International Health Exhibition Official Guide*, 1884; the Old London Street is white.

The main entrance to the Old London Street, an attraction at the International Health Exhibition in South Kensington, was through Bishopsgate, an imposing Norman arch sliced through the city wall of the Romans (fig. 1).[1] The wide opening, above which towered a statue of William the Conqueror, was framed by two monumental towers. Narrow slits of windows hinted at the dark, confined prison cells contained within its massive and weather-worn masonry walls.

Through the gateway, the picturesque sweep

Figure 2. View of the Old London Street at the Health Exhibition, from *The Illustrated London News*, 1884.

of the archaic street was breathtaking (fig. 2). Buildings of four or five stories cast their darkening shadows across the narrow passageway to Elbow Lane. Crowds jostled their way in and out of reconstructions of popular commercial establishments such as the Rose Inn and the Cock Tavern, passing beneath half-timbered façades whose heaviness was relieved only by bands of tiny, discolored windowpanes. A sudden widening of the street just past a re-

construction of Isaac Walton's house afforded a generous view of an old wooden church tower.

A small exterior staircase on the south side of the street ascended to the second-floor level of the buildings, where "darksome little upper rooms" were filled with a mismatched array of tapestries, furniture, and utensils.[2] The windows would not open; the thick panes of glass distorted the view of the crowd below, slowly making its way toward Elbow Lane.

The Old London Street was a brilliant ploy on the part of the executive council of the 1884 International Health Exhibition. Billed as a means of illustrating the overcrowded spaces, dark interiors, and inflammable building materials common in London before the Great Plague of 1665 and devastating fire of 1666, this reproduction of a medieval street—composed, as fairgoers were told, of "honest structures," rather than "pasteboard and painted canvas delusions"— was the most popular attraction of the exhibition, appealing in its picturesqueness to "lovers of Art."[3] The Old Street was part of a group of special displays comprising fireworks, flower shows, and illuminated fountains, intended to lure crowds to the exhibition in the hope that they might perhaps go on from there to explore the vast displays of drainpipes and ventilators or to attend one of the lectures on sanitation that formed the official educational program of the fair. Equally instructive of current notions of health, however, was the juxtaposition of the Old London Street with spaces and structures at the fair based on the theme of abundant water.

The International Health Exhibition (IHE), or "The Healtheries," as it was called at the time, was intended by its promoters to celebrate international progress in the scientific study of health.[4] "Sanitary science" was a relatively new field in the late nineteenth century; by the 1880s it was a fairly autonomous discipline, as illustrated by events like the IHE.[5] By this time courses in sanitation were taught in most schools; hygiene was the subject of royal commissions and government boards; Sanitary Institutes were common in many English cities. Divided into two main sections, "Health" and "Education," the focus of the International Health Exhibition was on recent reforms in food, dress, the dwelling, the school, and the workshop.[6]

The International Health Exhibition followed the fisheries Exhibition of 1883 in the series of

Figure 3. Site plan of the International Health Exhibition, London, 1884, from *The International Health Exhibition Official Guide*, published that year.

thematic fairs sponsored by Queen Victoria and the Prince of Wales. It was largely accommodated within the buildings and courts constructed for its predecessor, although fair organizers pointed with pride to "the intricacy of the ground plan," made possible by the "large number of new annexes, courts, corridors, and detached buildings" constructed for the IHE.[7] The health exhibition took place on the grounds of the Royal Horticultural Society, between the Royal Albert Hall and the Natural History Museum. The Royal Albert Hall and the City and Guilds of London Institute for Technical Education, on Exhibition Road to the east, were also appropriated for the health fair.[8]

Most of the displays at the IHE were housed in long, narrow galleries in the south end of the grounds, adjacent to the Natural History Museum on Cromwell Road (fig. 3). The north end comprised a grand terraced court and garden, boasting the Memorial to the Great Exhibition of 1851—a forceful reminder of the history of the area as the setting of other successful public exhibitions—and magnificent fountains; a grand axis, Central Avenue, bisected the site from north to south.

Figure 4. Miss South Kensington attracting theater crowds, from *Punch*, 1884.

recorded estimates, presumably drawing crowds away from many other cultural events. A satirical cartoon in *Punch* featured a huge "Miss South Kensington" luring people away from the city's theaters with a gigantic magnet called "The Healtheries" (fig. 4).

The crowds attending the health exhibition were a testament to the population's interest in the new field of sanitary science, as well as to the Victorian faith in the power of spaces and things—supposedly "useful productions"—to improve public health. Heating and cooking apparatus, clothing, shoes, machinery, food, ambulances, lighting, furniture, and baths, among other objects, were displayed by individual manufacturers, grouped by categories. Images of the fair show that most of the displays were arranged in large shop windows, or in small shoplike stalls constructed inside the open exhibition halls. Belgium, China, India, and Japan were represented by separate national pavilions in and around which were exhibited more objects, more or less related to health in those countries.[11]

Food, dress, furniture, and houses of the past were juxtaposed with similar contemporary productions in order to illustrate—and to celebrate—Victorian progress in the field of sanitation. This pointed juxtaposition of historical and contemporary artifacts communicated a clear message to fairgoers: living conditions in 1884 were much healthier than those of the past. This message was expressed not only by the architecture of individual buildings and the displays of objects within them, but also by the visitor's experience of moving through the entire grounds, directed by a fluid ground plan in and out of buildings, in a dynamic interplay of changing sights, smells, and sounds. The Old Street, the fountains, the buildings, and such displays as that of a room-ventilating tube could be read—at one level—as a lesson in the progress

The flurry of activity resulting from the fair, however, extended well beyond the boundaries of the exhibition site. Anticipating the four million visitors who attended the event, vendors filled the streets of South Kensington leading to the grounds with stands and displays of "useless productions." Stalls of cork mice, china dolls, and tin mechanical alligators hardly prepared the visitor for the plethora of hygienic devices exhibited within the boundaries of the IHE.[9] Railway companies also offered discounts to all districts within sixty miles of the metropolis, allowing their "country cousins to 'do' the exhibition in a day."[10] Fair attendance exceeded all

of sanitary science.[12] At the same time, the design of the IHE glorified the productive organizational capacities of the municipal government and manufacturers; it was the streamlined, rationalized structure of the industrial corporation and the city bureaucracy that seemed to offer hope in the present against what Victorians were warned to fear about the past.

In this sense, the display of water at the fair assumed special importance as a self-congratulatory promotional gesture by municipal water companies touting their role in the recent restructuring of London's sewer system, as well as a direct reference to the importance of clean water in the Victorian conception of disease control.[13] Decorative pools and drinking fountains could be found throughout the grounds of the IHE. This conspicuous consumption of water for apparently purely recreational use in the main court of the IHE was much more than an aesthetic choice; it was a public celebration of the city's good health in 1884.

In both its sheer quantity and its illumination, the water displayed at the exhibition was, in the words of one journal, "novel as well as ingenious" to the Londoner of the 1880s.[14] The magnificent Illuminated Fountains in the main courtyard of the fair, the "greatest attraction" of

Figure 5. View of the Illuminated Fountains at the International Health Exhibition, from *The Illustrated London News*, 1884.

the IHE, were visible from a great distance, as a single jet of water one hundred and twenty feet high rose from an island in the center of a water garden. Two hundred and fifty smaller jets and sprays of water "in the most fantastic designs" surrounded the island, changing constantly in their form and lighting (fig. 5).[15] The prime location of the fountains, on the axis between the Central Gallery and the Memorial to the Great Exhibition of 1851, was a further indication of the importance of water in the larger political agenda of the plan.

The sophisticated technology behind the elaborate water displays at the IHE was "invisible," intriguing the crowds with its seemingly magical qualities (fig. 6). Giant arc lights cast a range of colors upon the fountains, producing "the most varied effects to be attained, the water sometimes appearing red, at others purple, and again, when the white beam falls on it, the falling spray against the dark background of the sky resembles showers of diamonds." A journalist described the lighting effects as a "stream of fire," as electric lights were shot through the jet of water internally, so that the water itself appeared to be the source of illumination, rather than the reflecting surface.[16] Advertisements of the health exhibition claimed it was the "largest display of electric lighting in the world."

Colonel Francis Bolton, Examiner of the Metropolitan Board of Works, personally worked the display from the clock tower in the courtyard, sending signals to five men who controlled the lights from a cramped machine room under the island. Meters located on the western side of the center basin recorded the quantity of water displayed for the enthusiastic crowd.

In this magnificent use of electricity and waterworks, the Metropolitan Board of Works had succeeded in turning its mundane work into the stuff of fantasy and drama in the name of public health. "Londoners can no longer com-plain that they are deprived of all means of out-of-door enjoyment at night," claimed the author of the official guidebook to the exhibition.[17] Ernest Hart, an organizer of the IHE, pointed to the fountains as the exhibition's most important contribution, in his assessment of fair's overall influence. "The metropolitan water companies appeared in a new light at this Exhibition," he explained, "and entered the arena as caterers for pleasure, amusement, and instruction of the public." Hart claimed that London's parks were nothing more than "dreary desolate areas of darkness, . . . unused in the evenings for any wholesome or moral purpose." He saw the IHE as both a physical and moral model for the city:

Why should we not learn from the success of the music and the lighting of the gardens of the Health Exhibition, that our great parks should all be lighted by the electric light at night, . . . and should make those places, which are now not only useless but scandals to the metropolis, the sites of healthful and innocent recreation?[18]

In this way, the popularity of the Illuminated Fountains at night linked issues of urban safety and health, projecting an atmosphere of optimism for the use of public spaces at night in the city.

Undeniable as its value as both spectacle and model for the real city must have been, the health exhibition was condemned by critics who felt the connection to health had been interpreted by the commissioners and exhibitors far too broadly. The music, lighting, and water, as many visitors noted, drew the crowds away from the exhibition halls to the exterior spaces. But beyond their obvious role as an attraction to the overall event, the water gardens were also the vehicle of one of the IHE's most potent lessons.

Figure 6. "Behind the Scenes at the Fountains," from *The Illustrated London News*, 1884.

In 1854, John Snow had proven that cholera, which had raged through the city, killing thousands in 1832 and 1848, was transmitted primarily through infected water. He had been able to demonstrate that each victim in Westminster had consumed water from an infected pump in Broad Street. This discovery was followed by desperate calls to clean the Thames River, from which the water supply of London was drawn. Through massive urban restructuring—

a new sewer system, the embankment of the river, and widespread slum clearance—London had attempted to cleanse itself.[19]

As a subtle reference to this idea of sanitary progress, the clean-water theme was carried throughout the site plan of the International Health Exhibition in pools, fountains, and even in architecture. The Water Pavilion, for example, an octagonal building constructed especially for the fair, was jointly sponsored by the eight water companies supplying London at the time.[20] In the center of the building was a cast-iron fountain: a single jet of water rose from the mouth of a swan, whose neck was clasped by a young boy. An observer remarked that the statue was "an emblematic figure, no doubt, signifying the cupidity of the water companies." A journalist in *Punch* was even less sympathetic to what he read as pure hypocrisy, clearly disappointed with the building, following a rumor that "these monopolists were about to atone for a past of mismanagement and extortion, by affording a display that would soften the heart of the most indignant economist." As he shrewdly perceived, the architecture of the Water Pavilion was clearly intended to mask the general mismanagement of the city's water by the sponsoring companies with art and entertainment.[21]

The water theme was carried outward from this central motif through the rest of the building, recalling to *Punch* the "venerable squirts of Trafalgar Square." The basin surrounding the fountain was decorated with water lilies and other aquatic plants. From its edges, eight streams of water, representing each of the city's water companies, were directed toward the middle of the fountain. Scenes of the Thames River decorated the walls of the pavilion. Each company also displayed, "behind a glass screen, an actual section of the materials of its filter bed, and in each angle is a tap and a drinking-cup, so that

persons who feel that they 'may well abide it' can drink the water of all the different companies and compare them."[22] It is difficult to imagine Londoners of the 1850s drinking water that appeared to have been taken from the Thames River!

The elaborate use of water at the International Health Exhibition, even in its "artistic" guise, was a direct reference to the significance of clean water in the Victorian conception of disease control. But on another level, it operated as a subtle counterpoint to the quaint but lamentable picture painted by the architecture of the Old Street. The Water Pavilion, in its location and architecture, and in the sensual experience that it offered to visitors, was the antithesis of the Old Street.[23] In this way the water companies portrayed themselves as a means of relief, or even protection, from a horrific past.

As an amalgam of buildings from different time periods and different parts of London, the Old Street exhibition was less an accurate representation of an actual street than a creative recombination of "typical buildings, of which authentic drawings have come down to us."[24] The scale of the exhibit was equally misleading; the reproductions of medieval buildings that lined the street were much smaller than the original structures they were meant to represent.[25] Furthermore, realism in the Old London Street was invalidated by signs, advertisements, and evidence of modern technology at the fair. Old London, presented in this fictional, miniaturized model, clearly communicated to visitors that the mistakes of the past, which had resulted in horrifying plague and fire, were now understood and would, therefore, never be repeated. As one observer perceptively remarked, "as it stands, the sole relation of the old street to Health is a negative one."[26]

New London, the healthy city, was represented by more "positive" displays: the Water

Company Pavilion and the other displays of water in the site plan. In every way, the architecture of the building was a subtle rebuttal to the conditions simulated in the Old Street. While the Old Street was dark and overcrowded, the Water Pavilion was brightly illuminated and spacious; the Old Street was dry, while the new building was fresh and cool. Its lush decorative motifs, drawn from water and plant life, provided a counterpoint to the austere simplicity of medieval buildings, which recalled death and destruction from disease and fire. While the Old Street was essentially an enclosed space— its buildings were intended to be experienced like a stage set—the Water Pavilion was only one part of a complex series of relatively open spaces, linked by water, leading to the Illuminated Fountains, and eventually to the Memorial to the Exhibition of 1851.

The overall plan of the International Health Exhibition thus functioned as a lucid sketch of health issues as they were understood by the British middle class in 1884; like other large public exhibitions, the health fair simplified and clarified complex urban questions, codifying the relationships of power, disease, and recreation in physical form at a single moment in time. Its value cannot be overestimated as a compelling statement of current notions of health for historians of Victorian medicine.

For historians of architecture, too, an interpretation of the Old London Street in its larger context illustrates the critical relationship of nineteenth-century buildings to experiences, both outside their own physical boundaries and inside, and to the health of those who inhabited the spaces. It is only by examining urban projects in context and by locating ordinary people within these spaces that we can begin to understand the complexity of the nineteenth-century city. ∎

Notes

I am grateful to Eric Sandweiss and Dell Upton for their insightful readings of an earlier version of this paper; also to the staffs of the Wellcome Institute for the History of Medicine in London and to the Canadian Centre for Architecture and McGill University Libraries in Montreal.

1   This description of the Old London Street at the International Health Exhibition is based on observations reported in "The International Health Exhibition," *Builder* 46 (May 3, 1884): 601–2, and "The Health Exhibition," *Builder* 46 (May 17, 1884): 687–88; E. Hart, "The International Health Exhibition: Its Influence and Possible Sequels," *Journal of the Society of Arts* 33 (November 28, 1884): 35–58; G. A. Sala, "The Health Exhibition: A Look Around," *Illustrated London News* (hereafter *ILN*) 85 (August 2, 1884), 90–95; *The International Health Exhibition Official Guide* (London, 1884): 45–50; and D. Galton, "The International Health Exhibition," *Art Journal*, n.s. 4 (1884): 153–56, 161–64, 293–96.

2   *ILN* 85 (August 2, 1884): 94.

3   *Art Journal*, n.s. 4 (1884): 161.

4   *Official Guide*, 7.

5   Health exhibitions had already been held in England in conjunction with the annual meetings of the Social Science Association, beginning with that in Leeds (1871), followed by Norwich (1873), Glasgow (1874), Brighton (1875), and Liverpool (1876). The Sanitary Institute held a similar exhibition in 1879. See Hart, "International Health Exhibition," 35.

6   A guide to the Education section of the fair was published as *Special Catalogue of the Education Division* (London, 1884).

7   *Official Guide*, 11.

8   A detailed plan of the arrangements of exhibits in both these buildings was published in the beginning of the *Special Catalogue of the Education Division*.

No trace of the IHE has survived on the site; today the grounds are occupied by the Imperial College of Science and Technology, established in 1907 through the federation of the Royal College of Science, the

Royal School of Mines, and the City and Guilds College. See "Imperial College of Science and Technology," in *The London Encyclopaedia*, ed. B. Weinreb and C. Hibbert (London, 1983), 405. For an account of the history of the RHS garden, see F. H. W. Sheppard, ed., *Survey of London*, vol. 38 (London, 1975), 124–32. The area behind the Royal Albert Hall also had been used by the International Medical & Sanitary Exhibition of 1881; see *International Medical & Sanitary Exhibition Official Catalogue* (London, 1881).

9 "Our Insane-itary Guide to the Health Exhibition," *Punch* 86 (June 14, 1884): 277. For a description of the vendors along Exhibition Road in South Kensington, see *Architect* 32 (August 23, 1884): 114; the statistics on visitors are reported in *Architect* 32 (November 8, 1884): 296.

10 *Architect* 33 (August 23, 1884): 114.

11 For further information on the international pavilions, see *Architect* 31 (February 23, 1884): 129–30. The entry to the Belgian pavilion is illustrated in *ILN* 85 (August 2, 1884): 108; outside dining and a stand offering mineral waters were adjacent.

12 A comparison of public and domestic architecture at the IHE is offered in A. Adams, "Architecture in the Family Way: Health Reform, Feminism, and the Middle-class House in England, 1870–1900," Ph.D. diss., University of California, Berkeley, 1992. See also A. Adams, *Corpus Sanum in Domo Sano: The Architecture of the Domestic Sanitation Movement, 1870–1914*, ex. cat. (Montreal, 1991), 16–18.

13 Other health exhibitions also featured water fountains illuminated with colored light. See "The Manchester International Health Exhibition," *Sanitary Record* n.s. 16 (May 10, 1895): 1613.

14 *ILN* 85 (August 2, 1884): 106.

15 Hart, "International Health Exhibition," 55; *Official Guide*, 56.

16 *Official Guide*, 56; *Journal of the Society of Arts* 33 (November 28, 1884): 41.

17 *Official Guide*, 56.

18 Hart, "International Health Exhibition," 40, 56.

19 On John Snow and cholera, see J. J. Cosgrove, *History of Sanitation* (Pittsburgh, 1909), 91–98; F. Sheppard, *London, 1808–1870: The Infernal Wen* (Berkeley, 1971), 247–48; F. B. Smith, *The People's Health 1830–1910* (New York, 1979), 229–38. On the cleansing of London, see M. Brack, "The Architecture of Health: The Role of Hygiene in the Architecture and Planning of Nineteenth-Century London," unpublished paper, Dept. of Architecture, University of California, Berkeley, May 3, 1988. On the development of London's sewer system, see A. F. Green, "The Problem of London's Drainage," *Geography* 41 (1956): 147–54.

20 There are no extant images of this building; it is described in the *Official Guide*, 44.

21 *Builder* 46 (May 17, 1884): 688; "Our Insane-itary Guide to the Health Exhibition," *Punch* 87 (August 9, 1884): 65. The water companies failed to provide adequate water to poorer districts until after the formation of the Metropolitan Water Board in 1902. On the politics of London's water supply, see Sheppard, *London, 1808–1870*, 260–63.

22 "Our Insane-itary Guide," 65; *Builder* 46 (May 17, 1884): 688.

23 It was recommended to visitors that they first visit the Old London Street, then the Prince of Wales' and the Water Companies' pavilions. *Official Guide*, 13.

24 *Builder* 46 (May 3, 1884): 601.

25 This may have been due to contraints of the site, but it is also completely consistent with the style of other nineteenth-century exhibitions. Burton Benedict has described this common technique of miniaturization in the construction of models of cities, parks, and streets at world's fairs as a way of both impressing the public and expressing control of the simulated environment. See B. Benedict, *The Anthropology of World's Fairs* (Berkeley, 1983), 17.

26 *Builder* 46 (May 17, 1884): 687. See also "Our Insane-itary Guide," 49.

16

CARDIFF

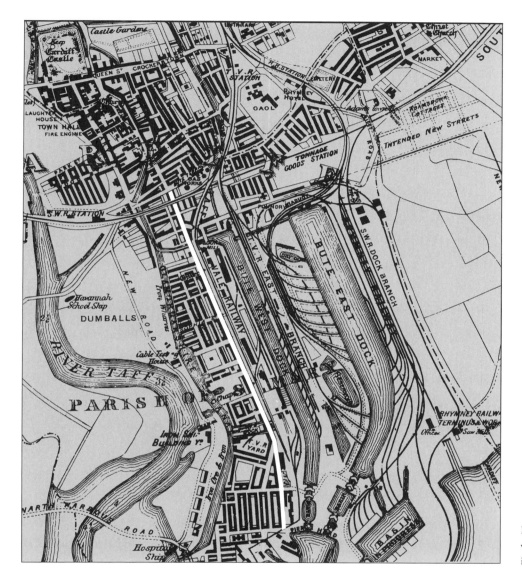

Bute Street

BRUCE THOMAS

Figure 1. Plan of Cardiff, with Bute Street marked in white.

In 1853 *The Cardiff and Merthyr Guardian* took stock of the recently built port on the mud flats outside the South Gate of old Cardiff:

Respectable parties are compelled to remove to other localities. The keepers of public-houses and brothels are gradually obtaining possession of [Bute Street]. . . . In short, Cardiff is gaining a world-wide reputation as one of the most immoral not only of towns but of seaports.[1]

Cardiff and Bute Street were not supposed to turn out that way. Rather, Bute Street was first imagined in the spirit of the grandest urban promenades, an answer to London's Regent Street, Paris's Rue de Rivoli, or St. Petersburg's Nevsky Prospect. Bute Street was conceived by Cardiff's hereditary landlord, John Crichton Stuart, the second Marquess of Bute

Figure 2. Paul Sandby, *Old Cardiff from South Moors*, 1776. Note ships aground at low water and Cardiff Castle in the distance at center.

(1793–1848), who envisioned a vibrant mix of commerce and gentility. As initially planned, Bute Street is an example of the singular vision of one of the most influential, powerful, and by most accounts benevolent of men. Its subsequent mutation is a demonstration of the limits of such a personal form of city design in the new urban world of laissez-faire capitalism (fig. 1).

In 1775, Cardiff's Customs Officer reported, "We have no coal exported from this port, nor ever shall, as it would be too expensive to bring it down here from the internal part of the country." As a prospectus for Cardiff's future, the statement was spectacularly wrong.[2] But the Customs Officer's prediction was in part based on the unprepossessing condition of the old settlement gathered to the south of a crumbling castle, a town that showed little hint of what it would become. Numbering less than two thousand people, Cardiff was, in the

words of one eighteenth-century tourist, "ill-built . . . nor is there anything very pleasing in its environs."[3]

But Cardiff was not without potential. The confluence of a booming iron (and later coal) economy and the most capable and powerful of landed aristocrats held great promise for the port. Only twenty-five miles to the north, the Valleys (as highland South Wales is known) were rapidly industrializing as an expanding iron industry exploited rich coal deposits and abundant water power. Located near the mouth of the River Taff, one of the principal watercourses running down from the Valleys to the Bristol Channel, Cardiff was well situated to become the heart of a Welsh commercial network. A half-century earlier, Defoe had noted that Cardiff "has a very good harbour opening into the Severn Sea."[4] But development of the waterfront was fraught with difficulties: the Taff regularly slipped its banks—so much so that buildings

Figure 3. View of Cardiff from the castle, 1841. Note St. Mary's Street (the High Street) at center, and the ship's mast at Bute Docks in the distance.

along the west side of St. Mary's Street—the High Street and Cardiff's principal thorough-fare—were swept away and St. Mary's Church was gradually undermined and reduced to ruin. More important, commerce was limited by the location of old Cardiff's quay, adjacent to St. Mary's Street, two twisting miles above the actual mouth of the river (fig. 2).

While in Elizabethan times Cardiff had been designated one of three "head ports" in Wales, by the early nineteenth century the town was overshadowed by Swansea to the west and Newport to the east. If quay activities could be moved closer to the mouth of the Taff, if St. Mary's Street could, in effect, run down to the open sea, the port would have the potential to be the economic foundation for a revitalized city.

This ambitious project was undertaken in the 1830s and 1840s by the Marquess of Bute, who boldly mortgaged the greater part of his fortune and all of his peace of mind to build new docks on the mud flats below the old South Gate of the city. The spine of development was to be a great commercial avenue, Bute Street, connecting the old town and the new docks. Because Bute built outside Cardiff's walls, the form of the old city remained intact, surviving to stand side by side with a more modern port town. Unique among provincial cities of its era, Cardiff retained its preindustrial form, with the castle at the head of St. Mary's Street, while concurrently spawning a separate, complemen-tary industrial and commercial focus, organize along Bute Street. In the Welsh geographer Harold Carter's words, Cardiff became "at once a market town grown large and a major indus-trial city" (fig. 3).[5]

As a young man, the future marquess had traveled extensively, becoming acquainted with glamorous European capitals contrived in the Grand Manner, great urban works of art that at once conveyed the power of social order and the grace of reigning fashion. In particular, young Stuart was intrigued by his visit to St. Petersburg, the Russian new town on the Baltic. He admired the manner in which the Czar had exercised his political and economic power to build a strategically important city, an economically viable port, yet at the same time had also been able to lay out a plan that, in fashionable conception at least, was a match for Sixtus V's Rome or even Louis XIV's Versailles.

Although Bute admired the physical grandeur and sophistication of the courts of Europe, by nature he had little interest in their surrounding social whirl. Moreover, a painful eye condition, irritated by even the dimmest candlelight, led him to shun the frivolous pursuits of his class, so often unfavorably contrasted by historians with the shrewd, driven new captains of industry. Frail and uninterested in society, Bute soon came to spend most of his time at his family's seat, the Isle of Bute in Scotland, where he pursued a talent and passion for estate management and land development. From there he reinvented his Welsh estate at Cardiff; in the apt phrase of John Davies, author of the most complete Bute biography, he "conduct[ed] an industrial revolution in South Wales through correspondence." Bute established a link of ideas and expertise between the Isle of Bute and Cardiff, exporting men of all stations, from surveyors to colliers to servants, from Scotland to South Wales to carry out his plans.[6]

In the nineteenth century, few individuals were as knowledgeable about estate planning as Bute. Few shared his finely balanced sense of noblesse oblige and understanding of the necessity for economic expansion. Nor was he blind to the prestige associated with sophisticated urban life. He knew that the urbane atmosphere for which he admired the modern European capitals would be difficult to foster in the narrow lanes of an old town. Yet nowhere were conditions as favorable as at Cardiff for an individual of his wealth, influence, and talent to realize his vision of a new urbanism.[7]

When Bute came into his inheritance in 1814, the Welsh holdings were primarily rural, with more than 80 percent of income derived from farm rents.[8] He immediately set about reconfiguring his holdings by an apparently conflicting policy of both expansion and consolidation. On the one hand, he purchased as much land with mineral potential as possible, throughout South Wales, and then linked trade exclusively to his holdings at Cardiff. On the other hand, he sold off agricultural land that was without mineral promise and used the proceeds to buy up property within and near Cardiff that might appreciate with the port development he already contemplated.[9]

Only the Marquess of Bute possessed the land, capital, influence, and perhaps skill to develop a port at Cardiff to take advantage of the Valleys' iron industry. As David Stuart, Bute's surveyor (transferred from Edinburgh), pointed out, "Neither the port of Cardiff nor the mineral country can be opened properly without the consent of Lord Bute. If the port of Cardiff is not made the best port in the Bristol Channel it must be because Lord Bute does not choose to exert his power."[10]

He chose to. Butetown, as the site for his development was to be called, was tightly circumscribed. To the west lay the river and the Glamorganshire Canal, the crucial lifeline that connected the Valleys' ironworks to the sea. To the east were to be the docks. The canal and proposed docks bracketed a strip of land approximately one-half mile across and three miles long. The easternmost one-third, the area adjacent to the docks, was reserved for the daily labor of the port—wharfs, warehouses, and later railway sidings. To the west, a more sedate mixture of businesses and residences was arranged in a long, narrow grid. Bute Street, a long, straight spine running southward to the channel, separated the two (fig. 4). To confirm his cornerstone principles of commerce and established order, the marquess provided £5,700 for construction and a £380 yearly endowment for a new Customs House and a new St. Mary's Church near the north end of Bute Street. At the other end of the street a glassworks, sealocks for both the canal and docks, a cluster of workers' houses, and, later, the Taff Vale Railway works and terminus formed a more motley southern anchor to development. Thus established, Bute Street's two ends encompassed both Cardiff's past and future: to the north, nearest the old town, fashionable institutional buildings evinced stability; to the south, new commerce and industry predominated.

Although shifted eastward in a slight jog, Bute Street effectively extended St. Mary's Street, connecting the old castle to its new economic adventure, the docks. Yet the two streets were not to be one. In addition to the jog (Bute Street aligned with The Hays, the most dense quarter of the walled town), a bridge over the Glamorganshire Canal outside the South Gate marked a clear dividing line, a separation recognized even today as the boundary between two distinct Cardiffs. St. Mary's remained the old street, a part of the old town; Bute Street was the avenue of Cardiff's future. Built respectively for a preindustrial market town and a nineteenth-century commercial and industrial city, St. Mary's Street and Bute Street were organizing elements of two different worlds.

It was most important to the marquess that Bute Street have an entirely different character than any street in old Cardiff: the new street, he hoped, would be Cardiff's answer to the sophisticated urban life of King Street in Bristol, South Wales's nearby metropolis. Butetown

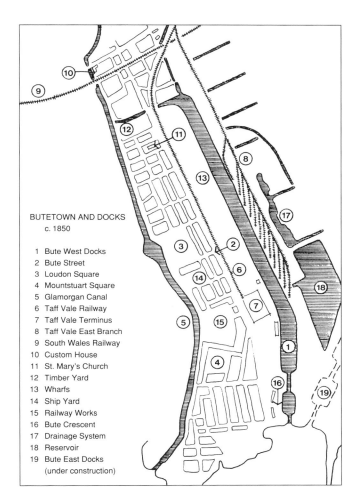

BUTETOWN AND DOCKS
c. 1850

1 Bute West Docks
2 Bute Street
3 Loudon Square
4 Mountstuart Square
5 Glamorgan Canal
6 Taff Vale Railway
7 Taff Vale Terminus
8 Taff Vale East Branch
9 South Wales Railway
10 Custom House
11 St. Mary's Church
12 Timber Yard
13 Wharfs
14 Ship Yard
15 Railway Works
16 Bute Crescent
17 Drainage System
18 Reservoir
19 Bute East Docks
   (under construction)

was to be not unlike the area around Bristol's Queen Square, where businessmen mingled with ladies and gentlemen amid the bustle and activity of the waterfront; where quays, warehouses, working-class cottages, and great houses combined in a vibrant city landscape (fig. 5).

The first manifestation of Bute's plans was an 1821 scheme by Thomas Telford. The famous engineer proposed to bypass completely the bends of the Taff, and in the process the town itself, by rerouting the river just west of the castle into a new channel. This would flow into the River Ely and out its mouth at Penarth, land

Figure 4. Plan of Butetown and docks, c. 1850.

Engd. & Pubd. by Newman & Co.

48. Watling St. London.

The Docks, Cardiff.

Figure 5. Idealized view of
the docks area at the foot
of Bute Street, in a print
of 1857.

owned by Bute on the west bank of the mouth
of the Taff, opposite the mud flats below Cardiff. The diversion would free St. Mary's Street
from the Taff's destructive flooding and the new
channel could accommodate the ever more common larger ships. Yet Bute hesitated, it was said,
at the estimated cost for the project of £20,000.
More important, he must have realized that
the Telford scheme would focus growth not on
Cardiff but on more remote empty tracts at
Penarth. Like any entrepreneur, he was driven
by the opportunity to make money. But unlike
so many of his contemporaries, the marquess's
plans were more complex than mere real-estate
speculation. He recognized that a principal
shortcoming of the new industrial landlords

who were his rivals (personified for Bute by
the ironmasters of the Valleys) was their refusal
to accept responsibility for building physical
and social order. Bute saw it as his paternal duty
to improve Cardiff.

After rejecting Telford's plan, he was unde-
cided as to how to proceed with improvements,
and was in no hurry to finance personally the
building of new port facilities. He believed, as
did most developers, that profits should be
realized from ground rents and that speculative building was best left to tenants. It was the
responsibility of those who might gain from
expanded commerce, in this case the Valleys'
industrialists, to step forward and finance development. Yet time and again, conflicts between

Bute's noblesse-oblige instinct and entrepreneurial zeal got in the way; he rejected the very schemes he solicited, distrusting development proposals that might darken his impressionistic image of what Bute Street ought to be.

Finding no one else who met his standards, Bute became resigned to assuming the expense of the planning work. In 1830 he sponsored a new scheme by Telford and James Green, an engineer noted for canal work, for development of the mud flats south of old Cardiff. The authorizing Bill of Parliament, issued the next year, noted that not only would "a new line of street, a new canal, [and] new wharfs" be built, but "almost a new town will be formed."[11]

By 1839, the new docks were complete. Initial cost estimates of £66,600 had been shockingly inaccurate; with construction costs topping £500,000, Bute was forced to mortgage most of his estate, spend £220,000 in cash, and provide an additional £130,000 in building materials from his land. Although he was rumored to have suffered "great anxiety," Bute had done his duty: the docks were the foundation on which a new Cardiff could rise. With these in place, he was ready for the return on his investment, for old Cardiff to flower, for a new Cardiff to take root, and for Bute Street to assume its place as one of the great streets of Europe.

Bute was reluctant to build in the old town, in part because of the expense and difficulty in making sweeping changes within an existing urban fabric. In contrast, Butetown was a clean slate. Bute Street, with its forty-foot roadway (although not as broad as St. Mary's Street in the old town, still one-third again as wide as any other Butetown street), was the axis of a formal scheme, with two great squares anchoring the elongated grid. Near the southern end, Mountstuart Square—named after the marquess's ancestral home—was designed to be the business center of Butetown. To the north, approxi-

mately at the center of Butetown, halfway along Bute Street was Loudon Square (or Luton, as it was originally called). Named after Bute's wife's ancestral home, it was to be a prestigious residential enclave, a complement to the business and commercial character of Mountstuart Square. Throughout the rest of the grid, Bute planned to scatter more humble terraces for dock-workers as well as more expensive two- and three-story blocks—houses that, in the Welsh historian John Hilling's phrase, "with their cast-iron balconies, must have looked quite elegant."[12]

Yet for Bute, the cityscape Hilling describes remained only a tantalizing dream. Despite the invigorating presence of the docks, Butetown's planned integrated community was slow to take shape. Throughout the 1830s, while the docks were being completed, the rest of Butetown remained only a surveyor's grid. By the 1840s, it was still little more than a motley collection of timber yards, shipyards, and similar waterfront businesses. The slow pace of residential construction was particularly distressing to Bute: two years after the completion of the docks only 5 percent of Cardiff's population of more than ten thousand lived in Butetown, where fewer than one hundred houses were recorded. Moreover, there was little evidence of the mixing of classes that Bute had desired. Even by 1850, a town directory listed among its "Nobility, Gentry, and Clergy" only two clergymen with Bute Street addresses.[13]

With significant parts of his scheme lagging, Bute was once again forced to take a greater financial role in development. Yielding to the repeated urging of his estate agent, Edward Priest Richards, to "set an example," at a cost of £8,250 Bute built a crescent of "better" houses along the east side of the docks' entry basin at the southern end of Bute Street (fig. 6). In keeping with his vision of a heterogeneous community, Bute added smaller houses for workmen for

Figure 6. Some of the extant original houses of Bute Crescent, Bute Street.

medieval layout, he dictated a minimum building frontage of fifteen feet; but in Butetown the minimum was an extravagant twenty-four feet. In addition, the standard Butetown lease was specifically written to allow Bute to set the tone of development. Within one year of the agreement, the tenant was required to improve the plot by building "with good and substantial materials." In many cases the marquess's agent would even supply plans, elevations, and bills of materials, which were to be strictly adhered to. For example, approved elevations for a building on Loudon Square carried the notation, "All the Cornices, Ballusters & Moulding, of every description are intended to be worked with Roman Cement which . . . is generally used in all our London buildings *Belgravia* included."[16]

In a few locations, Butetown reached the marquess's desired level of quality as commerce and gentility rested easily side by side. The head of Bute Street nearest the old town gained some imposing new buildings, fashionably styled by professionals familiar in sophisticated circles. For the new St. Mary's Church, the Liverpool architect John Foster designed a Neoromanesque façade with twin towers topped by stone pyramids. The Customs House, whose Palladian classicism spoke of the port's hoped-for prominence, may have been the work of Sydney Smirke.[17] By the early 1850s, brickyards and drydocks adjacent to Loudon Square had been cleared. Throughout the second half of the century, the square remained the most fashionable address in Butetown. In 1871, while the rest of Butetown was crowded with 7.5 persons per house, for the much larger houses in Loudon Square the number hovered near 5.5. Moreover, the census showed that buildings on the square housed a larger number of servants and were more often headed by members of a high social class than elsewhere in Butetown (fig. 7).[18] Meanwhile, to the south, Mountstuart Square

£175 each, behind the crescent. Furthermore, he began vigorous improvement of his property as an enticement to speculators. In the 1830s, his costs for preparing building ground in Butetown rarely exceeded £100 per annum. By the late 1840s, the figure ran between £1,000 and £3,000 per year. Stung by public criticism of sanitary conditions, Bute also took responsibility for providing Butetown with a sewer system.

As in the old town, regulations concerning speculative building in Bute Street and adjoining blocks were strictly enforced. Bute's control often extended to such apparently trivial matters as the naming of new streets, "to prevent any objectionable names being given by the occupiers of the houses."[14] More significantly, the marquess maintained a high ground rent in Bute Street. In the mid-1830s, the rate of 1s.6d. per foot of frontage was half again as high as the old-town rate.[15] Bute also controlled plot sizes. In the old town, in recognition of the

filled with ever larger office blocks, as Cardiff established itself as the world's leading coal port.

But everywhere else Butetown was turning into "Tiger Bay," a sink of legendary iniquity. No matter how diligently were enforced the regulations for minimum house size, no matter how skillfully were crafted the shop façades along Bute Street, no matter how carefully were designed the cornices and balustrades of Loudon Square, Tiger Bay stubbornly refused to imitate London's Belgravia or Bristol's Queen Square. Terraces overflowed with dock workers, often with multiple families and around-the-clock schedules of lodgers to a single house. Bute Street, the great thoroughfare of the new Cardiff, was renowned not as one of Europe's most prestigious boulevards, but as one of Europe's most infamous promenades of vice. Prostitutes came from as far away as Rotterdam and Hamburg to walk Bute Street, to meet ships at the Bute docks. Many of Butetown's "better" merchants, although maintaining their businesses in Bute Street and near the docks, began to live elsewhere. Even Bute's sewer project was a failure. H. J. Paine, Cardiff's Medical Officer, reported squalid physical conditions: "Nearly the whole of [Butetown's] streets are unpitched, very inefficiently drained, and, being situated on a very low level, usually contain stagnant water and much mud, mixed with refuse vegetable matter. The area behind most of the houses occupied by labourers, being a large proportion, is frequently flooded with foetid water and cesspool soakings."[19]

Bute witnessed neither the complete degradation of his vision, nor its later, unexpected economic revival. He died in 1848, twenty-five years after first seriously considering his plan, and with the economic and social success of the venture still very much in doubt. Despite Bute's enormous investment in the new docks, during his lifetime the increase in trade did not meet expectations. Because of antipathy fostered by the marquess's obstructionist attitude toward development plans other than his own, and high Bute Dock rates, the Valleys' iron-masters continued to use inferior facilities at the old canal basin. Moreover, by mid-century the railroad boom that had lifted South Wales's iron industry from the depression of the 1830s was over.

Soon after Bute's death, with the enormous expansion of the coal trade in the second half of the century, Butetown attained a degree of commercial success beyond Bute's wildest dreams. But the cost of that success was the degradation of Bute's social vision through the emergence of conditions that justified Tiger Bay's reputation. How is the emergence of a Bute Street from which "respectable parties are compelled to remove to other localities" to be accounted for? What turned Butetown into Tiger Bay?

Nineteenth-century industrialization and urbanization must be described as mixed blessings. A few industrialists and aristocratic landlords made fortunes; legions of workers made more money than they ever could have hoped for in a rural, agrarian world. Yet, as Engels and Marx warned, a social price was also to be paid. Familiar physical and cultural patterns, many essentially unchanged for centuries, were obliterated almost overnight. Social norms encapsulated in and reinforced by urban forms likewise disappeared. And even the best-laid plans were inadequate to direct and control progress.

Bute's assiduously enforced development regulations, imposed to assure a desired level of quality, were in many instances self-defeating. In addition, nineteenth-century demographics were at odds with preindustrial urban visions. In most rapidly growing nineteenth-century British cities, laborers far outnumbered all other segments of the population. In Cardiff, thousands of workers were needed to build and

Figure 7. The Loudon Square area, Butetown. Bute Street, at right, separates residential Butetown from docks.

then to operate the docks. The socially conscious Bute might put up a terrace of workers' cottages behind Bute Crescent, but for speculators, large plot sizes, high ground rents, and tight building restrictions made it unattractive to erect less expensive houses for the working class. Houses built to the marquess's specifications at Butetown rented at twice the rate of those in the courts and back lanes of the old town or on the developing fringe southeast of old Cardiff. It was no surprise that most workers chose to live in the old courts or new fringe, despite ever-worsening physical conditions there. Few of those laborers who did live in Butetown could afford to live "properly" in the larger houses. Their consequent doubling, tripling, or quadrupling—not to mention subletting to transients—threw Bute's envisioned social mix hopelessly out of balance. Although elsewhere the degradation of the nineteenth-century street must be charged to laissez-faire capitalism, at Bute Street the lagging growth rate, lack of appropriate housing for the working class, and skewed social mix may be attributed, ironically, to Bute's social consciousness, and to the land economics and building regulations he imposed.

Bute also failed to foresee the effect that ethnic diversity would have on his plans. The large numbers of Africans, Levantines, and Asians drawn by Cardiff's expanding commercial economy accounted for Butetown's unofficial but universal name of Tiger Bay. The rising tide of immigrants was clear in decennial census figures: in 1841 more than half of Butetown's population was native to Cardiff's county of Glamorgan; ten years later, only 37 percent were Glamorgan-born. As Bute must have foreseen, work at the docks guaranteed a continual flow of new arrivals. Yet most did not blend smoothly with the native Welsh (or even with the English), and instead clustered to-

gether ethnically and culturally for social and economic reasons, surrounding Bute Street and the two great squares with a zone of unassimilated foreigners. Butetown thus achieved the heterogeneity sought by Bute, but in a mutated form.

Thus, two of the elements that most characterized nineteenth-century urban life, the assembly of large numbers of people and the conduct of commerce, contained within them the seeds of both Cardiff's flowering and its degradation. The marquess's dream of a new Cardiff centered on Bute Street came to pass, but at the cost of the imagined physical and social landscapes that were the heart of his vision.

From the distance of a nascent post-industrial suburban society, infused with a well-developed romantic, nostalgic view of the city and the country, it is easy for us to damn places such as Bute Street as bad examples of the expansion of urban industry or commerce. Yet in the nineteenth century, although there was a price to pay, the traditional attractions of city life, enhanced by increased wealth and greater job security (admittedly often an illusion) were irresistible for hundreds of thousands. If the street stubbornly resisted shaping by the likes of the Marquess of Bute, and instead took its own form, that was simply the reality of city life.

Touring Manchester in the 1840s with a middle-class gentleman, Friedrich Engels directed his companion's attention to the "disgusting condition" of the streets through which they moved. After walking several blocks in silence, as they parted, the gentleman replied, "And yet there is a great deal of money made here. Good morning, Sir."[20] They might have been in Bute Street. ■

Notes

1   *The Cardiff and Merthyr Guardian*, January 8, 1853.

2   As quoted in W. Davies, *Agriculture and the Domestic Economy of South Wales*, 1814, in C. Evans, S. Dodsworth, and J. Bennett, *Below the Bridge: A Photo and Historical Survey of Cardiff's Docklands to 1983* (Cardiff, 1984). Less than one hundred years after the prediction, Cardiff was exporting 3 million tons of coal each year. By the first decades of the twentieth century, when coal shipments peaked, the figure was 10,500,000 tons annually, with an additional 11,750,000 tons shipped from nearby docks at Penarth and Barry.

3   Anonymous [H. P. Wyndham], *A Gentleman's Tour of Monmouthshire and Wales, in the Months of June and July, 1774* (London, 1775), 32.

4   D. Defoe, *A Tour through the Whole Island of Great Britain,* 1724–26 (repr. Harmondsworth, 1971), 378.

5   H. Carter, *The Towns of Wales* (Cardiff, 1965), 264.

6   J. Davies, *Cardiff and the Marquesses of Bute* (Cardiff, 1981), vii; 47–48.

7   Davies writes, "There can be few cities where the imprint of a single family is as legible as that of the Bute family at Cardiff," in *Cardiff*, 249.

8   Ibid., 146.

9   M. J. Daunton, "Aristocrats and Traders: The Bute Docks, 1839–1914," *Journal of Transport History* n.s. 3, no.2 (September 1975): 69.

10 Cardiff Public Library, ms. 4.850, cited in Davies, *Cardiff*, 247.

11 . *Parliamentary Report of the Commissioners*, London, 1831.

12 J. B. Hilling, "Cardiff," in S. Williams, ed., *South Glamorgan: A County History* (Barry, 1975), 80.

13 *Slater's National and Commercial Directory and Topography* (London, 1850), 21–27.

14 Letter, Collingdale to Bruce, July 27, 1850, cited in Davies, *Cardiff*, 186.

15 M. J. Daunton, *Coal Metropolis: Cardiff 1870–1914* (Leicester, 1977), 85.

16 Letter, A. Rees to E. P. Richards, June 1, 1853, Cardiff Public Library ms.

17 The authorship of the mid-century Butetown Customs House is unclear. Noting the similarities between it and one built eight years earlier in Bristol by Smirke, Hilling suggests the possibility that the same architect may have worked in Cardiff. The fact that Smirke was responsible for a similar customs house in Newcastle, and was married to the daughter of the architect John Dobson of Newcastle, a city to which Bute regularly looked for reference, lends fuel to the speculation.

18 R. G. Jones, "Butetown, Cardiff: Change in a Dockyard Community from the Early Nineteenth Century to the Present," unpublished master's thesis, 1980, Cardiff Public Library.

19 H. J. Paine, *Report to the General Board of Health on a Preliminary Inquiry into the Sewerage, Drainage, and Supply of Water and the Sanitary Condition of the Inhabitants of the Town of Cardiff* (London, 1850).

20 F. Engels, *The Condition of the Working Class in England* (Stanford, 1958), 312.

17

RABAT

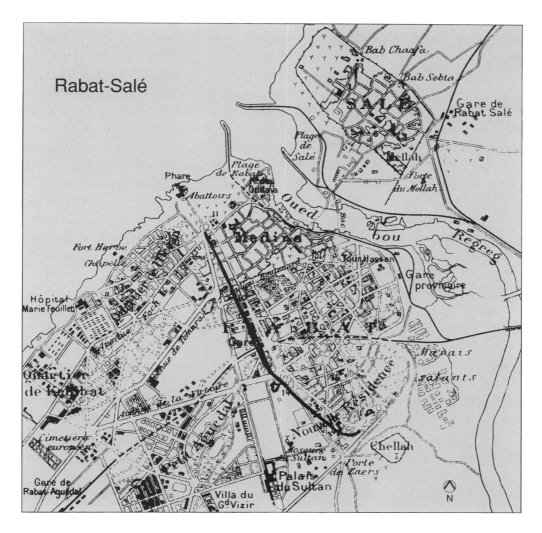

GWENDOLYN WRIGHT

Figure 1. French map of Rabat-Salé, 1936. Boulevard Muhammad V and its continuation, Avenue des Touergas, in the *ville nouvelle*, are marked in black. Note the extent to which later development followed the first colonial master plan (see fig. 3).

The major artery of Rabat, Morocco's capital city, bears the imprint of French colonial urban design in its assertive linearity (fig. 1). One also finds a multiplicity of references to Morocco's own indigenous culture, palpable not only in the years since independence in 1956, but from the first projection of the new French metropolis in 1914, with this as its principal thoroughfare. A massive wall from the seventeenth century rises to the north, where Boulevard Muhammad V connects to the medina, or original Arab town; the stately grounds of the sultan's palace and his mosque, Al Faeh, all continually altered since their mid-eighteenth-century construction, terminate the axis; the ruins of a fourteenth-century fortress can be seen below the wide plateau, as the roadway curves to the east. In addition, Islamic motifs feature prominently in most of the newer buildings on both sides of the street all along its length.

Yet even this inclusiveness forms part of the colonial history that defines much of contem-

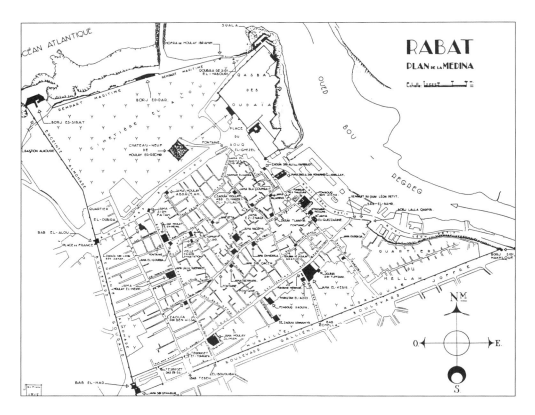

Figure 2. Plan of the medina in Rabat, c. 1940. Rue El Gza is at left, and leads from the cemetery to the Andalusian Wall, connecting there with Avenue Dar al-Maghzan.

porary Rabat. Romantic conceptions of the culture that had been overpowered, as well as the dominant status of the colonizers, frame the entire setting of the boulevard, and that of the city as a whole.

The French considered Rabat the supreme expression of their imperial accomplishments, an opinion shared by many visitors. Writing in the *Encyclopédie de l'Islam* in 1936, the anthropologist Evariste Lévi-Provençal proclaimed the city "an unqualified masterpiece, famed throughout the world for its successful town planning and architecture."[1] That success proved long-lasting, substantial enough in its formal clarity and symbolic significance to transcend the colonial system it supposedly embodied. Indeed, the change of name from Avenue Dar al-Maghzan to Boulevard Muhammad V pays

homage to the king who returned from exile in 1955 to win his nation's fight for independence.

What then were the goals, techniques, and results of colonial urbanism in Rabat, and how are they made manifest along this major axis?[2] first one must consider the historical role of this particular city. Although commercial ties between Europe (especially France) and Morocco had developed throughout the nineteenth century, the French did not invade Morocco militarily until 1907. In the small coastal settlement of Rabat's medina, they found an exceptionally beautiful setting with significant antecedents. The Casbah of the Uudaïas, facing the Atlantic, dated to the tenth century. In 1195 the Almohad ruler Yaᶜkub al-Mansur had initiated splendid mosques and immense protective ramparts far to the west and south for an expanded royal capital, to be called Rabat al-Fath (Camp of Conquest). Rabat again grew in size and prestige after the influx of Andalusian Moors fleeing the Spanish Inquisition during the seventeenth century. With the founding of the ʿAlawi dynasty in 1666, it became one of four imperial (*maghzan*) capitals, through which the sultan maintained control over different regions of the country.[3]

After five years of warfare, the French established a protectorate over Morocco in 1912. This system nominally "protected" the Muslim ruler from other European intrusions, but in fact dictated the terms of political and economic life under an artificial dual power.[4] President Poincaré named Maréchal Louis Hubert Lyautey both resident-general and head of the army, thereby giving him virtually complete control over the country. The nascent French capital was soon transferred from inland Fez to coastal Rabat, which facilitated ties to France. Rabat's lineage as an imperial capital, like that of Fez, gave symbolic historical continuity to the new colonial government.

Lyautey asserted two basic principles of governance. first, his "native policy" emphasized respect for indigenous mores and cooperative local officials. Whether at home or abroad, enlightened French leaders should assiduously protect traditions and traditional leaders. Second, he believed that urban design could serve as an exemplary political tool, far more effective than armies.[5] His urbanism encompassed historic preservation as well as modern social services and economic development. To achieve the maximum effect, it was necessary to insist upon the rigid "separation of European from indigenous Moroccan settlements."[6]

Within a year of taking office, the resident-general invited the architect Henri Prost to join his administration. Prost's Architecture and Urbanism Department—the first such governmental agency in the French world—was com-

missioned to determine the form of French settlements and industrial sites, and their relationship with existing Arab towns. Prost helped to develop the legal procedures for achieving his formal plans, as author of a section in the 1914 decree that required master plans with strict design guidelines for all Moroccan cities.

Rabat remained the favorite city of both the architect and his patron. Lyautey fondly called it his Washington, D.C., often juxtaposing this characterization with negative references to Casablanca as New York or the Wild West.[7] Avenue Dar al-Maghzan formed the major axis and the symbolic core of Prost's 1914 plan for the capital. Suggesting continuity between the old city and the new, it cut through the *ville nouvelle* from the historic medina to the sultan's palace and administrative quarters (*maghzan*), from which the street took its name.

Prost's design emphasized this connection of old and new by continuing the trajectory of rue El Gza, a major route within the medina (fig. 2). Here the local residents still come together in and around artisanal shops, fountains, bread ovens, and other communal services. One of only two straight thoroughfares running north–south, rue El Gza looks markedly different from the narrow, winding roads and impasses of the residential neighborhoods. Likewise, the intricate detailing of its façades contrasts sharply with the blank walls of houses.

Here, too, the French imposed design controls. Lyautey was determined to preserve the appearance and cultural milieu of everyday settings in the Arab medina. Early barracks for his officers, constructed in the northwestern part of the medina, adjacent to rue El Gza, had purposefully adapted the style of their surroundings. Alarmed by later French military structures in the vicinity, Lyautey established a Bureau of Fine Arts within months of taking office. The agency came under the direction of

Maurice Tranchant de Lunel, the young student from the Parisian Ecole des Beaux-Arts who had designed Lyautey's barracks "in the Arab style, making them tolerable"—or so he assumed—to the Moroccans.[8]

The Bureau of Fine Arts had the authority to safeguard the appearance and cultural life of Moroccan cities, initiating procedures that preservationists in France would have welcomed. From the start, officials asserted the need to protect entire streets like rue El Gza, rather than only a few isolated buildings. By 1925, they had fixed specific codes: a maximum height of four stories, sizable courtyards, a whitewash finish for all façades, flat tile roofs, and exacting proportions for doorways and windows; no western signage or visible utilities were permitted. It did not go unnoticed that a picturesque and seemingly authentic landscape would attract a strong tourist economy to Morocco.[9]

The majestic gate of Bab Teben frames the link between the medina's main street and that of the new city. Officially, Avenue Dar al-Maghzan begins at Boulevard Gallieni (today the Avenue Hassan II), a broad thoroughfare running parallel to the Andalusian Wall. A small landscaped island, designated Triangle Park, marks the intersection of the two streets. No construction was permitted in this *non edificandi* sector, 250 meters wide, in order to demarcate the two distinct cities. Empty of buildings, the space sets off two scales of construction, two cultures, and two periods of history. The term *cordon sanitaire*, applied to this strip, also suggests the health precautions inherent in this familiar colonial policy of separation. In an unguarded moment, Prost acknowledged that a no-man's-land would speed the mobilization of troops in the event of violence.[10]

Avenue Dar al-Maghzan cut through the center of a vast *ville nouvelle*, or new city, built for French residential and commercial settle-ments (fig. 3). Here all the benefits of modern urbanism could be applied and appraised. The colonial government acquired the necessary land in various ways: claims to the extensive domanial orchards and gardens of the sultan (which in theory belonged to the state); purchases and appropriations through the redefinition of private land ownership; and, later, outright expropriation for "public purposes."[11]

To assure visual continuity along the major thoroughfares of the *ville nouvelle*, Prost established numerous design controls for building construction. The regulations, called *police des constructions*, did not directly legislate style, but set rigorous guidelines for scale, materials, alignment, and services. Mandatory height limits were based on the width of the street, with an absolute limit of four stories during the first decade of French construction. Street façades were required to harmonize with the architectural character of Morocco, as interpreted by Prost and his staff. Along the length of Avenue Dar al-Maghzan, buildings were uniformly white over stone bases. Arcades were obligatory, providing unity to the street wall on both sides and protection from the bright sun. In order to assure "great architectural liberty," architects were free to interpret this requirement as they wished; some used heavy square columns; others, graceful arches with geometric patterns imitative of Islamic motifs.[12] Encouraged by Prost, European designers freely adapted the traditional white stucco walls of Arab architecture, together with details like interlaced wooden screens; porcelain or tile mosaics on columns or at the cornice line; prayer niches indicating the direction of Mecca; pointed or horseshoe arches; and vaulted corbeling.

Nearest the wall and the low houses of the medina, Boulevard Muhammad V consists of small-scale apartment buildings with porticoes. It then widens majestically, with a formal

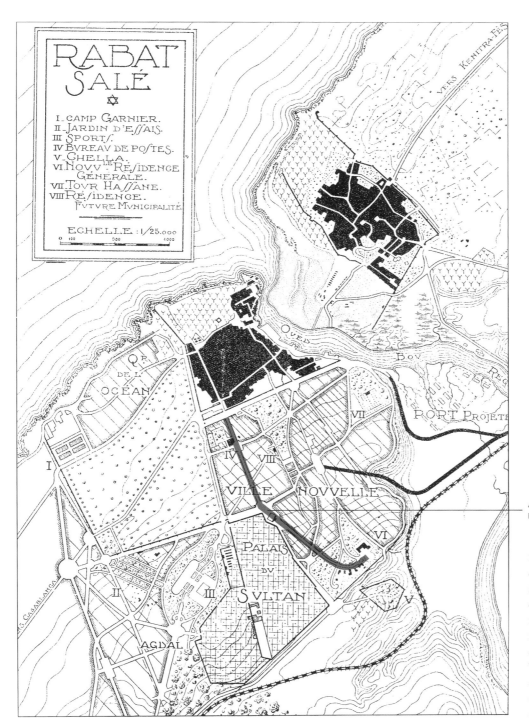

Avenue Dar al-Maghzan (now Boulevard Muhammad V)

Figure 3. Master plan of colonial Rabat and Salé in 1918, showing the development, since 1914, of newly acquired French land in the *ville nouvelle*, alongside the sultan's palace. The Arab medina and the adjacent town of Salé are darkened, as unchanging— and restricted—sites.

Figure 4. The Cours Lyautey, looking toward the Avenue Dar al-Maghzan, c. 1930. As the street moves from the medina, it expands in scale, and has larger public buildings, beginning with the state bank at left.

esplanade down the center and an allée of palm trees along the spacious sidewalks. This section, called the Cours Lyautey under the French, provides a proper setting for luxury hotels and important public buildings: the treasury, the state bank, the appellate court, the main post office (fig. 4). Halfway down this grand promenade, the Place des Alaouites faces the cathedral and the modern train station. Prost decided to locate all the railroad tracks underground, so that this convenient depot would not mar the elegance of the district.

At the center of the next major junction stands the imposing eighteenth-century Grand Mosque of Jame ᶜAl-Sunnah, where the French later added a new Koranic School and a *collège* for Muslim students (fig. 5). Farther to the south are the spacious grounds of the sultan's palace, encompassing the Supreme Court, offices, stables, schools, and another mosque. Sidi Muhammad ibn Abd-Allah began

construction of an imperial residence on this site in 1765, after the French bombardment of pirate strongholds near the coast, but, like the other *maghzan* complexes, it had never been a primary abode. All Moroccan rulers had moved in splendor from one imperial city to another, followed by an entourage of thousands. Now the French wanted the sultan fixed in one spot. Stifling his ceremonial journeys would diminish the *baraka*, or charismatic power, associated with his predecessors.[13] While carefully delimiting the force of his power, Lyautey also intended to strengthen the authority of Moulay Youssef, the ruler who had accepted the colonial presence. Accordingly, he hired the Frères Pertuzzio, French architects born in Algeria, to restore and enlarge the earlier palace as a permanent residence.[14]

Alongside the palace, the boulevard once more changes in name and form, becoming Avenue des Touergas (Tawareg). This gently

Figure 5. The Collège Musulman, built by the French architect Fernand Baud in 1916, faces the Grand Mosque Jame ʿAl-Sunnah and the grounds of the sultan's palace, at the juncture where the Boulevard Muhammad V curves to the east.

curving street passes what were once a small French military barracks and a sequence of administrative offices for the French protectorate, ending in the Résidence de France, formerly the office and home of the resident-general, now the French embassy. The parallel placement of the two administrations symbolized the myth of a dual government shared by French and Moroccan leaders.

In the French Administrative Quarter (now called the Ministries) along Avenue des Touergas, the imagery of efficient western life again sought a counterbalance with sensual Islamic design motifs. Here Prost hoped to soften both the appearance and the actual day-to-day process of political administration, at least for colonial functionaries—who constituted almost half of Rabat's fourteen thousand Europeans in 1926.[15] Rather than one massive complex, separate pavilions housed each branch of the bureaucracy (fig. 6). A curved colonnade with vine-covered pergolas,

five hundred meters long, linked the pavilions. Each of these harbored lush courtyards, where gardens and fountains offered a contemplative refuge. The decision to make each building a separate commission reinforced the pleasing effect of diversity within a strong overall plan.

Prost chose the site over an earlier location because of its strategic associations and visual assets. The plateau offers "a superb panorama of Rabat, Salé, and the estuary of Bou-Regreg."[16] A picturesque vista, like axiality, is not simply a matter of European aesthetics; here it represented European domination over the scene below. In addition, Lyautey's remarkable residence, with its marble colonnades and mosaic courtyards, overlooks the ramparts of the Chella, a fourteenth-century Merinid fortress, then in ruins, built on the remains of the Roman town of Sala. This view amplified the precedents of Roman colonization and the decline of previous Arab power.

Figure 6. Aerial view
showing several
pavilions in the French
Administrative
Quarter and, at center,
Albert Laprade's grand
Résidence de France,
which terminates
Avenue des Touergas.

Prost and Lyautey elected to highlight the historic monuments preserved in the *ville nouvelle*. Land was cleared around the walls of the Chella, visible from the Avenue des Touergas, and likewise around the Jame ʿAl-Sunnah. No construction was allowed near these sequestered structures; landscaping alone served to focus the observer's line of vision on these isolated objects. Since this concept of setting off monuments was entirely foreign to the Islamic sense of history and urban design, the French could use it as a strategy to reinforce a sense of cultural superiority. Selective preservation signaled respect for a bygone Arab civilization, in distinct contrast to the seeming disregard for the past on the part of the Moroccans themselves.[17] Furthermore, an emphasis on the timeless continuity of Islamic life implied no need to provide modern amenities for Moroccans. Prost spoke of the need to "maintain in its setting a civilization intact for centuries."[18]

In its parts and its whole, the composition was a resounding success—a success gauged on many levels, though overestimated by the colonial powers. "And thus, little by little," wrote Joseph Marrast, a French architect on Prost's staff, "we conquer the hearts of the natives and win their affection, as is our duty as colonizers."[19] The designs did win the affection of the city's residents, if not their souls. Imperialism, while evident, is by no means inherent in the urbanistic forms. The same streets and buildings can convey different messages, as they have come to do since independence. The half-hour walk from one end of Boulevard Muhammad V to the other reminds the careful observer of the complex historical narrative imprinted here. The images, close and far, like the meanings they evoke, can be read in many ways. The architecture and the spaces that surround it thus echo the multiplicity of voices and diversity of languages to be heard along the urban street. ∎

Notes

1 E. Lévi-Provençal, "Rabat," *L'Encyclopédie de l'Islam*, 1st ed. (Paris, 1936), 1164, cited in "Rabat," *Mimar* 22 (October–December 1986): n.p.

2 For an elaboration of this discussion, as well as a comparison with other French colonies, see G. Wright, *The Politics of Design in French Colonial Urbanism* (Chicago, 1991).

3 The other three were Fez, Meknes, and Marrakesh. See in particular J. Caillé, *La Ville de Rabat jusqu'au protectorat français*, 3 vols., Publications of the Institut des Hautes Etudes Marocaines (Paris, 1949).

4 "All administrative measures are taken in his name," Lyautey wrote of the sultan. "But in practice he has no real power. . . . His advice is requested only for the sake of form." From "Politique du protectorat," statement of November 18, 1920, in P. Lyautey, ed., *Lyautey l'africain—textes et lettres du Maréchal Lyautey*, 4 vols. (Paris, 1962), vol. 4, 28.

5 Lyautey had formulated his philosophy of governance during previous colonial service in Indochina and Madagascar, working under General Joseph-Simon Gallieni. The original statement of policy is Gallieni's famous "Instructions" to his staff in Madagascar in 1898. See Wright, *Politics of Design*, 76.

6 H. Prost, "Le Développement de l'urbanisme," in J. Royer, ed., *L'Urbanisme aux colonies et dans les pays tropicaux*, 2 vols. (La-Charité-sur-Loire, 1932), vol. 1, 60.

7 See Lyautey's letter of June 17, 1913, in *Lyautey l'africain*, vol. 1, 145–58; and L. Vaillat, *Le Visage français du Maroc* (Paris, 1931), 27.

8 Lyautey, speech at the Université des Annales, Paris, December 10, 1926, in his *Paroles d'action: Madagascar—Sud Oranais—Oran—Maroc (1900–1926)* (Paris, 1927), 453.

9 Ibid., 451.

10 P. Pelletier, "Valeurs financières et urbanisme au Maroc," *Bulletin économique et sociale du Maroc* 19 (June 1955): 39. Also see J. Abu-Lughod, *Rabat: Urban Apartheid in Morocco* (Princeton, 1980), 147.

11 Guillaume de Tarde and Henri de la Casinière spelled out the legal definitions of property ownership under French colonialism, which "modernized" the supposedly archaic Islamic system. In 1927, after Lyautey's departure, new *dahir*s (imperial decrees) declared that European settlement itself was one of the principal "public purposes" that justified expropriating land from Moroccans. By 1937 the French owned almost twice as much land as Moroccans in terms of both surface area and value, with urban landholdings in Rabat and Casablanca slightly higher.

12 Prost, "Développement de l'urbanisme," vol. 1, 62.

13 Walter Harris noted the Moroccan saying, "The king's throne is in his saddle" in *The Morocco That Was* (London, 1921), cited in C. Geertz, "Centers, Kings, and Charisma: Reflections on the Symbolics of Power," in J. Ben-David and T. N. Clark, eds., *Culture and Its Creators: Essays in Honor of Edward Shils* (Chicago, 1977), 162–67.

14 In 1916 this same pair were commissioned to design a lavish new palace in Casablanca, completed in 1919, in recognition of this city's new role as the economic capital of the colony.

15 A. Colliez, *Notre protectorat marocain, la première étape, 1912–1930* (Paris, 1930), 204.

16 Prost, "Le Développement de l'urbanisme," vol. 1, 70.

17 Emile Pauty, writing in the official journal of the Institut des Hautes Etudes Marocaines, chided Muslims "for whom the passage of time is nothing, [who] let their monuments fall into ruin with as much indifference as they once showed ardor in building them." "Rapport sur la défense des villes et la restauration des monuments historiques," *Hesperis* 2 (1922): 449.

18 Prost, "L'Urbanisme au Maroc," unpublished lecture notes, Prost Papers, Académie d'Architecture, Paris, 4.

19 J. Marrast, "Dans quelle mesure faut-il faire appel aux arts indigènes dans la construction des édifices?" in Royer, ed., *L'Urbanisme aux colonies*, vol. 2, 24.

CUZCO

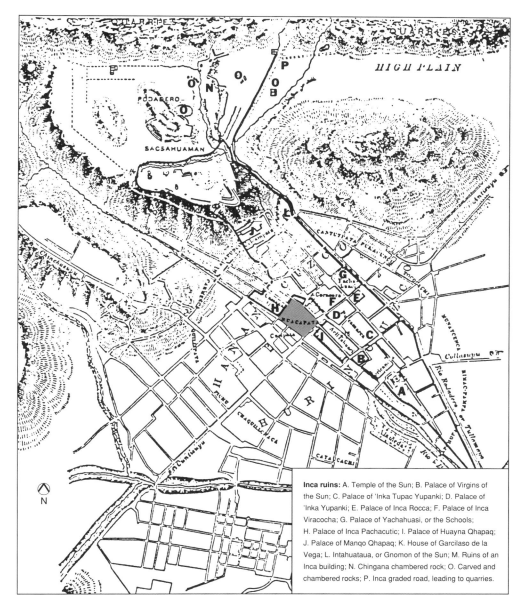

Inca ruins: A. Temple of the Sun; B. Palace of Virgins of the Sun; C. Palace of 'Inka Tupac Yupanki; D. Palace of 'Inka Yupanki; E. Palace of Inca Rocca; F. Palace of Inca Viracocha; G. Palace of Yachahuasi, or the Schools; H. Palace of Inca Pachacutic; I. Palace of Huayna Qhapaq; J. Palace of Manqo Qhapaq; K. House of Garcilaso de la Vega; L. Intahuataua, or Gnomon of the Sun; M. Ruins of an Inca building; N. Chingana chambered rock; O. Carved and chambered rocks; P. Inca graded road, leading to quarries.

Hawkaypata

The Terrace of Leisure

JEAN-PIERRE PROTZEN
&
JOHN HOWLAND ROWE

Figure 1. Map of Cuzco, after Squier, with the outline of the puma added. Black lines indicate ancient Inca walls; Hawkaypata Square is marked in gray. Not all of Squier's identifications of Inca buildings are reliable.

The Incas called their empire Tawantinsuyu, the Four Quarters. From Cuzco, four major roads ran out to the four quarters, Chinchaysuyu, 'Antisuyu, Qollasuyu, and Kuntisuyu, practically and symbolically marking the city as the center of the empire (fig. 1). In the eyes of Pedro Sancho de la Hoz, Francisco Pizarro's personal secretary, Cuzco "was so large and so beautiful that it would be worthy to be seen even in Spain."[1]

The Cuzco that Sancho saw in 1535 occupied a low ridge between two rivers, the

Figure 2. Cuzco viewed
from the road to
Chinchero. Hawkaypata
is at lower left, framed by
the cathedral (left) and
the Jesuit church of
La Compañía.

Huatanay and Tullumayo, at the head of the
Huatanay valley, some 3,300 meters above sea
level, in the southern Andes of Peru (fig. 2). To
the north, on a hillside above the city and
dominating it, was the formidable fortress of
Saqsawaman (fig. 3). A number of distinct residential settlements surrounded the city on the
other sides. Cuzco proper may have had a population of forty thousand or more residents,
and the valley may have counted as many as a
quarter-million inhabitants.[2]

The Cuzco that the Spanish encountered is
said to have been planned by Pachakuti 'Inka
Yupanki, who acceded to the throne in around
1438. He laid it out in the shape of a puma, with
Saqsawaman as its head, Hawkaypata its belly,
and the confluence of the two rivers its tail (see

fig. 1).[3] The city streets were straight and
crossed at right angles. Yet to accommodate
the puma shape and the site's specific topography, the street pattern was not entirely regular.
As a consequence, the city blocks varied in size
and none was strictly rectangular. The blocks
were occupied by residential or religious compounds called *kancha*. Sancho wrote that the
city was "full of palaces of the lords, for in it
there lived no poor people."[4] Some palaces and
their owners, as well as some religious compounds, have been positively identified.

The streets were paved with flagstones, and
a stone-lined water channel ran down their
middle. In the eyes of Sancho, the streets were
very well made, but had one major flaw: they
were so narrow that only two horsemen could

ride abreast through them, one on either side of
the water channel (fig. 4). Even that must have
been difficult, to judge from the scraped marks
made by horsemen's spurs that still can be seen
on Inca walls in Cuzco.

Street life was probably limited to the movement of people from one place to another, with
a stop perhaps for a bit of gossip, or to fetch water
from the canals. There was no mercantile activity in the streets and there were no storefronts.
Most residential and religious compounds were
surrounded by walls with only one doorway
giving access to the street. Supplies for the sus-
tenance of daily life were delivered directly from
the state warehouses to the compounds. All
production, weaving, wood and metal working,
pottery, brewing, baking, and so forth was car-

ried out within the compounds. On official
occasions, civil or religious, the street scene may
have been animated by parades and processions: the Inca being carried around town in
his litter with the requisite entourage of nobles
and bodyguards; the arrival of a dignitary from
the provinces accompanied by llama trains
loaded with gifts of all kinds; the triumphant
return of a war party, with soldiers displaying
their loot and parading prisoners; or a solemn
religious procession, with priests in colorful
attire carrying idols and other paraphernalia.

As the major ceremonial center of Inca
state religion, Cuzco held some of the holiest
places in the empire. In the southeast part of
the city, on a terrace overlooking the Huatanay River, stood the Qorikancha, "the richest,

Figure 3. The ruins of
the fortress of
Saqsawaman, with Cuzco
in the background.

other nonroyal.[6] The families officiated at the shrines in their care and provided appropriate sacrifices on the designated days.

The *zeq'e* were probably organized according to *khipu* reckoning. The *khipu* was an ingenious accounting device consisting of a tassel of knotted cords. The cords and knots represented things and quantities recorded in a decimal system. The *zeq'e* system can be seen as an analogue to a *khipu* used in tracking calendar events, with the lines representing cords and the *wak'a* standing for knots. The cords of a *khipu* are flexible, so there is no presumption that the *zeq'e* were straight lines.[7] On the other hand, there is no doubt that the *zeq'e* were radially arranged. It is obvious that the *zeq'e* system did not influence the general physical structure of Cuzco; nothing in the city's layout would lead one to suspect a radial pattern. Yet the *zeq'e* system must have played an important role in how the city's residents perceived and understood its spatial organization, and influenced the way they oriented themselves in it.

In an attempt to construct a set of performance scales for the spatial form of cities, Kevin Lynch has identified five major dimensions: vitality, sense, fit, access, and control. Of particular interest here is that of sense. It measures "the degree to which a settlement can be clearly perceived and mentally differentiated and structured in time and space by its residents." Sense, in turn, is composed of several dimensions, of which "congruence, transparency, and legibility are the components . . . which describe explicit connections of settlement form to nonspatial concepts and values."[8] An argument can be made that the ideal, radial pattern of the *zeq'e* provided the landmarks by which one remembered locations in town and beyond. The material, orthogonal pattern of streets supplied the pathways by which the landmarks were reached. Together, the two structures make the connec-

Figure 4. The old street of Hatunrumiyoq, with Inca masonry on the left.

most sumptuous, and principal temple in this kingdom" (fig. 5).[5]

In addition to the Qorikancha, a great many other holy places, known as *wak'a*, were distributed throughout the city and its immediate surroundings. These *wak'a* were arranged along imaginary lines, called *zeq'e*, radiating out from the Qorikancha into all four quarters and the cardinal compass directions. The *zeq'e* provided a sophisticated organization for the attendance at and maintenance of the shrines, since a group of three *zeq'e* was the responsibility of two *'ayllu*, or family groups, one royal, the

Figure 5. The Spanish church of Santo Domingo is built over the remains of the holiest of Inca temples, the Qorikancha.

tion between the religious concepts and values, the social organization, and the physical form of the city and its surrounding landscape.

Hawkaypata Square formed the space of the belly, between the fore- and hindquarters, of the crouching puma figure. It was surrounded by the city on three sides, the northwest, northeast, and southeast. To the southwest, the square flanked the corrected and canalized course of the Huatanay River and opened onto another square, Kusipata, the "fortunate terrace," on the other bank, to which it was probably connected by two bridges. The two squares served different functions. Kusipata appears to have been a kind of Campus Martius, where military reviews and exercises were held; Hawkaypata, the "leisure terrace," was the place for "festivals, amusements and drinking bouts."[9] There is a description of Hawkaypata as it was within weeks after Francisco Pizarro entered Cuzco on November 15, 1533, reported by an eyewitness

who accompanied him. What the reporter took for a drunken orgy most likely was a ceremonial drinking ritual in celebration of the important Inca festival of Qhapac Raymi, the initiation rite for young Inca noblemen.

There were so many people and [they were] such good drinkers, men as well as women, and such were the quantities that they poured into their skins—for all they do is drink and not eat—that it is certain, without any doubt, that two wide channels more than half a *vara* wide, covered with slabs, . . . flowed all day with the urine of those that pissed into them, in such abundance that it seemed they were fountains. Certainly, given the quantity of what they drank and of the people who drank, this is not to be marveled at, though to see it is a marvel and a thing never before seen.[10]

The unknown author of the "Noticia" remarked that "the plaza of the city was almost square,

Figure 6. Today's Plaza de Armas was the Inca Hawkaypata. The Jesuit church, an example of exquisite colonial Baroque, occupies the site of 'Amarukancha, one of the Inca palaces.

neither big nor small," and his contemporary Sancho wrote, "The plaza is square and most of it is level."[11] With dimensions of about 190 by 210 meters, Hawkaypata was large—probably larger than anything the Spaniards had seen in their own cities at the dawn of the sixteenth century. If today's Plaza de Armas is any indication (and there is no reason to believe that its topography was radically altered after the conquest), the Inca plaza was anything but level (fig. 6). It had a significant slope in both its main axes, with a difference in elevation along its diagonal, from its highest north corner to its lowest south corner, of about eight meters.

Attempts to establish what Hawkaypata Square looked like in Inca times are frustrated by the fact that Cuzco was systematically burned by Manqo 'Inka and his troops after he rebelled against the Spanish and laid siege to Cuzco in 1536. It was further altered by the decision of the

Spanish to turn Cuzco into a Christian city. This involved the destruction or disaffection of pagan shrines and temples. As a consequence, much of the archaeological record has either been obliterated or is now buried under Spanish buildings. There may have been from four to six streets leading from the square into the city. Only two of these are well enough defined today to leave no doubt about their original course: Callejón de Loreto (fig. 7) and Calle Triunfo and its extension, Hatunrumiyoq, which also was the road to 'Antisuyu. Callejón de Loreto and its continuation, the Pampa del Castillo, connected Hawkaypata to the Qorikancha and a small square in front of it.[12]

The entire square was covered with a layer of sand about a half-meter thick. The sand had been brought in from the Pacific coast—more than 90 leagues (about 450 kilometers) away—in reverence to the Creator. Buried in and dispersed throughout it were offerings of gold and silver dishes, small animal and human effigies, and other votive objects. To the great chagrin of the Incas, this layer of sand was removed by Juan Polo de Ondegardo, Corregidor of Cuzco, between December 1558 and December 1560, to make mortar for the construction of the cathedral. So upset were the Indians by this action that they would have paid the Spaniards handsomely to leave the plaza as it was, since it was the object of great veneration throughout the empire.[13] Set in the square was a ceremonial object known as an 'usnu. This was described by Pedro Pizarro (although he does not name it):

A round stone, which they took to be an idol, [placed] in the middle of the plaza; around it was a small pool. . . . This stone had a sheath of gold that fitted and covered it completely, and it also had a sort of small, round shed made of woven mats, with which they covered it at night.[14]

'Usnu were a recurrent feature of Inca towns. According to other sixteenth-century writers, an 'usnu was a sugarloaf-shaped stone set atop a platform with stairs. With time, the term came to designate the entire structure and not only the stone on top of it. These platforms served ceremonial as well as administrative functions; from their height the Inca lords spoke to their people, presided over festivities, reviewed their armies, or offered sacrifices to the deities. Guaman Poma de Ayala has depicted Manqo 'Inka sitting on the 'usnu in Cuzco (fig. 8).[15]

The other monuments in and around the plaza were a fountain, in which it was said that the Thunder bathed; the palace of Wayna Qhapaq, named Q'asana; a shrine to the Wind, placed in the doorway of Q'asana; and two round structures in front of it. Pizarro describes these:

. . . One on one side, the other on the other [of the door]—I want to say nearly at the corners of this block. These towers were of very well worked masonry, and very strong; they were round, roofed with straw very strangely set; the eaves of straw projected a fathom from the wall, so that when it rained, it favored those who on horseback made the rounds in the shelter of theses eaves.[16]

And finally, there was a wak'a called Ñan, meaning road, at which universal sacrifice was made for travelers.

The northwestern and southeastern edges of the square were defined by palaces. Nearest the Huatanay River, on the northwest side, was Q'asana, and to the east of it a complex probably called Qoraqora, which may have belonged to Thupa 'Inka. Opposite these, on the southeast side, stood 'Amarukancha, the palace of Waskhar, and Hatunkancha, the residence of Chosen Women.

These palaces were not individual buildings, but rather entire compounds, kancha, each occupying an entire city block, surrounded by a wall of fine masonry approximately four meters high, and harboring many other structures. Of the façades these compounds offered to the plaza, we only know that the doorway to Q'asana was "clad with pieces of silver and other beautiful metals."[17] Of the appearance of the other buildings and structures facing the square nothing is known, with one exception. In describing how Francisco Pizarro assigned his people to lodgings around the square, Pedro Pizarro notes that "most people settled in a large galpón that adjoined the plaza." Further on, he explains what a galpón is:

Galpón means a very long room with an entrance on the short side, from which one can see all that is inside, because the entrance is so big . . . it is all open from one wall to the other and up to the

Figure 7. The old Street of the Sun, today called Callejón de Loreto, connected Hawkaypata to the temple of Qorikancha. The view is from the southeast, with Hawkaypata at the far end of the street.

the modern literature on Inca architecture. When Pizarro said that *galpones* were very large buildings, he really meant it. Bernabe Cobo, describing the second type of great hall, has given us some measurements:

> They were large houses, or *galpones,* of a single room, from one hundred to three hundred feet long, and at least thirty and at most fifty wide, completely disencumbered and free, without division of rooms, nor apartments, and with two or three doors, all in one wall at equal intervals.[20]

We gather from Pizarro that at least one *galpón* adjoined Hawkaypata; where and of which type it was he did not say. He also mentioned that a Cuyus Mango was part of the complex of Q'asana, and Garcilaso de la Vega wrote of a *galpón* among the buildings of 'Amarukancha. We know that the great halls served a primarily public function. Garcilaso recounts that in Cuzco on rainy days celebrants in ceremonies took refuge in them to continue their festivities and ritual drinking bouts.[21]

Very little is left of the Inca square's northeastern edge. Its remains have been mostly obliterated by the construction of the cathedral and its adjoining chapels. Originally, the square was marked on this side by a great terrace on which stood other monumental structures. The existence of two of these, two *galpones,* has been established. One stood near the eastern corner of the plaza bordering the modern Calle Triunfo. On the foundations of this *galpón* stands the church of El Triunfo, with probably the same orientation as the original building; that is, with its longitudinal axis perpendicular to, and the great opening facing, the plaza. The other stood somewhere toward the northwestern end of the terrace (separated by a street from the southwestern part). It served as a foundry and for a short time as the meeting place for Cuzco's city

roof. There were other [*galpones*] that had the small ends closed and many doorways in the middle, all on one side. These *galpones* were very large, with no blockages inside, but unobstructed and clear.[18]

Pizarro clearly establishes two types of *galpones.* The first, with only one large opening in one of its short walls, bears a striking resemblance to a building type labeled "Cuyus Mango" and depicted by Guaman Poma de Ayala.[19] The second type, with multiple doorways in one of its long sides, is often referred to as a *kallanka* in

council.[22] Of what type this *galpón* was is not known, nor is its orientation.

From these descriptions and the archaeological evidence, it would appear that the built-up perimeter of Hawkaypata had a fairly uniform appearance: a continuous wall, about four meters high, of exquisitely fitted stonemasonry, regularly coursed on compound enclosure walls on the northwest and southeast sides, and perhaps of a polygonal bond on the terrace wall on the northeast side. This continuous wall was perforated only by doorways and interrupted by the mouths of the alleyways that gave access to the square.

Wherever structures faced the plaza, the façade wall was crowned by enormous thatched roofs, which in the case of great halls may have been up to five times as high as the wall itself.[23] In other words, these roofs may have reached heights of twenty-four meters above ground, the equivalent of an eight-story building. The eaves of these immense roofs created considerable overhangs, perhaps as much as six feet. They must have cast impressive shadow lines onto the façades, structuring and adding depth to them.

The "towers" in front of Q'asana added further depth to the northwestern enclosure of Hawkaypata. Whether they also marked vertical accents is difficult to say. Their walls may have been no higher than the enclosure wall of the compound before which they stood, and their roofs no higher than the other roofs.[24]

The slope on the right bank of the Huatanay, opposite Hawkaypata, was terraced; it was known to the Spanish as *los andenes* (the terraces), and to the Incas as Kusipata. Its exact dimensions are not known; Gasparini and Margolies, however, suggest that it was closed off on its southwestern side by a high terrace along today's Recocijo and Heladeros Streets.[25] Visually, the two squares would not have been perceived as separate entities, but as a single urban space. The sloping of the two plazas toward the river must have given this space the character of an amphitheater. People standing around the space's perimeter looked down at its optical center, near the river, where presumably stood the *'usnu.*

To judge from the historical accounts, Hawkaypata was the center of almost every important event in the life of the empire and its people. Strictly speaking, the plaza may not have been the holiest of the holy places, but it was so to the common people. "Because the temples had such a sacred character that only priests and very important persons could enter them, the public ceremonies took place out of doors, and preferably in the plaza, on the layer of sacred sand and around the *'usnu,* using principally temporary installations to complement those of the permanent elements."[26] Thus, it was in Hawkaypata that the people gathered to rejoice and mourn, to sacrifice and pray, to implore and adore, to reward or punish, to prepare for war and revel in victory, to parade and dance, to eat and drink.

The Incas had two kinds of festivals and religious ceremonies, ordinary and extraordinary:

The first were enacted at certain times of the year, to each month its own, in their order, for different purposes and with particular rites and sacrifices; the second had no determined times, because they were held only for incidental reasons: for example, when the rains failed, when some important war was about to begin, for the coronation of the king, and on other similar occasions.[27]

Among the regular ceremonies that took place in Hawkaypata were daily rituals such as the sacrifice to the Sun of a white llama at sunrise, noon, and sunset, and the cult worship of ancestral mummies.[28] Others were performed monthly, according to a set calendar. Although each festival had its own purpose and rituals, and differed

Figure 8. Guaman Poma de Ayala, Manqo 'Inka sitting on the 'usnu in Cuzco, illustration from *El primer nueva corónica*, 1615.

chical organization of civil servants, through which they mobilized a large labor force, distributed arable lands, directed the economy, established social order, meted out justice, and spread their language, culture, and religious values to conquered peoples. The chronicles say little about just where in each Inca town these civic functions were performed; hints here and there suggest that some were carried out in the main square. The role of Hawkaypata in civic government is not known, but on occasion the Inca probably ate in public in the plaza, performed collective wedding ceremonies there of his subjects, and administered justice.

Cieza de León repeatedly wrote that the Inca used to meet with his war council at the *'usnu* (or *piedra de guerra*, as he calls it), to which he summoned the principals and lords from the provinces, in order to choose and appoint from among them his commanders and captains.[29]

According to Inca history, as reported in the chronicles, the existence of Cuzco was threatened by the Chancas, her neighbors to the northwest. The Incas, under the rule of Wiraqocha, were about to surrender, when 'Inka Yupanki, one of his sons, rallied them and inflicted a devastating defeat on the Chancas. Sung as a hero by his people, 'Inka Yupanki wrested the crown from his father and took the throne, assuming the name Pachakuti, or "cataclysm."

Immediately, Pachakuti set out to redesign and rebuild Cuzco and its surroundings, and to lay the foundation of what was to become the largest empire in the New World. It is said that he started by replacing an earlier, modest temple to the Sun with the majestic Qorikancha, the remains of which one can still admire today. He also corrected the courses of the rivers, laid out the city, built storehouses in the vicinity, and terraced the city's larger surroundings to provide more arable land.

Pachakuti's innovations reached far beyond

from others in duration, there were some common features. Each festival was accompanied by sacrifices, although the kind and amount varied. Many involved a period of fasting, during which the participants abstained from seasoning their food with salt and *ají* (*capsicum* pepper), refrained from drinking *chicha*, and avoided sexual intercourse. Several ceremonies called for the banning of all foreigners, and even of animals, from the confines of the city for their duration. The mummies of ancestors were brought into the square to participate in most, if not all, festivities. And most major ones ended in a fiesta to which the whole population was invited, including the foreigners, who were invited to return. These usually lasted a couple of days and nights.

It is well recognized that the Incas were superb administrators. They had a very efficient hierar-

physical planning, into social engineering. He revised the Inca calendar, reorganized the pantheon, and conceived the festivals, with their rituals and sacrifices. He devised new laws, and invented much of the famed administrative structure. In short, Pachakuti embarked on a massive effort to bring into congruence the physical, social, and religious orders of Inca society.

Spiro Kostof has written of Greece that, after she suffered and repelled the Persian invasion, she became "aware and confident, more so than at any other time in her history."

The invasion had been sobering for the boastful Greeks. It taught them . . . the benefits of unity, creating legends of superhuman valor that would sustain generations of Greeks to come. A quickening of the spirit and a consciousness of the human frame . . . were now evident in everything the major cities produced—in art and building, drama and poetry.[30]

The Inca history recorded by the chroniclers was the official history recounted by nobles, dignitaries, and other individuals in the service of the Inca state. This history most likely was revisionist, designed to suit the purposes and ambitions of the builders of the Inca empire. What is fact and what myth is thus open to question, and one may wonder whether Pachakuti should be credited with all the feats attributed to him. Be that as it may, under his reign, the Incas experienced a *prise de conscience* analogous to that of the Greeks. The vision offered here of Hawkaypata, its surrounding buildings, and the activities in the square, is a small but significant window onto the manifestations of this emerging and doomed awareness. ■

Notes

1 P. Sancho de la Hoz, "Relación para S.M. de lo sucedido en la conquista y pacificación de estas provincias de la Nueva Castilla y de la calidad de la tierra, despues que el capitàn Hernando Pizarro se partió y llevó a su Magestad la relación de la victoria de Caxamalca y de la prision del cacique Atabalipa," 1535. *Biblioteca de cultura peruana*, 1st series, no. 2, *Los Cronistas de la conquista*, 117–85 (Paris, 1938), 176.

2 J. H. Rowe, "What Kind of a Settlement was Inca Cuzco? *Ñawpa pacha* 5 (1967): 59–76.

3 Ibid., 60.

4 Sancho, "Relación," 176.

5 B. Cobo, *Historia del nuevo mundo*, 1653, ed. P. F. Mateos, *Biblioteca de autores españoles desde la formación del lenguaje hasta nuestros días*, tomes 91, 92, *Obras del P. Bernabé Cobo* (Madrid, 1964), vol. 2, 168.

6 Ibid., vol. 2, 169.

7 Even a superficial analysis of the location of shrines along a specific *zeq'e* demonstrates that they are not strung out along a straight line. See B. Bauer, "Ritual Pathways of the Inca: An Analysis of the Collasuyu Ceques in Cuzco," *Latin American Antiquity* 3, no. 3 (1992): 183–205.

8 K. Lynch, *A Theory of Good City Form* (Cambridge, Mass., 1981), 118, 141.

9 J. H. Rowe, "The Lost Monuments of the Great Square of Inca Cuzco," unpublished manuscript. Garcilaso de la Vega's claim that the river was entirely covered with stone slabs between the two plazas is very doubtful.

10 Anon., "Noticia del Perú," in "El Descubrimiento y la conquista del Perú; Relación inédita de Miguel de Estete," 1535, ed. C. M. Larrea, *Boletín de la Sociedad Ecuatoriana de Estudios Históricos Americanos* 1, no. 3 (October–November 1918): 300–350.

11 Anon., "Noticia," 31; Sancho, "Relación," 177.

12 Some monuments that were within the Inca square are well established: "A layer of sand [covering the entire square], an 'usnu, where offerings to the Sun were made and which served other functions as well, a fountain in which the Thunder was supposed to bathe, a shrine to the Wind, and two freestanding round structures," Rowe, "Lost Monuments," 10.

13 Rowe, "Los Monumentos perdidos de la plaza mayor del Cuzco incaico," *Revista del Museo e Instituto de Arqueologia* (Cuzco), no. 24 (1991): 83–100.

14 P. Pizarro, *Relación del descubrimiento y conquista de los reinos del Perú*, 1571, ed. G. L. Villena (Lima, 1986), 90. Pizarro was a soldier in the Spanish expeditionary corps, under the command of Francisco Pizarro, his distant relative.

15 F. Guaman Poma de Ayala, *El primer nueva corónica y buen gobierno*, 1615, ed. J. V. Murra and R. Adorno (Mexico, 1980), 370.

16 Pizarro, *Relación*, 161.

17 "Noticia," 31.

18 Ibid., 88, 160.

19 Poma de Ayala, *Primer nueva corónica*, 321 [331]. "Cuyus Mango" was probably not the name of a specific building somewhere on Hawkaypata, but rather a generic building type.

20 Cobo, *Historia*, vol. 2, 130.

21 Garcilaso de la Vega (El Inca), *Comentarios reales de los Incas* (Caracas, 1976), vol. 2, 108.

22 Rowe, "Monumentos perdidos," 95, 96. The presence of other buildings on the terrace, northwest of the great hall that became the church, has also been confirmed. The block in which the great hall and these buildings stood was called Uchullo. It is said that Wayna Qhapaq lived in Uchullo before he had Q'asana built, ibid., 84–87.

23 J.-P. Protzen, *Inca Architecture and Construction at Ollantaytambo* (New York, 1993), 228–33. Terrace walls, as a rule, were not built with regularly coursed masonry. There are, however, some notable ex-ceptions, for example, the terrace walls of the Qorikancha.

24 If the tower walls were the same height as the enclosure walls, that is, some four meters, there would have been plenty of room for the mounted cavaliers mentioned by Pizarro to ride under the eaves.

25 G. Gasparini and L. Margolies, *Inca Architecture* (Bloomington, 1980), 54, fig. 43, and 55, fig. 44.

26 Rowe, "Monumentos perdidos," 93.

27 Cobo, *Historia*, vol. 2, 207.

28 Rowe, "Lost Monuments," 63; Pizarro, *Relación*, 89, 90.

29 P. Cieza de León, *El señorio de los incas (Segunda parte de la crónica del Perú)*, 1553, ed. C. Aranibar (Lima, 1967), 80, 156. Cieza uses the expression *piedra de guerra* because he may not have been told the object's real name, but it is clear from his own description of the stone that he was referring to the 'usnu.

30 S. Kostof, *A History of Architecture: Settings and Rituals* (New York, 1985), 137.

19

WASHINGTON, D.C.

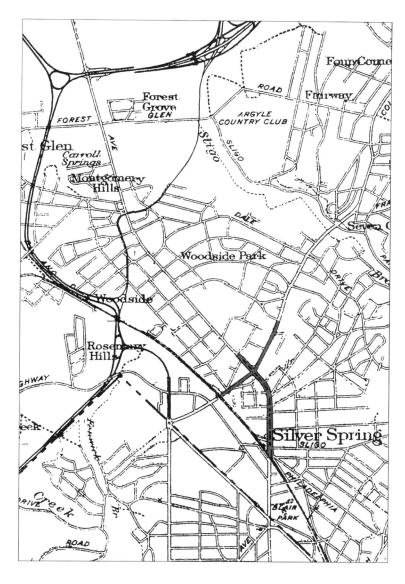

Silver Spring

Georgia Avenue,
Colesville Road,
and the Creation of
an Alternative
"Downtown"
for Metropolitan
Washington

RICHARD LONGSTRETH

Figure 1. Map of Silver
Spring, Maryland, 1945,
showing unrealized bypass
route at left. Georgia
Avenue and Colesville Road
are marked in gray.

Passing through the heart of Silver Spring, Maryland, is not an experience likely to spark interest in the community's past. At first glance, the place does not seem to have much of a past, or at least one of any consequence. Silver Spring has the kind of business district long ridiculed by persons who profess concern about the design of cities. It is a stereotype of settings used to illustrate the alleged evils of urban sprawl. It seems to have no true center or memorable spaces; it is bereft of distinguished architecture; it is visually discordant; it appears to lack purpose—beyond a quick financial return—and certainly lacks any sense of civic identity. Downtown Silver Spring is, in short, a testament to what many believe is wrong with the expansion of metropolitan areas over the past half-century.

Yet even a cursory probe into the history of Silver Spring's commercial development indicates that it merits closer examination. The community, which, like most others in Montgomery County, has never been incorporated, lies at a strategic point just beyond the uppermost reaches of the District of Columbia, six miles north of the Washington city center (fig. 1). A major north–south thoroughfare, Georgia Avenue, links the two zones. During the late nineteenth and early twentieth centuries, the greatest thrust of Washington's middle-class residential development took place along this corridor. Beginning in the 1910s, growth continued northward into Montgomery County. A decade later, several blocks of Georgia Avenue in Silver Spring had become a concentrated commercial district, with businesses catering to everyday needs of nearby residents—a place similar to many others further south along the street that served Washington neighborhoods. Following the worst years of the Depression, Silver Spring again experienced rapid growth, so that by the end of World War II it was touted as the second largest community in the state, with an estimated population of seventy thousand, exceeded only by that of Baltimore. In response to this influx of people, the commercial center expanded well beyond the traditional role of providing basic goods and services to become a magnet of trade for the region, it was the first such place seriously to pose a shopping alternative to downtown Washington. Silver Spring drew national attention as a business center created to meet the demands of a mobile, prosperous middle class—an entirely new district, with large, modern stores and ample parking, that set the pace for future urban growth. Between 1945 and 1950, Silver Spring was transformed from just one

in a chain of bedroom communities around Washington to a major focus of business activity for the metropolitan area (fig. 2).

Much of Silver Spring's significance lies in its representational attributes.[1] Far from being the product of uncontrolled growth, for example, the business district has been shaped by planning initiatives for much of its existence—a kind of planning that is the norm in thousands of communities. Furthermore, like many places at the urban periphery, Silver Spring became a proving ground for new ideas in retail development and in accommodating large numbers of automobiles. The site also reflects the fragile economic existence, where decline can be as swift as ascendancy, that has become common to such districts.

Silver Spring's meteoric rise in stature was part of a pattern that has become characteristic of cities throughout the United States since World War I. The first generation of major outlying centers emerged during the 1920s in the very largest metropolitan areas.[2] Places such as Jamaica in New York and East Orange, nearby in New Jersey, Ardmore and Upper Darby outside Philadelphia, Englewood and Uptown in Chicago, Midtown in St. Louis, and Hollywood in Los Angeles grew to provide effective surrogates for a number of the functions traditional to the city center. These new business magnets provided a substantial range of choices in shopping (chain stores, branches of major downtown stores, specialty shops), recreation (restaurants, theaters, ballrooms), and professional services (financial institutions, law firms, medical offices). While the range never came close to duplicating that found in the urban core, it was sufficient to address most needs most of the time for the burgeoning middle class that was its target audience. The appeal of outlying centers stemmed from the fact that, with rapid, lateral metropolitan expansion, they

lay much closer to where a major portion of the middle class now lived and hence were much easier to reach than downtown. Initially, these places escaped the intense vehicular congestion that plagued city centers, and they also seemed more socially homogeneous, lacking the conspicuous presence of lower-income groups and other segments of the community deemed undesirable.

Although the rate of growth in outlying centers plummeted during the Depression, a substantial rebound occurred after the mid-

1930s. By the eve of World War II, retail decentralization was seen as a serious threat to the economic future of many downtown districts across the country. The trend came to a halt during the war, when gasoline rationing greatly reduced consumer mobility, but thereafter it reached a new level of expansion. Postwar development was channeled not so much into established outlying centers as into creating new ones situated farther yet from the urban core.

Since the 1920s, outlying centers have elicited interest primarily as contemporary phe-

Figure 2. Aerial view of the Silver Spring business district in the early 1960s, looking north, with the intersection of Georgia Avenue and Colesville Road at center.

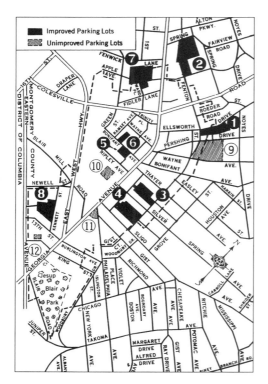

Figure 3. Map of municipal parking lots, Silver Spring, in the early 1950s.

of outlying center to the next, just as they can in other forms of urban development and building types. These differences encompass not only physical form and the processes by which it is shaped, but also the relative importance of various functions. Prior to World War II, for example, the office component of most outlying centers was quite limited; only in recent decades has it characteristically included concentrations of major business headquarters or branch offices. But irrespective of shifts over time, the outlying center has existed as a significant destination point for business within metropolitan areas for almost three quarters of a century. The span of this legacy is greater than the literature suggests; examples have proliferated and increased dramatically in their relative importance to the modern metropolis. Outlying centers have had a profound effect upon urban form, on daily routines of work and pleasure, and on our very notion of what a city is.

During the 1920s, outlying centers developed at prominent intersections of mass-transit lines, where large numbers of people with disposable incomes lived in the surrounding area. Even then, the momentum needed for intense commercial development did not exist without at least one, perhaps two or three, independent parties risking capital to erect facilities important enough to attract additional building. But even as it was emerging, this pattern began to be rendered obsolete by the growth in automobile usage. Vehicular congestion became a problem in outlying centers, albeit to a lesser degree than in the urban core. As a result, once commercial expansion began to resume in the years immediately preceding World War II, much of it occurred on scattered sites that were removed from established business centers. Prominent chain outlets or branches of downtown stores could trade on their reputation to attract patronage; cars put those stores within easy reach;

nomena. Discussion of the subject tends to occur either as news accounts by those interested in the advance of business, or as statistical analyses prepared by geographers, planners, and others concerned with quantifying trends in urban development. Study of outlying centers from a historical perspective, however, is rare—so rare that the subject matter itself is not generally viewed in the past tense. Among the now numerous accounts of current examples—places misleadingly given such names as "urban villages" and "edge cities"—few authors even suggest that development of this kind preceded the 1970s. Some early examples, such as Hollywood, remain well known, but, remarkably, they are not thought of as precursors to contemporary developments, such as that at Irvine–Costa Mesa, in Orange County, California.

Changes can be found from one generation

and ample space existed for parking on or near the site. This shift meant that if commercial development was to be concentrated again, new techniques would have to be devised so that the motorist could be accommodated easily. Furthermore, some coordination had to exist so that many stores would benefit, instead of just one. Silver Spring was in the first wave of communities in the postwar United States to conceive and execute an effective strategy in this regard. That strategy depended upon public-sector planning.

The planning that helped stimulate Silver Spring's postwar boom was not the sort that gets memorialized in history texts. There was never a grand design or a truly comprehensive blueprint for development. Initiatives were neither visionary nor even particularly novel. Instead, the approach represented a middle ground. It was planning of a kind practiced in many communities nationwide that has had a profound effect upon their complexion: it had a limited agenda, addressed immediate and concrete needs, and served a specific constituency. In Silver Spring, there were two interrelated programs: to expand the commercially zoned core with adequate room for large-scale business development; and to acquire land for a network of sizable (2,200 spaces), publicly administered parking lots, so that as the business district grew motorists would continue to find it a convenient destination point (fig. 3). If neither component was innovative, the two in combination distinguished this program from many others in the country at the time; first, because they were adopted *before* large-scale development occurred, instead of after the fact, to ameliorate already difficult conditions; second, because they were fully implemented within in a mere five years, rather than being realized partially or not at all, after a protracted and divisive struggle, as was more common.

The success of the scheme was in large part due to the aggressiveness of its sponsoring agency, the Maryland–National Capital Park and Planning Commission, which enjoyed considerable authority in local land-use decisions. The initiative's author was E. Brooke Lee, who was appointed chairman of the commission in 1942. A powerful figure in the local Democratic party, Lee had been prominent in both state and county politics for over two decades. He campaigned tirelessly to implement his plans because he saw them as the key to significant commercial growth. Events proved him correct. After the county Board of Commissioners approved his proposals in 1946, a number of national chains and leading Washington stores made bids to establish branches in the community. The sites they coveted lay along or near Colesville Road, which intersected Georgia Avenue at the northern edge of the existing business area. At that juncture lay the Silver Spring Shopping Center. When it opened in 1938, with twenty-one establishments, this was the largest drive-in, integrated retail development in the region. As a result of Lee's initiatives, the complex became the site around which new construction occurred, transforming Colesville Road into a "Main Street" for Montgomery County (fig. 4). In contrast to the shopping center, where off-street parking provisions determined the entire layout, postwar development was more traditional. The street remained the anchor for development, even though many customers were now motorists, rather than pedestrians. Most retailers still firmly believed in the street façade, and expansive display windows across it, as the principal means of establishing their presence in the world. Buildings abutted one another and occupied most of their respective properties. The nine car lots created by the county in the 1940s lay removed from the main arteries and had

Figure 4. Colesville Road, looking east from the Georgia Avenue intersection, in the early 1950s.

little frontage on side streets. Space allocated to the automobile thus was primarily of a residue kind. Most lots occupied block interiors, and had few, if any, direct links to adjacent buildings. After leaving their cars, patrons had to take a circuitous route from lot to sidewalk to store.

By the time the network of parking lots was completed in 1949, Silver Spring was firmly established as the region's foremost outlying center for shopping (indeed, nothing comparable could then be found between Philadelphia and Raleigh); it was the site of proposed office buildings and a hotel as well. The extent to which Lee's strategy was catalytic may be measured by comparing Silver Spring to nearby Bethesda, which, although better situated for such development, retained a far narrower trade orientation. Lee made similar proposals to that community, concurrent with those to Silver Spring; however, they met vigorous opposition. Not until Silver Spring's hegemony was clear did some contingents in Bethesda begin to press for change (fig. 5).

At the heart of Lee's effort lay an altruistic desire to see Silver Spring emerge as the leading Maryland community in the metropolitan area. He wished it to be the centerpiece in both symbol and fact of an expansive, well-ordered, and prosperous chain of residential enclaves around Washington. Silver Spring would, in effect, become the core of a new kind of urban realm, better than the traditional city. Pragmatic concerns weighed heavily in this equation. Lee felt that if a community did not continue to grow, it would decline and eventually decay. Good planning enabled growth. Planning was not a giver of form, but the instrument of a supposedly natural progress in which private-sector forces could flourish. That condition, in turn, yielded public benefit. Planning was guided by statistics and calculations such as those that gave retailers and automobiles enough space in the right locations. The appearance of a store, a car lot, or of the precinct as a whole never seems to have been an issue. Nor was there a sense of civic presence. Lee's agenda embraced business. There was no need for a municipal center, since most government functions were housed in Rockville, the county seat. Libraries, schools, churches, parks, and playgrounds, he felt, were best situated in the residential areas outside the commercial core. The Planning Commission spent considerable effort in acquiring public open space, but it was all for use as parking areas. The traditional notion of a strong public identity for the urban core was absent and no provisions were made for the private sector to compensate for its lack. This was something of a departure from the 1920s model of the large, integrated retail complex, such as Country Club Plaza in Kansas City, which again surfaced in regional shopping malls of the 1950s, such as Shopper's World in Framingham, Massachusetts. In Silver Spring, store and parking signs, more than any other element, were used to represent the precinct (fig. 6). But whether the object of pride or derision, this commercial landscape was not the product of unbridled laissez-faire. Silver Spring's physical character was directly linked to a strong system of controls and a coherent view of what those controls could accomplish.

Silver Spring further affords insight as a proving ground for significant changes in commercial development itself, especially in the retail sphere. Much can be learned, for example, about general tendencies, such as the extent to which the number of major chain stores present had come to define the relative importance of a new business precinct. Outlying centers also began to outpace the urban core as hearths of innovation in retail design by the mid-1920s. Silver Spring's major contribution in this regard was the Hecht Company department store (1946–47). A leading downtown emporium, Hecht's was among the first retailers to announce postwar plans for building in Silver Spring—a move which, combined with Lee's

initiatives, helped to attract other stores. The building was the earliest very large (160,000 square feet, increased to 214,000 in 1949–50) branch of a major downtown department store to be realized outside a sizable, established retail district anywhere in the United States, with the exception of two prewar examples in Los Angeles. The success of the Hecht store showed that expansion on this scale could be very profitable in its own right and could give the parent company a decisive advantage among competitors. The project also demonstrated that building a single store could spark intense business development, given adequate space for other new buildings and for cars. It was now clear that such a project could be targeted to a broad middle market, rather than to the upper end, as were its few predecessors and the other, much smaller examples then in existence. finally, the scheme showed that such a building need not be elaborate. A no-nonsense design that looked efficient and modern but had no frills was quite adequate and might even be an advantage in appealing to the budget-conscious consumer (fig. 7).

The location of the Hecht Company Silver Spring store was practically without precedent. Unlike any previous example, whether in the urban core or an outlying district, the site did not front on a major artery. Instead, it lay one block removed, at the intersection of Fenton Street and Ellsworth Drive, so that the building turned its back on existing and most future retail space. The decision to do this may have been prompted by an inability to secure adequate land for the huge store along either Georgia Avenue or Colesville Road within the business zone. Perhaps, too, Hecht's planners believed it advantageous to locate away from the most crowded routes, so that nearby lots could be used for parking, and customers could walk from their cars to the store without having

Figure 5. Editorial cartoon on parking conditions in Silver Spring and Bethesda, 1949.

comings of unintegrated business development. Company officials, in a rare public admission of strategic error, expressed regret that the wave of building their project had fostered made store or parking-lot expansion nearly impossible (lots provided by the county were not, as it turned out, sufficient). Moreover, they had no influence over the kind or quality of retail growth around them. The sorts of merchants, the quality of goods sold, the caliber of services offered were uncontrolled. A few weak links in this merchandising chain could undermine their own business. Hecht's would never put itself in the same position again.

This episode gained national attention among retailers and the business world in general during the early 1950s, concurrent with the swift rise of the regional shopping mall as a preferred alternative to those outlying centers where merchants could function unilaterally. Many factors contributed to this shift. Among the appealing aspects of such integrated development was the presence of a master plan at the outset: the mall complex was set well back from its access routes and surrounded by an enormous parking area, giving patrons convenient access to all its parts. An object of this arrangement was to give every merchant a good location, but, as the anchor tenant, the department store was assured the best place. The Hecht Company's problems probably influenced department-store executives, few of whom previously had shown much inclination to participate in the complicated and expensive process of planning a regional shopping center.

Other problems arose in Silver Spring, due to overly high expectations. The booster spirit that lay behind the creation of outlying centers from the 1920s on fostered a belief that, once having gained the strategic advantage, a place would remain in the limelight indefinitely. Those who participated in Silver Spring's post-

to pass through streams of moving vehicles. finally, it may have been hoped that a new core shopping area would develop facing the store, away from the principal streets altogether. If this last idea was entertained, it came to naught. Hecht's location remained peripheral, yet was close enough to other emporia not to hurt sales.

As the Hecht Company project illustrates, outlying centers can be informative about the errors as well as the successes in development, as they were understood in their time. Between the 1920s and 1950s, many experimental projects were undertaken in these precincts, owing to the rapid pace of growth and change generally. Developers had few appropriate models from which to draw. Under the circumstances, it is not surprising that some of the results became object lessons in what to avoid. While it yielded profits beyond expectation and helped to propel a new genre of retail facility into the limelight, Hecht's also underscored the short-war boom conceived its shopping area as the only substantial alternative to downtown Washington for most of those residential areas north of the Potomac River. Yet its hegemony lasted for only a brief period. Silver Spring was still brand new as a retail magnet when merchants began to complain that trade was now going to two large shopping centers (1950–51, 1954–56) at Langley Park, three miles to the east. Even more ominous were the plans, announced in 1954, for Wheaton Plaza, the metropolitan area's first regional shopping mall, situated off Georgia Avenue, five miles to the north. Strategically, this complex was not only closer to new areas of residential development, it lay near the path of the proposed Capital Beltway, for which the initial plan was unveiled in 1952 and which was completed a dozen years later. Proximity to this high-speed route meant that people living some distance to the east or west also enjoyed easy access. When Wheaton Plaza opened in 1958, Silver Spring's businesses were already struggling to maintain the status quo. The cycle is a common one: a new type of retail development is introduced to a metropolitan area; at first the project is extremely successful, not just because of its inherent attributes, but also because it is unique; success spawns emulation; the more competitors enter the scene, the smaller their respective shares of the market become. Competition is further intensified as newcomers improve upon the model, which thus may soon start to seem outmoded.

To remain economically viable once competition is well established, the original development itself must change. That process, however, can be extremely difficult when it requires the cooperation of many parties, public and private. Very little new retail development occurred in Silver Spring after the early 1950s because such change proved difficult to bring about. County lawmakers increasingly balked

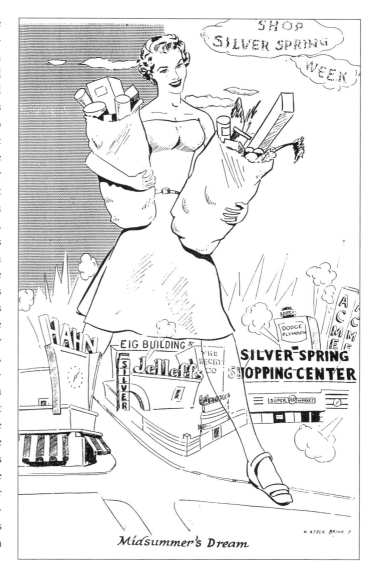

Midsummer's Dream

H. STECK BRINK 7

at the Planning Commission's proposals, which included an expanded business zone. Enlarging the once-innovative network of car lots became a laborious procedure, in part because of a sharp rise in the cost of land, but also because of diverging opinions about the best course of action to reach a common goal. Disputes between property owners and county officials

Figure 6. "Midsummer's Dream," editorial cartoon, 1956.

Figure 7. The Hecht
Company Silver Spring
store, 1946–47, Abbott,
Merkt & Company,
architects, altered.

arose. One of Silver Spring's principal developers, Sam Eig, conspicuously worked elsewhere during the mid-1950s, out of frustration over the local situation.

Few outlying centers have enjoyed sustained prestige. Often their heyday lasts less than a quarter-century. Most examples created during the 1920s and in the post–World War II era have experienced a pronounced decline. Some, such as Cleveland's Euclid Avenue and 103rd Street district, have been leveled; the site now bears almost no trace of its former function. In Silver Spring, stagnation was turning to decay by the early 1970s. A decade later, the area had lost all

its attraction as a retail center. Most leading merchants had left, replaced by marginal enterprises, or sometimes by no business at all. On the other hand, Silver Spring has prospered as an office center, a component envisioned in the mid-1940s that began to coalesce some dozen years later. The greatest growth in this sphere came in the 1980s, on the heels of the new Metro rapid-transit system, which opened a major station on Colesville Road, just to the west of the shopping district. The fact that Silver Spring's retail area all but collapsed at the same time reveals that the two functions can act independently of one another. Yet it is doubtful whether the precinct's appeal among white-collar firms will endure if a conspicuous part of the whole continues to be blighted.

Attempts to rejuvenate "old" outlying centers have not met with great success on the whole. Most such programs have focused either on cosmetic changes or on wholesale removal of the existing fabric. Progress has been stymied in Silver Spring for nearly a decade over proposals, since abandoned, for an ill-conceived multistory shopping mall that would have eliminated most of the commercial legacy of the postwar era, and completely divorced retail activity from the street.

Can Silver Spring be restored to its former economic vitality without an expensive transformation that eradicates the past? What lessons can be learned from its dilemma? Is drastic physical change necessary, or even desirable?

The first generation of fully integrated business developments in outlying areas occurred during the 1920s; these have continued to flourish as long as they are well managed. At the same time, both Georgia Avenue and Colesville Road in Silver Spring are so heavily traveled that they resist the regeneration of street-oriented development. If one cannot draw from tradition or return to it, if the outlying center that lacks business integration becomes disposable and valueless, what are the implications for our sense of community? Whatever the answers, we can ill afford to remain ignorant of the subject. To study the urban-core surrogates that have proliferated since World War I will not only tell us much about a century almost past, but will aid us to form reasoned, long-term strategies for the future. ■

Notes

1 A full discussion of Silver Spring's ascent to commercial prominence and the erosion of its stature is beyond the scope of the present essay. This is a prolegomenon to a further inquiry into these salient issues. It draws upon a larger study I have undertaken of retail decentralization in the Washington, D.C., metropolitan area after World War II. Generous funding for this research has come from the Center for Washington Area Studies at George Washington University. I am grateful to Howard Gillette, Jr., Dorn McGrath, and Richard Striner for reading this essay in draft form and providing many useful suggestions for its improvement.

Space limitations here also preclude a full citation of sources. The archival record from the public and private sectors alike is slim. The best contemporary sources found to date are local newspapers, including the *Maryland News, Silver Spring Post, Record of Bethesda–Chevy Chase, Washington Post,* and *Evening Star* (Washington, D.C.). Among trade journals and other publications, *Women's Wear Daily* gives some of the most extensive coverage of the community. A historical overview of the subject is presented in M. Walston, "The Commercial Rise and Fall of Silver Spring . . . ," *Maryland Historical Magazine* 81 (Winter 1986): 330–39. R. Longstreth, "The Neighborhood Shopping Center in Washington, D.C., 1930–1941," *Journal of the Society of Architectural Historians* 51 (March 1992): 5–34, discusses a key aspect of retail decentralization in the area prior to World War II. For general background on growth in the metropolitan region during the mid-twentieth century, see F. Gutheim and National Capital Planning Commission, *Worthy of the Nation: The History of Planning for the National Capital* (Washington, 1977), chaps. 9–11.

2 For purposes of this essay, I use "outlying center" to indicate a commercial district that on a frequent basis provides significantly more than the basic goods and services demanded by a localized, or neighborhood, market, and thus attracts a substantial portion of its trade from well beyond the immediate precinct. Fully developed, such places can function as an equivalent to the traditional city center, at least for a large middle range of the populace, much of the time. Outlying centers have seldom been the subject of historical inquiry. Useful overviews of developments during the 1920s in one city are afforded by H. M. Mayer and R. C. Wade, *Chicago: Growth of a Metropolis* (Chicago, 1969), 325, 342–48; and N. Harris, "Shopping— Chicago Style," in J. Zukowsky, ed., *Chicago Architecture 1872–1922: Birth of a Metropolis* (Munich, 1987), 137–55. Contemporary accounts are much more detailed, including case studies such as I. K. Rolph, *The Location Structure of Retail Trade Based on a Study of Baltimore,* Bureau of Foreign and Domestic Commerce, U.S. Department of Commerce, 1933; M. J. Proudfoot, *Intra-City Business Census Statistics for Philadelphia, Pennsylvania,* Bureau of Census, U.S. Department of Commerce, 1937; H. M. Mayer, "Patterns and Recent Trends of Chicago's Outlying Business Centers," *Journal of Land and Public Utility Economics* 18 (February 1942): 4–16; S. B. Cohen and G. K. Lewis, "Form and Function in the Geography of Retailing," *Economic Geography* 43 (January 1967): 1–42; and E. W. Kersten, Jr., and D. R. Ross, "Clayton: A New Metropolitan Focus for the St. Louis Area," *Annals of the Association of American Geographers* 58 (December 1968): 637–49. Much useful information also can be gleaned from journals related to real-estate development, retailing, and public works, as well as planning reports, economic bulletins, and newspapers.

CHICAGO

**Planning
Wacker Drive**

JOAN E. DRAPER

Figure 1. Aerial
photograph of downtown
Chicago and the Chicago
River. Wacker Drive
is marked with a heavy
black line.

Wacker Drive is a two-level street in downtown Chicago, running along the south bank of the main branch of the Chicago River, from Lake Michigan to the point just over a mile distant where it turns ninety degrees to run parallel to the river's South Branch (fig. 1). It defines the north and east sides of the Loop, the city's central business district. The original portion of Wacker Drive, running from Michigan Avenue west to Lake Street, was designed in 1917 and built between 1925 and 1927 for $21,584,576, including both land acquisition and construction costs. Its builders boasted that it was the first such bilevel street in the world, and its complexity was increased by the necessity to mesh it with eight different bridges over the river, one also double-decked and two carrying

elevated trains.[1] Wacker Drive's riverside façade was designed by Edward H. Bennett, consulting architect for the Chicago Plan Commission, to emulate the embankments of the Seine in Paris (fig. 2). Bennett's ideas for rebuilding all the rivers' banks in the downtown area in a similar manner had first been essayed in the 1909 *Plan of Chicago*, which he co-authored for the Commercial Club with Daniel H. Burnham (figs. 3, 4). In subsequent years, the club, the commission, and Bennett devoted themselves to promoting the particular vision of Chicago embodied in this 1909 plan. Wacker Drive, which accomplished some of their street transportation goals, was named for Charles H. Wacker, the long-time president of the Chicago Plan Commission.

Undoubtedly because of this and because of the vast amount of promotional literature about Wacker Drive issued by the commission, historians have interpreted it simply as the partial fulfillment of the 1909 plan. In the popular imagination also, this feat of engineering and urban design continued to be depicted as one of the most conspicuous manifestations of Burnham's famous plan.[2] This is the sole context within which historians have discussed Wacker Drive and the redevelopment of Chicago's downtown riverfront in the early twentieth century.

But the reality is more complicated. The story of Wacker Drive starts before 1909, and many people were involved in its planning and design. Chicagoans representing various interests had been advocating the redevelopment of the Chicago riverfront at this point since the 1880s. A number of related infrastructure improvements in and around the Loop were proposed, and in some cases executed, by individuals and organizations other than the Plan Commission prior to 1925. Furthermore, the fate of the Wacker Drive site was linked to the planning and development of harbor facilities throughout the Chicago region, activities in which the commission took little part. In other words, it was but one of many groups—public, quasipublic, and private—involved in the transformation of this stretch of riverbank from a dilapidated wholesale produce market and obsolete port facility to an elegant boulevard lined with some of Chicago's most prestigious skyscrapers (figs. 5, 6).

The commission succeeded in advancing its own designs for the street because of three factors over which it had, at best, limited control: a shift occurred in the economic base of Chicago and its land-use patterns during the 1890–1925 period; governmental authority was fragmented, which made infrastructure im-provement, especially at a locale such as the riverbank, difficult; and the other local riverfront redevelopment advocates had less effective organizational and communication skills, and were unable to realize their intent to preserve the status quo—the Chicago River as a major international port. Wacker Drive thus is as much a monument to the failure of planning as a symbol of the tenacity of the Plan Commission.

This case study illustrates how different readings of city form can result from, on the one hand, a view that emphasizes the achievements of great men, the rhetoric of planning professionals, and progress toward clear goals, and on the other, a viewpoint that analyzes urban form in relation to actual city building processes. In this instance, the process was characterized by barriers to action, from the time the problems were defined, around 1890, until construction on Wacker Drive began, in 1925. Delays resulted not from open hostilities among rival factions, but because no effective mechanism could be found to cope with the administrative, legal, technical, and financial complexities posed by this project until after 1920. The previous three decades had been, of course, a period in which members of the Chicago elite had effectively cooperated to carry out other big planning and public-works projects, including the 1893 World's Columbian Exposition and the expansion of public parks.[3] But the story of redeveloping the downtown riverfront is different. Here, we find no clear programs and many conflicting interests, none of which achieved ascendancy until the 1920s.

The Wacker Drive story reveals the degree to which attitudes of privatism and the fragmentation of authority, both characteristic of the nineteenth century, persisted into the twentieth. In this respect, Wacker Drive is probably more representative of Chicago planning than parks development, for which administrative

Figure 2. Alexander III Bridge and the Grand Palais, Paris, constructed for the 1900 International Exposition.

and financial patterns were much more rational and streamlined.[4]

Some sort of redevelopment would probably have taken place by 1925 at the northern edge of the central business district, along what is now Wacker Drive, even without the Plan Commission's initiative. In the 1910s and 1920s, various construction projects in downtown Chicago furthered land-use changes taking place there. The Loop, completely encircled by elevated trains by 1900, became a center for finance, retail sales, entertainment, and culture, while less profitable activities were increasingly forced out by high land values. The replacement of obsolete buildings accelerated. By 1920, the elegant boulevard proposal appeared entirely feasible, while rival plans for the same site faded from public consciousness. Earlier proposals for commercial harbor facilities on the river at this site seemed dated and irrelevant. Thus the

cumbersome, inefficient processes of planning and infrastructure building had as much to do with the appearance of Wacker Drive as the Burnham plan did.

Before the 1925 redevelopment, buildings crowding the shoreline faced onto South Water Street, an east–west thoroughfare. By mid-decade, South Water Street Market, the city's principal center for wholesale produce, was a congested and obsolete district, and had to be completely cleared in order to build Wacker Drive. Already by 1890, conditions there were frequently decried. Carts, crates, sacks, and seething crowds thronged the streets and side-walks. Wagons clogged nearby Rush Street Bridge, which had frequently to swing open to allow passage of schooners through the turgid river waters, toward docks further inland. Congestion here was exacerbated by the fact that the produce market had no special railroad-

Figure 3. Chicago, 1909, view looking north on the South Branch of the Chicago River, showing the suggested arrangement of streets and ways for teaming and reception of freight by boat, at different levels.

terminal facilities. Perishables had to be transported over the streets to and from the market. In the first two decades of the twentieth century, pollution and traffic problems at this spot grew worse, while the character of the central business district just to the south changed. Following trends in the development of American central business districts generally, wholesaling and warehousing moved to outlying locations, while more prestigious and profitable retailing and office uses became more prevalent. Chicago, like other modern industrial cities, became characterized by districts of more specialized land uses, all linked by transportation networks of increasing sophistication.

Port facilities along the Chicago River were also obsolete and their redevelopment subject to larger market forces that no one group could effectively manipulate. In 1890, the Chicago River in the central district had comprised one of the world's busiest commercial ports. In tonnage it ranked second in the United States only to New York City. Traffic on the river reached a peak in 1889. The next year, twenty-two thousand vessels passed in and out of the river's mouth, bearing lumber, coal, grain, salt, and other cargoes, as well as passengers. In 1900, dock frontage along fifteen navigable miles totaled seven to ten miles, all of it privately owned. Forty-one bridges crossed the stream.

Riverfront lots throughout the downtown were occupied not only by docks, but also by railroad terminals, warehouses, coal and lumberyards, and factories. Prominent features were the Illinois Central grain elevators at Lake Michigan and the passenger and package freight docks at Rush Street, further inland, where the eastern end of Wacker Drive was later constructed.[5]

After 1890, however, shipping tonnage on the Chicago River began a steady decline relative to other regional ports and to the railroads. Concerned observers identified four physical conditions that threatened the lifeblood of "the most important navigable stream for its length on the globe."[6] first, many center-pier bridges blocked the passage of ships. Bridges were frequently swung open to allow their passage, and all land traffic came to a standstill. As late as 1909, an engineer who had studied river problems for decades lamented that "interruptions due to opened bridges for the accommodation of river traffic are met with maledictions loud and deep."[7]

Second, encroachments by private riparian owners cut the clear channel to no more than one hundred feet across in places. Virtually all riverbanks were privately owned. Regulation of encroachments—docks built out into the channel—proved impossible, and there was no inventory of private land ownership here until 1899. Third, the many natural bends in the river's original meander line made passage difficult for the larger ships, which could exceed four hundred feet in length. finally, until after about 1910–12, three streetcar tunnels ran under the river to and from the Loop at a depth of only sixteen feet. For years before this time, the largest lake freighters had a draft of twenty feet.[8] An additional problem arose after January 1900, when the Sanitary District of Chicago completed and opened the Drainage Canal, later called the Sanitary and Ship Canal (fig. 7).

This uniquely expensive public-works project connected the South Branch of the Chicago River to the Des Plaines River. It reversed the Chicago River's flow so that it ran out of the lake and ultimately into the Illinois and Mississippi Rivers, carrying with it the city's sewage. Given the many narrows and bends in the river remaining unimproved, the current now ran too swiftly in places to permit freight-filled ships to operate without expensive tugboats.[9]

Five groups of Chicagoans attempted to remedy these problems. All had a hand in planning Wacker Drive. These were "river men," who included grain-elevator owners, shipping agents, and the like; the Army Corps of Engineers; the engineers and elected trustees of the Sanitary District of Chicago; the members and staff of the Chicago Plan Commission, a semipublic agency; and other city officials, including the mayor, aldermen, council committee members, and the Board of Local Improvements. Some groups made redevelopment proposals, and some had partial powers to enact them, though power was very fragmented. The laissez-faire attitude of the nineteenth century persisted. As the more modern bureaucratic mode came into being in the twentieth century, the situation was not necessarily simplified. New, narrowly focused special authorities and regulatory bodies appeared, none of them able adequately to coordinate with each other. Nor could any one entity by itself deal with the complexity of the problems of the riverfront. Not until the 1920s did the pieces fall into place, at least temporarily, while economic prosperity lasted.[10]

Men representing Chicago's shipping interests proved to be ineffective planners. In 1894 they founded the Chicago River Improvement Association to try to prevent freight traffic from going to other Great Lakes ports and to keep the city's waterborne transport economically competitive with the railroads. Association members actively lobbied Congress, the state legislature, and the city council through 1909, demanding nothing less than the complete redevelopment of Chicago's river harbor as a modern commercial port, at public expense. They argued that the port could not be moved from the river to the lakefront or to South Chicago, as others had suggested. Relocating the existing railroad tracks, docks, grain elevators, and warehouses that lined the river's banks would be too expensive, they claimed.[11]

The Chicago River Improvement Association sought unsuccessfully to preserve the pattern of the nineteenth-century city, in which land uses in the central district were mixed, and where manufacturing and wholesaling interests maintained a close proximity to lines of transport because of the high cost of moving goods relative to moving people.[12] The association could not effect this goal for a number of reasons. Competition from railroads was sharp. Transhipped cargo, which in the 1890s had accounted for about 30 percent of total lake traffic, was driven away by the relatively high costs associated with navigation on the Chicago River before the association could act; by 1905, total tonnage of all types on the Chicago River was down more than 50 percent, to five million tons. Wagon, and later automobile, traffic in and out of the Loop steadily increased, exacerbating the longstanding "bridge nuisance." Public opinion ran against the association, whose wealthy members were popularly resented.[13]

The River Improvement Association could not overcome this bias, nor rouse many other Chicagoans to take up its cause. Its members never moved beyond supplying anecdotal evidence of their woes. They never hired an expert consultant to promote their interests by making a plan, nor did they form productive coalitions with other private interest groups or with the

most powerful public agencies with authority over the river. They could not build a new private port independently, although one such proposal did surface in the city council in 1909 and in the Illinois legislature in 1910. The river harbor was never rebuilt to accommodate modern cranes and docks. Instead, marine shipping, associated facilities, and piecemeal public investment gradually migrated out of the city and to the Calumet Harbor in South Chicago.[14]

The river men failed to make use of their potential allies in the Army Corps of Engineers. The officers stationed in Chicago over the years were among the most expert people who had authority over the planning and redevelopment of the river and its banks. The scope of their concern was defined by a congressional mandate to promote interstate navigation. Federally financed dredging activities at the mouth of the Chicago River date to 1833, but not until the end of the century did the corps involve itself with what happened inland. The River and Harbor Act of 1888 empowered the Secretary of War and his agents, the district engineers, to control obstructions to navigation throughout the United States. In the same piece of legislation, Congress gave the secretary jurisdiction over the navigable portions of the Chicago River, in addition to the "outer harbor" on Lake Michigan.

Subsequently, Chicago's marine interests expected that more federal funds would flow for river development, but their hopes were frustrated by William Marshall, the Chicago district engineer from 1888 to 1899. His annual reports from 1890 to 1899 recommended little or no investment to develop the Chicago River as a commercial harbor. He proposed that no improvements be made until the city stopped dumping sewage and began to regulate dumping by slaughterhouses. Year after year, he catalogued the river's navigational problems, including the lack of public docks. As early as 1890,

CHICAGO PLAN COMMISSION
PROPOSED WACKER DRIVE & RIVER FRONT IMPROVEMENTS
VIEW LOOKING SOUTHWEST
EXECUTED 1924 - 1926
January 1926
Bennett Parsons & Frost
Consulting Architects

he predicted that the land along the down-town riverfront, where Wacker Drive was later constructed, would become too expensive for warehousing and freight handling, while the distant and relatively undeveloped Calumet area to the south, already a zone of manufacturing, would have more potential as the site of a new, modern harbor and terminal on the projected Great Lakes–Mississippi River route.

The river men fought proposals to build a modern port away from the Chicago River. They fumed in the press and lobbied Congress, together with the Chicago Real Estate Board. This activity had some result. Marshall was replaced in 1899 by someone more conciliatory to local interests. Federal appropriations for dredging the Chicago River channel to a six-teen-foot depth had begun in 1896; in 1897, Congress approved funds for purchasing land from owners of riparian encroachments; and the 1899 River and Harbor Act adopted a twenty-one-foot depth.

Between 1900 and 1925, the federal government's stance toward harbor improvements in Chicago was inconsistent. Tonnage on the Chicago River continued to decline, but army engineers attributed the drop to inadequate harbor facilities rather than to competition from the railroads. The district engineers' reports continued to express doubts about the harbor potential of the Chicago River, except for passenger and local freight traffic. Nevertheless, modest congressional appropriations for improvements to the Chicago River continued to flow. Additionally, the Secretaries of War demanded that the municipality and the Sanitary District help to widen and straighten the river channel and to remove impediments to navigation. For example, in 1904, the secretary ordered the city to lower streetcar tunnels under the Main Branch, and both the district and the municipality were forced to remove the old swing bridges and to construct new movable bridges over the widened channel at many

Figure 4. Aerial-view drawing of Chicago, 1926, showing proposed Wacker Drive and riverfront improvement.

Figure 5. The Chicago
River and Wacker Drive,
aerial view eastward, 1931.

streets, including some that later connected with Wacker Drive. Federal regulations required a clear span of 140 feet, and to this day federal law requires that bascule bridges in the center of Chicago be kept in working order, even though commercial shipping long ago deserted this river.

By 1925, when construction began on Wacker Drive, the river's Main Branch was finally able to accommodate the passage, if not the docking and unloading, of large lake freighters. But the volume of shipping had continued to decline as other ports developed superior facilities, as rail transportation became cheaper, and as lumbering operations moved away from the shores of Lake Michigan.[15] From the successful lobbying of Congress by river interests had come navigational improvements all along the river, but not in time to make the construction of publicly financed commercial docks anywhere on its length a feasible proposition. So when the downtown riverfront was finally reconstructed, it was

Figure 6. View across the Chicago River to the embankment west of the Michigan Avenue Bridge, c. 1927.

as an elegant boulevard, and the only docking facilities below Wacker Drive were for occasional use by passenger and pleasure craft.

The local public agency most responsible for river improvements before 1925 was the Sanitary District of Chicago. Formed by the Illinois legislature in 1889, it was charged with disposing of the city's sewage without contaminating its water supply, drawn entirely from Lake Michigan. This single-purpose special district had boundaries that ultimately exceeded those of the municipality. Its taxing and administrative powers were analogous to those of a city. The solution the district took to metropolitan sanitation problems was to build a $30 million, twenty-eight-mile-long canal connecting the South Branch of the Chicago River to the Des Plaines River, thereby reversing the former river's flow and diverting diluted sewage into the Illinois River Valley, instead of into Lake Michigan (see fig. 7). The Drainage Canal, which opened in January 1900, was over twenty feet deep and varied in width from 110 to 201 feet.

This canal had enormous importance for Chicago River navigation and for Wacker Drive. Despite the legislative mandate to focus on public health, the renamed Sanitary and Ship Canal became part of the Lake-to-Gulf inland waterway system. Its dual function created both problems and possibilities. Of necessity, the Sanitary District trustees' and officers' undertakings were subject to regulation by the Secretary of War, who had assumed responsibility for navigation on the Chicago River in 1888. Jurisdictional conflicts developed as these two entities sought to reconcile navigational with sanitation needs.[16] In 1895 a federal commission was appointed to investigate the canal's effect on lake water levels and on the river's current. Its report suggested that the impact would be deleterious in both respects, although later experience showed that only the rate-of-flow problem was real. In May 1899, when the Secretary of War issued a permit authorizing the Sanitary District to open the canal, he stipulated that not only would the speed of the river's flow be subject to federal regulation, but that the district bore all responsibility for damages due to the induced current.

Consequently, the Sanitary District was required to spend millions of dollars on Chicago River improvements in its first decades. Alterations included dredging, dock reconstruction to widen the channel to 200 feet, and the construction of new bridges. Some turn-of-the-century optimists hoped that the district would be granted full responsibility for planning and funding all river and harbor improvements. Its independent taxing and bonding powers made the idea seem feasible. One such optimist was the engineer Albert H. Scherzer, who in 1901 issued a pamphlet to advertise his patented "Scherzer Rolling Lift Bridges" and to outline a plan for the comprehensive rebuilding of the entire internal harbor along the miles of the North and South Branches and the Drainage Canal. Scherzer offered this proposal to Sanitary District trustees. He claimed it would improve navigation and free the lakefront and riverfront from rail lines, docks, and warehouses, so that it could be used for park land and public buildings. His brochure shows Grant Park, on the lakefront, developed along the lines of the 1893 fairgrounds and a Parisian-style bridge at Michigan Avenue that closely resembles the structure built there nearly twenty years later (see fig. 5).[17] Various other proposals and legislative bills were occasionally advanced, but they had no success.

The Sanitary District trustees never took on this larger harbor planning role, although they were not above touting the navigational importance of their work when petitioning Congress for financial assistance with river improve-

ments. In all, Chicago River projects undertaken by the district before 1930 cost about $12 million. Along the Main Branch, where Wacker Drive was later built, less reconstruction seems to have been undertaken than on the South Branch. Dredging undermined the foundations of the privately owned docks and buildings along the shore, many built in the 1870s. However, they remained in place until the 1925 Wacker Drive redevelopment. Two new Scherzer rolling-lift bridges were also constructed at this site by the Sanitary District: that at State Street was completed in 1903; that at Dearborn Street in 1907. Neither was as "artistic" as Scherzer's proposed Michigan Avenue Bridge, and both bridges were subsequently replaced with more modern and decorative structures. Their significance here lies in the fact that their abutments established both the vertical and horizontal placement of Wacker Drive, when it was designed and constructed between 1917 and 1927.

The actual design of Wacker Drive came from the Chicago Plan Commission, a 328-member body appointed by the mayor in 1909. This semiofficial, quasipublic organization existed as an advisory body to the city council until 1939. Planning, in this context, meant persuading Chicagoans to conform to the 1909 Burnham and Bennett plan. The plan, which dealt primarily with public works and focused on central city redevelopment, had been sponsored by the Commercial Club, a selective businessmen's club. The club also partially funded the commission's activities through 1920. These club men, a number of whom also served on the commission, claimed to represent the public interest and to be above the antagonisms of the ten separate taxing bodies within the boundaries of Cook County. In fact, their biases are evident in their documents and actions. An executive committee, chaired until 1926 by Charles Wacker, tightly controlled the business of this volunteer organization between 1909 and 1939.

The Plan Commission, along with its paid professional staff, undertook two types of tasks, publicity and technical assistance. Under the guidance of Walter Moody, a former advertising man, and his successor, Eugene Taylor, it issued a stream of promotional publications whose persuasiveness and ubiquity has led some historians to attribute all planning in Chicago in the 1910s and 1920s to the commission itself. In actuality, its specific project designs were heavily conditioned by other agencies' plans; not all were executed as proposed—or ever built. Edward H. Bennett, appointed consulting architect in 1909, and Hugh H. Young, appointed consulting engineer in 1920, prepared detailed designs for the public-works projects that the commission decided to advance. Wacker Drive was among these. Both the executive committee and the staff then lobbied assiduously behind the scenes to convince the responsible public agencies—the federal government, the Sanitary District, the park districts, the city council, the Board of Local Improvement, and the Department of Public Works—to follow those designs and to conform to the guidelines of the 1909 plan.[18]

Despite its apparent comprehensiveness, the *Plan of Chicago* mentioned harbor planning only briefly, while railroad consolidation received a thorough analysis. It illustrated two proposed sets of new piers projecting into Lake Michigan, one at the Calumet River and the other north of the Chicago River. In between these industrial and commercial piers was indicated a continuous band of parks along the lakefront. The rebuilding of the riverfront, however, was proposed in a different context: in the "Streets within the City" chapter, as part of a comprehensive traffic plan (see fig. 3). Burnham and Bennett recommended boulevards along both sides of the river on the Main Branch

and on the North and South Branches for about two miles in either direction. These streets, they claimed, would help relieve downtown traffic congestion. By building roadways above grade, they added, warehouses accessible to riverside docks could be constructed below. But they did not elaborate on any of the functional details which had so animated the river men and the engineers of the army and the Sanitary District.[19]

Why such a lack of concern for the river? The *Plan of Chicago* clearly reflects the interests of its makers. No river men served on the original Plan Commission, although there were two lumber merchants and a yacht broker. In contrast, railroad interests were well represented, especially in the person of the long-time executive committee member Frederic A. Delano, president of a railroad company. The commission as a whole in its early years included at least nineteen men in the real-estate business, as well as many lawyers, bankers, and merchants, all of whom could be considered to represent downtown landed interests, not marine interests.

These men envisioned the Loop, doubled in size, as the vital headquarters of a modern, integrated city. Although the text acknowledges that implementing land-use zoning legislation was out of the question in 1909 (Chicago got zoning in 1923), the plan did envision differentiations in land use. The "Heart of Chicago," in their mind's eye, could no longer accommodate warehousing, wholesaling, cargo handling, and other such activities still clustered around the main branch of the Chicago River, where Wacker Drive rose in 1925. It would, instead, consolidate its position as the financial, administrative, retail, and cultural hub of the Chicago region. The Heart is described as a dense core, filled with highrise structures:

These buildings will be used for offices by corporations whose plants are scattered throughout the

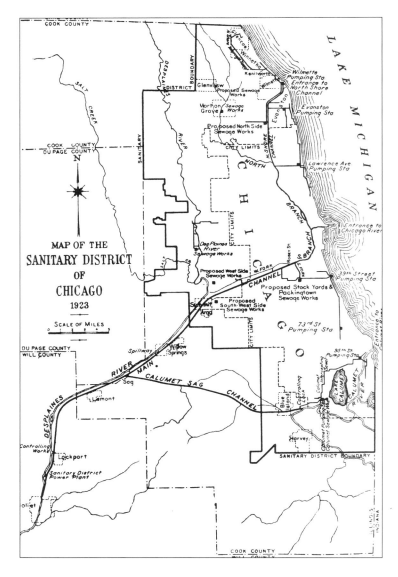

Burnham, Bennett, and the Commercial Club understood that market forces were already changing land use. Their plan fostered that transformation by illustrating with maps and beautiful renderings how the Loop could be redeveloped for more profitable and prestigious uses, none of which were port activities. Their park expansion plans also conflicted with other proposals for harbor development. They remained devoted to the idea of a single band of parkland stretching along Chicago's lakefront from north to south, a concept supported, and gradually executed over the years, by the park district. Consequently, the commission vehemently opposed proposals for commercial harbor development along the lakefront or at the mouth of the river.

The *Plan of Chicago* sketched out the future Chicago in broad strokes. More detailed suggestions issued copiously from the commission in the years after 1909. Among the improvements the commission approved, downtown traffic-relief projects received top priority. Bennett planned both the Michigan Avenue Bridge and Wacker Drive to complete a quadrangle of widened and improved streets allowing more efficient movement around the congested Loop.[21] The bridge (see fig. 5) completed the so-called "Boulevard Link" between the north and west sides of Chicago. It replaced the narrow, rickety Rush Street Bridge, long condemned as a bottleneck and potential disaster site. The new bridge fulfilled a need for a safer and more dignified intersection at a point where thousands of vehicles, crossing the river daily, met the traffic associated with the produce market and the railhead to the east, across Michigan Avenue. Proposals for eliminating this bottleneck included a suspension bridge and a tunnel; however, a more practical movable bridge, of a type invented in Chicago around 1900 by Department of Public Works engi-

Figure 7. Chicago Sanitary District regional map, 1923. The Sanitary and Ship Canal is labeled "Main Channel."

wide territory of which Chicago is the metropolis; for shops and banks; for hotels; for theatres and other places of entertainment; for railroad passenger terminals; for churches and public or semi-public structures, all of which will be resorted to by hundreds of thousands of people who must pass daily into and out of this comparatively small area.[20]

neers, was chosen. The elegant double-decked, double-leafed, trunnion bascule bridge was designed by Bennett and the city engineer Thomas Pihlfeldt in 1911–12, but not completed until 1920. It is one of eight bridges connected to Wacker Drive, and it established exactly the new grade levels for the two roadways at its eastern end. Both the bilevel bridge and the bilevel drive were embellished with the same elegant architectural details inspired by the Alexander III Bridge and its embankments along the River Seine in Paris (completed in 1900, see fig. 2).

The Michigan Avenue Bridge set precedents for Wacker Drive in two other ways. Both projects provoked a furious legal controversy over who would pay. When the bridge was completed, it had a positive influence on surrounding property values. The rapid rise in the early 1920s of prestige skyscrapers like the Wrigley Building and the Tribune Building, adjacent to the Michigan Avenue Bridge, foreshadowed similar development along Wacker Drive in the late 1920s, although some Chicagoans had been skeptical about the ability of the real-estate market to absorb so much high-priced commercial space at one time.[22]

The Chicago Plan Commission announced its Wacker Drive project in 1917, in another of its many promotional brochures: *South Water Street Must Go.* The publication contained photographs and drawings of Bennett's proposed redevelopment of the Chicago River's south bank. Statistics and bold prose brought home the message: South Water Street "is an economic waste, a burdensome charge on all the people; a drawback to Chicago's progress; obstructive to its prosperity; and a conflagration danger to the whole Loop." The Commission claimed, "This improvement will pay for itself in one year." The plan outlined in the brochure was more elaborate than that finally constructed. It called for rail lines on the lower level, along with a vehicle roadway, both connecting to rail terminals to the east. A proposed car ferry at Lake Street would transfer railroad cars across the river to connect with rail terminals there, enabling freight to reach west-side warehouses or to continue on to other destinations. In the completed plan, these features were eliminated; the reinforced-concrete structure was designed to carry only horse-drawn wagons and motor vehicles.[23]

Responsibility for public works within the municipal bureaucracy was also extremely fragmented. The Board of Local Improvements, which oversaw construction of Wacker Drive, was but one of several independent agencies with the power and the means to influence its planning during the 1900–25 era. One political historian has characterized Chicago's municipal government then (and now) as a "a tortuous and cumbersome maze of overlapping administrative and fiscal authorities." Chicago's situation was not atypical of American cities, only more acute because of its size and the fact that it lacked home rule until 1970.[24] Some public agencies, like the BLI, helped further the Wacker Drive scheme; they actively supported the Plan Commission's twin obsessions, lakefront parks and efficient traffic circulation through a redeveloped downtown.

On the other hand, the city council's Harbor Commission, appointed in 1908, attempted to collect and channel the energies of the river men, energies that were still directed toward commercial harbor development along the river and the lakeshore. The commission's 1909 harbor plan was a landmark document because of its regional scope, but it had limited influence. It was narrowly focused on shipping interests, technical in tone, and weakened by its attempt to reconcile too many conflicting demands. The report also bore little relationship to the

Commercial Club's more famous plan of the same year, even though Frederic Delano and Charles Wacker served on the Harbor Commission. Among the concepts endorsed by the 1909 harbor plan was the idea of outer (lakefront) harbor development. This put a stop to efforts by the Chicago River Improvement Association and the Chicago Association of Commerce to elicit public funds for commercial docks along the river, including the three-quarter-mile stretch where Wacker Drive was later built. Subsequent harbor-plan reports, made between 1909 and 1914 by the city council's Committees on Harbors, Wharves, and Bridges, outlined five piers jutting out into Lake Michigan at Chicago Avenue, north of the river, although only one was ever constructed. Between 1914 and 1916 the Municipal Pier (later Navy Pier) was constructed there. The three-thousand-foot pier was planned for both commercial freight and passengers, but it never fulfilled its advocates' hopes. Passenger boats still preferred to dock on the river. Freighters still had difficulties finding places to unload goods in Chicago throughout the 1920s, because only one rail line served the Municipal Pier. Nevertheless, by 1916, shipping interests no longer had reason to oppose the redevelopment of South Water Street into that elegant boulevard, Wacker Drive.[25]

While the Harbor Commission's approach to planning was technical, one municipal department exerted an influence on Wacker Drive planning for highly political reasons. The Board of Local Improvements enthusiastically allied itself with the Chicago Plan Commission to carry out the Wacker Drive project and other street improvements throughout the city. This agency had been authorized by the city council in 1897 to oversee all street improvements paid for through assessments. The BLI, whose members were appointed by the mayor, had three responsibilities: to condemn properties and fix compensations; to fix assessments on properties affected by improvements; and to supervise construction. Michael Faherty, board president from 1915 to 1931, was an especially enthusiastic supporter of the Plan Commission's work. Faherty was a close associate of Mayor "Big Bill" Thompson (1915–23 and 1927–31). Both men were former real-estate developers. They recognized the political advantages of promoting big building. They compared themselves to Baron Haussmann, and produced lavish reports claiming that the Plan Commission had been helpless to proceed without their intervention. These machine politicians also recognized in the multimillion-dollar construction projects an opportunity to hand out favors to laborers, contractors, and real-estate appraisers. In 1921, the *Tribune* newspaper filed suit against both men, charging that they and their associates had conspired to overpay assessors working on Michigan Avenue by $2,876,063. This and other scandals contributed to the hiatus in Thompson's mayoralty. However, Charles Wacker winked at Thompson's demagoguery and corruption. Both men were master coalition builders; Thompson helped win passage of the two bond issues passed by voters in 1919 and 1924, which raised $13.8 million for the conversion of South Water Street Market into Wacker Drive.[26]

In addition to cheerleading for public-works bond issues, the BLI determined the assessments against adjacent properties, which paid a portion of the costs of street improvements. Redevelopment of the former South Water Street Market ran into opposition after the city council approved the project in 1917, as had the Michigan Avenue improvements. Some market tenants grumbled in the press about relocation to a new site on the south side.[27] More serious resistance came in the form of legal challenges to the assessments imposed upon the 12,500 parcels of property that the corporation counsel and the BLI had determined to be within the area benefiting from the Wacker Drive improvement. Determining the assessments required several years' time. When they were finally announced in 1922, the assessees filed suit against the city, challenging its determination that they should pay 65 percent of the $22 million improvement, while only 35 percent would be financed by all the citizens of Chicago through revenue bonds. The suit dragged on until 1924, when the assessment was revised at 52 percent for the adjacent property owners and 48 percent for the city; only then could bids for demolition and construction be let.

The Wacker Drive case signaled a shift in fiscal responsibility for public-works construction costs away from local property owners and to Chicago taxpayers generally. This was consistent with trends in other American cities in the early twentieth century. In the nineteenth century, as the historian Robin Einhorn has demonstrated, American city governments were designed to minimize the redistributive effects of general funding and to keep property taxes low. Therefore, street building was kept off-budget, through the use of special assessments, and services were privatized whenever possible. Einhorn's study of Chicago demonstrates that before 1865 local property owners successfully controlled street improvements, based on their perceptions of what would or would not bring a rise in property values. Such a practice, of course, made "comprehensive planning" and centralized control of public works incompatible with the aims of municipal government. Einhorn argues that the system began to break down in the 1870s, as wealthy businessmen became more adept at finding the means to shift the public-works burden onto all taxpayers, without reference to ward boundaries. As this occurred, advocates of centralization of public-works functions elevated their own interests to the public interest.[28]

The Wacker Drive planning process clearly demonstrates this thesis. The wealthy business-men and property owners who comprised the Commercial Club and controlled the Chicago Plan Commission sold the project to the public in 1917 by proclaiming that it would benefit everyone in the city, while predictions about property values in the assessment district were equally rosy—experts predicted increases of 200 to 300 percent.[29] Litigious property owners quoted Plan Commission propaganda. And so it was decided that taxpayers throughout the city should pay a larger share of the $22 million price tag for Wacker Drive.

This case study of one street redevelopment project demonstrates the actual city building processes at work in early-twentieth-century Chicago. It shows that although the city had a "comprehensive plan" and a plan commission, the planning process scarcely resembled the centralized and rationalized model that became the norm in later decades. Nor are the myths about the agency of Chicago's heroic and visionary architects and planners entirely accurate.[30] On the contrary, the process was characterized by administrative fragmentation and rivalry among the public agencies that had jurisdiction over the spot where Wacker Drive was constructed after 1925. Barriers to action were overcome by the superior financial resources and organizational skills of the Chicago Plan Commission. This special-interest group formed effective ad hoc coalitions with others in order to get things done. The commission members also astutely understood changes taking place in the economic geography of the city—changes upon which they sought to capitalize. Nevertheless, their patience and tenacity were required to accomplish the redevelopment of Chicago according to the Burnham plan. The Wacker Drive story, although it could be told as a stirring narrative of architects and planners overcoming adversities, was actually more a matter of collaboration, good timing, and muddling through. ■

Notes

This is a revised version of a paper presented at the Annual Meeting of the Society of Architectural Historians, April 16, 1988, in Chicago.

1 H. E. Young, "The South Water Street Improvement," *Journal of the Western Society of Engineers* 30 (March 1925): 73–95; "Design and Structure of Double-Deck Street, Chicago," *Engineering News-Record* 95 (October 15, 1925): 632–35; "Construction Methods on Double-Deck Street, Chicago," ibid., 662–65; R. W. Priest, "Building a Two-Level Street in Downtown Chicago, Part I," *Concrete* 30 (January 1927): 41–45; R. O. Benson, "Building a Two-Level Street in Downtown Chicago, Part II," *Concrete* 30 (March 1927): 44–47; S. H. Lomax, "Building a Two-Level Street in Downtown Chicago, Part III," *Concrete* 30 (May 1927): 31–34; H. E. Young, "Wacker Drive," *Nation's Traffic* 2 (May 1928): 17–18, 51.

2 C. Condit, *Chicago 1910–1929: Building, Planning and Urban Technology* (Chicago, 1973), 75, 98, 250; H. M. Mayer and R. C. Wade, *Chicago: Growth of a Metropolis* (Chicago, 1969), 310–15; S. Shepherd, "Fastest Route Thru Loop Still 'Lower Level,'" *Chicago Tribune*, March 14, 1965; *Central Area Plan* (Chicago, 1983). For examples of the Plan Commission's literature, see the articles by H. Young, Plan Commission engineer, n. 1, and Chicago Plan Commission, *South Water Street Must Go* (Chicago, 1917); E. H. Bennett, *South Water Street Improvement* (Chicago, 1921); Chicago Plan Commission, *The Chicago Plan in 1933, Twenty-five Years of Accomplishment* (Chicago, 1933).

3 See M. P. McCarthy, "Politics and the Parks: Chicago Businessmen and the Recreation Movement," *Journal of the Illinois State Historical Society* 65 (Summer 1972): 158–72; H. L. Horowitz, *Culture and the City: Cultural Philanthropy in Chicago from the 1880s to 1912* (Lexington, 1976); F. A. and M. E. Cassell, "The White City in Peril: Leadership and the World's Columbian Exposition," *Chicago History* 12 (Fall 1983): 10–27; F. C. Jaher, ed., *The Urban Establishment: Upper Strata in Boston, New York, Charleston, Chicago and Los Angeles* (Urbana, 1982).

4 On nineteenth-century infrastructure in Chicago, see R. L. Einhorn, *Property Rules: Political Economy in Chicago, 1833–1872* (Chicago, 1991); C. M. Rosen, *The Limits of Power: Great fires and the Process of City Growth in America* (Cambridge, Eng., 1986); A. D. Keating, *Building Chicago: Suburban Developers and the Creation of a Divided Metropolis* (Columbus, 1988). On park planning, see D. Bluestone, *Constructing Chicago* (New Haven, 1991), 37–61.

5 H. M. Mayer, *The Port of Chicago and the St. Lawrence Seaway* (Chicago, 1957), 12; J. W. Larson, *Those Army Engineers: A History of the Chicago District U.S. Army Corps of Engineers* (Washington, D.C., 1980), 192; T. S. Charney, "Chicago Harbor a Century Ago," *Sea History* 47 (Summer 1988): 12–15; M. A. Lane, "Good Stories of Chicago's River," *Harper's Weekly* 36 (January 2, 1892): 9; R. B. Wilcox, "The River and Harbor of Chicago," *Journal of the Western Society of Engineers* 5 (November–December 1900): 499–535.

6 Chicago City Council, Commission on the Chicago River, *Report*, December 11, 1899, 4.

7 Isham Randolph, quoted in J. Ewen, "The Chicago Harbor," *Journal of the Western Society of Engineers* 14 (December 1909): 776.

8 U.S. War Department, Engineer Department, *Annual Report of Engineers*, 1893, 4 vols. (Washington, D.C., 1893): 2791–2809; G. A. M. Lilliencrantz, "Obstructive Bridges and Docks in the Chicago River," *Engineering News* 40 (July 21, 1898): 44; W. Artingstall, "Chicago River Tunnels, Their History and Method of Reconstruction," *Journal of the Western Society of Engineers* 16 (November 1911): 869–921. Many other reports and journal articles catalogue the inadequacies of the Chicago River harbor.

9 "The Improvement of the Chicago River," *Journal of the Western Society of Engineers* 6 (February 1901): 1–25.

10 See J. W. Konvitz, *The Urban Millennium: The City-Building Process from the Early Middle Ages to the Present* (Carbondale, Ill., 1985), 100–110, 129–30, 132–34.

11 Chicago River Improvement Association, *Chicago: Where Railroad Traffic and Lake Transportation Meet*, 1896; ibid., *Annual Report and Constitution*, 1897; *Memorial to Congress by the City of Chicago with Reference to the Improvement of the Chicago River* (brochure) Chicago, December 30, 1897; "Chicago River Improvements," *Engineering News* 4 (January 26, 1899): 55; "Ask Help of Congress to Improve the River," *Record-Herald*, February 14, 1905, 14.

12 R. L. Fales and L. N. Moses, "Land-Use Theory and the Spatial Structure of the Nineteenth-Century City," *Regional Science Association, Western Division, Papers and Proceedings* 28 (1972): 49–80. The article uses data from Chicago in the 1870s to test the theory.

13 U.S. War Department, Engineer Department, *Annual Report of Engineers*, 1893, 2796; ibid., 1896, 2574; R. W. Putnam, "Chicago's Need for a Comprehensive Water Terminal Plan," *Journal of the Western Society of Engineers* 28 (September 1923): 416.

14 R. S. MacElwee, *Ports and Terminal Facilities* (New York, 1926): 417–19; Mayer, *Port of Chicago*, 17–22.

15 E. O. Griffenhagen, "Water-Borne Commerce of the Chicago Region and Its Requirements," *Journal of the Western Society of Engineers* 30 (April 1925): 191–92.

16 See I. Randolph, *The Sanitary District of Chicago and the Chicago Drainage Canal: A Review of Twenty Years of Engineering Work* (Chicago, 1909); C. A. Williams, *The Sanitary District of Chicago: History of Its Growth and Development as Shown by Decisions of the Courts and Work of Its Law Department* (Chicago, 1919); L. Pearse, "The Sanitary District of Chicago," *Journal of the Western Society of Engineers* 28 (May 1923): 179–94; Sanitary District of Chicago, *Engineering Works: The Sanitary District of Chicago* (Chicago, [1928]); L. P. Cain, *The Search for an Optimum Sanitary Jurisdiction: The Metropolitan Sanitary District of Greater Chicago, A Case Study*, Public Works History Essay No. 10 (Chicago, 1980).

17 Scherzer Rolling Lift Bridge Company, *Scherzer Rolling Lift Bridges* (Chicago, 1901); "Plans a Great Internal Harbor," *Record-Herald*, June 11, 1901, 12.

18 See H. Whitehead, ed., *The Chicago Plan Commission: A Historical Sketch, 1909–1960* (Chicago, 1961); M. P. McCarthy, "Chicago Businessmen and the Burnham Plan," *Journal of the Illinois State Historical Society* 63 (Autumn 1970): 228–56; R. P. Akley, "Implementation of the 1909 Plan of Chicago: An Historical Account of Planning Salesmanship," Master's thesis, University of Tennessee, 1973; J. Zukowsky, S. Chappell, and R. Bruegmann, *The Plan of Chicago, 1909–1979* (Chicago, 1979); J. E. Draper, *Edward H. Bennett: Architect and City Planner, 1874–1954* (Chicago, 1982), 16–22; T. J. Schlereth, "Burnham's *Plan* and Moody's Manual: City Planning as Progressive Reform," in *The American Planner: Biographies and Recollections*, ed. D. A. Krueckeberg (New York, 1983), 75–99; J. E. Draper, "Paris by the Lake: Sources of Burnham's Plan of Chicago," in J. Zukowsky, ed., *Chicago Architecture 1872–1922: Birth of a Metropolis* (Munich, 1987), 108–19.

19 D. H. Burnham and E. H. Bennett, *Plan of Chicago* (Chicago, 1909), 97.

20 Ibid., 99.

21 See Chicago Plan Commission, *South Water Street Must Go*.

22 See J. Stamper, *Chicago's North Michigan Avenue*; Commercial Club of Chicago, *Plan for a Boulevard to Connect the North and South Sides of the River on Michigan Avenue and Pine Street* (Chicago, 1908). The Franklin–Orleans Street Bridge at the other end of Wacker Drive also opened in 1920. The Wells Street Bridge, one block west, opened in 1922; see Chicago, Department of Public Works [J. E. Draper], *Chicago Bridges* (Chicago, 1984). For the comparison to Parisian types, see M. Gaillard, *Quais et Ponts de Paris* (Paris, 1982), 157–58.

23 Chicago Plan Commission, *South Water Street Must Go*, 7; Young, "South Water Street Improvement"; "Design and Structure of Double-Deck Street, Chicago."

24 M. A. Flanagan, *Charter Reform in Chicago* (Carbondale, 1987), 23, 154.

25 Chicago Harbor Commission, *Report to the Mayor and Aldermen* (Chicago, 1909); ibid., minutes, typescript, August 11, 1908. Municipal Reference Library, Chicago; Mayer, *Port of Chicago,* 14; Chicago, Harbor and Subway Commission, *Report on Dock and Pier Development Harbor District No. 1* (Chicago, 1912); Chicago, Commission on Harbors, Wharves, and Bridges, *Chicago Harbor Development* (Chicago, 1915); "Chicago Municipal Pier," *Engineering News* 74 (July 29, 1915): 193–97; U.S. Congress, House, *Report on Transfer Facilities and Terminals,* 66th cong., 2nd sess., 1919, House Document 652, 1706–20; M. G. Barnes, "The Waterway Terminal Situation in Illinois," *Journal of the Western Society of Engineers* 28 (September 1923): 404–12; B. R. Kogan, "Chicago's Pier," *Chicago History* 1 (Spring 1976): 28–38.

26 Chicago, Board of Local Improvements, *Chicago Plan* (Chicago, 1922); idem, *The Work of M. J. Faherty and Associates* (Chicago, 1923); idem, *A Sixteen Year Record of Achievement, 1915–1932* (Chi-cago, 1931); eight thousand lawsuits were filed in the process of purchasing properties and making assessments for the Michigan Avenue Bridge.

27 Chicago Plan Commission, *South Water Street for All the People,* Chicago, November 1917; "South Water Street," *Economist* (July 24, 1920): 182; F. J. Herlihy, "How Wacker Drive Was Built," *Chicago Realtor* 39 (December 1926): 12.

28 Einhorn, *Property Rules,* 14–26, 215, 227–40.

29 "Will Double Values," *Economist* (January 26, 1924): 217.

30 See R. Miller, "Burnham, Sullivan, Roark, and the Myth of the Heroic Architect," *Art Institute of Chicago Museum Studies* 13, no. 2 (1988): 86–96; D. Dunster, "The City as Auto Didact: The Chicago Plan of 1909," *AA files* [London] 23 (Summer 1992): 32–38.

NEW ORLEANS

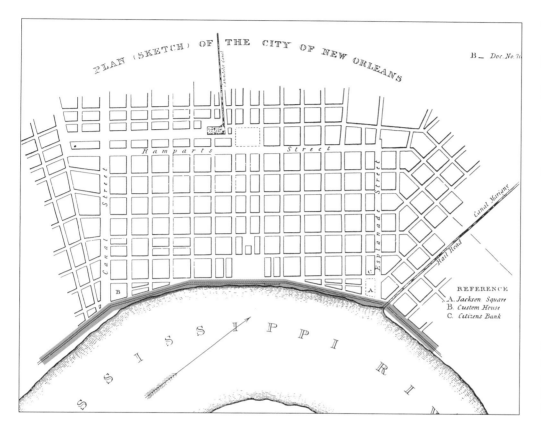

The Master Street of the World

The Levee

DELL UPTON

Figure 1. Plan (Sketch) of the City of New Orleans, c. 1835. The Vieux Carré is at center. The levee is marked in gray.

Antebellum travelers came to New Orleans by way of the Mississippi River; there was no overland route. As they approached the city, the levee made the first and most striking impression (fig. 1). Here steamboats and flatboats from upriver and oceangoing ships from downriver were berthed four or five vessels deep the length of the city. Beyond the crowding vessels travelers saw swarms of people surrounding the mountains of goods piled on the levee—cotton bales, lumber, hogsheads of sugar and tobacco, bags of rice, barrels of pork, casks of molasses, sacks of corn, farm machinery (fig. 2). Near the *place d'armes*, the main square, were the principal market houses, while peddlers sold oysters, cigars, fruit, cheap clothing, and other incidentals from tables and sheds set up along the levee and in the adjacent square. Many probably observed as well that the broad levee was strikingly open, devoid of the densely built wharves and warehouses that characterized most ports.

Some visitors accepted the scene as that of an ordinary waterfront, "a modest commercial plain," an impression reinforced by a cursory walk through the city behind it. At first glance, New Orleans followed a highly conventional plan: that of a gridded commercial city bracketed by gridded speculative suburbs, added intermittently after 1788. The Vieux Carré, the original city, was planned by the engineer Pierre Le Blond de la Tour and laid out by his assistant Adrien de Pauger in 1721. A regular grid ten squares, or blocks, long by six deep stretched along the river. The *place d'armes* (now Jackson

Figure 2. The levee in 1860. The spire of St. Louis Cathedral at the left and the meat (French) market on the levee at the upper center mark the location of Jackson Square.

Square) was set at the center of the riverfront, recalling European commercial ports such as Amsterdam and resembling even more closely the plans of New World administrative and commercial centers such as Spanish St. Augustine in Florida and French Mobile in Alabama. The city grid was enclosed by defensive ditches and earthworks, as often as not in disrepair until they were finally demolished in the early nineteenth century.[1]

Despite its apparent conventionality, New Orleans was not what it seemed. For Orleanians, the peculiar topography of the site gave the riverfront an inordinate significance even for a commercial port. For visitors and for the itinerant merchants who played such an important role in the antebellum city, expecta-

tions of a conventional commercial waterfront were undermined in the Crescent City. While the appearance and function of the waterfront changed noticeably in the half-century after 1803, following in some respects the pattern of other American seaport cities, the intersection of insider and outsider views gave the development of the levee its distinctive trajectory. New Orleans's antebellum identity was forged on the levee.

Orleanians had deeply ambivalent feelings about the Mississippi. The city was planted on the natural levee, a low, fragile ridge of earth, a small dry spot poised between the river's edge and its backswamp a quarter-mile away. Because it was created by the river's annual inundations, the natural levee sloped back from the

Figure 3. Basil Hall, *The Mississippi at New Orleans*, 1828, engraving. Hall noted that at the time the view was made the river was six or seven feet higher than the city.

river (figs. 3, 4). The city lay lower than the river's crest, and constant landfill was required to keep the urbanized area habitable. First and foremost, then, the levee held the Mississippi at bay, making the city's existence possible. To prevent the river from overflowing or breaking the levee, as it sometimes did, the natural levee was continually reinforced with an ever-growing artificial levee, constructed of earth-filled timber pilings.[2]

The day-to-day depredations of the river were even more frightening than its episodic disasters. In antebellum New Orleans, an elaborate mythology of guilt developed out of common medical theories that attributed epidemic disease to miasmas, or emanations from damp earth. To its citizens, the Crescent City was peculiarly unsuitable for human occupation because the high water table preserved putrefying remnants of the primeval forest beneath the swamps, on the riverfront, and under the city itself. Physicians and laypeople believed that whenever the earth was disturbed, the decaying organic matter exposed combined with the bodily effluvia of humans in a torrid cli-

mate and caused the death rate to soar. Edward H. Barton, the premier epidemiologist of mid-nineteenth-century New Orleans, codified forty years' wisdom in a sanitary map that linked the geography of yellow fever to excavations for drainage and navigation canals: the more people dug, the sicker they became (fig. 5). The more the city strove to improve itself, the more dangerous it became for its occupants.[3]

The river claimed the unwary by accident as well as by flood and disease. On the levee, "if a man falls in, he is lost beyond all doubt, the undercurrent is so strong. When our Stevadoor fell in, no one moved to save him, he never rose again," wrote Caroline Hale to her sisters in Massachusetts. To the extent that watery death haunted the city, New Orleans was a "Wet Grave." Indeed, the city's poorest dead were consigned to the water in cemeteries on the edge of the backswamp, where they were lowered into water-filled graves, "dreadful to the imagination of a sick stranger."[4]

The water, then, had some of the qualities traditionally attributed to a wilderness. Pervasive, ominous, chaotic, it demanded that a

Figure 4. Schematic
section of (a) the
Mississippi River channel
and (b) the natural levee.

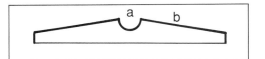

human realm be won from it: the levee "con-quer[ed] the solid earth from the inunda-tions" of the Mississippi. As a wilderness, it was also a waste, an unimproved common available for any purpose. Benjamin Henry Latrobe laid the intake pipe for the city's first waterworks, completed in 1820, far out into the river channel to "escape the vast impurities which were near the shore, where every species of disgusting filth was hourly deposited." This included "dead bod-ies of animals and other filthy matter," notably the contents of chamber pots and privies, dumped freely, despite recurrent, justified fears about the risk to urban hygiene. The unrestrained pollution of the waterways was a practice shared with other port cities, and resembled as well the treatment of unimproved land in less water-bound cities. In antebellum New Orleans the habit was unshakable. A carriage excursion along the Carondelet Canal in 1862 turned into a disgusting outing for the Union general Ben-jamin Butler and his wife, who found themselves assaulted by "the most noxious and offensive stenches possible—so noxious as almost to take away the power of breathing. The whole surface of the canal and the pond [turning basin] was covered with a thick growth of green vegetable scum, variegated with dead cats and dogs or the remains of dead mules on the banking." The director of public works pronounced the smell "no more than usual."[5]

The water was, in equally important senses, New Orleans's life. The levee was the contact point between the vast Mississippi Valley hin-terland and the Caribbean basin. Its econ-omic functions were as carefully guarded as its protective ones.

New Orleans's Creole-dominated city gov-ernment vigorously defended the openness of the levee and its batture (an alluvial deposit left between the levee and the riverbank by the annual rise and fall of the river), treating them as public space in the broadest sense: no alter-ation for private purposes was allowed (see fig. 3). Private structures erected on either were instantly demolished, since the spaces were "to serve for the public in general, and in no man-ner for a private person to make profit thereof." The first rank of private buildings stood well back from the waterfront on the far side of Levee (now Decatur) Street. Only with the arri-val of the railroad after the Civil War, signaling the end of the river's dominance of New Or-leans's economy, did private interests take over the waterfront. Throughout the antebellum pe-riod, the levee was a sacrosanct public space.[6]

The Americans who flooded the city after 1790 brought a different conception of the wa-terfront.[7] It was customary in northern ports for the waterfront to be engrossed by private own-ers soon after a city's founding. Throughout the colonial and early national periods, for ex-ample, New York City periodically sold off its shoreline property, and eventually gave up all pretense of control over the use made of the land, which was seen as a source of municipal revenue, rather than as a public resource to be directed to the general good.[8]

The contrast between American and Creole definitions of the public interest and public space on the waterfront were brought into high relief by a bitter legal battle that arose immedi-ately after the Louisiana Purchase, precipitated by a former mayor of New York City. Edward Livingston suffered a severe financial setback and moved to New Orleans, where he pur-chased the right to the batture of the upriver Faubourg Sainte-Marie from the heirs of a Creole resident, Bertrand Gravier, subject to the

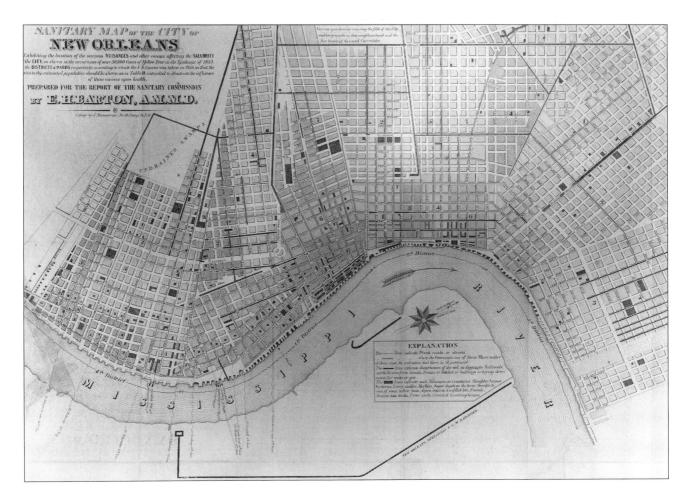

SANITARY MAP OF THE CITY OF
NEW ORLEANS
Exhibiting the location of the various NUISANCES and other causes affecting the SALUBRITY
the CITY, as shown in the occurrence of near 50,000 Cases of Yellow Fever in the Epidemic of 1853,
the DISTRICTS & WARDS respectively, according to which the U.S. Census was taken in 1850, so that the
ratio to the estimated population should be shewn as in Table B, intended to illustrate the influence
of these causes upon health.
PREPARED FOR THE REPORT OF THE SANITARY COMMISSION
BY E. H. BARTON, A.M. M.D.

court's recognition of his right of ownership (fig. 6). A heated public controversy paralleled the courtroom maneuvers, exposing the assumptions behind the Creole and American viewpoints. The Creole position, enunciated by the city council and its representatives, presupposed a public good that transcended any private interest. The public good encompassed the safety, salubrity, and commercial well-being of New Orleans. It recognized public rights in a common land, the batture, used as a landing, work, and recreational space, and as a source of earth for filling city lots. Livingston's control of the batture threatened all these uses. He intended to construct a kind of private port by moving the levee out beyond the batture and constructing canals through the drained land. According to the council, these actions threatened the health of the city by disturbing the earth and impeding the free passage of air. They endangered New Orleans's trade even more severely, by removing the customary landing place of flatboats and possibly by forcing the river current out of its natural channel, which would ruin the port. In addition, Livingston's works would deprive individual citizens of

Figure 5. Edward H. Barton, *Sanitary Map of the City of New Orleans*, 1854. The darker the shading, the greater the threat. Most of the waterways and the levee are black.

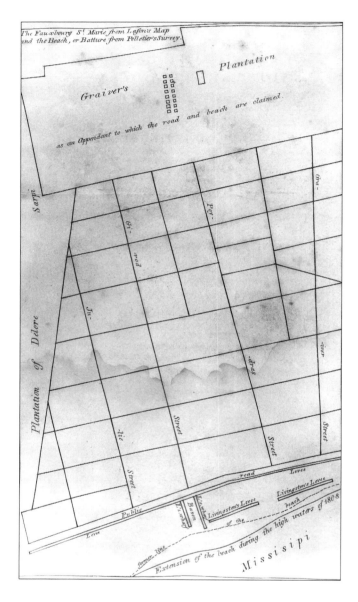

The Faubourg St. Marie from Lafon's Map and the Beach, or Batture from Pelletier's Survey.

Graiver's   Plantation

as an Appendant to which the road and beach are claimed.

Sarpi

Plantation of Ddore

Mississipi

former line

Extension of the beach during the high waters of 1808

Figure 6. Map of the Faubourg Sainte-Marie, showing the disputed batture and Edward Livingston's abortive development.

delightful aspect of the harbor and city, which extends itself along the river in a regular semi-circular form, with elegant houses in front, would have been destroyed. It would have intercepted the view which the city now enjoys of the river and opposite country, and the view from the river and country of the city and harbor; while the loathsome appearance of irregular and filthy store houses and stinking canals would have made it look like the doleful abode of death and desolation; and, in truth, it would soon have become so." Indeed, Livingston's "unnatural contrivance" would "take from the view of the inhabitants every object fitted to cheer their spirits and gratify their senses."[9]

The city's representatives branded Livingston's actions "criminal speculations" by a "Hercules of chicane," aimed to commandeer "a public property so useful, so indispensably necessary to all the inhabitants of this territory" that its loss would be economically fatal. The Americans, on the other hand, recognized no such common rights or interests. All land was available to be owned privately, and the function of the city government was to protect individual property rather than collective right. If the people had enjoyed the privilege of taking earth or of promenading on the waterfront, it was because the true owners had not chosen to exclude them at that time. Now, however, if the citizens needed the land, let them buy it. Where the Creoles understood the case in terms of private greed opposing the public good, Livingston cast his plight in terms of "the destruction of personal liberty."[10]

Although the batture case was the most dramatic incident of conflict between Creole and American views of public space, the development of the levee continued to be shaped by the conflict. In common with most pre-industrial port cities, New Orleans's waterfront was originally the site of important institu-

customary rights, including the right to a place for "an evening walk, so necessary in that hot country," and even the right to "enjoy the freshness of the river air, and the agreeable view of the water, and of the country on the opposite shore." Livingston's development promised severe damage to the urban image: "The

tions and elite residences, in addition to serving its commercial functions. In planning the city, de la Tour had distributed its major political and religious buildings—the Roman Catholic church, the guardhouse, prison, barracks, warehouses, and high officials' residences—around the *place d'armes* and along the length of Levee Street (fig. 7). These gradually attracted company, as wealthy merchants joined the government officials at the waterfront.[11]

In most early-nineteenth-century American seaports, the intensification of commercial activity on the waterfront combined with a growing suspicion that waterfronts were sources of epidemic disease to prompt a retreat of the wealthy from their waterfront residences. By 1830 they were gone, and the wharves were left to the ships, warehouses, sailors' taverns and boardinghouses, and a few poor folk.[12]

A limited abandonment of the waterfront characterized New Orleans as well. No really large houses were built along Levee Street after the early nineteenth century, and some of those that remained fell into decay or were converted to hotels, while side streets accumulated the brothels and barrooms endemic to waterfronts. Large stretches of Levee Street were rebuilt with stores and warehouses, while similar structures, as well as cotton presses and other industrial buildings, occupied New Levee Street, upriver.[13]

Yet the abandonment of the waterfront to pure commerce was never as complete in antebellum New Orleans as elsewhere. The Roman Catholic church retained its original location and its importance as a ceremonial center for the city's large Catholic population. New houses, genteel if not necessarily elite, continued to be built along Levee Street. The architects Gurlie and Guillot erected a row of three-story balconied houses with ground-floor stores for the Ursuline nuns on the Levee Street side of

their property, while high-quality, exclusively residential development continued around (old) Jackson Square, a brief-lived amenity that occupied the former site of Fort St. Charles at the downriver end of the Vieux Carré, until it was replaced by the United States Mint in the mid-1830s.[14]

Most striking was the gradual gentrification of the *place d'armes*, renamed Jackson Square in 1851. Originally an integral part of the waterfront, it was a rough-hewn parade ground used for public executions, mass spectacles, and as a kind of informal marketplace. A major improvement campaign of 1819–20 involved an iron-and-stone fence, landscaping by the city engineer Joseph Pilié, and a fountain by Benjamin Henry Latrobe. Yet a quarter-century later, the square had been drawn back into the levee's dissipated milieu. In 1846 the New Yorker Abraham Oakey Hall recorded the remnants of the Latrobe-Pilié beautification: "A very neat railing, one or two respectable aged trees, a hundred or two blades of grass, a dilapidated fountain, a very naked flag-staff. . . . It has a water view, and with a judicious expenditure of a few thousand dollars might be made an inviting promenade; it is now but a species of cheap lodging-house for arriving emigrants, drunken sailors, and lazy stevedores." In short, thought Hall, the name "Place des Armes may be freely translated 'the beggar's retreat.'"[15]

Four years later, however, the square was improved again. The Baroness Micaela Almonester de Pontalba, a member of the family that had dominated New Orleans in the late Spanish regime, constructed two rows of houses with ground-floor shops along two sides of the square. In response, the city redesigned the square, erected a new fence, and created the genteel park we now know. Yet this renewal was effected only a few feet from the levee, which remained in the realm of gentility much as the *place d'armes* had been part of the working levee. The dual spheres of the waterfront did not mesh smoothly and conflicts arose as commercial development proceeded on the levee.[16]

As the city gentrified some parts of the levee, it commercialized others. New Orleans's original grid was set tangent to a wide curve in the river, with the river's edge curving away from Levee Street at both ends, leaving broad triangular areas called the quays (see fig. 7). While preserving the openness of the levee proper, the city attempted to build up the quays by erecting a vegetable market adjacent to the meat (now French) market on the downriver quay in 1823, and by selling the upriver quay to private individuals a year later.

The city met with resistance to these plans both from the federal government and from adjacent property owners. In a tactical move designed to thwart Livingston, the city council had declared the riverfront federal property, and it now found the federal government claiming the land, particularly the quays, where its customhouse stood, and the central part of the levee and batture, where it maintained workshops for repairing naval vessels. The city brought suit and won in the Supreme Court in 1836, and the national government surrendered the quays to the municipality and moved its naval operations downriver. In opposing the federal government, the city used two different (and rather contradictory) arguments, objecting on the one hand to the naval operations on the same grounds it had used to oppose Livingston: that they deprived the people of their customary access to the waterfront. On the other hand, the city argued that the quay land ought to belong to it because the revenues were needed for street paving and other improvements elsewhere in New Orleans. In using the waterfront land in this way, the city emulated New York's sale of its waterfront for revenue purposes.[17]

In selling the quay lands, however, the city laid itself open to opposition on private-property grounds. Adjacent landowners on Levee Street objected both to the construction of the city's vegetable market and to private developers' erection of the so-called Blue Stores, a commercial block on the upriver quay, as infringements of property rights—the same argument Livingston and his allies had made—while citing the same disadvantages that the city had made against the batture purchase. The Widow Carrick claimed that the vegetable market stood between her house and the river on "a spot so long viewed as *Sacred and inviolable*." Its construction infringed upon her "free, direct and uninterrupted *view of* and intercourse with the river . . . as well for purposes of commerce. . . as for all other purposes of business or pleasure." It was, she said, "a solitary instance of Public aggression on Private right unexampled in any other part of the front of the city within its ancient limits." Carrick lost her battle, as did those property owners of upper Levee Street who objected to the construction of the Blue Stores.[18]

As the urban population, the legal structure, and government personnel absorbed increasing American influence, levee development was affected. The city's official position, while continuing to maintain a core belief in the common right to the waterfront, was tinged with the newer American notions of urban polity, in which government was seen not as a player in its own right, but as a facilitator of private activity.[19] Within these shifting terms specific alterations to the levee were debated. Opposition to new development, while often posed in the newer language of private-property rights, was based equally in the traditional belief in the inviolability of the levee. Moreover, the very existence of these conflicts over commercial development is a sign that the

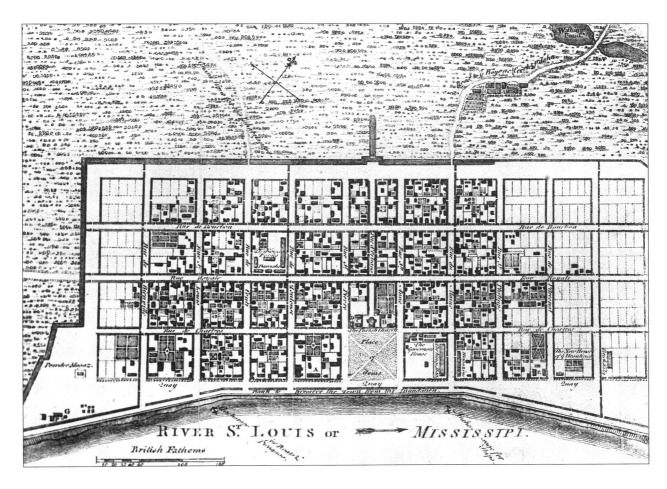

RIVER St. LOVIS or MISSISSIPI.

British Fathoms

waterfront continued to be important in New Orleans public life, in contrast to that of American port cities elsewhere at this time, where waterfronts were declining. In New Orleans the riverfront was not absolutely abandoned to sailors and longshoremen.

Indeed, the levee was one of New Orleans's principal social spaces. As the European urban habit of open-air promenading took on an increasingly pedestrian aspect in the late seventeenth and eighteenth centuries, and spread through many levels of urban society, New Orleans found itself with no gardens, squares, boulevards, or other customary sites for such

activities. The *place d'armes* was unsuitable, and the city was hemmed in by earthwork fortifications and surrounded by swamps and fields that left little space around the edges for informal socializing. For a brief time, "lanes formed of trees and serving as public walks" had been laid out inside the upriver ramparts, but this land was granted to private builders in 1797 and lost to public use. Thus the levee was the place adopted for the promenade, and orange trees (later, Pride of China trees) were planted along the downriver portion of the Vieux Carré to enhance the setting. After the demolition of the fortifications, Canal, Ram-

Figure 7. Plan of New Orleans in the mid-eighteenth century. The *place d'armes* and the government buildings clustered around it and along the levee are clearly visible, as are the quays at either end of the levee.

part, and Esplanade Streets were laid out on their sites as tree-lined "Promenade[s] Publique[s]," but the levee remained the favorite place of evening resort.[20]

Throughout the antebellum years, then, the waterfront grew increasingly commercial, yet genteel residences hung on along Levee Street and older forms of public sociability continued on the levee. It was a natural, if tense, juxtaposition for Orleanians, for it brought together on the sacred space of the levee the qualities that were distinctive to New Orleans: its ethnic variety, its sociable proclivities, the commercial frenzy fed by its critical location at the intersection of the Caribbean and Mississippi basins, and its necessary, precarious relationship to the river.

Outsiders saw these qualities of the levee through eyes accustomed to the more complete separation of commerce and social life already accomplished in northern and European cities. They were initially impressed by the variety and profusion of goods that passed over the levee and through the markets, goods brought not only from far upriver, but from around the Caribbean, making the levee "the master street of the world." They were equally charmed by the human variety of commerce and sociability: "In perambulating the Levee you will observe men of every hue & Clime Shade &c the black from Bombay & Ethiopia, the Swarthy Son of Italy & benighted Spain, the brunette from Chivalrous France, the Copper Colour from China & Japan: also from Mexico & South America, the ruddy Sons of Hibernia the honest Scot & the proud Englishman, and our own fair & enterprising Country men from Yankee Land," wrote the Northerner James Edwards.[21]

Ultimately, though, they were repelled. New standards of gentility and social order made such mixture suspect. Respectable peo-

ple increasingly held themselves not only socially but physically aloof from the corrupting, the base, and the ordinary. The levee had plenty of all three. Flatboats were commonly converted to "saloons, gambling houses and bad places." One encountered "a great deal of rudeness, and a great deal of swearing, among the carmen or carters, and among the persons delivering goods from the vessels and loading them." In the market, the linguistic cacophony and the rough-hewn company were overpowering.[22]

The sinister associations of the northern waterfront informed visitors' readings of the space. Because respectable people avoided such scenes, the implication was that no one there was respectable. Increasingly, visitors stressed the questionable character of promenaders, reading the crowd as entirely male and hostile. "Every, or nearly every gentleman carried a sword cane, apparently, and occasionally the bright hilt of a Spanish knife, or dirk, would gleam for an instant in the moon-beams from the open bosom of its possessor, as, with the lowering brow, and active tread of wary suspicion, he moved rapidly by us. . . . In groups—promenading, lounging, and sleeping upon the seats along the Levée—we passed several hundred of this *canaille* of Orleans."[23]

Most tellingly, outsiders were disturbed by the levee's apparent use as a site of sexual commerce, an undisguised "traffic de coeur," as Thomas Ashe called it, that paralleled in its openness and ethnic profusion the variety of the market. Ashe noted that on the levee, quadroon (mixed-race) women and their mothers gathered each evening and chatted easily with passing men. Although these discussions appeared innocent enough, Ashe, like many travelers, was convinced that they were business negotiations intended to establish sexual liaisons.

The mothers always regulate the terms and make the bargain. The terms allowed the parents are generally fifty dollars a month; during which time the lover has the exclusive right to the house, where fruit, coffee, and refreshments may at any time be had, or where he may entirely live with the utmost safety and tranquillity.[24]

Although not all travelers accepted this story, it embodied the critical difference of the Anglo-American and Creole views of New Orleans and emphasized the levee's centrality to both. For the Americans (and their British contemporaries), the apparently free and easy common ground of the levee deprived New Orleans of the careful spatial distinctions of class and function they had come to prize in a nineteenth-century city. Lacking a clear sense of boundaries, the levee was read as a place of commercial and sexual expediency in a city whose values and society were ephemeral.

Orleanians (and a few perceptive visitors) knew that social and ethnic bounds were rigidly maintained in their city; there was no need to demonstrate the divisions spatially. Consequently, they saw the frenetic mixture of people and goods on the levee in a much different light: New Orleans was itself ephemeral. The river constantly threatened to wash away its economic and physical existence. To gather on the levee was to celebrate the city's collective ability to resist annihilation. ∎

Notes

1 A. Oakey Hall, *The Manhatter in New Orleans; or, Phases of "Crescent City" Life* (1851), ed. H. A. Kamen (Baton Rouge, 1976), 5. The best description of the development of the plan of New Orleans's old city is S. Wilson, Jr., *The Vieux Carré, New Orleans: Its Plan, Its Growth, Its Architecture* (New Orleans, 1968), supplemented by the relevant neighborhood volumes of the Friends of the Cabildo's survey *New Orleans Architecture*, 7 vols. to date (Gretna, La., 1971–). Although the original city of New Orleans was sometimes called the Vieux Carré in the nineteenth century, it was most commonly referred to simply as *le carré de la ville*, the city square, to distinguish it from the surrounding faubourgs.

2 Peirce F. Lewis has explained New Orleans's topography and urban morphology brilliantly and succinctly in *New Orleans: The Making of an Urban Landscape* (Cambridge, Mass., 1976).

3 A. A. Gros and N.-V.-A. Gerardin, *Rapport fait à la Société Médicale sur la fièvre jaune* (New Orleans, 1818), 6–7; P.-F. Thomas, *Essai sur la fièvre jaune d'Amérique* (New Orleans and Paris, 1823), 62–65, 72. Barton's map and report were included in *Report of the Sanitary Commission of New Orleans on the Epidemic Yellow Fever of 1853* (New Orleans, 1854).

4 C. Hale to M. Hale and A. L. March, March 14, 1844, Tulane University Library (*TUL*); C. J. Latrobe, *The Rambler in North America, MDCCCXXXII–MDCCCXXXIII* (New York, 1835), vol. 2, 238; T. flint, *Recollections of the Last Ten Years, Passed in Occasional Residences and Journeys in the Valley of the Mississippi* (Boston, 1826), 312.

5 E. Livingston, *Address to the People of the United States, on the Measures Pursued by the Executive with Respect to the Batture at New-Orleans* (New Orleans, 1808), i; M. E. Latrobe, "Memoir of Mary Elizabeth Latrobe," in *The Correspondence and Miscellaneous Papers of Benjamin Henry Latrobe*, vol. 3, *1811–1820*, ed. J. C. Van Horne (New Haven, 1988), 1065; New Orleans Municipal Papers [*NOMP*], *TUL*, box 3, folder 15 (June 6, 1819); B. Butler, *Autobiography and Personal Reminiscences of Major-General Benjamin F. Butler: Butler's Book* (Boston, 1892), 397–98. For

many Orleanians, the filth was nearly an asset. Butler discovered a widespread rebel hope that an epidemic would arise to exterminate the occupying army.

6 *Pièces probantes à l'appui des droits des habitants de la cité d'Orléans et de ses faubourgs, sur la batture en face du faubourg Sainte-Marie* (New Orleans, 1807), 4, 6; New Orleans, Conseil de Ville, Resolutions and ordinances of the Conseil de Ville, vol. 1, 1805–15, New Orleans Public Library, orders of June 22, July 13, 1805; P.-A.-C.-B. Derbigny, *Mémoire à consulter, sur la réclamation de la Batture, située en face du Faubourg Sainte-Marie à la Nouvelle-Orléans* (New Orleans, 1807), 3–4.

7 In antebellum usage, "American" referred to English-speaking residents who had emigrated from the north and east. French- and Spanish-speaking native-born residents were Creoles.

8 H. Hartog, *Public Property and Private Power: The Corporation of the City of New York in American Law, 1730–1870* (Chapel Hill, 1983), 104–10.

9 J. Poydras, *Speech of Julien Poydras, Esq., The Delegate from the Territory of Orleans, in Support of the Right of the Public to the Batture in Front of the Suburb St. Mary* (Washington, 1810), 20–24.

10 J. Poydras, *Further Observations in Support of the Right of the Public to the Batture of New Orleans* (Washington, 1809), 12; J. B. S. Thierry, *Reply to Mr. Duponceau* ([New Orleans], 1809), 47; P. S. Duponceau, *A Review of the Cause of the New Orleans Batture and of the Discussions that Have Taken Place Respecting It* (Philadelphia, 1809), 32–33, 39–41; Livingston, *Address,* iii–iv.

11 Wilson, *Vieux Carré,* 89.

12 D. diZ. Wall, "The Separation of Home and Workplace in Early Nineteenth-century New York City," *American Archaeology* 5, no. 3 (1985): 186–87.

13 Wilson, *Vieux Carré,* 89–90; W. Brand, letter to mayor, November 25, 1820, *NOMP,* box 7, folder 5.

14 J. Boze to H. de Ste.-Gême, July 21, 22, 1830, Ste.-Gême papers [*SGP*], Historic New Orleans Collection.

15 *NOMP,* box 2, folder 7 (May 9, 1812); box 2, folder 8 (May 23, July 18, 1812); box 3, folder 12 (February 13, 20, 1819); folder 13 (March 13, 20, 1819); box 8, folder 8 (August 11, 1820); Latrobe, *Correspondence,* vol. 3, 1028, 1029n–30n; L. V. Huber, *Jackson Square through the Years* (New Orleans, 1982), 36–39; Hall, *Manhatter,* 89–90.

16 L. V. Huber and S. Wilson, Jr., *Baroness Pontalba's Buildings: Their Site and the Remarkable Woman Who Built Them,* 2d ed. (New Orleans, 1966), 36–47; Wilson, *Vieux Carré,* 88–89; Huber, *Jackson Square,* 63–68.

17 Wilson, *Vieux Carré,* 90; Boze, "Suite au bulletin," March 28, 1836, *SGP,* folder 248; *NOMP,* box 1, folder 3 (March 14, 1808); box 2, folder 5 (February 16, 1811).

18 Wilson, *Vieux Carré,* 90–91.

19 My understanding of this transformation derives from Hartog, *Public Property,* an extended analysis of the process in New York City.

20 Wilson, *Vieux Carré,* 90, 59; Latrobe, *Correspondence,* vol. 3, 1061.

21 A. J. Pickett, *Eight Days in New-Orleans in February, 1847* (Montgomery, Ala., 1847), 19; James Edwards, New Orleans, to Eliza Edwards, Cincinnati, January 8, 1842, James Edwards letters, 1841–42, *TUL.*

22 R. L. Bushman, *The Refinement of America: Persons, Houses, Cities* (New York, 1992), esp. 354–70; *NOMP,* box 2, folder 7 (May 12, 1812); J. Stuart, *Three Years in North America,* 3d ed., rev. (Edinburgh, 1833), vol. 2, 205.

23 J. H. Ingraham, *The South-West: By a Yankee* (New York, 1835), vol. 1, 90.

24 T. Ashe, *Travels in America, Performed in the Year 1806* (London, 1809), 315.

About the Contributors

Annmarie Adams is assistant professor of design and architectural history in the School of Architecture, McGill University, Montreal. She has published articles on the history of housing in *Perspectives in Vernacular Architecture* and *Urban History Review.* She was curator of a 1991 exhibition at the Canadian Centre for Architecture, Montreal. Her current research focuses on Victorian hospitals, wartime housing, and Canadian women architects.

Nezar AlSayyad, an architect, planner, and urban historian, is associate professor at the University of California, Berkeley, where he teaches courses on housing, urban design, and the history of Islamic architecture. He is co-founder of the International Association for the Study of Traditional Environments (IASTE), and edits the association's journal, *Traditional Dwellings and Settlements Review.* His publications include *The Streets of Islamic Cairo* and *Cities and Caliphs: On the Genesis of Arab Muslim Urbanism.*

Eleni Bastéa is assistant professor in the School of Architecture, Washington University, St. Louis, where she teaches architectural and urban history and architectural theory. Her writing has appeared in *Places, Design Book Review, Journal of Architecture and Planning Research,* and *Twentieth-Century Art and Culture.* She is writing a book on the planning of modern Athens.

Charles Burroughs teaches architectural history at Binghamton University, State University of New York. His book *From Signs to Design: Environmental Process and Reform in Early Renaissance Rome* was published in 1990; other writings include articles on Leon Battista Alberti, Michelangelo, and Andrea Palladio. He is currently engaged in a contextual study of architectural and urban developments in Rome during the pontificate of Paul III, with a focus on Michelangelo's project for the remodeling of the Campidoglio.

Greg Castillo is a doctoral candidate in the Department of Architecture at the University of California, Berkeley. His publications include "Cities of the Stalinist Empire," in *Forms of Dominance: On the Architecture and Urbanism of the Colonial Experience,* and, in collaboration with Spiro Kostof, *The City Assembled.* He is currently preparing the second edition of Spiro Kostof's *A History of Architecture: Settings and Rituals.*

Zeynep Çelik teaches architectural history at the New Jersey Institute of Technology. She is author of *The Remaking of Istanbul: Portrait of an Ottoman City in the Nineteenth Century* and *Displaying the Orient: Architecture of Islam at Nineteenth-Century World's Fairs,* as well as articles on cross-cultural topics. She is completing a book on French colonial architecture and planning in Algiers.

Joan E. Draper is a historian of architecture and urban planning who focuses on the development of professional practice and ideology in late-nineteenth and early-twentieth-century America. She is associate professor in the New College of Architecture and Planning at the University of Colorado, Denver and Boulder. She has published widely on American urbanism and architecture.

Diane Favro is associate professor in the Graduate School of Architecture and Urban Planning, University of California, Los Angeles. Her most recent book, *The Urban Image of Augustan Rome,* explores the physical and conceptual transformations of Rome at the millennium. In addition to studies of Vitruvius, ancient urban management, and Roman latrines, she has published on women in architecture. Current projects include co-authorship of a texbook on Roman architecture and a study of women architects in early California.

Paul Groth, a historian of rural and urban cultural landscapes, is associate professor in the Department of Architecture ant the University of California, Berkeley. His studies of the American street include articles on parking spaces and street grids. He is author of *Living Downtown: A History of Residential Hotel Life in the United States.*

Heng Chye Kiang teaches design and history of architecture at the National University of Singapore. His current research interests include medieval Chinese architecture and cities and he has published articles on architectural design and urban planning.

Krystyna von Henneberg is a doctoral candidate in history at the University of California, Berkeley. She is completing a dissertation on the role of modern architecture and urban planning in the Italian colonization of Libya. In addition to Fascist architecture, her work deals with the official memory of, and justifications for, Italian colonialism; the rise of experts and social engineering in the Fascist period; and the impact of empire on modern state formation.

Richard Ingersoll teaches architectural history at Rice University, Houston. He has published widely on contemporary architecture and urbanism and is the editor of *Design Book Review*. His books include *Le Corbusier: A Marriage of Contours* and *Nivola Sculture.*

Spiro Kostof was educated at Robert College of Istanbul and Yale University. He taught architectural history at the University of California, Berkeley, from 1967 until his death in 1991 and supervised numerous dissertations. The editors of this volume and many of its contributors are former students of his. Among his best-known works are *A History of Architecture: Settings and Rituals, The City Shaped, The City Assembled,* and the five-part television series and accompanying volume *America by Design*. His wide range of publications includes books and articles on the architecture and planning of Rome, religious architecture of medieval Cappadocia, and the history of the architectural profession, as well as literary criticism, short stories, and poems (mostly in Turkish).

Richard Longstreth is professor of architectural history and director of the Graduate Program in Historic Preservation at George Washington University, Washington, D.C. He has authored *On the Edge of the World: Four Architects in San Francisco at the Turn of the Century, The Buildings of Main Street: A Guide to American Commercial Architecture,* and other books and articles. He is completing a study of retail decentralization in Los Angeles before 1950.

Jean-Pierre Protzen is professor in the Department of Architecture, University of California, Berkeley, and an architect registered in Switzerland. His writing cuts across disciplinary lines. He has published articles in architectural journals and others, such as *Scientific American*. His most recent book is *Inca Architecture and Construction at Ollantaytambo*.

Deborah Robbins is lecturer in architectural history at the Southern California Institute of Architecture, Los Angeles. Her dissertation is "A Case Study of Medieval Urban Process: Rome's Trastevere, 1250–1450." Specializing in medieval urbanism and vernacular architecture in Italy, she has also published writings on medieval Siena and Florence.

Bruce Thomas is assistant professor of architecture at Lehigh University, Bethlehem, where he teaches architectural history and the occasional design studio. He is also a registered architect. His most recent publication is an opening essay in *The Company Town: Architecture and Society in the Early Industrial Age,* an account of the Welsh iron town of Merthyr Tydfil. His doctoral work was on urban patterns in British industrial cities.

Stephen Tobriner is professor of architectural history in the Architecture Department of the University of California, Berkeley. He is author of *The Genesis of Noto: An Eighteenth-Century Sicilian City* as well as articles on Baroque architecture, legal history, and historical aspects of reconstruction after earthquakes. His newest book, on the reconstruction of San Francisco after fires and earthquakes, is *Fate of the Phoenix*.

Marc Treib is professor of architecture at the University of California, Berkeley, a practicing designer, and a frequent contributor to architecture and design journals. He is author of *Sanctuaries of Spanish New Mexico,* editor of *Modern Landscape Architecture: A Critical Review,* and co-author of *A Guide to the Gardens of Kyoto.*

Dell Upton is professor of architectural history at the University of California, Berkeley. He is author of *Holy Things and Profane: Anglican Parish Churches in Colonial Virginia,* editor of *America's Architectural Roots: Ethnic Groups that Built America,* and co-editor of *Common Places: Readings in American Vernacular Architecture.* He is completing a study of the urban cultural landscapes of antebellum Philadelphia and New Orleans, and an edition of the diary and essays of Madaline Selima Edwards of New Orleans.

Gwendolyn Wright is professor in the Graduate School of Architecture, Planning, and Preservation at Columbia University, New York. She is the author of *Moralism and the Model Home: Domestic Architecture and Cultural Conflict in Chicago, 1873–1913, Building the Dream: A Social History of Housing in America,* and *The Politics of Design in French Colonial Urbanism.*

Fikret K. Yegül is professor of architectural history in the Art History Department, University of California, Santa Barbara. Trained as an architect, he is a member of the Sardis Archaeological Expedition and worked on the restoration of the Marble Court of the Roman bath-gymnasium complex; currently he is undertaking a full architectural recording of the Temple of Artemis. His two recent books are *Gentlemen of Instinct and Breeding: Architecture at the American Academy in Rome, 1894–1940* and *Baths and Bathing in Classical Antiquity.*

Credits

His Majesty the Pick: The Aesthetics of Demolition, by Spiro Kostof, originally appeared in *Design Quarterly* 118–119 (Fall 1982): 32–41, and is reprinted here by gracious permission of MIT Press Journals and the Walker Art Center, Minneapolis. Figures 1, 7: courtesy of the Archivio Comunale, Rome; 5: from S. Kostof, *The Third Rome,* ex. cat., University Art Museum, University of California, Berkeley (Berkeley, 1973); 6: from *L'Illustration* (Paris) 51 (February 8, 1868).

1

Figure 1: United States Geological Survey, San Francisco North, 1947; 2, 5, 9: collection of the San Francisco History Room, San Francisco Public Library; 3: Lewis W. Hine Collection, United States History, Local History & Genealogy Division, New York Public Library, Astor, Lenox, and Tilden Foundations; 4, 8: drawings by Dorothée Imbert from drawings by the author; 6: John W. Proctor Collection, San Francisco Maritime Museum National Historic Park; 7: the author.

2

Figures 1–5, 7: the author, 1971; 6, 8: Ron Herman, 1974; 9: collection of the University Art Museum, University of California, Berkeley, gift of William Dallam Armes Estate, 1919.110.

3

Figure 4: Xiao Mo, *Dunhuang jianzhu yanjiu* [Architectural Research of Dunhuang Grottos] (Beijing, 1989), 110; 5: Denman Waldo Ross Collection, courtesy of the Museum of Fine Arts, Boston; 6, 7: courtesy of the Palace Museum, Beijing.

4

Figures 2, 8: the author; 3: from V. Tolstoy, I. Bibikova, and C. Cooke, *Street Art of the Revolution: Festivals and Celebrations in Russia, 1918–33* (London: Thames and Hudson and Vendome, 1990), 59, fig. 19, originally published by Iskusstvo, Moscow, 1984; 4, 6, 7: from B. Kreis, *Moskau 1917–35* (Munich: Marzona, 1985), 186, 159, 206, figs. 228, 193, 260; 5: after S. Boldyrevand, P. Goldenberg, "Rekonstruktsiya Ulitsy Gorkogo v Moskvye," *Arkhitektura SSSR* 6 (1983): 17.

5

Figures 2–5: the author; 7: from P. Coste, *Architecture Arabe ou monuments du Caire* (Paris, 1838), pl. xx.

6

Figures 1, 2, 7: the author; 3: Istanbul University Library; 4, 5, 6: Gülersoy; 8: Bibliothèque Nationale, Départment des Estampes et de la Photographie, Paris.

7

Figures 1, 2: drawn by the author, after Alzinger; 3–9: the author.

8

Figure 1: from E. Curtius and J. A. Kaupert, *Atlas von Athen* (Berlin, 1878); 2: courtesy of the Staatliche Graphische Sammlung, Munich; 3: from H. Beck, *Monuments antiques et vues d'Athènes: Photographies d'après nature* (Berlin, 1868); 4: M. P. Vrèto, *Athènes moderne: Album contenant les vues des principaux monuments de la capitale de la Grèce* (Paris: C. Reinwald, 1861); 5: courtesy of the National Gallery, Athens; 6: Hellenic Literary and Historical Archive Society, Alma Cerezole Collection, Athens; 7: Benaki Museum, Photographic Archive, N. Xanthopoulos Collection, Athens; 8: drawing by John Travlos, 1838, courtesy of the Archaeological Society of Athens, repr. in J. Travlos, *Poleodomike exelixis ton Athenon* (Athens, 1960).

9
All figures drawn or photographed by the author.

10
Figure 1: from "Tripoli," *Enciclopedia Treccani* (Rome: Treccani, 1937), vol. 34, 366; 2: from A. Ghisleri, *Tripolitania e Cirenaica dal mediterraneo al Sahara: Monografia storico-geografica* (Milan, Bergamo: Società Editoriale Italiana, Istituto Italiano d'Arti Grafiche, 1912), table 3; 3: from L. V. Bertarelli, *Guida d'Italia del Touring Club Italiano: Possedimenti e colonie* (Milan: Touring Club Italiano, 1929), 280, reproduction authorized September 7, 1993; 4: from F. Ravagli, "Il Viaggio del sovrano in Libia," *Annali dell'Africa italiana* 1, no. 2 (August 1938): 430; 5, 7: from Lore and Nikolaus Richter, *Lybien: Libya* (Heidelberg, Munich: Keysersche Verlagsbuchhandlung, 1960), pls. 2, 4; 6: photograph by Armando Maugini, courtesy of the Istituto Agronomico per l'Oltremare, Florence; 8: from M. Moore, *Fourth Shore: Italy's Mass Colonization of Libya* (London: Routledge and Kegan Paul, 1940), 169.

11
Figures 1, 6, 7: drawn Richard H. Abramson; 3: after T. Schreiber, *Die hellenistischen Reliefbilder* (1894), pl. 89; 4: after J. Klein, *Bonner Jahrbuch* 87 (1889): 85, Rheinisches Landesmuseum, Bonn; 5: private collection.

12
Figures 1, 3: Biblioteca Apostolica Vaticana; 2, 5: the author; 4: Oscar Savio, Archivio Fotografico Comunale, Rome, inv. A.F. 6049, albumin print, photograph by Parker, 233; 6: Escurialensis, fol. 56v, courtesy of the Warburg Institute, London.

13
Figures 1, 6: from J. H. Aronson, ed., *Rome 1748: The Nolli Plan in Facsimile, with an Introduction by Allan Ceen* (Highmount, N.Y.: J. H. Aronson, 1991); 2, 4: the author; 7: Biblioteca Apostolica Vaticana.

14
Figure 1: from J. H. Aronson, ed., *Rome 1748: The Nolli Plan in Facsimile, with an Introduction by Allan Ceen* (Highmount, N.Y.: J. H. Aronson, 1991); 2: from G. F. Bordini, *De rebus praeclaris gestis . . . a Sixto V* (Rome, 1588), 48, courtesy of the Metropolitan Museum of Art, New York; 3, 7: Alinari/Art Resource; 4: Biblioteca Apostolica Vaticana; 5: courtesy of the Kroch Library, Cornell University, Ithaca, N.Y.; 6: Bibliothèque Nationale, Paris; 8: Trustees of the British Museum, London.

15
Figures 1, 3: Collection of the Centre Canadien d'Architecture/Canadian Centre for Architecture, Montreal; 2, 5, 6: from *The Illustrated London News* 85 (August 2, 1884): supplement, 112, 93, all Collection of the Centre Canadien d'Architecture/Canadian Centre for Architecture, Montreal; 4: from *Punch* 87 (July 26, 1884): 39, courtesy of the Winterthur Library, Printed Book and Periodical Collection, Winterthur, Del.

16
Figure 1: detail from a plan of Cardiff by T. Waring, M. Inst. C.E., 1869, repr. by D. Brown and Sons, Cowbridge and Bridgend, South Wales; 2, 3, 5: Welsh Industrial and Maritime Museum, Cardiff; 4, 6: the author; 7: British Ordnance Survey, 1880, by permission of the British Library, London.

17

Figures 1, 3: Library of Congress; 2: from J. Caillé, *La Ville de Rabat jusqu'au protectorat français* (Paris: Vanoest, 1949), fig. 186; 4, 5: from L. Vaillat, *Le Visage français du Maroc* (Paris: Horizons de France, 1931), facing pp. 10, 41; 6: from *L'Art vivant* (Paris, February 1938): 23.

18

Figure 1: After Squier, 1877, p. 428.

19

Figure 1: United States Geological Survey; 2: photograph courtesy of the Lee Development Corporation; 3: from American Automobile Association, *Parking Programs* (Washington, D.C., 1954), 174; 4: Photograph by Joseph Allen, Library of Congress, Prints and Photographs Division; 5: from *Record of Montgomery County*, December 2, 1949, 1; 6: from *Maryland News*, July 25, 1956, 4; 7: photograph from the *Evening Star* (Washington, D.C.), 1947, Washington, D.C., Public Library.

20

Figure 1: United States Geological Survey; 2: courtesy of the Art Institute of Chicago; 3: plate CVII, *Plan of Chicago* (Chicago: Commercial Club, 1909), courtesy of the Art Institute of Chicago; 4: Bennett, Parsons &

Frost, consulting architects to the Chicago Plan Commission, January 1926, courtesy of the Art Institute of Chicago; 5, 6: courtesy of the Chicago Historical Society; 7: from L. Pearse, "The Sanitary District of Chicago," *Journal of the Western Society of Engineers* 28 (May 1923): 179.

21

Figure 1: Library of Congress; 2: courtesy of the Historic New Orleans Collection, Museum/Research Center, 60.58.Re; 3: from B. Hall, *Forty Etchings, from Sketches Made with the Camera Lucida, in North America, in 1827 and 1828* (Edinburgh: Cadell, 1829), pl. XXX, courtesy of the Historic New Orleans Collection, Museum/Research Center, 1974.25.17.13; 4: redrawn by the author from *The Batture Question Examined, by a Member of the Louisiana Bar* (New Orleans: F. Cook and A. Levy, 1840), 8; 5: from *Report of the Sanitary Commission of New Orleans on the Epidemic Yellow Fever of 1853* (New Orleans: at the *Picayune* office, 1854), Louisiana Collection, Tulane University Library; 6: from T. Jefferson, *The Proceedings of the Government of the United States, in Maintaining the Public Right to the Beach of the Missisipi[sic], Against the Intrusions of Edward Livingston* (New York: Ezra Sargeant, 1812), frontispiece, Louisiana Collection, Tulane University Library; 7: courtesy of the Historic New Orleans Collection, Museum/Research Center, 1974.25.18.25.

Designer: Alisa Bales Baur

Text: Garamond with Garamond Expert

Display: Franklin Gothic No. 2

Printer: Malloy Lithographing, Inc.

Binder: John H. Dekker & Sons